Wrongful Convictions and Forensic Science Errors

Wrongful Convictions and Forensic Science Errors: Case Studies and Root Causes provides a rigorous and detailed examination of two key issues: the continuing problem of wrongful convictions and the role of forensic science in these miscarriages of justice. This comprehensive textbook covers the full breadth of the topic. It looks at each type of evidence, historical factors, system issues, organizational factors, and individual examiners.

Forensic science errors may arise at any time from crime scene to courtroom. Probative evidence may be overlooked at the scene of a crime, or the chain of custody may be compromised. Police investigators may misuse or ignore forensic evidence. A poorly trained examiner may not apply the accepted standards of the discipline or may make unsound interpretations that exceed the limits of generally accepted scientific knowledge. In the courtroom, the forensic scientist may testify outside the standards of the discipline or fail to present exculpatory results. Prosecutors may suppress or mischaracterize evidence, and judges may admit testimony that does not conform to rules of evidence. All too often, the accused will not be afforded an adequate defense—especially given the technical complexities of forensic evidence. These issues do not arise in a vacuum; they result from system issues that are discernable and that can be ameliorated.

Author John Morgan provides a thorough discussion of the policy, practice, and technical aspects of forensic science errors from a root cause, scientific analysis perspective. Readers will learn to analyze common issues across cases and jurisdictions, perform basic root-cause analysis, and develop systemic reforms. The reader is encouraged to assess cases and issues without regard to preconceived views or prejudicial language. As such, the book reinforces the need to obtain a clear understanding of errors to properly develop a set of effective scientific, procedural, and policy reforms to reduce wrongful convictions and improve forensic integrity and reliability.

Written in a format and style accessible to a broad audience, **Wrongful Convictions and Forensic Science Errors** presents a root cause analysis across all of these issues, supported by detailed case studies and a clear understanding of the scientific basis of the forensic disciplines.

Wrongful Convictions and Forensic Science Errors

Case Studies and Root Causes

by

John Morgan

CRC Press
Taylor & Francis Group
Boca Raton London New York

CRC Press is an imprint of the
Taylor & Francis Group, an **informa** business

Designed cover image: The 1895 train derailment at Montparnasse train station, Paris, France. A famous case of both mechanical failure and human error.

First edition published 2023
by CRC Press
4 Park Square, Milton Park, Abingdon, Oxon, OX14 4RN

and by CRC Press
6000 Broken Sound Parkway NW, Suite 300, Boca Raton, FL 33487-2742

CRC Press is an imprint of Informa UK Limited

British Library Cataloguing-in-Publication Data
A catalogue record for this book is available from the British Library

ISBN: 978-1-032-06497-0 (hbk)
ISBN: 978-1-032-06350-8 (pbk)
ISBN: 978-1-003-20257-8 (ebk)

DOI: 10.4324/9781003202578

Typeset in Sabon
by Deanta Global Publishing Services, Chennai, India

This book is dedicated to my parents,
Jim and Sue Morgan,
whose love and teaching remain.

Contents

Acknowledgments

The author would like to recognize the support of the National Institute of Justice (NIJ) for the research project that subsequently led to the development of this textbook. That research was supported by the National Institute of Justice through Research and Evaluation Technical Assistance Contract GS10F0114L/OJP2002BF. In addition, the author would like to thank the many individuals who took the time to provide materials or insights into the issues in wrongful conviction cases.

Author

Dr. John Morgan is internationally recognized for his work in forensic science, body armor, special operations technology, and police technology. He has conducted research in optoelectronic materials, countering weapons of mass destruction, and a wide variety of police and forensic technologies. Previously, Dr. Morgan was Senior Director of the Center for Forensic Sciences at RTI International. He has served as a member of the Maryland House of Delegates and Congressional Science Fellow of the American Physical Society. He also served in the U.S. Department of Justice and the U.S. Department of Defense as a senior executive managing programs that encompass scientific research, public safety, military technology, special operations, information systems, and standards, including as Deputy Director for Science and Technology at the National Institute of Justice and the Combatting Terrorism Technology Support Office, as well as Command Science Advisor for the US Army Special Operations Command. He received the 2007 Service to America Medal for his work to improve the nation's capacity to conduct DNA analysis. ***Wrongful Convictions and Forensic Science Errors: Case Studies and Root Causes*** follows years of research on the topic for the Department of Justice as part of his research and teaching work to improve policing, forensic science, and the use of science to inform public policy.

CHAPTER 1

Context of Wrongful Convictions and Forensic Science Errors

INTRODUCTION

Since the beginning of human civilization, governments have adopted and enforced criminal codes. Governments derive legitimacy from the fair and effective management of their criminal justice systems. They may vary with respect to goals: some governments emphasize order and punishment and seek to establish a rule of law that prevents chaos; other governments emphasize freedom, equity, responsiveness, or other values related to their structure and place in history. Criminal justice systems usually act with impunity, which is the ability to act without fear of punishment or repercussions. There are limits to that impunity, which may lead citizens to seek redress or revolution. Although some totalitarian governments abuse impunity to impose terror on their citizens, such Orwellian dystopias have not proven to be long-lived. As a result, most criminal justice systems are designed to identify and punish those who offend against the law and err toward leniency when in doubt.

The idea is echoed in many religious texts, and it is notable that a major world religion—Christianity—is based on a story of wrongful conviction. The scholars shown in Figure 1.1 illustrate the breadth of the idea that wrongful convictions come at a high societal cost. Jewish scholar Moses Maimonides said, "It is better and more satisfactory to acquit a thousand guilty persons than to put a single innocent man to death" (Maimonides, c. 1200). Later, Benjamin Franklin advocated for a ratio of 100 to 1, while English jurist William Blackstone said, "It is better that ten guilty persons escape than that one innocent suffer" (Blackstone, 1893). It might disturb the reader to observe that the acceptable ratio appears to have been in decline over the centuries.

DOI: 10.4324/9781003202578-1

FIGURE 1.1A Three views of the importance of wrongful convictions: Moses Maimonides, Benjamin Franklin, and William Blackstone. Moses Maimonides. Source: Moses Maimonides. Photogravure. | Wellcome Collection.

FIGURE 1.1B Benjamin Franklin. Source: Library of Congress.

FIGURE 1.1C William Blackstone. Source: New York Public Library, CCO 1.0 Dedication.

Nonetheless, Blackstone and others have recognized the problem of wrongful convictions and attempted to establish legal frameworks that were intended to produce reliable verdicts. By the early 1900s, many legal scholars in Western societies were convinced that the legal system produced very few, if any, wrongful convictions. Although corruption and incompetence were recognized, it was believed that common law traditions and modern processes like appeals courts could prevent systematic injustice (Figure 1.1a, Figure 1.1b, Figure 1.1c).

During this period, there were high-profile exonerations, including several cases that resulted in presidential pardons. Most cases involved mistaken identity, in which a crime victim testified in error concerning the actual perpetrator. Others, such as the Oscar Krueger case (see box), included errors related to forensic evidence. The cases were usually considered isolated errors until the work of Edwin Borchard, a Yale law professor who wrote *Convicting the Innocent: 65 Actual Errors of Criminal Justice* (1932). Borchard highlighted the stories behind many wrongful convictions and was an early advocate for compensation for the wrongfully convicted. The father-daughter team of Jerome and Barbara Frank contributed *Not Guilty* 1957 following the style of Borchard in providing narrative descriptions of individual cases (Frank & Frank, 1957). These efforts established that wrongful convictions were more prevalent than was widely believed within the criminal justice community. The specific role of forensic science was not highlighted in these early works (Figure 1.2).

OSCAR KRUEGER

Oscar Krueger was wrongfully convicted in 1910 of mailing obscene material on the basis of an invalid handwriting examination (The Sheboygan Press, Sheboygan, Wisconsin, February 28, 1912) (Source: The Sheboygan Press, February 28, 1912.)

In 1910 in New York City, a young woman seeking employment received an anonymous, obscene letter. She took the letter to the Society for the Prevention of Vice, which had been founded by Anthony Comstock. Comstock was a well-known activist against pornography and sexual vice and for moralistic censorship. He agreed to help the woman. Comstock arranged to entrap the offending writer using a ruse that implicated Oscar Krueger, a married man with two children. Comstock believed that Krueger's handwriting matched that of the letter-writer, an opinion confirmed by a handwriting expert. They focused on the name "Waschak," which was the last name of the victim and had been written on

FIGURE 1.2 Picture of Oscar Krueger. The Sheboygan Press, 28 Feb 1912, page 7

the envelope that contained the offending letter. Krueger was then charged and convicted of violating Section 211 of the U.S. Code, which outlaws the mailing of any "obscene, lewd, lascivious, indecent, filthy or vile article." He did not have the funds to hire an independent handwriting expert.

After his conviction, Krueger wrote letters to the President and Attorney General protesting his innocence. An assistant US attorney, Daniel Walton, reinvestigated the case and retained noted handwriting expert William Kinsley, who determined that Krueger was not the writer of the offending letter. Despite Comstock's opposition, Walton's recommendation for pardon was accepted, and President Taft issued him a pardon on January 18, 1912. As Borchard put it, "Comstock's sincere, though often misguided, fanaticism induced in him gullibility and carelessness in fastening so serious an offense on an innocent man, and these characteristics were combined with exceptional stubbornness and unwillingness to admit error" (Borchard, 1932). Handwriting expert Kinsley wrote a book, *Tales Told by Handwriting*, that popularized handwriting examination. Nonetheless, the field would lack comparison and testimony standards for many decades afterward.

FORENSIC SCIENCE IN THE 20TH CENTURY

Around the same time as the Krueger case, Edmond Locard established the first police crime laboratory in Lyon, France in 1910. Locard developed basic standards for fingerprint identification, including the standard of using 12 points to establish a definitive latent print match. In the United States, Calvin Goddard established the FBI Laboratory in 1924. Goddard's work in ballistics had been heavily influenced by the experience of wrongful convictions. On Sunday evening March 21, 1915, between 10 and 11 o'clock, Charles B. Phelps, an aged farmer residing in the town of Shelby, Orleans County, and Miss Margaret Wilcott, his housekeeper, were both murdered by being shot with a revolver containing 22-caliber cartridges and bullets (People v. Stielow, 1916). The case involved Stielow's false confession, prosecutor misconduct, and inadequate defense. Stielow owned a 22-caliber revolver, which was matched to four autopsy bullets by self-taught firearms expert Albert Hamilton. Hamilton had awarded himself a phony medical degree and advertised as a criminologist with expertise in chemistry, cause of death, anatomy, and firearms identification (Borchard, 1932). Hamilton did not show his findings to the jury at trial, contending that the work was so technical that only an expert could understand it. At the time, there were no standards for the forensic profession in general or the practice of ballistic identification specifically. Stielow was sentenced to death, Green to 25 years to life in prison. While awaiting his execution at Sing Sing prison, Stielow related his case to prison officials, who conducted their own investigation. Stielow came within 40 minutes of execution when a stay was ordered. Afterwards, alternative suspect Erwin King was identified and eventually confessed to the crime, but Stielow's conviction was not overturned. Governor Whitman took an interest in the case and ordered an investigation by a former district attorney, George Bond. Bond hired Charles Waite from the New York Attorney General's office to reexamine the ballistic evidence. In turn, Waite enlisted Henry Jones, a firearms expert with the New York City Police Department. Waite and Jones conducted test fires, in which several rounds from the Stielow revolver were fired into cotton batting. Further assisted by optician Max Poser, they established that the bullets were dissimilar from the autopsy bullets in every regard. Stielow and Green were subsequently pardoned by the Governor. King was never indicted for the murders. Waite would go on to work with Calvin Goddard, physicist John Fisher, and chemist Philip Gravelle to establish a Bureau of Forensic Ballistics in New York City and develop the comparison microscope, which is still used today in ballistic identification.

With the support of influential police executives—including FBI Director J. Edgar Hoover—Goddard and his colleagues established the training and practice standards that ushered in an era that was associated with scientific crime detection. They were heavily influenced by Sherlock Holmes and scientific positivism, which held that all true knowledge is scientific. They believed that forensic science could definitively establish the facts of a crime. Their view was neatly summarized by Locard's exchange principle: "Every contact by a criminal leaves a trace." The job of the forensic scientist was to find and characterize these traces and associate them with sources or activities at the crime scene. Criminologists adopted their own brand of positivism, holding that an individual's personality or background would make the person more prone to antisocial or criminal behavior. This view was reinforced by the growing evidence that crime was often committed by repeat offenders. Although scientific positivism led to many improvements in forensic science and law enforcement, it failed when pseudoscientific theories were given inordinate credibility. For example, the Bertillon system used morphological characteristics, such as face shape, as a method of identification. Bertillon identification was successful for a time but eventually was supplanted by fingerprint identification. There remained a belief that criminals would have morphological characteristics that would make them look like a comic-book villain, a pernicious view that may have contributed to wrongful convictions in many cases. Oscar Krueger had what was called a "mesomorphic" body type, being muscular and big-boned, which was theorized to be associated with a propensity to criminal delinquency.

At the same time, police agencies adopted a professional-policing model that emphasized a constrained role for law enforcement. Summed up by the "just the facts, ma'am" Dragnet detective, the professional policing model emphasized rapid response and solving crime. Agencies avoided community interaction or prevention efforts, which were thought to lead to police corruption (and often did). Forensic science in the Locard-Goddard model was a natural adjunct to professional policing because it also emphasized fact-finding and solving crime. Police agencies started crime laboratories or standalone units to support investigation in the mid-20th century in the expectation that forensic science would support the law enforcement mission. In fact, crime laboratory directors and forensic discipline scientific working groups were originally organized by the FBI Laboratory. The close relationship between forensic science and law enforcement continues to this day and has been the subject of criticism from wrongful conviction researchers who believe that it leads to biased decision-making (Giannelli, 2011). Many forensic scientists defend the practice. Historically, the relationship has led to more resources for the development of laboratories. Many police leaders have been strong supporters of research and scientific standards. Most notably, Berkeley, California police chief August Vollmer (Figure 1.3) is widely considered the founder of professional policing and introduced many new ideas into policing including radio systems, records systems,

FIGURE 1.3 August Vollmer pioneered professional policing and influenced the development of crime laboratories as important tools to support police investigation. Source: Library of Congress, (1929) August Vollmer [photograph].

and lie detectors. He encouraged the development of crime laboratories and was largely responsible for the establishment of the Los Angeles Police Department laboratory and the International Association for Identification. The International Association of Chiefs of Police still gives an annual August Vollmer Excellence in Forensic Science Award for innovative use of forensic science.

As the Krueger and Stielow/Green cases demonstrate, the fields of ballistics and handwriting identification required significant development of their scientific foundations and practice standards. These gaps existed across the disciplines. For many disciplines, individual innovators would play key roles. For example, Albert Osborn is often considered the "father of questioned document examination." Among other innovations, he recognized individual variations in the ability to discern visual patterns and developed the "form blindness" test to predict the ability of novices to become good handwriting examiners (Osborn, 1939). As disciplines matured, professional associations and scientific working groups produced consensus standards to govern training, certification, methods, and testimony. These governance mechanisms established the scope and best practices associated with a wide range of disciplines and worked well when connected to public laboratories that were well-led and well-funded. They also had significant limitations. The groups seldom had sufficient representation from scientific researchers, leading to standards based on the experience of practitioners, not empirical scientific research. Because practitioners had limited feedback concerning errors, they could have unrealistic expectations about the reliability of their methods. Also, professional associations possessed weak enforcement mechanisms, meaning incompetent or fraudulent examiners were able to continue to practice with insufficient accountability. Even when disciplinary actions were taken, an examiner could continue to work in many jurisdictions. Many examiners worked without sufficient training or meaningful certifications. This phenomenon was most clearly demonstrated in fingerprint units, which were (and remain) often located within police departments, not independent crime laboratories. The units were primarily staffed with examiners who possessed the ability to do ten-print checks to identify a suspect but often were insufficiently trained to do the much more difficult task of latent print identification. These individuals may have been police officers themselves, so they were susceptible to making biased, inculpatory, and, possibly, erroneous identifications. Local jurisdictions seldom possessed sufficient review mechanisms to identify these problems, and the national governance bodies were even weaker. In some disciplines, even certified examiners may not have had the ability to perform difficult comparisons. The professional associations relied on revenue from training and certification regimes and had the perception that difficult testing would disincentivize participation by practitioners. The associations were particularly reluctant to decertify practicing forensic scientists. Many wrongful convictions were related to these gaps in forensic science governance.

Governance gaps remain to varying degrees to the present day. The scientific working groups are now managed by the National Institute of Standards and Technology (NIST) under the Organization of Scientific Area Committees (OSAC, The Organization of Scientific Area Committees for Forensic Science | NIST, see Figure 1.4). Some professional associations have stronger certification and standards structures, particularly in chemistry and toxicology. DNA evidence standards are enforced in connection with the national DNA index, although the FBI continues to play the central management role (see www.swgdam.org). Most public laboratories are now accredited and enforce professional and practice standards through formalized quality assurance. Some jurisdictions have oversight boards—such as forensic science commissions—that have direct enforcement

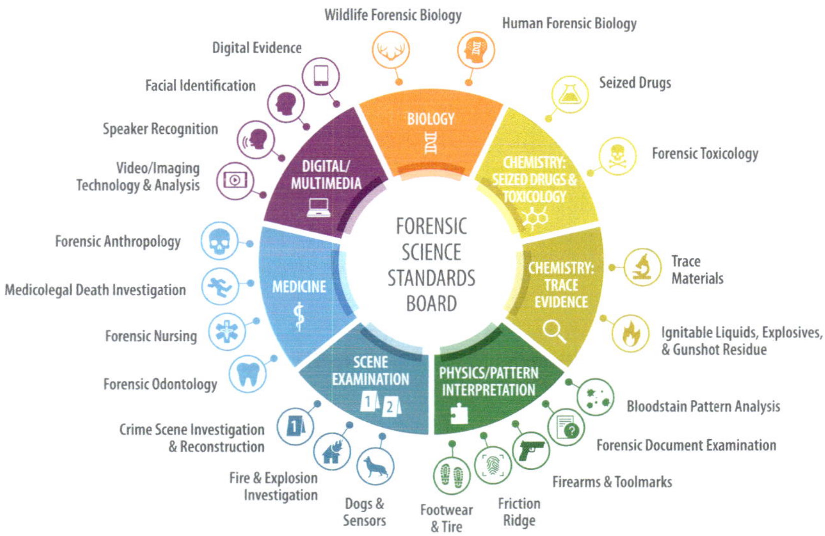

FIGURE 1.4 The structure of the NIST-managed Organization of Scientific Area Committees for Forensic Science. Note that OSAC does not include DNA, which is managed by a scientific working group under FBI authority, and forensic pathology. Source: National Institute of Standards and Technology.

powers. Outside the United States, national forensic regulators have been established and enforce standards with varying levels of success. Nonetheless, many disciplines continue to rely on weak governance. For example, bite mark examiners are governed by the American Board of Forensic Odontology (ABFO), which is connected to the American Academy of Forensic Science (AAFS). ABFO moved slowly to recognize the well-established limitations of bite mark comparison to identify an individual biter. It lacked the power to enforce the standards it did put in place, even when it decertified an examiner.

FORENSIC EVIDENCE STANDARDS IN CRIMINAL CASES

Legal scholars maintain that the courts are best positioned to enforce meaningful scientific standards. Before the Frye rule was established in 1923, courts accepted an expert opinion if it was based on "special experience or special knowledge." The Frye court extended this concept when it was faced with the admission of lie detector testing based on the measurement of systolic blood pressure (Frye v. United States, 1923). Although the lie detector test was administered by an expert, the scientific foundation for polygraphy was lacking. The Frye court held that scientific evidence could be admitted only when it was "sufficiently established to have gained general acceptance in the particular field in which it belongs." On this basis, it rejected the systolic blood pressure deception test. In response to Frye, polygraphers established a professional organization, the American Polygraph Association (APA), which provides training and standards for the field and publishes a scientific journal, *Polygraph* (see Home (polygraph.org)). Although the work of the APA and similar organizations may be considered by some to meet the Frye general acceptance test, polygraphy is not accepted in court in many jurisdictions today. Almost a century after Frye, the scientific consensus holds that polygraph has some value to discriminate lying from truth-telling when used to investigate specific incidents such as crimes, but the technique is subject to many confounding factors and can be abused as a screening tool (National Research Council, 2003). The Frye general acceptance rule has many weaknesses. First, judges are in a poor position to determine whether a particular method is generally accepted by the relevant scientific community. Also, advocates or self-described experts could misuse or exaggerate the value of a method. In 1976, the Supreme Court of California adopted the Kelly-Frye test to address these issues to a limited extent (People v. Robert Kelly, 1976). The court was considering voiceprint identification, a technique used to associate a recording with an individual's voice. As practiced at the time, voiceprint relied on analog tracings of the intensity of a recording within frequency bands. The Kelly-Frye court rejected the testimony of a voiceprint examiner who was primarily a "technician," not a scientist, and was an advocate, not an impartial judge of the scientific merit of the method. The Kelly-Frye test requires that scientific techniques must show general acceptance and be presented by a qualified expert using the correct scientific procedures. The test also prohibits the expert from speculating concerning an opinion outside the bounds of the subject. Many wrongful convictions include forensic testimony that would violate the Kelly-Frye standard if applied properly by a judge at trial. The courts may fail to recognize the novelty of methods or allow experts to speculate on matters that are outside their expertise or the bounds of validated science.

DAVID SHAWN POPE (POPE V. STATE, 1988)

On July 25, 1985, a young woman was raped in her apartment in Dallas, Texas. The rapist called her later that day and again on July 27, at which time her answering machine recorded the call.

A ten-minute phone conversation with the rapist on August 2 was fully recorded. David Shawn Pope was a former resident of the same apartment complex. He had been found by the management of the complex loitering in the neighborhood on multiple occasions after his eviction in June. On August 28 at 6:30 a.m., Pope was arrested by police while wandering the premises of the complex. He was found with a 9-1/2" knife similar to the weapon used by the attacker. His white pants and general description also matched the victim's description.

Investigators attempted to match Pope's voice to the recordings from the victim's answering machine (see Figure 1.5 for an example of voiceprint analysis at the time of the Pope trial). Houston police officer Larry Howe Williams, who had performed 1000 voiceprint comparisons, and Dr. Henry Truby, an expert with a Ph.D. in acoustic phonetics, testified that a

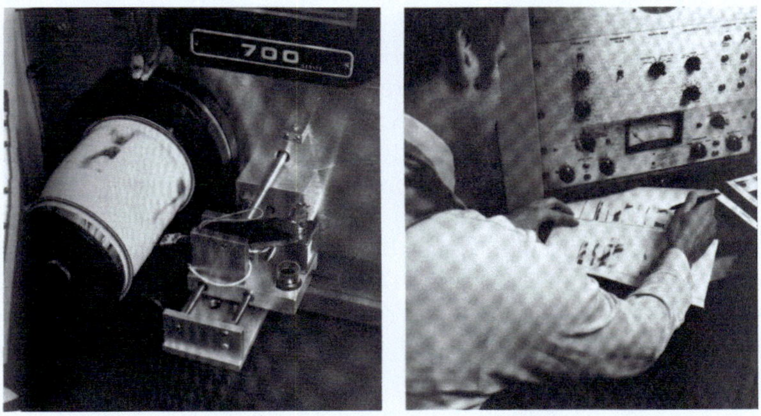

FIGURE 1.5 An examiner compares spectrograms for similarities. These two images are from a January 1980 *FBI Law Enforcement Bulletin* article on *Speaker Identification*, which was published after the Kelly-Frye decision and immediately after a National Research Council report that criticized the scientific validity of voiceprint analysis (Koenig, 1980). The Pope wrongful conviction occurred five years later. The same issue of the *FBI Law Enforcement Bulletin* highlighted the FBI's "team approach" to the use of hypnosis, which has also been associated with many wrongful convictions. Source: FBI Law Enforcement Bulletin, January 1980. (Koenig, 1980)

reference voice recording and the voice from the answering machine were from the same source, David Shawn Pope. Truby further testified that voice spectrography could identify an individual to the exclusion of all others in the world, just like fingerprints. Pope's defense lawyer called Stuart Ritterman, a professor from the University of Florida, who questioned the scientific validity of the technique. The trial judge accepted the identification testimony under the Frye standard then in use in Texas. Pope was convicted.

The Texas appeals court noted that Truby's testimony was contradicted by the most important research then extant on voiceprint spectrographic analysis, that of Oscar Tosi at Michigan State University (Tosi, et al., 1972). Tosi found false identification error rates of 2.4% under ideal conditions. The court also cited a 1976 National Academy of Sciences study of voiceprint identification, which raised serious concerns about confounding factors, including deliberate attempts to disguise a voice, recording fidelity, and the subjectivity of examiner decisions. The appeals court wrestled with how to apply the Frye standard in the case and cited 25 different cases in which state and federal courts had come to wildly divergent conclusions about the admissibility of voiceprint analysis. Although the court held that voiceprint evidence was improperly admitted, the majority held that the error was harmless.

Eleven years later, the Dallas district attorney followed up on a tip about the case with a DNA test on the rape kit from the crime. Pope was exonerated, received a pardon from the governor, and received $385,000 in compensation plus a $6,500/month lifetime annuity.

The case demonstrates the limitations of the Frye standard but more fundamentally shows that the courts are poorly equipped to review scientific evidence. Voiceprint spectrographic analysis is not a singular method that is applied in the same way by all practitioners. The technology has changed over the years. Practitioners use digital analysis to examine different patterns and frequency bands. The research has revealed many confounding factors and suggested many strategies to account for those limitations. Even if Truby had correctly described the research and cited Tosi's work, he was not applying the same technique that Tosi used. No voiceprint identification technique has been validated to the point of establishing a reliable error rate in practice.

In 1975, the federal government adopted the Federal Rules of Evidence (FRE). FRE Section 702 is the primary rule that relates to forensic evidence. FRE 702 emphasizes the background of the expert, the relevance of the experts' testimony, and the reliability of the expert's methods in principle and as applied. The term, "in principle," relates to the ideal application of the method. The term, "as applied," relates to the way the method is actually applied by the expert. Specifically, FRE 702 states:

> A witness who is qualified as an expert by knowledge, skill, experience, training, or education may testify in the form of an opinion or otherwise if:
>
> (a) The expert's scientific, technical, or other specialized knowledge will help the trier of fact to understand the evidence or to determine a fact in issue
> (b) The testimony is based on sufficient facts or data
> (c) The testimony is the product of reliable principles and methods and
> (d) The expert has reliably applied the principles and methods to the facts of the case
>
> (Legal Information Institute)

Although FRE 702 formally applies in federal court, its principles are incorporated into most state rules of evidence through the Daubert standard or other mechanism. The US Supreme Court established the Daubert standard in a civil case in 1993 relating to whether the drug Bendectin could cause birth defects (Daubert v. Merrell Dow Pharmaceuticals. Inc., 1993). The Daubert court adopted FRE 702 by reference and added a series of tests for scientific validity:

1. Has the theory or technique has been tested?
2. Has it been subjected to peer review and publication?
3. What is the known or potential error rate?
4. Are standards maintained controlling its operation?
5. Is it widely accepted with a relevant scientific community?

In his decision, Justice Blackmun clarified that the standards were flexible and should be judged based on the principles and methodology of the theory or technique. The Daubert decision was heavily influenced by the ideas of philosopher of science Karl Popper. Popper emphasized that the validity of scientific hypotheses required that they be falsifiable

(Popper, 2005). He pointed out that adherents tend to make observed reality fit their predictions. As a result, even if you verify a hypothesis many times, it has not truly been tested until you try to prove it was wrong. In forensic practice, this implies that a method should not be accepted solely on the basis of its success in casework. The underlying assumptions of the method should be tested as falsifiable hypotheses. For example, toxicologists assume that a level of alcohol observed in breath measurements directly correlates with levels of alcohol in the blood. The principle could be verified using roadside testing machines and blood sampling that shows the relationship, but Popper would hold that to be an insufficient empirical test. Instead, the researcher should conduct a controlled experiment to produce known levels of blood alcohol in test subjects, predict breath alcohol results, and determine whether the predictions were valid.

Although Daubert and FRE 702 provide a more thorough approach to the review of forensic science by the courts, wrongful convictions demonstrate that significant gaps remain in the review of scientific testimony. Judges and lawyers continue to lack education and training in the increasingly sophisticated science and technology that is presented in trials. Dubious methods may be accepted. Faulty testimony may be presented without objection. In many circumstances, defendants may be faced with an adversarial deficit in which their counsel has fewer resources or capabilities than the prosecutor. Forensic science issues exacerbate adversarial deficits because an adequate defense requires thorough review of forensic reports and testimony. An unprepared defense counsel may not recognize problems in laboratory analysis or interpretation or raise appropriate objections.

THE MODERN ERA: ADVENT OF DNA

DNA forensic technology was developed during the 1980s and 1990s and came into common practice in the 2000s. The first DNA exoneration in 1989 was a landmark in the recognition of the problem of wrongful convictions. Gary Dotson had been convicted of sexual assault and kidnapping on the basis of the testimony of 16-year-old Cathleen Crowell (Connors, Lundregan, Miller, & McEwen, 1996). Both Dotson and Crowell were B secretors, and semen on the victim's undergarment had type B blood group substances consistent with an assailant who was a B secretor. Crowell recanted postconviction and maintained that she had lied about the rape to cover for a presumed pregnancy after consensual sex with her boyfriend, David Bierne. The case received substantial media attention, and the Governor of

Illinois ordered a review that found errors in the original serological analysis and testimony. DNA technology in 1989 was very limited, so the initial analysis using variable number tandem repeat (VNTR) testing was unsuccessful. PCR testing was then used to exclude Dotson. Although PCR testing at the time could not be used to identify a source, the results were consistent with Bierne. On August 4, 1989, the prosecution agreed to vacate the conviction. Dotson was pardoned based on innocence in 2003 and awarded $120,300 by the Illinois Court of Claims. Crowell gave Dotson $17,500 from the profits on her book about the case.

DNA technology has now been used to exonerate over 300 defendants. The definitive database, the National Registry of Exonerations (NRE), has documented over 3,000 wrongful convictions overall in the United States (University of California Irvine Newkirk Center for Science & Society, University of Michigan Law School, and Michigan State University College of Law, 2020). The NRE provides summary information on each case, including descriptive coding of factors that contributed to the wrongful conviction. Faulty eyewitness identifications, false confessions, false or misleading forensic evidence, official misconduct, inadequate legal defense, perjury/false accusations, and jailhouse informants are the primary factors cited by the NRE. They publish annual reports that provide an overview of wrongful convictions added to the database each year (National Registry of Exonerations, 2021). While DNA played a major role in exonerations up to 2010, most exonerations in recent years were based on other evidence. The number of exonerations recorded by the NRE peaked at 183 in 2016 and has been steadily declining. The number of exonerations associated with false or misleading forensic evidence has also been in decline. The use of DNA, other new technologies, and improved standards may have contributed to these trends.

The number of wrongful convictions associated with false or misleading evidence has been the subject of significant debate. Currently, the NRE attributes false or misleading forensic evidence as a contributing factor in approximately one-quarter of all post-1989 wrongful convictions. Past estimates have estimated that as many as 63% of wrongful convictions were associated with forensic errors (Saks & Koehler, 2005). These estimates may have been inflated because of the early prevalence of DNA exonerations, which required the availability of biological evidence in the case. As a result, the first detected wrongful convictions were disproportionately associated with sexual assault and the use of forensic hair comparison and serology. Hair comparison and serology had significant challenges with respect to their selectivity, i.e., the ability to differentiate sources from a population. As a result, early estimates yielded inflated numbers for the prevalence of forensic science errors. Further, many wrongful conviction analyses have relied on subjective judgments about the assessment of errors in wrongful conviction cases, leading to flawed interpretations (LaPorte, 2017). In general, wrongful conviction researchers have been limited by the lack of empirical data on which to base reliable conclusions (Cole, 2011). The reader is cautioned that this limitation is relevant to the discussion of forensic science errors and wrongful convictions presented here.

Innocence organizations have played a central role in advocacy on behalf of innocent defendants who have been wrongfully convicted. Most prominently, the Innocence Project—started by Barry Scheck and Peter Neufeld—has been involved in over 200 exonerations (Innocence Project, 2022). Both Scheck and Neufeld have influenced the consideration of forensic science errors related to wrongful convictions (Scheck, Neufeld, & Dwyer, 2000). Scheck has worked on the development of DNA analysis and scientific testimony standards. Neufeld co-authored an extensive analysis of DNA exonerations with legal scholar Brandon Garrett (Garrett & Neufeld, 2009). There is now an Innocence Network of 69 organizations worldwide that advocate for exonerations and criminal justice reform (Innocence Network, 2022). In addition, prosecutors have formed over 90 conviction integrity units that work to prevent, identify, and remedy false convictions (National Registry of Exonerations, 2022).

Most importantly from a forensic science perspective, some states have formed innocence commissions and forensic science commissions in response to the problems of forensic science errors and wrongful convictions. The most active such commission is the Texas Forensic Science Commission, which has reviewed over 100 complaints since 2009 and has established a licensing requirement for forensic scientists to practice in that state. The commission played a key role in the prohibition of the use of bite mark comparison testimony in Texas (Texas Forensic Science Commission, 2016). Innocence commissions tend to work in conjunction with courts to review postconviction petitions. For example, the North Carolina Innocence Inquiry Commission (NCIIC) investigates claims of innocence and makes recommendations to a three-judge panel (North Carolina Innocence Inquiry Commission, 2022). They have reviewed over 3,000 claims and produced 15 exonerations.

THE BUNCOMBE FIVE (NORTH CAROLINA INNOCENCE INQUIRY COMMISSION, 2011)

On August 18, 2000, Walter Bowman was murdered in the small town of Fairview in Buncombe County, North Carolina. A local CrimeStoppers tip line collected many leads to possible suspects, including Kenneth Kagonyera and Larry Williams. Robert Wilcoxcon and Teddy Isbell were soon implicated as police elicited information and false confessions from Williams and his supposed accomplices. A fifth defendant, Damian Mills, was identified based on a shotgun purchase and a jailhouse informant. A bandana and gloves had been found near the house where the murder occurred and was presumed to be associated with the assailants, and Kagonyera requested DNA testing of that evidence. The evidence was analyzed and excluded all five defendants, but that result was not shared with them. All five defendants eventually pled guilty to elements of murder, armed robbery, and conspiracy and were sentenced to various prison terms.

In 2003, Robert Rutherford confessed to federal agents that he, Bradford Summey, and Lacy Pickens committed the crime. Rutherford, Summey, and Pickens had been identified in a CrimeStoppers tip at the time of the crime, but local police did not follow up on that tip sufficiently. In 2007, the DNA profile from the bandana and gloves were reanalyzed, uploaded to the Combined DNA Index System (CODIS), and matched to Summey. Kagonyera and Wilcoxson filed claims for actual innocence, but the claims were not acted upon until the NCIIC found that there was sufficient evidence to merit a judicial review. Among other evidence, the NCIIC found that Pickens' car, a 1971 Olds Cutlass Supreme, was found on a gas station surveillance tape near the murder scene. Kagonyera and Wilcoxson were judged innocent by a panel of North Carolina Superior Court judges on September 23, 2011. In 2015, a new Buncombe County district attorney agreed that the DNA evidence exculpated all five defendants, and they were found factually innocent. A formal gubernatorial pardon was issued in 2020.

The case demonstrates many aspects common across wrongful convictions, including official misconduct related to the suppression of evidence, mistaken eyewitness identification, false confessions, and investigative tunnel vision. The district attorney suppressed the DNA exclusion found by the North Carolina State Bureau of Investigation (NCSBI) laboratory (seen in Figure 1.6). The actual forensic analysis was valid, but the management and communication of the DNA evidence were severely lacking. The DNA profile had been eligible for CODIS upload at the time of trial. It is unclear why NCSBI failed to conduct that search, which would have identified known, alternate suspect Summey and might have exculpated the innocent defendants prior to their false conviction (Figure 1.6a, Figure 1.6b)

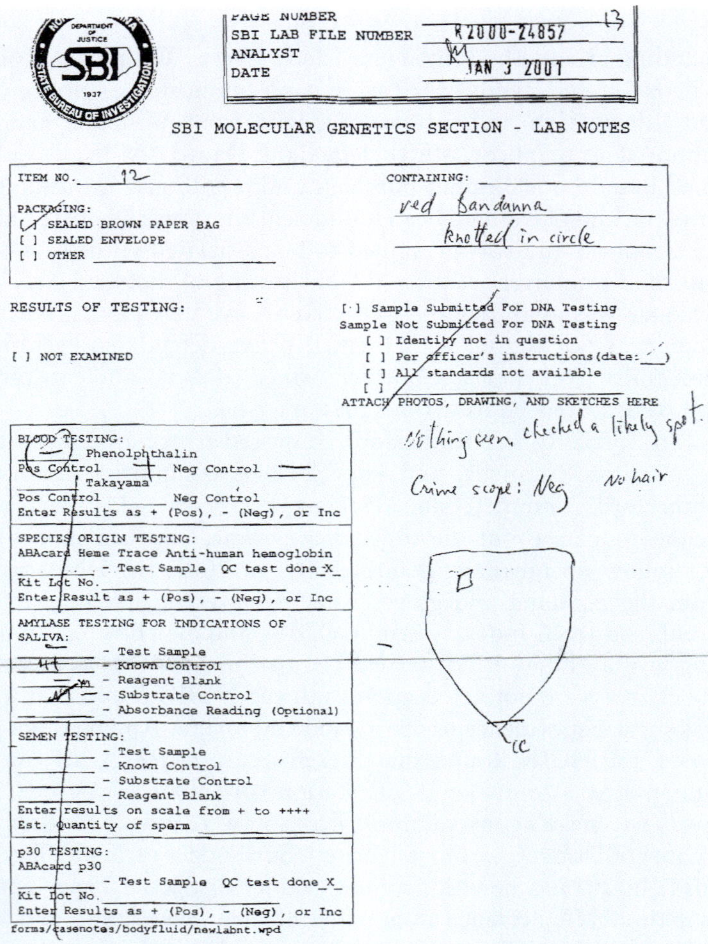

PAGE NUMBER 13
SBI LAB FILE NUMBER R2000-24857
ANALYST
DATE JAN 3 2001

SBI MOLECULAR GENETICS SECTION - LAB NOTES

ITEM NO. 12 CONTAINING: red bandana knotted in circle

PACKAGING:
[✓] SEALED BROWN PAPER BAG
[ ] SEALED ENVELOPE
[ ] OTHER

RESULTS OF TESTING:

[ ] NOT EXAMINED

[ ] Sample Submitted For DNA Testing
Sample Not Submitted For DNA Testing
[ ] Identity not in question
[ ] Per officer's instructions (date:)
[ ] All standards not available
[ ]
ATTACH PHOTOS, DRAWING, AND SKETCHES HERE

Nothing seen, checked a likely spot.

Crime scope: Neg No hair

BLOOD TESTING:
Phenolphthalin
Pos Control + Neg Control —
Takayama
Pos Control Neg Control
Enter Results as + (Pos), - (Neg), or Inc

SPECIES ORIGIN TESTING:
ABAcard Heme Trace Anti-human hemoglobin
- Test Sample QC test done X
Kit Lot No.
Enter Result as + (Pos), - (Neg), or Inc

AMYLASE TESTING FOR INDICATIONS OF SALIVA:
— - Test Sample
++ - Known Control
— - Reagent Blank
— - Substrate Control
- Absorbance Reading (Optional)

SEMEN TESTING:
- Test Sample
- Known Control
- Substrate Control
- Reagent Blank
Enter results on scale from + to ++++
Est. Quantity of sperm

p30 TESTING:
ABAcard p30
- Test Sample QC test done X
Kit Lot No.
Enter Results as + (Pos), - (Neg), or Inc

forms/casenotes/bodyfluid/newlabnt.wpd

FIGURE 1.6A Extracts from the 2001 forensic reports in the Buncombe Five case were presented during the NCIIC hearing. The figure shows the lab notes on the bandana and summary report on the findings, which showed "no matches observed." Page 42 of the report from the SBI label to the bandana "cartoon." (Source: North Carolina State Bureau of Investigation Lab File Number R2000-24857, January 3, 2001.)

State Match Result Report
Target ID: R200024857#10-1
Laboratory: NCBCI0094
Specimen Type: KEYBOARD
Index: None

p.19 MTB

Target Profile:

CSF1PO:	12	
TPOX:	9,	11
THO1:	6,	8
vWA:	16,	17
D16S539:	12,	13
D7S820:	7,	8
D13S317:	12,	13
D5S818:	11,	13
FGA:	25,	26
D8S1179:	13,	16
Penta E:	5,	8
D18S51:	15,	17
D21S11:	28	
D3S1358:	16	

Match Summary:

Total Candidates: 0 *no matches observed. MTB*

Match Details:
Specimen ID: Not a Match
Laboratory:
Specimen Type:
Index:

Match Date: 03/07/2001 08:32
Match Stringency: Not a Match

Match Window in Effect:
Above 10,000 BP: ±6.5%
Between 10,000 BP and 2,000 BP: ±2.5%
Below 2,000 BP: ±2.5%

Minimum number of loci required to report a match: 4
Include Candidate specimens that match on all but 1 loci.
Maximum number of candidates to return from search: 0

Printed by: MARK T. BOODEE on 03/07/2001 1 Searcher Ver 5 2

FIGURE 1.6B DNA match results with the notation of "no matches observed," indicating that the biological evidence did not match any of the Buncombe Five. Source: North Carolina State Bureau of Investigation, Lab File Number R200024857, March 7, 2001.

WRONGFUL CONVICTION RESEARCH

There is now an extensive literature of legal academic reviews, descriptive studies, and analyses related to wrongful convictions and forensic science errors (Garrett, 2020)(Huff & Killias, 2008) Because studies usually rely on retrospective case reviews, there is limited empirical research that can identify causative factors (Leo & Gould, 2009). The University of Michigan has studied capital cases as an empirical framework for wrongful conviction research (Gross & O'Brien, 2008). Other studies have also examined the capital case framework as a method to study wrongful convictions, demonstrating a variety of causative factors, such as inadequate defense (Liebman, Fagan, West, & Lloyd, 2000). In building the NRE, Gross and Shaffer discovered forensic errors that ranged from simple mistakes to outright fraud. They also pointed out that it is often "impossible to distinguish one type of forensic error from another" (Gross & Shaffer, 2012).

In a separate paper, Gould et al compared erroneous convictions with "near misses" in which a defendant was cleared prior to trial (Gould, Carrano, Leo, & Young, 2013). Their study found 10 causative factors, including forensic evidence errors, which included omission of key information (such as masking considerations in serology), poor statistical characterization, and exaggeration of the scientific and probative value of techniques (such as bite marks or canine scent identification). Most forensic errors were found at the testimony stage and were not necessarily errors in the testing itself. Hence, the report recommends, "As a result, previous policy recommendations that have focused on improving the quality of forensic laboratory procedures should be revisited to emphasize quality control at the interpretation and testimony stages." Although the study examined these forensic issues, it coded only for forensic discipline and whether an error was present, so it did not examine the nature and incidence of specific error types within the forensic science context.

Two notable studies have examined forensic errors in wrongful convictions more closely. Cooley and Oberfield examined over 50 case studies in which "unreliable forensic evidence" contributed to wrongful convictions (Cooley & Oberfield, 2007). Although the authors did not seek to provide systematic analysis, they did establish a baseline of claims concerning factors that cause forensic errors. The paper outlines cases that used bite mark identification, hair microscopy, serology, DNA, fingerprint identification, fiber analysis, fire debris analysis, firearms identification, bullet lead analysis, forensic pathology, lip print identification, and fraudulent testimony. They recommended:

1. Improved judicial oversight of unreliable forensic techniques
2. External and independent crime laboratory oversight
3. Accreditation under international standards
4. Professional certification

The paper did not attempt to provide a direct link between wrongful convictions and these recommendations.

Brandon Garrett has established a database of exonerations based on DNA testing (https://www.convictingtheinnocent.com/) and published a book on the topic (Garrett, 2011b). The database relies on information from the Innocence Project and The Innocence Record, which provides more detailed trial transcripts and other information about the cases, including information about forensic testimony (Garrett, 2011a). In general, the data is based on older cases and is presented in summary form, although a widely cited 2009 law review article did provide more details (Garrett & Neufeld, 2009). That article states, "[O]ne cannot determine whether invalid forensic science testimony was common in the past two decades or today." In part, this limitation arises because the data are generally limited to older rape cases, in which DNA evidence is more common and probative. Also, it is impossible to know whether other innocent defendants *should have been* exonerated but were not.

Garrett and Neufeld produced the most comprehensive examination of forensic errors to date in their 2009 paper (Garrett & Neufeld, 2009). They limited their data set to DNA exonerees with available trial transcripts, which at that time included 137 cases, 85 of which included "invalid forensic science testimony." Thus, 63% of cases in their study set included forensic errors—as expected, given that they limited their analysis to DNA exonerations. Cases included the use of a wide range of pattern evidence, physical evidence, and biological evidence. They found errors in most serology and bite mark comparison testimony and in many hair comparison and DNA cases. They found an error in only one fingerprint comparison case out of the 13 they reviewed. Notably, they state, "almost half of the valid forensic testimony was not inculpatory and likely did not significantly support the conviction." In other words, there is uncertainty with respect to the weight given to the various forms of forensic evidence and testimony in these cases. In hair and serology cases, the forensic evidence was usually secondary to victim testimony that identified the defendant. DNA exonerations reinforce research findings concerning the unreliability of eyewitness testimony, especially in cases of cross-racial identification (Loftus, 2019).

They also published an appendix that defined the type of forensic error in each case and a website, www.convictingtheinnocent.com, that provides their documentation, including trial transcripts. Interestingly, the classic case of an outright error is present in only six cases. In most of their data set, wrongful convictions are associated with misinterpretation or miscommunication of the evidence. The study authors performed most of the case analysis themselves, with only limited, published justification. They did not specify a methodology for their categorization or discuss the resolution of conflicting views, if any existed. They did establish two important points. First, forensic errors can contribute to wrongful convictions and be described and categorized. Second, clear and scientifically sound communication of forensic results is just as important as reliable forensic analysis at the lab bench. Miscommunication can lead to miscarriages of justice.

In general, forensic science practitioners and their critics among exoneration advocates disagree about the implications of wrongful convictions (Innocence Project, 2020). The forensic science community has emphasized the realities of the criminal justice system and value of current forensic science practices. Exoneration advocates have suggested many reforms but have had limited success in linking those reforms to research data or convincing forensic science leaders to agree with their recommendations. The criminal justice system continues to face challenges relating to the admissibility and use of forensic evidence.

In 2009, the National Academy of Sciences (NAS) issued a landmark report (Committee on Identifying the Needs of the Forensic Sciences Community, National Research Council, 2009) that recommended forensic improvements because "faulty forensic science analyses may have contributed to wrongful convictions of innocent people." (Committee on Identifying the Needs of the Forensic Sciences Community, National Research Council, 2009). The report recognized that DNA had played an important role in exonerations while acknowledging that other forensic disciplines lacked the scientific foundation, standards, and probative value associated with DNA forensics. The report made recommendations for the establishment of improved governance mechanisms in forensic science, particularly for research, education, laboratory development, and the establishment and enforcement of standards. The NAS recommended the use of standards to improve the precision and thoroughness of forensic reports and testimony and to limit the misinterpretation or misuse of forensic science by the courts. The report also recognized that forensic disciplines could be impacted by contextual bias and recommended the development of science-based procedures to limit bias and human error in forensic practice. In addition to improvements in forensic certification, accreditation, and education, NAS advocated for substantial investment in scientific studies "address issues of accuracy, reliability, and validity in the forensic science disciplines." In particular, the report discusses the importance of validation studies to establish the reliability and accuracy of forensic analyses.

Although the NAS report has been very influential, none of its recommendations have been realized in the manner envisioned by the authors in the 13 years since its publication. In particular, its recommendations to establish a separate "National Institute of Forensic Science" at the federal level and to remove public crime laboratories from the administrative control of law enforcement have not been implemented. The federal government did operate a National Commission of Forensic Science (NCFS) from 2013 to 2017 (National Commission on Forensic Science, 2017). NCFS published influential documents on accreditation and proficiency testing, quality assurance, ethics, medicolegal death investigation, testimony and reporting standards, scientific research, and human factors. NCFS documents are referenced throughout this textbook where appropriate. Like the NAS, the NCFS has been influential but lacked any enforcement or oversight powers. Some jurisdictions and laboratories have implemented aspects of NCFS recommendations, but only to a limited extent. State-level forensic science commissions have been the most effective mechanism to promulgate NCFS standards and recommendations, but such organizations exist in only 10 states and the District of Columbia (Morgan, Ropero-Miller, McCleary, & McLendon, 2016). Other state reforms have been considered or implemented (Norris, Bonventre, Redlich, Acker, & Lowe, 2017).

The National Institute of Standards and Technology (NIST) established the Organization of Scientific Area Committees (OSAC) in 2014 to guide and develop forensic science standards (National Institute of Standards and Technology, 2020). Over 500 forensic scientists and researchers collaborate within the consensus-based OSAC process. OSAC has developed and published standards across a wide range of forensic disciplines and works with other standards bodies to promulgate the completed work. OSAC addresses an issue that has arisen frequently in wrongful convictions, the failure by a forensic practitioner to follow best practices.

In 2016, the President's Council on Applied Science and Technology (PCAST) issued a report that highlighted the vulnerability of pattern evidence disciplines to subjectivity and forensic error in their 2016 report (PCAST Working Group, 2016). As the PCAST report states:

> By objective feature-comparison methods, we mean methods consisting of procedures that are each defined with enough standardized and quantifiable detail that they can be performed by either an automated system or human examiners exercising little or no judgment. By subjective methods, we mean methods including key procedures that involve significant human judgment—for example, about which features to select or how to determine whether the features are sufficiently similar to be called a proposed identification.

In the view of PCAST, "human error, bias, and performance variability across examiners" are important contributors to forensic errors and wrongful convictions. Like the NAS, PCAST sought to establish validation studies to determine the accuracy and reliability of forensic disciplines. Building on that idea, PCAST made recommendations concerning the construction of validity studies. The PCAST report highlighted the differences between the scientific process and the processes followed within forensic disciplines. In summary, PCAST recommended that forensic science laboratories build close relationships with research laboratories and follow protocols similar to those found in general scientific practice. It is the case that DNA analysis, toxicology, and drug chemistry follow standards that are similar to (or even the same as) those in the broader scientific community, but other disciplines do not. Some forensic scientists have been critical of the PCAST report because it overemphasized the role of subjective interpretation in the pattern evidence disciplines. Every forensic discipline—indeed every scientific discipline or other professional field—is vulnerable to human error, bias, and performance variability, so the primary concern should be the most appropriate strategy to mitigate these risks, not "eliminate" them. Further, the idealized PCAST vision of a scientific research facility may not be an effective model for the management of a forensic science organization. In fact, some wrongful convictions have arisen from scientific research laboratories that did not follow the stringent quality assurance mechanisms associated with forensic science practice. These mechanisms reflect the challenges associated with sample quality, contamination, and the inherently uncontrolled nature of crime scenes (Organization of Scientific Area Committees for Forensic Science, 2020).

STUDY QUESTIONS

1. Consider the Krueger and Stielow/Green wrongful convictions. What were the contributing factors to the forensic science errors in those cases? Would current forensic science reforms have prevented the errors in those cases?
2. Public crime laboratories are government organizations that usually report to a law enforcement agency. Discuss the benefits and risks of the close relationship between police and crime labs.
3. Like society as a whole, the criminal justice system faces challenges related to the increasing complexity of science and technology. What should the courts do to make sure that their decisions are based on reliable scientific methods? Do current evidence standards provide a rigorous set of rules to review forensic evidence? Why or why not?
4. Many observers believe that forensic science organizations should reflect a "research culture" like a scientific laboratory. Others hold that medical organizations—such as hospitals—may be a better model. What kinds of organizations should forensic science organizations emulate? What are the key attributes of these organizations?

FURTHER READING

The literature of wrongful convictions has become quite extensive and may be difficult for the new student. Among the references cited in this chapter, the student may want to start with the Borchard or Frank & Frank historical volumes. More recently, *Actual Innocence* by Scheck, Neufeld, and Dwyer remains relevant and highlights some forensic science issues. The 1996 Connors report was a comprehensive resource looking at DNA exonerations at that time. Simon Cole's book on fingerprints, *More Than Zero*, (Cole, 2005) and his summary on forensic evidence in the New England Law Review are both excellent examinations of forensic science issues in wrongful convictions. Most importantly, the National Registry of Exonerations provides comprehensive resources on wrongful convictions, including annual reports that summarize new exonerations and trends. See https://www.law.umich.edu/special/exoneration/Pages/about.aspx.

The reader should review the key documents related to forensic science reform. These documents start with the 2009 National Academy of Sciences report. The work of the National Commission on Forensic Science is archived at https://www.justice.gov/archives/ncfs. The OSAC is producing a large and useful set of work on forensic standards; see https://www.nist.gov/organization-scientific-area-committees-forensic-science. Similarly, the European Network of Forensic Science Institutes (ENFSI) is an excellent example of governance in the international community. See https://enfsi.eu/.

REFERENCES

(2022). Retrieved from North Carolina Innocence Inquiry Commission: https://innocencecommission-nc.gov/

Blackstone, W. (1893). *Commentaries on the Laws of England*. Philadelphia: J. P. Lippincott Co.

Borchard, E. M. (1932). *Convicting the Innocent: Sixty-Five Actual Errors of Criminal Justice*. Garden City, NJ: Garden City Publishing.

Cole, S. A. (2005). More Than Zero: Accounting for Error in Latent Print Identification. *Journal of Criminal Law and Criminology*, *95*, 985–1078.

Cole, S. A. (2011). Forensic Science and Wrongful Convictions: From Exposer to Contributor to Corrector. *New England Law Review*, 46, 711–736.

Committee on Identifying the Needs of the Forensic Sciences Community, National Research Council. (2009). *Strengthening Forensic Science in the United States: A Path Forward*. Washington, DC: National Academies Press.

Connors, E., Lundregan, T., Miller, N., & McEwen, T. (1996). *Convicted by Juries, Exonerated by Science: Case Studies in the Use of DNA Evidence to Establish Innocence After Trial*. Washington, DC: National Institute of Justice.

Consortium of Forensic Science Organizations. (2013, December). *Accreditation of Entities Providing Forensic Science Services*. Retrieved from American Society of Crime Laboratory Directors: https://www.ascld.org/wp-content/uploads/2014/02/CFSO-Accreditation-Paper-December-2013.pdf

Cooley, C. M., & Oberfield, G. S. (2007). Increasing Forensic Evidence's Reliability and Minimizing Wrongful Convictions: Applying Daubert Isn't the Only Problem. *Tulsa Law Review*, *43*(2), 285–380.

Daubert v. Merrell Dow Pharmaceuticals. Inc., 92–102 (Supreme Court of the United States June 28, 1993).

Frank, J., & Frank, B. (1957). *Not Guilty*. Doubleday & Company.

Frye v. United States, 293 F. 1013 (Court of Appeals of the District of Columbia December 3, 1923).

Garrett, B. L. (2011a). *Characteristics of Forensic Testimony at DNA Exonerees' Trials*. Retrieved from Convicting the Innocent: https://www.convictingtheinnocent.com/wp-content/uploads/2016/10/garrett_forensics_appendix.pdf

Garrett, B. L. (2011b). *Convicting the Innocent: Where Criminal Prosecutions Go Wrong*. Cambridge, MA: Harvard University Press.

Garrett, B. L. (2020). Wrongful Convictions. *Annual Review of Criminology*, *3*(1), 245–259.

Garrett, B. L., & Neufeld, P. (2009, March). Invalid Forensic Science Testimony and Wrongful Convictions. *Virginia Law Review*, 1–97.

Giannelli, P. C. (2011). Daubert and Forensic Science: The Pitfalls of Law Enforcement Control of Scientific Research. *University of Illinois Law Review*, *2011*(1), 1–39.

Gould, J. B., Carrano, J., Leo, R., & Young, J. (2013). *Predicting Erroneous Convictions: A Social Science Approach to Miscarriages of Justice*. NCJRS. Retrieved from https://www.ncjrs.gov/pdffiles1/nij/grants/241389.pdf

Gross, S. R., & O'Brien, B. (2008, December). Frequency and Predictors of False Conviction: Why We Know So Little, and New Data on Capital Cases. *Journal of Empirical Legal Studies*, *5*(4), 927–962.

Gross, S. R., & Shaffer, M. (2012, June). *Exonerations in the United States, 1989–2012*. Retrieved from National Registry of Exonerations: https://www.law.umich.edu/special/exoneration/Documents/exonerations_us_1989_2012_full_report.pdf

Huff, C. R., & Killias, M. (Eds.). (2008). *Wrongful Conviction: International Perspectives on Miscarriages of Justice*. Philadelphia, PA: Temple University Press.

Innocence Network. (2022). Retrieved from https://innocencenetwork.org/

Innocence Project. (2020, January 28). *Overturning Wrongful Convictions Involving Misapplied Forensics*. Retrieved from Innocence Project: https://www.innocenceproject.org/overturning-wrongful-convictions-involving-flawed-forensics/

Innocence Project. (2022). *Innocence Project.* Retrieved January 7, 2022, from Explore the Numbers: Innocence Project's Impact: https://innocenceproject.org/exonerations-data/

Koenig, B. E. (1980). Speaker Identification (Part 1) Three Methods--Listening, Machine, and Aural-Visual. *FBI Law Enforcement Bulletin*(January), 1–4.

LaPorte, G. (2017, September). Wrongful Convictions and DNA Exonerations: Understanding the Role of Forensic Science. *NIJ Journal*, 1–10.

Legal Information Institute. (n.d.). *Rule 702. Testimony by Expert Witnesses.* Retrieved from Cornell Law School: https://www.law.cornell.edu/rules/fre/rule_702

Leo, R. A., & Gould, J. B. (2009). Studying Wrongful Convictions: Learning from Social Science. *The Ohio State Journal of Criminal Law*, *7*, 7–30.

Liebman, J. S., Fagan, J., West, V., & Lloyd, J. (2000). Capital Attrition: Error Rates in Capital Cases, 1973–1995. *Texas Law Review, 78*, 1839–1865.

Loftus, E. F. (2019). Eyewitness testimony. *Applied Cognitive Psychology*, *33*(4), 498–503.

Maimonides, M. (c. 1200). translation by Charles Ber Chavel and Moses ibn Tibbon*The book of divine commandments.* (the Sefer Ha-mitzvoth of Moses Maimonides) London: Soncino Press, 1940

Morgan, J., Ropero-Miller, J., McCleary, N., & McLendon, M. (2016). *State Forensic Science Commissions.* National Institute of Justice.

National Commission on Forensic Science. (2017). *National Commission on Forensic Science: Reflecting Back--Looking Toward the Future.* National Institute of Standards and Technology.

National Institute of Standards and Technology. (2020, February 13). *OSAC Organizational Structure.* Retrieved from The Organization of Scientific Area Committees for Forensic Science: https://www.nist.gov/topics/organization-scientific-area-committees-forensic-science/osac-organizational-structure

National Registry of Exonerations. (2021). *Annual Report.* Newkirk Center for Science & Society at the University of California Irvine, the University of Michigan Law School & Michigan State University College of Law.

National Registry of Exonerations. (2022). *Conviction Integrity Units.* Retrieved from National Registry of Exonerations: https://www.law.umich.edu/special/exoneration/Pages/Conviction-Integrity-Units.aspx

National Research Council. (2003). *The Polygraph and Lie Detection.* Washington, DC: The National Academies Press. https://doi.org/10.17226/10420

Norris, R., Bonventre, C., Redlich, A., Acker, J., & Lowe, C. (2017). Preventing Wrongful Convictions: An Analysis of State Investigation Reforms. *Criminal Justice Policy Review, 30*(4), 597–626.

North Carolina Innocence Inquiry Commission. (2011). *State v. Kagonyera/Wilcoxson.* Retrieved from North Carolina Innocence Inquiry Commission: https://innocencecommission-nc.gov/cases/state-v-kagonyera-wilcoxson/

Organization of Scientific Area Committees for Forensic Science. (2020, March 23). *OSAC Research and Development Needs.* Retrieved from National Institute of Standards and Technology: https://www.nist.gov/topics/organization-scientific-area-committees-forensic-science/osac-research-and-development-needs

Osborn, A. S. (1939). Form Blindness and Proof (Sight Defects in Relation to the Administration of Justice). *Journal of Criminal Law and Criminology* (1931–1951), *30*(2), 243–249.

People v. Robert Kelly, 19028 (Supreme Court of California May 28, 1976).

People v. Stielow, 160 N.Y.S. 555 (Supreme Court of New York, Special Term, Erie County July 30, 1916).

Pope v. State, 756 W. S. 2d 401 (Court of Appeals of Texas, Dallas August 4, 1988).

Popper, K. (2005). *The Logic of Scientific Discovery.* London: Routledge.

Saks, M. J., & Koehler, J. J. (2005). The Coming Paradigm Shift in Forensic Identification. *Science, 309*, 892–895.

Scheck, B., Neufeld, P., & Dwyer, J. (2000). *Actual Innocence.* New York: Random House.

Texas Forensic Science Commission. (2016). *Forensic Bite mark Comparison Complaint Filed by National Innocence Project on Bhealf of Steven Mark Chaney - Final Report.* Austin, TX: Texas Forensic Science Commission.

Tosi, O., Oyer, H., Lashbrook, W., Pedrey, C., Nicol, J., & Nash, E. (1972). Experiment on voice identification. *The Journal of the Acoustical Society of America, 51*(6B), 2030–2043.

University of California Irvine Newkirk Center for Science & Society, University of Michigan Law School, and Michigan State University College of Law. (2020, January 28). Retrieved from The National Registry of Exonerations: https://www.law.umich.edu/special/exoneration/Pages/about.aspx

CHAPTER 2

Assessment of Forensic Science Errors

WHAT IS FORENSIC SCIENCE?

Forensic science is the use of scientific methods or expertise to investigate crimes or examine evidence that might be presented in a court of law (Forensic Science | NIST). In legal proceedings, forensic science may be considered a subset of expert witness testimony, which includes any opinion on a technical or scientific topic, as set forth in Rule 702 in the Federal Rules of Evidence (Legal Information Institute). The forensic sciences include many disciplines used in the investigation and adjudication of crime and that cover different aspects of the natural sciences. Most crime laboratories examine physical evidence collected from crime scenes, but the methods used to extract information from that evidence might include any of the physical sciences. A cell phone from a crime scene might be dusted for fingerprints, swabbed for DNA, sampled for trace evidence, and examined for digital evidence. Other forensic examiners work within the medico-legal death investigation system in medical examiner or coroner offices. Many examiners work closely with law enforcement, particularly those who do crime scene investigation. Others work entirely outside traditional forensic science organizations doing medical or psychological assessments. Regardless, all of these professionals are forensic scientists.

Some criminal justice practitioners use science and technology but are not considered forensic scientists. For example, polygraphers conduct lie detection interviews and are subject to the same expert evidence standards as forensic scientists, but they are not generally viewed as forensic scientists. Many police and security professionals use dogs for screening or tracking, in which case the work is outside a forensic context. On the other hand, if a dog handler testifies in court, then the canine detection work may be considered a forensic technique.

DOI: 10.4324/9781003202578-2

Forensic science sits at the intersection of two worlds—science and justice—that have different rules for investigating problems and making decisions. The forensic scientist must resolve the conflict between these two, very different ways to determine truth. Science produces reliable knowledge, especially when one applies established theories that have been subject to rigorous experimental confirmation. The scientist builds knowledge by testing hypotheses against observations and experiments. Science advances by adopting new generalizations that fit the reproducible results observed in the natural world. The scientist can then apply properly tested theories to build reliable bridges or perform a forensic analysis. The scientist remains a skeptic about all theories because new observations may cause one to rethink the implications of prior work and because there are inherent uncertainties in all real-world observations. It is not necessary to have epistemological certainty to apply science successfully. When forensic scientists testify, they should convey the uncertainties associated with their method. Proper communication of the limitations of a method should reinforce confidence in the validity of forensic science testimony. That is how science works—or it's how science is supposed to work. The scientist must retain doubt about any experiment or theory that may be contradicted by new information.

The justice system relies on a very different model to elucidate truth. The court relies on human experience and judgment to reach verdicts that are uncertain by definition. Decisions are reached on the basis of "reasonable doubt" or "preponderance of evidence." Information is collected from witnesses, whose recollection and testimony are both fallible and potentially dishonest. Many strategies are employed to minimize this problem, from moral strictures in society against false witness to the adversarial system of American jurisprudence. The judge and jury consider the testimony based on their own experience, education, and point of view. It is less important that they are learned than that they are perceived as fair and impartial.

Thus, the justice system produces reliable knowledge based on the perception of the fairness of its processes and verdicts. The justice system must assume it is infallible, even though it is clear that some doubt may remain and that errors can be made. For example, the prison system can't treat one convicted person differently due to doubts about a verdict. Once the court says the person is convicted and sentenced to a term in prison, then the system is designed to follow that verdict as if it were absolute truth. This legal principle is called the doctrine of finality. In other words, the verdict is assumed to be true and correct unless the court process was flawed in some demonstrable and significant way. The courts have little room for the doubts of forensic scientists about a theory or method after a trial has been completed.

Of course, the court may produce erroneous verdicts, but it is essential that the process is deemed as fair and reliable by the public and therefore retain its legitimacy. Criminal proceedings must produce judgments that resolve matters conclusively. Hence, appeals are based on procedural matters, such as the treatment of the suspect or the fairness of the trial. In general, new evidence does not produce a new trial unless it calls into question the soundness of the original proceeding. Whether it is a conviction or acquittal, the original verdict becomes an accepted "Truth." The rest of the criminal justice system proceeds as if the result is an absolute fact, regardless of any doubt that may have arisen during a trial. In the context of wrongful convictions, this behavior may seem callous or ignorant, even if it is necessary for the proper functioning of the system.

FORENSIC SCIENCE CONCLUSIONS

Forensic science may be used in a variety of ways to assist the fact-finder in criminal proceedings. It may produce an identification or individualization, which is a conclusion that two samples derive from the same source (Organization of Scientific Area Committees for Forensic Science, 2018). As a practical matter, individualization may be determined if samples from two sources cannot be distinguished within the sensitivity of the comparison process. This implies that a sample from a crime scene and a reference sample from a known source possess the same characteristics. From a theoretical perspective, a particular technique may lack the selectivity required to do an individualization. For example, bite mark evidence is limited by the ability of skin to be used as a registration medium for bite mark impressions. A particular dentition source can be associated with many bite marks. So, bite mark comparison cannot be used to produce individualizations, although bite mark examiners have testified to individualizations in many wrongful convictions.

Alternatively, forensic science may be used to produce a classification, which is a conclusion that two samples derive from a common population of sources. All forensic methods rely on the interpretation of populations of sources. For example, we may consider the human population as a set of possible sources of a piece of biological evidence. We can characterize the biological sample using DNA analysis and derive the value of the allele at a particular genetic locus, such as the short-tandem-repeat (STR) D7S820, which contains between 5 and 16 repeats of the sequence GATA. There is a subpopulation or "class" of humans with D7S820 of five repeats, another class with six, and so on. Initially, DNA analysts using PCR could only produce a classification because they were largely limited to the dqAlpha locus. They could describe the subpopulation that could be associated with biological evidence and use it to eliminate or exonerate an individual but they could not use dqAlpha to produce an individualization. After the development of multiplexing and the introduction of databases based on many STR loci, DNA could be used to individualize and even produce cold hits. Many forensic techniques have purported to produce individualizations but are in fact limited to classification. Many hair examiners testified that their comparisons were individualizations and by doing so contributed to wrongful convictions. These examiners should have limited their testimony to the characterization of a class of sources who could have contributed the evidence hair, an approach which remains valid and reliable.

Forensic science may be used to describe events that may have occurred in connection with a crime. These conclusions may be considered types of classification. For example, a medical professional may conclude that a child has been abused based on a set of observed injuries. The child's injuries are said to belong to a class of injuries that are associated with abuse. The medical professional should provide context concerning the likelihood that the injuries are associated with abuse relative to the possibility that the injuries are not associated with abuse. Further, a differential diagnosis would be required to determine if other conditions may have contributed to the observations and would change the ratio between the possibilities. Similarly, a fire debris investigation may result in the classification of the cause of a fire as incendiary, i.e., arson. It may also produce descriptive information about the spread of the fire, the time sequence of events, or the possibility of smoke inhalation or carbon monoxide poisoning. Each description is a separate conclusion that requires a classification of the debris patterns in some form. In reports and testimony, these distinctions may not be clarified for investigators or the court. This miscommunication may also contribute to a wrongful conviction.

Many attempts have been made to improve the standards for the formulation of forensic conclusions. One recent example involves the testimony standards promulgated by the European Network of Forensic Science Institutes (ENFSI) (Champod et al., 2016). The ENFSI guidelines require forensic scientists to use a likelihood ratio approach based on the consideration of a hypothesis and an alternative proposition. For example, the forensic scientist may consider the likelihood that a shard of glass came from a particular broken window relative to the possibility that the shard of glass came from an unknown source of glass (European Network of Forensic Science Institutes, 2015). ENFSI also recommends a hierarchy of propositions that distinguishes among conclusions related to crime, activity, source, and sub-source (Aitken et al., 2011). In general, a forensic scientist should avoid making a conclusion about a crime proposition. It is unlikely that forensic evidence will permit the conclusion that

"John Doe murdered the victim." Forensic pathologists may make a conclusion of "homicide" on a death certificate, but that conclusion should be limited to the activity-level proposition that the death was the result of actions by another individual. Also, such determinations of manner of death are public health decisions, not legal ones. Other activity-level propositions might be "John Doe shot the gun" or "John Doe broke the window." Most commonly, forensic science can make source or sub-source propositions. Source propositions relate to physical evidence. For example, was John Doe the source of the biological evidence or was an unknown individual the source of the biological evidence? Sub-source would then relate to the particular element of the evidence that was the subject of an analysis. For example, was the suspect the source of the DNA in the biological evidence or was an unknown individual the source of the DNA? The clear distinction of propositions was prominent in wrongful convictions associated with serological profiling before the advent of DNA. In most cases, the serological profile of a biological stain is associated with a wider population of sources than the serological profile of a particular suspect. Some serologists confused the source-level population (relating to class of sources that could have contributed to the biological sample) with the sub-source population (relating to the class of sources that had the same serological profile as the suspect). This type of miscommunication contributed to wrongful convictions.

BOX 1: RONJON CAMERON (COMMONWEALTH V. CAMERON, 2007, 2015)

Robert Lanphear was forced to vacate his apartment in Pittsfield, Massachusetts when he was sentenced to jail. His girlfriend lived in the same building and agreed to keep an eye on the place. In the meantime, Lanphear allowed Ronjon Cameron to live there. On September 13, 1999, the girlfriend visited the apartment to retrieve some items for Lanphear. She alleged that Cameron grabbed her from behind, threw her to the floor, and then dragged her to a recliner, where he raped her vaginally and anally for several minutes. Two days later, the victim reported the incident to Pittsfield police, who collected the dress and underwear she said she wore on the day of the assault. Berkshire Medical Center physician Dr. Mark Liponis examined her later and noted healing scratches and bruises. A rape kit was also collected. Cameron was identified by the victim, arrested, and then released on bond. He was arrested again in November of 2001 in Key West, Florida after having left the state in violation of the bond.

The Massachusetts State crime laboratory examined the evidence and found seminal residue on the crotch of the underwear. They sent the underwear to a widely respected commercial laboratory, Orchid Cellmark, for DNA testing. DNA analyst Kathryn Colombo testified at Cameron's 2003 trial that she performed Y-STR DNA testing on the underwear stain. Y-STR testing was designed to analyze only DNA markers from the male-specific Y-chromosome, so it is considered useful in sexual assault testing to differentiate a male assailant from a female victim. Y-STRs were not in common use at the time, although some commercial test kits were available from two manufacturers, Reliagene and Promega (Butler, 2003). See Figure 2.1. It is likely that results could have been obtained using DNA kits that looked at a broader range of STR markers. The STR kits available in 2003 might not have had the sensitivity needed to analyze the samples, especially if they turned out to be mixtures. At trial, Colombo reported that she indeed found a mixed sample of two contributors. Cameron was excluded from what Colombo called the "primary source." For the

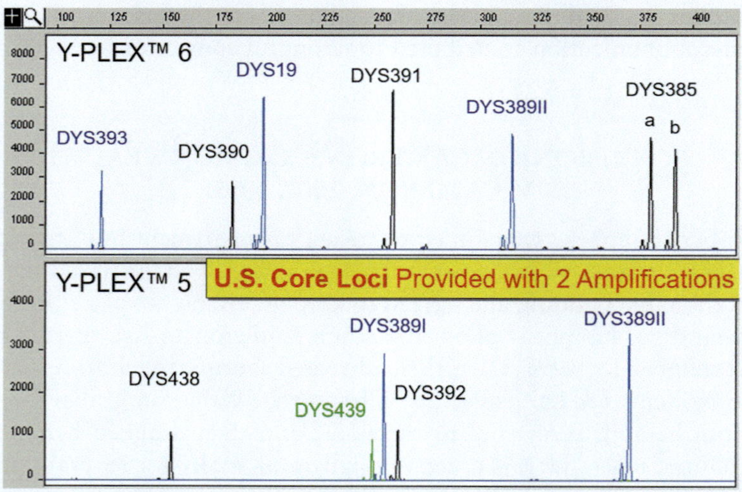

FIGURE 2.1 A typical, high-quality Y-STR result from the Reliagene Y-PLEX 6™ kit. Note that peak artifacts can be seen near the peaks associated with the single primary source. It is unclear if Colombo misinterpreted artifact peaks or mishandled the actual testing. It is also unclear if Orchid Cellmark had protocols for technical and administrative reviews of DNA analyses or testimony. Source: John Butler, National Institute of Standards and Technology (Butler, Y Chromosome Workshop, 2004.)

secondary source, she reported four Y-STR results. The secondary source DYS19 marker was 19, consistent with Cameron. The DYS 389-I marker was consistent with Cameron but was masked by the identical type in the primary source. The DYS 389-II marker failed. The DYS 390 marker produced a 21, but Cameron was typed to be a 24. The Reliagene and Promega kits were capable of typing several more markers at the time, but for unknown reasons Colombo did not report those results. Based on the results reported, Colombo should have excluded Cameron as a sub-source contributor to either the primary or secondary DNA profiles. Instead, she discounted the exclusion at DYS 390, saying:

> We know that sometimes with these systems we may lose types. So, I – I'm not saying we did in this case, I'm just saying we can't make that determination about the secondary source, we can't make any conclusion about the secondary source.
>
> *(Commonwealth v. Cameron, Appeals Court of Massachusetts, September 30, 2014, Case No. 10-P-692)*

Colombo clarified that she would not include or exclude Cameron as a donor of the seminal material on the underwear.

The trial rested on the victim eyewitness testimony, and Cameron was convicted. Years later, he was able to obtain DNA testing on an evidence slide that had been preserved from the underwear sample. That DNA testing again excluded him as a source from the "primary" profile. The testing then found that the "secondary" profile was actually from a female contributor. In other words, the Y-STR data reported on the secondary source was completely spurious. As it happens, Orchid Cellmark had other issues that came to light around the time of trial involving another DNA analyst, Sarah Blair, who had allegedly altered data for control samples in 20 instances over nine months (Cadiz, 2004). In 2015, the Massachusetts Supreme Judicial Court ordered a new trial for Ronjon Cameron, and the prosecution chose to drop the charges rather than retry him.

FORENSIC SCIENCE STANDARDS

Forensic science leaders have recognized that gaps in governance and standards have contributed to forensic errors and wrongful convictions. The development of standards has been a particular focus in recent years. ENFSI is one of many sources of standards for forensic science practice and communications. In the United States, the Organization of Scientific Area Committees (OSAC) develop consensus standards, (National Institute of Standards and Technology, 2020) but additional standards are promulgated by standards bodies (e.g., National Fire Protection Association (NFPA)), forensic science associations (Academy Standards Board | American Academy of Forensic Sciences (aafs.org)), and accrediting bodies, among others. The US Department of Justice (USDOJ) has established a Uniform Language for Testimony and Reports (ULTR) that governs the scope of forensic science communications from USDOJ examiners (US Department of Justice, 2019). In the United Kingdom, a Forensic Science Regulator establishes "an appropriate regime of scientific quality standards" for forensic science services (Forensic Science Regulator—GOV.UK (www.gov.uk)). Some medical associations, such as the American Academy of Pediatrics (AAP), promulgate guidelines that are relevant to many criminal cases.

Standards are a critical consideration in the assessment of forensic science errors in wrongful convictions. The examiner's work or testimony may not have conformed to the standards in place at the time of trial. The examiner's organization may have failed to establish or enforce standards. In some cases, standards may not have existed for the discipline at the time of trial. The standards may have existed but were based on an insufficient scientific foundation. When one assesses wrongful convictions, it is important to recognize the state of science and practice when the trial took place and consider the standards that were in place at that time. In hindsight, it is apparent that improved standards based on empirical research could have prevented many wrongful convictions.

SYSTEM ISSUES

A wrongful conviction may arise from a variety of factors that may or may not include a problem related to forensic evidence. Also, the reliable use of forensic evidence depends on competent work from the crime scene to the courtroom. At the crime scene, forensic evidence must be identified and collected. This requires investigators to understand whether a particular piece of evidence could be probative, ensure that it is collected and preserved, and maintain its chain of custody during storage and transport. The evidence may be mislabeled, mixed up with other evidence, or even lost. Later forensic analysis may be compromised by contamination or poor crime scene investigation. In many cases, police may not recognize that a crime could have taken place, such as when it is assumed that a death was a suicide or accident. Then, the scene is not secured and important evidence not collected. In the case of the death of a victim, the autopsy may be an important part of evidence collection. The pathologist may misinterpret artifacts on the body (e.g., confusing bruising due to resuscitation efforts with injuries inflicted during the crime) or may fail to properly collect and store evidence from the body.

Investigators may exhibit tunnel vision and become convinced that a particular suspect committed the crime. They will—consciously or unconsciously—develop false theories of the case and try to make the evidence fit into their preconceived ideas. At times, they will ignore or suppress exculpatory forensic results that counter this narrative. This "continuation bias" is common in all human cognition and is not unique to police investigators. We tend to have assumptions and expectations about the world. Cognitive biases help us to navigate complexity and social networks and are an inevitable part of any human decision-making. In criminal investigation and forensic science, cognitive biases may prevent the objective consideration of a case from the first moments of police response all the way through to conviction and beyond. Cognitive biases may be important in criminal investigation because detectives spend much more time building a case against known suspects than attempting to solve "unsub" (unknown subject) cases with unknown perpetrators. Forensic scientists may be vulnerable to contextual bias when they are aware of case information that is not relevant to their analysis. This issue is especially acute in forensic disciplines—such as forensic pathology and fire debris investigation—that consider contextual information in their analysis and produce subjective interpretations about activity-level propositions. Cognitive biases may contribute to forensic errors, but it should be recognized that the problem is relevant across the criminal justice system. In addition to limiting bias issues within the laboratory, forensic science organizations must foster clear and complete communication with police investigators and officers of the court. Communication should ensure that labs understand the probative value of evidence from the crime scene and other criminal justice practitioners understand the implications of forensic results.

FORENSIC SCIENCE ORGANIZATIONS

Of course, many forensic errors occur in the crime laboratory (National Institute of Standards and Technology, 2015). Some errors occur at the organizational level. Forensic science organizations may be dysfunctional in whole or in part because of poor management or inadequate resources. Labs in Houston, Chicago, and Detroit have contributed to multiple wrongful convictions—and there have been major laboratory scandals in Boston, New York, Delaware, and many other jurisdictions. It should be recognized that any organization may be susceptible to errors. Crime laboratories are in a special category with other high-reliability organizations (HROs), which are organizations that perform complex tasks with life-or-death consequences (Roberts, 1990; Houck, 2016). For example, other HROs include hospitals and airlines, both of which are vulnerable to error and must function with extremely high reliability on a daily basis. HROs are preoccupied with errors and will implement strategies to identify and mitigate risks. Wrongful convictions represent an important type of error for crime laboratories—similar to an airplane crash for an airline company. Although many crime laboratories now accept the possibility of forensic errors, fewer labs use HRO strategies to determine the root causes of errors and develop mitigation strategies closely connected to those root causes. All accredited laboratories are required to have a policy for "corrective action" when an audit finds work that fails to conform with policies and procedures. ISO 17025 is a general standard for testing and calibration laboratories and is applied in accredited crime laboratories (SO/IEC (International Organization for Standardization/International Electrotechnical Commission), 2017). When a nonconformance or adverse event occurs, the standard requires that the lab initiate an investigation to determine the "root cause(s) of the problem." The National Commission on Forensic Science (NCFS) recommended policies and procedures for the implementation of root cause analysis (RCA) in crime laboratories (Interim Solutions Committee, 2016). Properly done, RCA includes consideration of causes at the individual, physical/environmental, organizational, and system levels. Organizational issues may include resource management, organizational climate (or context), and organizational processes. As envisioned by the NCFS, the initiation of an RCA depends on the severity and probability of the error. For example, a minor clerical nonconformity that does not affect a reported result may not require an RCA, while a catastrophic system error related to misconduct and a wrongful conviction will always require an RCA. A thorough and transparent RCA may be difficult for a forensic laboratory in the context of a high-visibility wrongful conviction. Media attention, law enforcement influence, and the adversarial justice system may discourage transparency and lead to organizational defensiveness, thus exacerbating negative perceptions. Many crime laboratory directors recognize these issues and have established leadership programs for forensic professionals to help them navigate the challenging HRO environment (see ASCLD—ASCLD Leadership Academy: https://www.ascld.org/ascld-leadership-academy/.)

FORENSIC ANALYSIS

A forensic analyst may fail to follow best practices or standards, even when they have been clearly established in the organization. The analyst may fail to conduct the correct tests or may conduct them incorrectly. The tests may be unvalidated, based on insufficient science, or misinterpreted. The failures may be due to inadequate training, poor quality management, or fraudulent work. Misinterpretations may relate to the data, the probative value of the evidence, exaggerated statements about the results, or failures in statistical characterization. In some cases, a test may be in error due to the limitations of the method or the technology. Every scientific technique is associated with some error rate. The hallmark of a validated technique is a quantified characterization of its error rate at the test and/or system level (Ulery et al., 2011). The error rate may be difficult to determine in forensic science because the field involves samples that are inherently unpredictable. For example, drug analysis changes from year to year based on the introduction of novel psychoactive substances, new drug mixtures and adulterants, and new approaches to evade detection and prosecution.

Even if a forensic result was accurate and reliable, it may not be communicated correctly in reports or testimony. A forensic report may be incomplete or unclear, especially in light of miscommunications with investigators and officers of the court. Many fact-finders will not understand the implications or limitations of a forensic result. This issue has been exacerbated by the increasing complexity of science and technology. A failure to document data and methods in a forensic report may lead to its misuse in court. Most critically, defense lawyers often rely on forensic reports to formulate trial strategy, so poor documentation may lead to inadequate defense for the accused and a wrongful conviction. In other cases, the report may be missing background data or may have relied on an interpretation that did not have sufficient reference data. For example, the evidence may have been tested correctly, but elimination samples may not have been obtained or tested. In extreme cases, exculpatory results may not have been included in a report or recognized in the interpretation. Exculpatory results may also be discounted later in the investigation or trial. For example, in fingerprint cases, it is common for latent prints from crime scenes to match no suspect or other person known to be present at the scene. The nonmatches may be irrelevant if they were incidental to the crime. On the other hand, a nonmatch may be highly exculpatory if it is found on the murder weapon, or a surface known to have been touched by the perpetrator.

BOX 2: MICHAEL SERI

Michael Seri's father was a former state representative and gaming commissioner. His uncle was FBI agent Richard Macko. In 2001, Seri was living in Connecticut, earning money as a house painter, and studying for a bachelor's degree in English literature. On March 13, Seri visited the Newtown Public Library, as he had done on many days. He viewed some books on Greek tragedies that had been reserved for him. At the same time, a 15-year-old Girl Scout studying in the reference room of the library reported that a man had exposed himself to her and masturbated. The police were called, but the perpetrator was not found that day. The girl described the man as a 30–40-year-old male of average height, with dark skin, and black hair. She also identified a stack of books the suspect had handled. A librarian noted that Seri's name and phone number were on a note in a different stack of books he had returned to the reference desk. Police questioned Seri that day. The lead police investigator then went on sick leave for a month, during which time the investigation was not pursued.

The books that were handled by the perpetrator were sent to the State Forensic Laboratory. The lab found prints on the books and compared them to Seri's prints in July and October 2001. Both times, they reported that they could not match Seri to the latent prints from the books. The victim and her mother identified Seri as the perpetrator, despite differences in his appearance from the description given on the day of the crime. Seri and his lawyer asked police to do a database search on the unknown prints, but they refused (see Figure 2.2). In fact, at trial, a fingerprint examiner said he could not rule out Seri as the source of the prints because not enough of Seri's reference palmprint had been collected for a complete comparison. Seri was convicted, sentenced to jail, and required to register as a sex offender.

As it happens, a man named Angel LaPorte was arrested in June 2002 after exposing himself in a similar manner to a teenage girl at the same library. LaPorte matched the physical description of the perpetrator and had a prior history of sexual offenses. Police were aware of LaPorte at the time of Seri's arrest. LaPorte had been involved in a similar incident in Brookfield, but Newtown police did not follow up on that lead. Seri's uncle—the FBI agent—tried to get them to compare the latent prints from the books with LaPorte, but they refused. After Seri's lawyer went to court to get the latents, Macko arranged for a fingerprint comparison, which found a match to LaPorte.

Had police followed up on the obvious lead, they would have solved the case easily. Instead, the print was used to produce

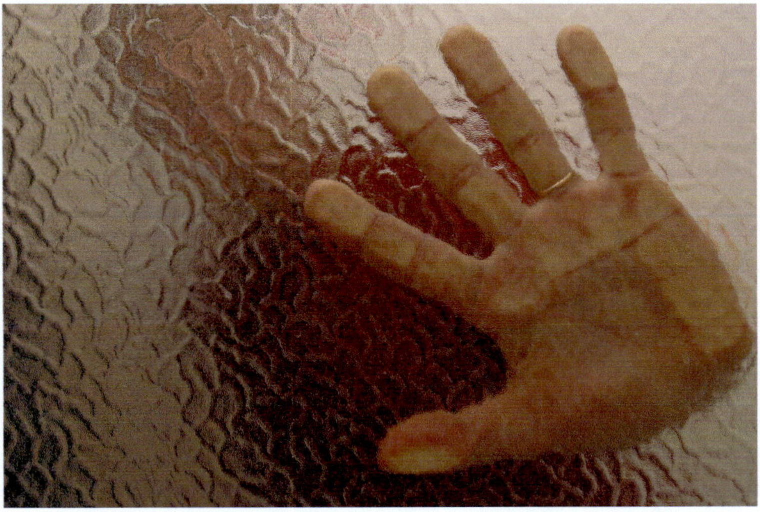

FIGURE 2.2 The FBI launched the National Palm Print System (NPPS) in 2013. Although many police agencies could perform local palmprint searches prior to 2013, the NPPS greatly expanded the scope and capabilities available to law enforcement. Typically, palmprint systems need 15 points of comparison to make a reliable cold hit. In the Seri case, a palmprint search would have helped but would not have been necessary if police had investigated known alternative suspects, such as LaPorte. (Source: Federal Bureau of Investigation.)

misleading testimony that appeared to inculpate Seri, even though the print was not a match to him.

Seri's conviction was vacated in February 2003. He received $370,000 in compensation.

Most wrongful conviction research relating to forensic evidence has studied forensic testimony (Garrett & Neufeld, 2009; Garrett, 2020). In part, this is due to the availability of trial transcripts. Also, forensic testimony is the linchpin of forensic science, which is after all the application of scientific methods in legal proceedings. Forensic testimony will reflect system failures outside the scope of the courtroom, such as failures to collect evidence or analyze it correctly. On the other hand, misleading forensic testimony may undermine otherwise reliable forensic work. In their landmark 2009 review of DNA exonerations, Garrett and Neufeld presented six categories of error in forensic testimony:

1. Non-Probative Evidence Presented as Probative, 48 cases
2. Exculpatory Evidence Discounted, 23 cases
3. Inaccurate Frequency or Statistic Presented, 13 cases
4. Statistic Provided Without Empirical Support, 5 cases
5. Non-numerical Statements Provided Without Empirical Support, 19 cases
6. Conclusion that Evidence Originated from Defendant, 6 cases

Most category one cases involved inculpatory serological interpretations in which Garrett and Neufeld found that the biological evidence was not sufficient to exclude any suspect. Categories three, four, and five involved the mischaracterization of statistics. For example, some hair comparison examiners quoted random match probability statements that were not supported by scientific research. A later FBI review found that many of their examiners had made misstatements about the probative value of hair comparisons, including misleading statistical characterizations (ABS Group, 2018). The review found three types of errors that exceed the limits of science:

Error Type 1. The examiner stated or implied that the evidentiary hair could be associated with a specific individual.

Error Type 2. The examiner assigned a statistical weight or probability to the opinion that a questioned hair originated from a particular source.

Error Type 3. The examiner cited the number of cases or hair analyses worked in the laboratory to bolster the predictive value of a conclusion that a hair belonged to a specific individual.

In most cases, the actual analysis by the examiner was valid, but the testimony exaggerated the value of the result. Error Type 2—statistical mischaracterization—was the most common problem. Some of these errors led to wrongful convictions.

There is a disconnect among the various standards and reviews of forensic evidence. For example, ENFSI guidance requires that each forensic result be conveyed in the form of a statistical likelihood ratio. The guidance allows some leeway for the examiner to use qualitative language when quantitative statistical estimates are not possible. This guidance runs counter to the Garrett and FBI reviews of hair comparison cases. Like many scholars, they held that statistical characterization should not be provided if there is no foundational scientific research to support it. A statistical statement implies a level of knowledge about the method and the population of sources that the method is characterizing. If those source populations have not been empirically studied, the examiner has no objective basis to communicate any statistical formulation, whether it be qualitative or quantitative. In many wrongful convictions, examiners provided invalid statistical testimony without adequate empirical foundations. Although many well-meaning researchers continue to advocate for the development of statistically based testimony standards, they should recognize that this goal can only be realized *after* the completion of the necessary empirical research. The premature adoption of statistical requirements may lead to faulty testimony. The premature adoption of sophisticated but unvalidated statistical approaches may undermine public trust in the criminal justice system and forensic science (Gittelson, 2013).

Testimony errors may include a misstatement of the scientific basis for a conclusion. This problem has arisen in many cases in which a novel forensic technique has been introduced but not sufficiently validated. Voiceprint analysis and lip-print comparison fall into this category. In other cases, an examiner may be an advocate for a new method that is not accepted in the field. For example, bite mark examiner Michael West thought he could visualize subcutaneous bruises using ultraviolet light, but no researcher could duplicate his results. Finally, an examiner trained in old methods may not use validated science in forming conclusions. The field of fire debris investigation was revolutionized by the NFPA 921 standard, which was introduced in 1992 and revised substantially in the years since then (National Fire Protection Association, 2017). The standard has been heavily influenced by wrongful convictions in arson cases and the development of fire science to inform interpretation. Some examiners resisted the adoption of NFPA 921 and continued to rely on outdated ideas without a scientific foundation to interpret fire scenes. Their testimony misstated the scientific basis for their conclusions and led to wrongful convictions.

SYSTEMATIC REVIEWS OF FORENSIC ERRORS

The scientific community has conducted extensive research to improve the understanding of errors and uncertainties (Joint Committee for Guides in Metrology, 2008). These methods are most clearly represented in forensic methods involving chemical analysis, such as toxicology or chemical analysis of fire debris. Forensic errors may be assessed on a broader, systems basis as well. For example, legal academic Paul Roberts has proposed a 20-item typology of forensic science errors, as outlined in Figure 2.3 (Roberts, 2015). Roberts' approach includes the consideration of factors related to the use of forensic science in the courts, including the failure of lawyers or jurors to understand and use scientific testimony reliably. The typology reflects that valid scientific work may be undermined if it is not communicated clearly and accurately.

1. *Junk science.* Tests do not measure what they purport to measure.
2. *Invalidated method.* Techniques lack validation or sufficient statistical support.
3. *Operationally deficient processing.* Lab protocols are inadequate and may lead to contamination or sample degradation.
4. *Unscientific methodology.* The method lacks scientific objectivity and is susceptible to cognitive bias effects.
5. *Human fallibility.* Forensic experts are human, have cognitive biases, and make mistakes.
6. *Charlatanism.* Examiners may be incompetent or produce fraudulent results.
7. *Overreaching.* Experts stray beyond the bounds of their legitimate area of expertise.
8. *Institutional distortion.* Organizational policies and procedures may compromise the performance and communication of forensic testing.
9. *Lawyer ignorance/misuse.* Lawyers and courts mishandle or misuse science due to poor understanding or deliberate manipulation.
10. *Communication failures.* Experts communicate their work in a manner that is not fully understood by the non-specialist.
11. *Lax admissibility standards.* Courts accept questionable and misleading scientific evidence.
12. *Overly restrictive admissibility standards.* Courts exclude novel but valid scientific evidence that could provide relevant, probative information.
13. *Testimonial silencing.* Experts must conform to courtroom procedures that prevent the clear communication of scientific evidence and the limits of its reliability.
14. *Adversarial deficit.* Defendants do not have access to sufficient scientific expertise to use forensic evidence effectively.
15. *Manufactured disagreement.* Adversarial trials mislead fact-finders concerning agreements or differences among expert interpretations of forensic evidence.
16. *Institutional incompetence to resolve genuine disagreement.* The criminal trial process is a poor forum to resolve scientific disagreements.
17. *Excessive jury deference.* Juries defer too readily to experts.
18. *Excessive jury skepticism.* Juries discount valid scientific evidence due to unfounded skepticism.
19. *Number-blindness.* Nonexperts may not understand the statistical basis of scientific evidence.
20. *Two antithetical cultures.* Law and science are methodologically incompatible.

FIGURE 2.3 The Roberts Paradigm of forensic science errors in legal processes (Roberts, 2015). Source: Adapted from Roberts' list, with significant modifications by the author.

Alternatively, NIST sponsored the 2015 International Symposium on Forensic Science Error Management, which largely focused on the role of the forensic scientist (National Institute of Standards and Technology, 2015). The proceedings included a useful set of examples of errors in forensic science, as reproduced below.

ANALYST/EXPERT ERROR

- Errors due to human bias (i.e., cognitive bias, confirmation bias)
- Forensic examiner variability
- Errors due to improperly collected or improperly labeled evidence from crime scenes
- Errors due to break in the chain of custody

- Errors due to contamination and mislabeling of evidence
- Errors due to mishandling (i.e., losing samples, sample mix-ups, sample mislabeling, and sample contamination)
- Errors due to misinterpretation of evidence
- Errors due to misinterpretation of data
- Errors in poorly following best practices, processes, and methods
- Errors due to poor documentation and transcriptions
- Errors due to inadequately trained personnel
- Errors due to analyst incompetence
- Errors due to failure to review the analysis of the original analyst
- Errors due to misinterpretation of post-mortem artifacts (i.e., artifacts due to resuscitation, exhumation, decomposition, embalming, rigor mortis, toxicological, environmental)
- Measurement errors (i.e., systematic and random)

FRAUD

- Errors due to examiner fraud
- Errors due to falsified reports
- Errors due to suppression of exculpatory evidence
- Errors due to exaggeration of test results
- Errors due to false testimony about test results

METHODS/PROTOCOL ERROR

- Errors due to invalidated methods
- Errors due to methods without scientific underpinnings
- Errors due to inaccurate and misleading statistics
- Error rates in scientific techniques
- Measurement errors (i.e., systematic and random)

INSTRUMENTATION/TECHNOLOGY LIMITATIONS

- Errors in software packages
- Error rates in technology solutions
- Laboratory equipment errors (i.e., poor or no calibrations)
- Errors due to deficiencies in laboratory reference materials
- Measurement errors (i.e., systematic and random)

Finally, the Canadian government conducted a review in 2011 of wrongful convictions associated with faulty expert testimony (FPT Heads of

Prosecutions Committee Working Group, 2011 (update)) They discussed several categories of error, including:

1. Prosecutorial bias or misleadingly presented evidence to support one theory alone
2. Evidence presented with exaggerated probative value
3. Poorly communicated evidence with excessive jargon and terminology
4. Testimony on contaminated or tainted evidence
5. Testimony on evidence reliant on scientifically out-of-date methodologies or evidence reliant on subjective judgments

There is significant overlap among the various approaches to error interpretation. Most importantly, it should be recognized that the etiology of expert errors is more complex than is generally recognized. While many observers assume that forensic errors arise primarily from fraud or junk science, the reality is far more complex. The assessment of wrongful convictions should reflect this complexity and the wide range of root causes that may lead to forensic errors.

OFFICERS OF THE COURT

Forensic evidence may contribute to a wrongful conviction even in cases in which the forensic work was valid and reliable and communicated correctly. As alluded to previously, officers of the court may misuse forensic evidence. A prosecutor may ignore, suppress, or mischaracterize the evidence. A defense attorney may fail to review the forensic evidence, raise appropriate objections to forensic testimony, or may even fail to recognize exculpatory evidence. A judge may allow invalid scientific testimony or fail to sustain valid defense objections to forensic evidence.

Forensic scientists usually have a close, working relationship with prosecutors. It is common for prosecutors to have a better understanding of the implications of forensic evidence than many defense attorneys. This may be due to the direct communication and collaboration of prosecutors with forensic science organizations during criminal investigations. Further, a prosecutor may rely on a forensic result to go to trial. For example, a prosecutor would have great difficulty getting a murder conviction in the absence of a homicide determination by a medical examiner or getting an arson conviction in the absence of a finding of incendiary cause by a fire investigator. Thus, forensic evidence tends to be "prosecution-friendly" in many cases, including many cases that end in wrongful convictions. Finally, a prosecutor has a responsibility on behalf of the state to make the best possible case against a defendant.

The prosecutor's theory of the case, characterization of evidence, direct examination, and summary will reflect a biased—in this case deliberately biased—view of the forensic evidence. In taking this approach, a prosecutor is not free to suppress evidence, mischaracterize the evidence, or misrepresent the scientific basis for the forensic result. The prosecutor is free to interpret the implications of probative evidence in the light most favorable to the state's case.

Inadequate defense is associated with a large number of wrongful convictions but may be more likely in cases involving forensic science. In many cases, defendants have few resources to counter prosecution claims, exacerbating an adversarial deficit caused by the increasing complexity of the science and technology of forensic evidence. As outlined above, inculpatory forensic conclusions may be needed to support the prosecution theory of a case, but those conclusions may often be based on subjective interpretation frameworks. A different examiner may look at the same evidence and come to a different conclusion. In such cases, it is imperative for defense counsel to understand the implications of the forensic evidence and seek independent review to determine if an alternative interpretation could be consistent with the defense theory of the case. For example, a fire debris investigator may make a conclusion that a fire had an incendiary cause—i.e., that it was arson—based on the physical debris and the presence of accelerant. A different investigator may conclude that the cause of the fire was "undetermined" because of uncertainties in the evidence or interpretation. The defendant would be much more likely to be convicted without the input from the independent examiner. This issue can be seen in cases involving forensic pathology and forensic medicine, which also involve subjective interpretation of complex fact patterns. Notably, these disciplines are susceptible to contextual bias effects because they may use case information to bolster a forensic interpretation.

Like a prosecutor, a defense attorney is not obligated to take an objective view of a case. The defense attorney is an advocate and will rely on the defense theory of the case and characterize the evidence in the best light consistent with that theory. To accomplish this goal, the defense will have several obligations relative to forensic evidence. First, the defense must conduct appropriate discovery of the forensic evidence and obtain a thorough understanding of the evidence prior to trial. If a novel forensic method is used, the defense must object to it and pursue appropriate judicial review. If an examiner testifies outside the rules for expert testimony, the defense must object to the testimony at the appropriate time. In wrongful convictions, a defense lawyer may not meet these challenging obligations. In many cases, the first appeal after a conviction will be based on a claim of inadequate defense, although convictions are seldom overturned on such a claim. It should be noted that the legal standard requires only that defense counsel act with reasonable diligence under "prevailing professional norms," but those norms generally do not require challenges to forensic evidence (Strickland v. Washington, 1984).

Judges can also play a role in the misuse of forensic evidence. A judge may accept a novel, unvalidated forensic method over the objections of defense counsel. The court may also allow invalid or exaggerated testimony that does not conform to rules for expert testimony. Also, courts seldom recognize the importance of the adversarial deficit between the prosecution and defense as it relates to forensic evidence. Because defendants may rely on public defense, they are also dependent on the allocation of resources by the court for the independent review of forensic evidence. Courts may provide limited or no funding for those reviews, even in cases in which the forensic interpretation is probative and clearly uncertain. Such reviews can cost thousands of dollars even before accounting for time and travel costs for the expert to attend a trial. Few defendants can afford those expenses, and few courts will allocate sufficient funds for those purposes. In many wrongful convictions, a defendant may have had limited or no access to an independent expert despite attempts by the defense to obtain one.

There may be concern that prosecutors or defense attorneys or other officers of the court are "blamed" for the shortcomings of the criminal justice system in the use of forensic evidence. That is not the implication of any meaningful discussion of wrongful convictions. In fact, a wrongful conviction usually has many contributing causes, and blaming a particular individual or part of the system should be avoided. As in the discussion of crime laboratories, the appropriate response should include the recognition that criminal courts are high-reliability organizations that deal with complex problems with life-or-death consequences. Wrongful convictions are the most severe mistakes they make, but courts also commit other errors. Courts use the adversarial and appeals processes to identify errors, but these mechanisms have limited utility in judicial reform. Court leaders should recognize the importance of RCA and other mechanisms used in other sectors of society to improve their processes. The handling of forensic evidence demonstrates that the courts have much work to do in this regard.

POST CONVICTION

Forensic science may also be relevant to postconviction proceedings. It is well-known that DNA has been used to exonerate many of the wrongfully convicted. Substantial government and private resources are now available for postconviction DNA testing. The impact of postconviction

DNA has been declining as DNA analysis has become more common and routine in criminal investigations. Other forensic technologies, such as automated latent fingerprint databases, have also produced exonerations. When a forensic science issue contributes to a wrongful conviction, it may be difficult for a defendant to discover the issue. Even if they are aware of the issues regarding forensic evidence in their case, they may not have access to forensic reports or the resources needed to perform an adequate review. Innocence organizations, conviction integrity units, and other experts are now available, but access to these resources is limited by the defendant's ability to articulate a case for innocence—or at least the possibility of a miscarriage of justice based on an unfair trial.

From a legal perspective, the "finality of verdicts" still applies. Once a court has reached a guilty verdict, an appeals court will only consider issues related to the fairness of the proceedings during direct appeals. Some wrongful convictions have been overturned on the basis of prosecutorial or judicial misconduct, a failure by a judge to review a novel forensic method, or a failure by the defense attorney to render effective assistance related to forensic evidence. Once direct appeals have been exhausted, a convicted person may file a petition for habeas corpus. A habeas corpus appeal will be based on "new evidence," which may include new forensic evidence or a new interpretation of a forensic result. This may be due to changes in the scientific consensus about a forensic method. These so-called "junk science" writs recognize that the inadequate scientific foundation of some disciplines has undermined the confidence in verdicts based on forensic evidence (Beety, 2020). Nonetheless, the defendant must show that the scientific basis for a forensic conclusion has shifted, that the change could have changed the original verdict, and that the defense counsel could not have been aware of the changes in science at the time of trial. Some states have implemented reforms that assist the defendant to obtain such writs. Texas law has a junk science statute that now considers changes in conclusions by a testifying expert, such as a forensic pathologist who revises a cause of death (Texas Code of Criminal Procedure, n.d.). California's junk science statute allows state habeas petitions to challenge "false evidence" that has been repudiated by the original testifying expert or undermined by new science or technology (California Penal Code, n.d.)

Many exonerations rely on the availability of forensic evidence for retesting. Jurisdictions have widely varying policies for postconviction evidence retention. Many wrongful conviction appeals have been compromised by policies and practices that caused the destruction of evidence that might have been exculpatory. Many police investigators and prosecutors take personal responsibility for the storage of evidence from their cases, a practice that undermines the integrity of the evidence and the ability to obtain postconviction relief.

Even when evidence is available, postconviction testing is not a priority for many public crime laboratories, which tend to focus on the immediate demands of pending casework. A defendant must have the resources to obtain an independent forensic examination, which usually depends on the level of external advocacy for the individual and not necessarily the merits of their claims. More states have implemented review commissions and other mechanisms to detect wrongful convictions, but most defendants are dependent on their own resources. Given the cost of forensic expertise, resource requirements are often the biggest impediment to postconviction testing.

STUDY QUESTIONS

1. In your own life, you have probably made some kind of mistake in the last few weeks. You may have gotten lost when driving or had an accident at home. You may have missed a deadline at work. Select one of your mistakes and perform a root cause analysis. What could you do differently in your life to mitigate the risk of making the same mistake again?
2. Consider the Cameron and Seri cases. How would you relate the forensic errors in those cases to the error typologies discussed in this chapter? You may consider the Garrett/Neufeld typology, the Roberts typology, the NIST error examples, or the Canadian government approach.
3. What were the root causes of the errors in the Cameron and Seri cases? Why did the errors occur and what parts of the criminal justice system contributed to the underlying issues? Put yourself in the hypothetical position of a crime lab director. What system improvements would you implement to address the root causes analysis you have developed?
4. We discussed the evidence standards used by the courts in Chapter 1, including Frye, Daubert, and FRE 702. Are these evidence standards sufficient to ensure that the testimony of a scientific expert is valid and reliable? How would you improve the standards to reflect the different ways that science and the criminal justice system operate?

FURTHER READING

The ABS Group was retained by the FBI to conduct a root cause analysis of hair comparison errors by FBI examiners. Their report is a good starting point to understand the analysis of forensic errors (ABS Group, 2018).

Another approach is sentinel event analysis, which relates root causes to system deficiencies. John Hollway has pioneered sentinel event reviews in policing, including an examination of a wrongful conviction in Philadelphia related to faulty digital evidence examination. His research report discusses the methodology and the results of the Philadelphia case review (Hollway, 2021). The Roberts paper is a model for clear thinking about forensic errors and the discordance between science and the law (Roberts, 2015).

There is an extensive literature from the legal academic community about the role of forensic science in wrongful convictions. The Saks and Koehler paper includes out-of-date analysis but remains an important reference to understand the general issues (Saks & Koehler, 2005). Paul Giannelli has been one of the most influential scholars highlighting deficiencies in forensic science practice. A good starting point to understanding his work would be his paper on the pitfalls of law enforcement control of crime laboratories (Giannelli, 2011). Brandon Garrett has conducted a wide range of research related to forensic evidence, juries, and wrongful convictions. His 2020 review paper on wrongful convictions provides a useful introduction to his work and the state of research (Garrett, 2020).

Testimony standards have developed considerably since the 2009 NAS report. The DOJ's ULTR standards are available from the Department of Justice website at https://www.justice.gov/olp/uniform-language-testimony-and-reports. The ENFSI testimony guide for evaluative reporting and other standards are available online and include ancillary training materials; see https://enfsi.eu/about-enfsi/structure/working-groups/documents-page/documents/forensic-guidelines/. The NIST OSAC standards include many testimony standards across the forensic disciplines; see https://www.nist.gov/organization-scientific-area-committees-forensic-science.

REFERENCES

ABS Group. (2018). *Root Cause Analysis of Microscopic Hair Comparison Analysis*. Washington, DC: Federal Bureau of Investigation.

Aitken, C., Roberts, P., & Jackson, G. (2011). *Fundamentals of Probability and Statistical Evidence in Criminal Proceedings*. London, UK: Royal Statistical Society's Working Group on Statistics and the Law.

Beety, V. (2020, April 11). Changed Science Writs and State Habeas Relief. *Houston Law Review*, *483*.

Butler, J. (2003). Recent developments in Y-short tandem repeat and Y-single nucleotide polymorphism analysis. *Forensic Science Review*, *15*(2), 91–114.

Butler, J. (2004). *Y Chromosome Workshop. American Academy of Forensic Sciences* (pp. 1–10). Gaithersburg, MD: National Institute of Standards and Technology STRBase.

Cadiz, L. (2004, November 18). Md.-based DNA lab fires analyst over falsified tests. *Baltimore Sun.*

Champod, C., Biedermann, A., Vuille, J., Willis, S., & De Kinder, J. (2016, March 12). ENFSI Guideline for Evaluative Reporting in Forensic Science, A Primer for Legal Practitioners. *Criminal Law & Justice Weekly*, *180*, 189–193.

Chapter 11. Habeas Corpus. (n.d.). *Title 1. Code of Criminal Procedure.* Texas. Retrieved January 13, 2022, from https://statutes.capitol.texas.gov/Docs/CR/htm/CR.11.htm

Commonwealth v. Cameron, 06-P-59 (Appeals Court of Massachusetts August 17, 2007).

Commonwealth v. Cameron, SJC-11835 (Supreme Judicial Court of Massachusetts October 28, 2015).

European Network of Forensic Science Institutes. (2015). *ENFSI Guideline for Evaluative Reporting in Forensic Science.*

FPT Heads of Prosecutions Committee Working Group. (2011 (update)). *Report on the Prevention of Miscarriages of Justice.* Department of Justice, Government of Canada. Retrieved from https://www.justice.gc.ca/eng/rp-pr/cj-jp/ccr-rc/pmj-pej/pmj-pej.pdf

Garrett, B. L. (2020). Wrongful Convictions. *Annual Review of Criminology*, *3*(1), 245–259.

Garrett, B. L., & Neufeld, P. (2009, March). Invalid Forensic Science Testimony and Wrongful Convictions. *Virginia Law Review*, 1–97.

Giannelli, P. C. (2011). Daubert and Forensic Science: The Pitfalls of Law Enforcement Control of Scientific Research. *University of Illinois Law Review*, *2011*(1), 1–39.

Gittelson, S. N. (2013). *Evolving from Inferences to Decisions in the Interpretation of Scientific Evidence.* Lausanne: University of Lausanne.

Hollway, J. F. (2021). *Instilling a Culture of Continuous Learning from Criminal Justice Systems Errors: A Multi-Stakeholder Sentinel Event Review Process in Philadelphia.* National Institute of Justice. NCJ256006.

Houck, M. (2016). Risk, Reward, and Redemption: Root Cause Analysis in Forensic Organizations. *Forensic Science Policy & Management: An International Journal*, 7(3–4), 106–112. https://doi.org/10.1080/19409044.2016.1224278

Interim Solutions Committee. (2016). *Recommendation to the Attorney General Root Cause Analysis (RCA) in Forensic Science.* National Commission on Forensic Science.

Joint Committee for Guides in Metrology. (2008). *JCGM 100: 2008, Evaluation of Measurement Data--Guide to the Expression of Uncertainty in Measurement* (First ed.). Saint-Cloud, France: International Bureau of Weights and Measures.

Legal Information Institute. (n.d.). *Rule 702. Testimony by Expert Witnesses.* Retrieved from Cornell Law School: https://www.law.cornell.edu/rules/fre/rule_702

National Fire Protection Association. (2017). *NFPA 921, Guide for Fire and Explosion Investigations.*

National Institute of Standards and Technology. (2015). Proceedings of the 2015 International Symposium on Forensic Science Error Management. In J. M. Butler (Ed.). Retrieved from https://nvlpubs.nist.gov/nistpubs/SpecialPublications/NIST.SP.1206.pdf

National Institute of Standards and Technology. (2020, February 13). *OSAC Organizational Structure.* Retrieved from The Organization of Scientific Area Committees for Forensic Science: https://www.nist.gov/topics/organization-scientific-area-committees-forensic-science/osac-organizational-structure

Organization of Scientific Area Committees for Forensic Science. (2018). *OSAC Lexicon.* Gaithersburg, MD: National Institute of Standards and Technology.

Roberts, K. H. (1990). Some characteristics of one type of high reliability organization. *Organization Science*, *1*(2), 160–176.

Roberts, P. (2015). Paradigms of forensic science and legal process: a critical diagnosis. *Philosophical Transaction of the Royal Society B*, *370*: 20140256, 1-11.

Saks, M. J., & Koehler, J. J. (2005). The Coming Paradigm Shift in Forensic Identification. *Science*, *309*, 892–895.

SO/IEC (International Organization for Standardization/International Electrotechnical Commission). (2017). *ISO/IEC 17025: General Requirements for the Competence of Testing and Calibration Laboratories.* Geneva, Switzerland: International Organization for Standardization/International Electrotechnical Commission.

Strickland v. Washington, 466 U.S. 668 (US Supreme Court May 14, 1984).

Title 12. Of Special Proceedings of a Criminal Nature. (n.d.). *Penal Code Part 2. Of Criminal Procedure.* California. Retrieved January 13, 2022, from https://leginfo.legislature.ca.gov/faces/codes_displaySection.xhtml?sectionNum=1473.&lawCode=PEN

Ulery, B. T., Hicklin, R. A., Buscaglia, J., & Roberts, M. A. (2011). Accuracy and reliability of forensic latent fingerprint decisions. *Proceedings of the National Academy of Sciences*, *108*(19), 7733–7738.

US Department of Justice. (2019, March 19). *Uniform Language for Testimony and Reports*. Retrieved from US Department of Justice: https://www.justice.gov/olp/uniform-language-testimony-and-reports

CHAPTER 3

Hair and Serology

Before DNA came into common use in the 1990s, hair comparison and serology were used to determine if individuals could be associated with or excluded as contributors to biological evidence. The two fields had significant statistical and scientific limits. When misapplied or misinterpreted, hair comparison and serology contributed to many wrongful convictions that were later overturned by DNA evidence. These disciplines have important lessons for forensic science in the use of validated science, statistical interpretation frameworks, and testimony standards.

Given that humans shed approximately 100 hairs per day, hair is one of the most important types of trace evidence available to the forensic examiner (Robertson, 1999) (Koch, Tridico, Bernard, Shriver, & Jablonski, 2019). There are observable differences between human and nonhuman hair, among types of hair from different places on the body, and among hairs from broad human population groups. There are variations in hair characteristics between individuals that may be used to differentiate the source of a hair. There are also variations among hairs from the same person and even among hairs from the same location on a person. A hair comparison examiner typically uses either scalp or pubic hairs that have an acceptable level of quality, samples many hairs from a suspect from the presumed body origin site, and characterizes morphological features of each hair microscopically. In some wrongful convictions, the examiner may have looked at fewer than the 10–24 characteristics that are typically used in the field. For example, they may have noted that an evidence hair was curly and black and concluded that an African American suspect was the contributor without further examination. This practice was never aligned with any professional standards in the field.

The 1970s and 1980s were the "heyday" of forensic hair comparison. The technique was used in a very wide range of homicide and sexual assault investigations and enjoyed wide acceptance in law enforcement and the courts. Studies at the Royal Canadian Mounted Police (RCMP) had established that well-trained examiners using a well-defined protocol could reliably distinguish among pairs of hairs (Gaudette &

DOI: 10.4324/9781003202578-3

Keeping, 1974). Other researchers presented research on the use of protein composition or elemental analysis to supplement or replace microscopic hair comparison in forensic examination. By 2000, it was clear that mitochondrial-DNA (mt-DNA) testing would provide more reliable results than microscopy alone (Houck & Budowle, 2002). Today, hair microscopy is used primarily as a screening presumptive test and mt-DNA or nuclear DNA is used to provide complementary information about the source of an evidence hair. Although this technical advance has provided more probative information in current cases, DNA has also highlighted the weaknesses of hair microscopy as it was practiced in its heyday. Many examiners exaggerated the probative value of hair comparisons or misrepresented scientific studies, such as the Gaudette work. Further, the field never developed and enforced practice and reporting standards. There were attempts to do so. The Scientific Working Group on Materials Analysis produced useful guidelines, but the adoption and enforcement of those standards was left to the discretion of individual laboratories (Scientific Working Group on Materials Analysis (SWGMAT), 2005). A conference on hair comparison was hosted by the FBI in 1985 (The Laboratory Division, Federal Bureau of Investigation, 1985). That symposium proposed standards that could be used in practice and testimony, but retrospective reviews have established that standards or guidelines were not enforced, even in the FBI Laboratory itself (ABS Group, 2018).

Serology had a more robust scientific foundation based on research work throughout the 20th century (Gaensslen, 1983). Serology relies on chemical tests that are specific to components of biological fluids. For example, a chemist can determine if a sample contains blood by using a reaction that is catalyzed by hemoglobin. These tests are very sensitive and still in use for screening purposes in forensic laboratories.

Serological typing attempts to distinguish the differences in characteristic proteins that may vary among individuals. The proteins in blood may be present in several forms, which we know now depends on the DNA coding for the protein in question. Small DNA variations will produce protein variants that are all functional in the body but may be distinguished by laboratory testing. The most well-known protein system is the ABO blood type. Long before it was applied to forensic science, ABO blood typing made blood transfusions much safer, as a mismatch in blood type can cause severe immune reactions in the recipient. The main ABO types are A, B, AB, and O, and their relative frequency in human populations was well-established by the middle of the 20th century. The discovery that roughly 80% of the population secretes the ABO blood group factors into bodily fluids other than blood was useful to forensic science in determining the blood type of an unknown semen source in rape cases under the right circumstances. Other blood typing systems were also common in forensic analysis, particularly the phosphoglucomutase (PGM) test, which could be typed in 10 different forms.

Serological typing cannot be used to individualize a biological sample. Most serological types can only be narrowed down to a percentage of a population. Sometimes the population of possible sources was one or two percent of the overall population; sometimes it was as much as 90%–100%. Therefore, serological typing was useful only for excluding suspects and was of very limited value as inculpatory evidence. In reports and testimony, examiners would typically state that a suspect was "in the population of males that could have contributed to the sample." That very broad statement could easily be misinterpreted by investigators or the courts to be inculpatory, even in cases when many jurors would also be included "in the population" of possible contributors.

The limited probative value of serological typing was a minefield for the forensic serologist. Forensic serologists and hair comparison examiners were under great pressure to be relevant and may have mischaracterized the probative value of the evidence in an effort to be helpful to law enforcement and prosecutors. This phenomenon—referred by social scientists as role strain—may be present in many wrongful convictions (Turvey, 2013). The forensic scientist may experience stress due to the conflicts between the demands of law enforcement to solve a case and the constraints of the scientific process. These stressors may be in addition to other personal and occupational stresses experienced by forensic scientists (Holt, Blevins, Foran, & Smith, 2016).

MICHAEL BLAIR: CASE EXAMPLE

The Michael Blair case involved a wide range of the typical factors seen in pre-DNA cases involving biological and trace evidence. It also demonstrates the deep influence of stress on forensic practitioners due to vicarious trauma. On September 4, 1993, seven-year-old Ashley Estell was murdered in Plano, Texas (In re Blair, 2013). The primary suspect was Michael Blair, who had a long criminal record that included indecency with a child. Blair admitted that he had sexually abused other children on many occasions but denied any involvement in the Estell murder.

Hair and fibers were recovered from the body of the victim, as well as a clump of hair from a nearby park that may or may not have been associated with the murder. The forensic examiner on the case was Charles Linch from the Southwestern Institute of Forensic Sciences (SWIFS) in Dallas. Two years earlier, Linch had helped in the recovery of 137 bodies from an airplane crash at the Dallas/Fort Worth airport (Becka & Swindle, 2000). Linch was deeply affected by the experience and fell into depression and alcoholism. His supervisor, Dr. Jeffrey Barnard, later became aware of the issue and helped to ensure that Linch received treatment in an in-patient psychiatric unit. During his hospitalization and afterward, Linch expressed anger at his supervisors at SWIFS, who also arranged for him to testify at two capital murder cases—including the Blair case—while he was hospitalized. Linch's state of mind was not disclosed to the defense in the Blair trial.

Linch gave extensive testimony on the hair and fiber evidence in the Blair case. Among other items, a stuffed bunny rabbit was recovered from Blair's vehicle when he was arrested. Linch testified that fibers from the victim were microscopically indistinguishable from fibers from the rabbit. This language implied a misleading level of probative value. Linch meant that he could not distinguish the fibers from each other using the microscopic features he examined. Jurors could easily have misinterpreted this language to imply that the fibers were in fact identical and had to be from the same source. He examined plant material from the ear of the rabbit using a scanning electron microscope and concluded that it was the same as plant material from the crime scene, clarifying, "It's a common Texas weed." Linch said the clump of hairs found in the nearby park had "a strong microscopic indication" that it came from the victim. A hair from the Blair vehicle was also associated with the victim. On that point, Linch gave unusual testimony. He noted that the victim's hair had microovoid bodies (see Figure 3.1). He said, "These are very small air inclusions that are smaller than a true

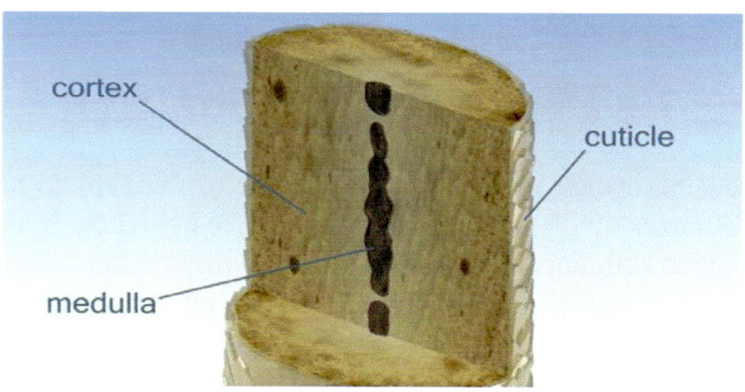

Microscopic layers of the hair shaft.

FIGURE 3.1 The hair shaft is divided into three primary layers: the outer cuticle, the cortex, and the medulla. Each layer may exhibit variable characteristics. The cortex may contain pigment granules, small air pockets called cortical fusi, or opaque structures called ovoid bodies. In the Blair case, Linch described "microovoid bodies" and other features that he described as unique to the victim's hair. His statements had little or no basis in scientific research. Source: Department of Justice (2018).

ovoid body. Ovoid bodies are mostly found in cattle hair and they're much larger, but [the victim] throughout her standard or known head hairs, has these microstructures." He also noted unusual damage in the evidence hair and the victim's hair. This testimony implied that Ashley Estell's hair was especially unique and supported the possibility that the hair comparison had definitively placed the victim in Blair's car. This implication was a critical piece of evidence in a case that had no eyewitness testimony to support it. Nonetheless, there is no statistical basis for the features Linch presented in the Blair trial, and it is unclear if his interpretation of "microovoid" structures was valid.

Blair was convicted and sentenced to death. Afterward, Governor George Bush signed Ashley's Law—named for the victim in this case—to extend punishments and registration of sex offenders in Texas. In 2001, DNA testing excluded Blair and inculpated another man in the murder. The conviction was vacated and charges dropped in 2008. Blair remained in prison on other child molestation counts. His lawsuit for wrongful conviction damages was denied by the Texas Supreme Court.

Linch was involved in at least one other wrongful conviction around this time, the 1994 conviction of Richard Kussmaul for a double murder in Moody, Texas. In that case, Linch gave confusing testimony about DNA analysis that failed to disclose an exculpatory dqAlpha report on rape kit samples. The defense lawyer knew about the result but failed to use it during the trial. Linch also testified that evidence hairs excluded Kussmaul and his codefendant. He associated fibers from a blanket used to wrap the bodies with carpet fibers from Kussmaul's home. Kussmaul's conviction was vacated based on postconviction DNA testing, but he wasn't given a finding of factual innocence due to his possible involvement in the murders. Linch recovered from his mental health issues and returned to forensic work elsewhere. The consideration of occupational stress and resiliency has been highlighted by forensic science leaders in recent years, although much work remains to be done to help forensic professionals in this regard.

ROLE OF HAIR COMPARISON AND SEROLOGY IN THE BALANCE OF EVIDENCE

Serological testing can be presumptive or confirmatory. For example, hemoglobin catalysis reactions are generally considered to be presumptive tests only. Confirmatory tests for blood are usually based on immunological reactions, such as enzyme-linked immunosorbent assays (ELISA). In sexual assault cases, the most important body fluid test is the determination of the presence of semen. The definitive confirmatory test for semen is microscopic detection of spermatozoa, which is usually semi-quantitatively characterized on a scale from 1 to 4, depending on how many sperm cells are seen in the field of view of a microscope at a particular magnification. No fully quantitative assay would be possible (or reliable), given that evidence samples are generally stored dry to prevent bacterial growth. Also, some males will not deposit spermatozoa due to vasectomy, medical conditions, or the use of birth control. The most common presumptive semen test relied on the enzyme acid phosphatase, abbreviated as AP or ACP. Semen contains large amounts of ACP, but small amounts may be detected in vaginal fluid and other bodily fluids. In the 1980s, forensic scientists started to use immunological detection of prostate-specific antigen, which is commonly referred to as PSA today and is referred to as P30 in forensic analysis. P30 is rarely present in blood or other bodily fluids and is more specific for detection of semen than ACP. In general, the confirmatory testing for spermatozoa or P30 is considered definitive proof that semen has been contributed by at least one male to a biological sample (Gaennslen, 2000). This determination was a critical element for the reliable interpretation of sexual assault samples, which were commonly a mixture of female and male bodily fluids. The interpretation required the analyst to consider masking, which occurs when female blood group substances are present and would "mask" the presence of male group substances. In those instances, a male contribution could be assumed to be present if there were markers foreign to the female in the sample. If the sample included the female blood group substances, then the analyst must confirm that the male fraction is present by finding microscopic spermatozoa or detecting P30. Before P30 was available, some analysts in the pre-DNA era interpreted sexual assault samples based solely on presumptive ACP testing. Like other presumptive tests, ACP should never be relied upon to make a forensic conclusion. Therefore, even if the analysts clarified the limits of ACP testing, they were potentially misleading fact-finders about the probative value of their conclusions. On the other hand, if they used microscopic confirmation of spermatozoa, they could make reliable interpretations and account for masking effects.

In their 2009 analysis of DNA exonerations, Garrett and Neufeld concluded that the large majority of serological interpretations included misleading or false masking interpretations (Garrett & Neufeld, 2009). In their view, no male could be excluded by the serological typing in these cases because masking from the female blood group substances could account for all of the observed markers. Garrett and Neufeld relied on a strict interpretation framework, which in some cases discounted even microscopic confirmation of spermatozoa. As a result, their work has been criticized by some observers (LaPorte, 2018). That said, it should be noted that serologists—like hair examiners—often provided incomplete reports and testimony that did not clarify masking or other methodological or interpretation issues. Because Garrett and Neufeld relied on trial transcripts, they had a very limited basis on which to give the testifying examiner the benefit of the doubt. Many examiners gave prosecution-friendly testimony that discounted exculpatory interpretations. Many prosecutors asked questions that led to misleading interpretations of the populations of possible contributors to evidence samples. Many defense attorneys did not understand the subtleties of serological interpretation or the limitations to microscopic hair analysis and failed to raise important issues on cross-examination that could have been helpful to their clients.

In sexual assault cases, hair and serology were often incidental to the overall case, which usually relied on victim testimony. In the 1980s and before, significant racial disparities existed in sexual assault cases. African American defendants were disproportionately represented among those who were wrongfully convicted for rape during that period. Research has established the unreliability of cross-racial eyewitness identifications, which are often associated with testimony errors (Scheck, Neufeld, & Dwyer, 2003). Hair comparison and serology lacked the probative value to counteract these effects. The techniques could only narrow down the possible suspects and would not necessarily exclude an innocent individual. In fact, *valid* serological analyses and hair comparisons supported many wrongful convictions. Although hairs from individuals of African descent could be distinguished microscopically, most research was based on study subjects of European ancestry. The methods, assumptions, and population estimates may not have been valid for interpretation across racial categories. Poorly trained examiners would associate evidence hairs with African American defendants on the basis of very few characteristics, producing prejudicial testimony with little or no scientific value. DNA has ameliorated the situation because it can be used to individualize contributors to a biological sample and has well-established population studies across racial and ethnic categories. That said, the problems of cross-racial identification and resulting racial disparities remain a challenge for the criminal justice system (Wilson, Hugenberg, & Bernstein, 2013).

CLYDE CHARLES

(State v. Charles, 1987)

The Clyde Charles case manifested many of these problems of cross-racial identification, hair comparison, and serological typing. On March 12, 1981 in Houma, Louisiana, a 26-year-old white woman left her parents' home between 2:00 a.m. and 3:00 a.m. to "watch the tugboats and think." Her car experienced a blowout which left her stranded on the railroad tracks behind Grand Caillou Road. She abandoned her car and walked for about twenty to thirty minutes, when she noticed a man approaching her. She told him about her car trouble and that she was meeting friends at a nearby restaurant. After making a series of suggestive remarks, the man grabbed the victim by the neck and dragged her from the roadway. As the victim screamed and struggled, the man punched her in the face, verbally threatened her, pulled her hair, dragged her behind some oil tanks, and raped her. Afterward, the man allowed her to go to the bathroom, and she took the opportunity to escape. A short time after the rape, a parish deputy passed the victim on the road, finding her visibly upset and clearly physically abused. She told the deputy that she had been raped by a black man who might still be in the vicinity. She was too upset to provide more details.

Shortly afterward, the deputy found Clyde Charles hitchhiking by the side of the road but did not arrest him at that time. The deputy returned to the victim, at which point he elicited details about the attacker's clothing that matched what Charles was wearing. The deputy already suspected that Charles might be the rapist and included a suggestive description of Charles' clothing in his questioning of the victim. Meanwhile, another officer found a blue denim jacket 50 feet from the highway and the victim's purse approximately 30 feet from the highway. Behind storage tanks where the rape occurred, Bergeron found a red baseball cap. The second officer found Charles and arrested him. The victim positively identified Charles as the assailant at the local hospital, where she had been transported for medical care and the collection of a rape kit.

The evidence was sent to the Louisiana State Police Crime Lab in Baton Rouge. DNA was not available at the time, so the samples were subject to hair comparison and serological analysis. The serologist reported that the rape kit sample showed the presence of spermatozoa and blood group substances from a type O individual. The victim's sweater and pantyhose had type O blood stains. If Charles had been blood type A or B, that should have been observed in the evidence and would have exculpated him. In fact, Charles was blood type B. But the analyst didn't bother take a reference sample from Charles because the results were all consistent with the victim's blood type. Two Caucasian hairs were removed from Charles' shirt and were similar to hair from the victim. The analyst said, "The probability exists that it could have come from the same individual." On cross-examination, the

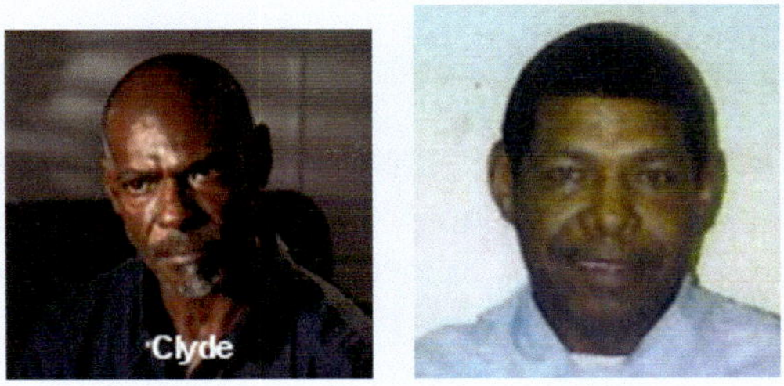

FIGURE 3.2 Clyde Charles and Marlo Charles. The white victim identified Clyde Charles as the assailant, but cross-racial eyewitness identification is inherently unreliable. The serological profile of the rape kit sample excluded Clyde Charles but did not exclude his brother, who was later implicated using DNA profiling. In the Marlo Charles trial, the victim testified that the assailant looked and sounded like Clyde Charles (a) but did not identify Marlo Charles (b) as the assailant. Credit: Illustrated by the Innocent in Prison Project International.

analyst approximately clarified, "It cannot be individualized to state with any degree of scientific certainty that a strand of hair found here came from any one individual." Charles was convicted by an all-white jury and sentenced to "life at hard labor."

Charles asked repeatedly for DNA testing but was denied. With the help of Barry Scheck and the Innocence Project, Charles was the first person to successfully use section 1983 of the Civil Rights Act to obtain DNA testing in 1999. The DNA profile excluded Clyde Charles and matched his brother, Marlo Charles, who was convicted in 2002 of the assault and sentenced to life in prison. Marlo Charles had blood type O, which was the same as the victim's blood type. Marlo Charles claims that he is innocent, and the DNA testing could not be used to inculpate him because the analysis was limited to only five STR markers (see http://cases.iippi.org/marlo-charles/). After his exoneration and release, Clyde Charles received $450,000 from state compensation and a civil suit settlement. He died in 2009 after experiencing post-traumatic stress disorder and other struggles related to his wrongful conviction (Figure 3.2).

SEROLOGICAL TYPING

Serological analysis is closely connected to postconviction DNA testing because both methods rely on samples of biological evidence. Many labs did not preserve biological evidence, making it impossible to detect wrongful convictions in those jurisdictions. Many prosecutors opposed postconviction DNA analysis. Sometimes, the DNA evidence would be more probative than the serology presented at trial but would not be sufficient to identify a "cold hit" to an alternate suspect. The prosecutor would then argue that an unknown male contributed to the biological evidence, but the convicted defendant was still the rapist. The Innocence Project came to refer to this claim as the "unindicted coejaculator" argument. In many cases, the resolution of the forensic analysis depended on the work of the original investigator and serological laboratory. Ideally, the serological analysis would have included reference samples from consensual partners or other suspects. The serologist could then establish the likelihood that any particular male contributed to the evidence sample. Later, this work could be used in combination with DNA analysis to determine any "unindicted coejaculators" and provide a definitive conclusion concerning the exoneration of the defendant. Many labs failed to perform the necessary reference testing to clarify either the serology or DNA analyses (Figure 3.3).

In one unusual situation, Virginia serologist Mary Jane Burton would preserve slides or evidence in her laboratory notebook. Later, this practice permitted comprehensive DNA reanalysis of 634 cases of sexual assaults and homicides resulting in 715 convictions. A comprehensive research project was conducted by the Urban Institute in coordination with the reanalysis (Roman, Walsh, Lachman, & Yahner, 2012). DNA analysis was successful in 230 cases, and the convicted offender was eliminated as the source of the evidence in 56 cases. The elimination supported a possible exoneration in 38 cases. This does not imply that there were errors in the serology in these cases. In many cases, the actual assailant and the defendant may have both been included as possible contributors to the serological profile of the evidence. The probative value of the serology was just insufficient to exculpate the defendant. For example, in the Willie Davidson case, the victim was an O secretor and Davidson was a nonsecretor. Burton confirmed the male fraction through microscopic detection of spermatozoa. Burton correctly concluded that 58% of males could have contributed to the sample, including O secretors and nonsecretors of any blood type. Burton also presented a hair comparison based on pubic hair combings from the victim. She said one hair "was consistent with and could have originated from the pubic area of the suspect." This testimony was in compliance with the standards of the time. Davidson was convicted at a bench trial,

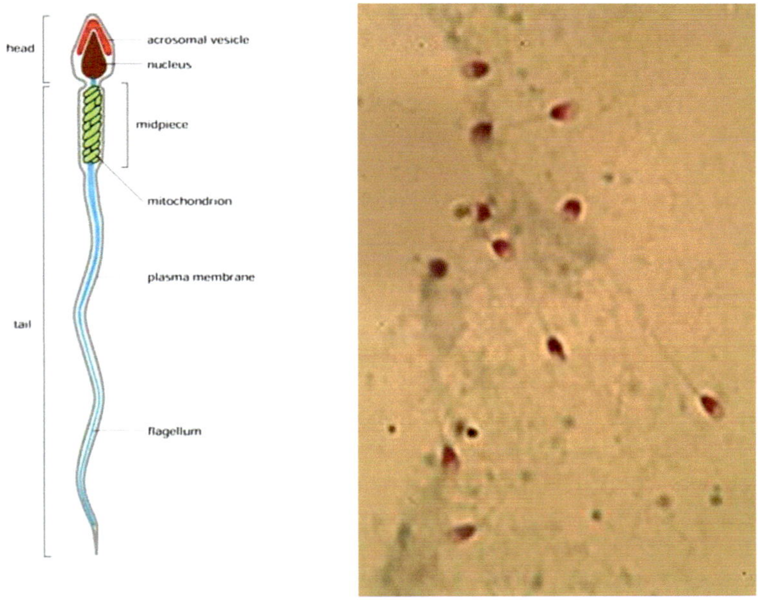

FIGURE 3.3 Sperm are visualized using a Christmas tree stain in which the tail shows up as a yellow-green and the head as red or pink. The slide would be examined at 100X or 400X. The presence of spermatozoa was reported on a semiquantitative scale: 4+ (many sperm in every field of view); 3+ (many sperm in some fields of view); 2+ some sperm in some fields of view (easy to find); 1+ hard to find, very few sperm over the entire slide; 1 one sperm observed on slide; 0 no sperm. This approach is the most definitive way to confirm the presence of a male contributor to a sexual assault sample. Source: District of Columbia Department of Forensic Sciences (2014).

meaning that the judge decided the verdict, not a jury. Unfortunately, the judge did not understand the nuances of Burton's characterization of the hair comparison and thought she was just exercising "scientific care." He compared the hair comparison to a fingerprint identification, but hair comparison never was considered nearly as statistically powerful as latent prints. Davidson was convicted but exonerated by a DNA analysis of a sample swatch from Burton's notebook in 2005. The Davidson case was typical, just as Burton's work was typical for hair comparison and serological testimony at the time. She generally accounted for masking appropriately and gave limiting testimony about hair. Nonetheless, there were many wrongful convictions in the cases she handled. This was not primarily due to errors in her analysis or testimony. Rather, it was related to the inherent limitations of hair and serology to exclude many innocent suspects and failures of the justice system to use forensic and other evidence effectively. Also, as demonstrated by the Urban Institute study, there is an inevitability of errors in casework. The risk of errors can be mitigated by well-considered reforms, but it cannot ever be entirely eliminated. The inevitability of errors may seem frustrating, but it provides a key insight. It means that the study of errors and wrongful convictions is an important priority for forensic scientists and the broader criminal justice community. The lessons learned provide a starting point to raise salient issues for reform.

TESTIMONY ERRORS RELATED TO SEROLOGY

Testimony errors in serology generally related to errors of interpretation. For example, almost all sexual assault cases involved male assailants and female victims. When calculating the percentage of the population that were included, some examiners divided the possibilities in half to account for the fact that only males could have contributed semen. The correct interpretation would have been to communicate the fraction of males who could be associated with the sample, and the divide-by-two interpretation was misleading in implying that the serology was more probative than was warranted. In the William Harris case, examiner Fred Zain went even further. Noting that the defendant was African American, he said that only 3% of West Virginians were African American—and males were only half of that population. The sexual assault kit evidence included blood group substances from a type O secretor and PGM 1+ contributor. Harris was blood type O and had a PGM type of 1+, which Zain said was associated with 11.8% of the population. Finally, he assumed that the evidence was pure seminal fluid and that the victim—who was also blood type O and had a PGM type of 1+—did not contribute any markers to the biological evidence, a clear failure to account for masking. These statements were completely invalid and misleading and led to Harris' conviction for sexual assault. Harris was exonerated by DNA testing and received $4.3 million from lawsuits related to his wrongful conviction. Zain was associated with many wrongful convictions in West Virginia and Texas. A review by the American Society of Crime Laboratory Directors Laboratory Accreditation Board (ASCLD-LAB) found that Zain repeatedly falsified lab reports, misinterpreted findings, and lied in testimony to inculpate defendants (McNamara & Linhart, 1993). Even after he was discredited in West Virginia, he was able to move to Texas and work as a forensic scientist. He testified falsely that a DNA match inculpated Gilbert Alejandro in a sexual assault in Uvalde County in Texas in 1990 (Associated Press, 1994). Alejandro was exonerated by postconviction DNA performed by another laboratory.

HIERARCHY OF PROPOSITIONS

Crime level: Statements concerning the perpetrator of the crime. "John Doe committed the rape."

Activity level: Statements concerning actions taken during the commission of the crime. "John Doe had intercourse with the victim."

Source level: Statements concerning evidence from the crime scene. "John Doe contributed to the biological evidence in the rape kit. "

Sub-source level: Statements concerning attributes of the evidence or sample. "The serological markers from the biological sample are of the same type as the serological markers of John Doe and could not have come from the victim."

In other cases, the examiner would confuse the population that had the defendant's serological profile with the population of people that could have contributed to a sample of biological evidence. When considering this issue, it may be useful to recap the concept of activity-level propositions. In a criminal case, there are questions concerning the crime, activities, sources, and subsources (European Network of Forensic Science Institutes, 2015; Champod, Biedermann, Vuille, Willis, & De Kinder, 2016). Example propositions that may be appropriate in serological typing are described in the box.

The distinctions among propositions may be very important to the interpretation of biological evidence, especially if there are uncertainties concerning multiple contributors to the evidence. In a serological analysis, an examiner may conclude that John Doe could have contributed to the evidence from a sexual assault kit. That conclusion is a source-level proposition about the sample. The conclusion may be based on a sub-source level analysis of John Doe's serological profile. For example, if John Doe were a type A secretor and A blood group substances were present in the sample, then it may be appropriate to conclude that John Doe could have contributed the A blood group substances to the sample. In this example, John Doe shares the same serological profile (A-type secretor) as approximately 32% of the population. That statement should be distinguished from the source-level conclusions about the evidence, which could have had contributions from A-type secretors or non-secretors of any blood type, thus including over 50% of the population. In addition, if the examiner didn't account for masking from a victim's blood group substances, it is possible that 100% of the population could have contributed to the evidence sample. An examiner must clearly delineate the possibilities in laboratory analysis and testimony. These distinctions were well-known to serologists in wrongful conviction cases, although forensic scientists were not trained to apply a formalized "hierarchy of propositions," and even today the distinctions are not commonly taught outside of Europe.

In many wrongful convictions, the analyst did not make the proper distinction among the possible hypotheses. In the William Harris case, Zain just assumed that the serological profile of the sample was one and the same with the serological profile of the defendant. Zain was an extreme case, but other examiners failed in a similar manner. In the Donald Good case, the serologist was Dr. Irving Stone, formerly of the FBI and then with the Southwestern Institute of Forensic Sciences in Dallas, Texas. Stone did serological typing of a blanket—showing O blood group substances—and a vaginal swab—showing A and O blood group substances. Good was an O secretor, but Stone did not report the victim's serological profile. Stone said Good was among the 30% of Caucasian males that are O secretors, an interesting fact but a misleading one because other males with different serological profiles could have contributed to the biological evidence. Especially in light of his failure to report reference testing on the victim or the victim's husband, Stone was not able to provide a reliable interpretation of the serological contributors to the evidence and instead gave the misleading fact about Good's serological profile. Good represented himself during the trial and did not attempt any cross-examination of Stone. He was convicted of burglary with intent to commit rape and sentenced to life in prison. In 2004, the Texas Department of Public Safety completed a DNA analysis of the vaginal swabs that excluded Good and the victim's husband. Good was exonerated and in 2007 settled his federal civil rights lawsuit for $1 million.

MORPHOLOGICAL HAIR COMPARISON

The limitations of microscopic hair comparison required great care by the forensic examiner during courtroom testimony. The 1985 FBI Symposium on hair comparison recommended the use of three possible statements of inclusion about hair comparison:

1. The questioned hair is consistent with having come from John Doe.

2. The questioned hair could have come from John Doe.
3. John Doe qualifies as being the donor of the questioned hair.

Further, symposium participants recognized that the scientific foundations for hair comparison were insufficient and advised against referring to specific studies to bolster jury acceptance of hair testimony (The Laboratory Division, Federal Bureau of Investigation, 1985). As noted previously, forensic laboratories did not adopt or enforce testimony standards, so individual examiners had minimal guidance about which statement to use to describe their comparison conclusions. It is likely that many examiners were influenced by prosecutors to adopt the strongest language possible, i.e., the "consistent with" statement. In many wrongful convictions, examiners did not follow this guidance and provided misleading or exaggerated testimony. Examiners would also cite past performance, a practice which is acceptable to demonstrate skills and experience but is not a valid basis to establish the reliability of the discipline. At the time, because detected wrongful convictions were unusual, examiners believed their work was highly reliable. That turned out to be a misconception, and dozens of wrongful convictions are now known to have included false or misleading hair comparison testimony.

Even highly capable examiners were subject to this problem. In the 1989 Central Park Five case, five teenagers were convicted in connection with a sexual assault. The case included official misconduct and false confessions. Hairs from the defendants' clothes were associated with the victim after a prolonged and careful analysis by respected examiner Nicholas Petraco. Petraco testified appropriately on direct examination in a manner that would conform to the stricter standards in place today. For example, in the Keith Richardson trial, he testified that a hair recovered from Richardson's clothing "was similar in all physical characteristics to the known sample K 1 [from the victim]. And in my opinion that questioned hair fragment could have originated from the source of the known specimen K 1." On cross-examination, he was challenged about the fundamental value of hair comparisons. While acknowledging the inadequacy of research, he also said,

> I have looked at thousands of hair standards over the course of my work and I haven't seen any that have the same range of physical characteristics yet. But I really haven't looked at them in the sense of exclude one from the other. But I have in fact looked at thousands of standards and haven't seen two that matched exactly.
>
> (Morgenthau, 2002)

Those statements implied that his experience could provide a basis for the frequency of hair characteristics or the individualization of hairs, which was invalid and misleading. The Central Park Five were exonerated after a DNA cold hit to an alternate suspect who was known to police at the time of the original investigation and trial (Morgenthau, 2002).

During the 2010s, the FBI conducted a thorough review of the hair comparison testimony in cases involving their analysts (ABS Group, 2018) (Federal Bureau of Investigation, 2015). That review found that most FBI hair analysts exaggerated their testimony, and the problem got worse as time went by. Right after the 1985 symposium, many analysts limited their testimony to "similar physical characteristics" in the manner demonstrated by Petraco in his direct examination in the Central Park Five case. Over time, almost all analysts used the strongest possible language—"consistent with" the defendant—that was suggested during the 1985 symposium. The root cause of this "probative value creep" was not the examiners themselves but the failure of the FBI Laboratory (and presumably other crime labs) to establish and enforce meaningful testimony standards. Lab managers reviewed testimony for comportment, such as proper attire and confident delivery, but they did not have a process to review the substance of the testimony. Thus, examiners tended to use the "strongest" statements in testimony that they could.

Arguably, competent examiners using "consistent with" testimony did not cause wrongful convictions even if the language of their testimony was later found to be in error. On the other hand, the failure to establish and enforce standards also meant that incompetent examiners could repeatedly produce errors that clearly contributed to miscarriages of justice. Among FBI examiners, Michael Malone was the clearest example of this issue. In Delaware in 1980, an all-white jury convicted Elmer Daniels, an 18-year-old African American, of sexual assault of a white child (Otterbourg, 2020). Malone linked Daniels to the victim by hair comparison of two evidence hairs from Daniels' home and the victim's clothing. Malone testified, "When you get a double, what we call a double match like this, it would increase the probability tremendously." That statement was not valid scientifically or statistically. Daniels was later exonerated in 2018 after an FBI review found that Malone had produced invalid testimony in 96% of the cases he worked. In another case, Malone produced hair and fiber testimony against noted drug kingpin, Juan Matta-Ballesteros, who was convicted for the murders of a DEA agent and pilot (Matta-Ballesteros v. United States, 2017). Malone said he could match an evidence hair to its source and had only seen two hairs that could not be distinguished in the 10,000 he had examined in his career. Postconviction, independent review by trace evidence expert Skip Palenik found that Malone had not only exaggerated his testimony but had also used a hair sample that was unsuitable for comparison, i.e., it was too short or damaged. Matta-Ballesteros' conviction was vacated, and the government did not retry him because he remained in prison for drug-smuggling offenses. In this case, Malone's testimony errors may have undermined the conviction of a possibly guilty defendant.

Since the advent of DNA, hair examiners have addressed many concerns related to wrongful convictions. The development of testimony and practice standards has progressed under the Organization of Scientific Area Committees. Reforms have included peer review, blind verification, testimony monitoring, and transcript review. Morphological hair comparison remains relevant as a low-cost, nondestructive tool for the examination of trace evidence. DNA and hair analysis are effective and complementary techniques when used in a valid manner by trained forensic scientists. A review of the relevant material is beyond the scope of this textbook. The interested reader should refer to materials from the American Society of Trace Evidence Examiners (www.asteetrace.org) or a review by leading expert Sandra Koch (Koch, Tridico, Bernard, Shriver, & Jablonski, 2019).

POLICE INVESTIGATION AND PROSECUTION BEFORE DNA

Police investigators often focus on a particular suspect and discount exculpatory information. This phenomenon was common in hair and serology cases because exculpatory results could be discounted and never pointed to a specific alternate suspect. This cognitive bias could extend to prosecutors and even defense counsel. One example is the case of Orlando Bosquette, involving a burglary and sexual assault in Monroe County, Florida in 1982. The forensic examiner found A and O blood group substances in semen on the victim's underwear, but Bosquette was an O nonsecretor, meaning he could not have been the source of either type of marker. The examiner found no blood group markers on pajama stains, which theoretically would be consistent with a nonsecretor assailant. However, the pajama stains did not contain detectable levels of semen, so they were not forensically useful. On cross-examination, the forensic analyst did clarify that some of the semen could not possibly have come from Bosquette but failed to clarify that Bosquette, as a nonsecretor, would not have been excluded from *any* biological evidence if one assumed the possibility of multiple contributors. Bosquette was convicted but later exonerated by DNA analysis in 2006.

The forensic evidence was also exculpatory in the Edward Honaker case. Honaker was accused of a sexual assault/kidnapping in Nelson County, Virginia in 1984. The analyst found spermatozoa on the vaginal slides from the victim and Caucasian hairs in the rape kit. Fingerprints from the victim's car did not match Honaker. Honaker had had a vasectomy so could not have produced the spermatozoa. In any case, only O blood group substances were found, and Honaker was blood type B. The hairs did not match Honaker except for one hair found on the victim's shorts that the analyst said "was unlikely to match anyone" other than Honaker. Postconviction, the defense lawyer said he was unaware of Honaker's vasectomy or the fact that the key witnesses were hypnotized to elicit their identification of Honaker. An independent hair expert said the hair from the shorts didn't match Honaker. DNA analysis excluded Honaker, who was pardoned by the governor and received $500,000 in compensation. The original forensic analyst, Elmer Gist, recanted his conclusions and said the error may have arisen because he had been influenced by contextual information about the case.

In some cases, the problems arose at the crime scene, the collection of evidence at an autopsy, or the chain of custody. Evidence management can still support or undermine reliable forensic science analysis across all disciplines and case types. In some wrongful convictions, poor evidence management prevented the reliable use of serological analysis. Most commonly, bacterial contamination was the problem. Bacteria may produce proteins that produce false positives in immunological assays. In ABO testing, spurious type A or type B results can be seen when a biological sample has been stored wet or when it is collected from a decaying corpse or contaminated with fecal matter (Culliford, 1971). In these cases, the sample does not contain A or B blood group substances but rather bacterial proteins that cause the tests to produce false results.

Degradation could also be misused to discount exculpatory results. The 1987 murder/rape trial of Barry Laughman in Adams County, Pennsylvania is instructive. Rape kit swabs and other evidence was collected at autopsy. The swabs sat for a month before they were opened by the crime lab analyst, Janice Roadcap. Roadcap found A antigens consistent with the victim on almost all of the evidence. The rape kit samples showed spermatozoa that were "nearly all intact." She found only A antigens in those samples. Given the confirmation of male fraction by the detection of spermatozoa, Roadcap should have concluded that the rape had been committed by nonsecretor or A secretor, a conclusion which would have exculpated Laughman, who was a B secretor. Instead, she discounted the results, saying that she had seen a "pinkish substance" on the swabs and that they were damp when she got them. She dried the swabs and performed a Benedict's test which showed the presence of a sugar-reducing substance and implied bacterial growth. She added a note to the margin of her laboratory chart about possible contamination. During her testimony, she said the serology was essentially worthless because bacteria could have broken down Laughman's B antigens. She also speculated—without any foundation—that the victim may have been on a medication that would interfere with the antigen tests.

There were several problems with this testimony. Bacteria would also break down spermatozoa and A antigens. Further, if the spermatozoa were intact, then the B antigens in the spermatozoa would have been unaffected. Roadcap was clearly influenced by case context and used the possibility of degradation to avoid an exculpatory interpretation of the serology. She hadn't noted the wet condition of the swabs until after she found that Laughman was a type B secretor. Her actions demonstrate the problem of confirmation bias in the interpretation stage of forensic analysis. Laughman's defense attorney challenged some of Roadcap's interpretation but did not recognize the importance of the intact spermatozoa undermining the theory of bacterial degradation.

The case included a similar misuse of fingerprint comparison. A cigarette pack was found at the scene. A latent print on the cigarette pack had level 1 detail showing a whorl pattern. Laughman's fingerprints had whorls, like 25 to 30% of the population. The incomplete print comparison was used to elicit a false confession from Laughman.

Laughman was convicted and sentenced to life in prison. DNA testing in 1993 failed to exonerate him because the methods at the time were not selective enough to produce a conclusive result. In 2003, the DNA tests were redone using STR profiling, and Laughman was exonerated. He received an undisclosed settlement from the state of Pennsylvania for his wrongful conviction.

STUDY QUESTIONS

1. Consider the case of Dennis Butler. The appeals decision that overturned his conviction can be obtained from https://www.govinfo.gov/content/pkg/USCOURTS-caDC-17-03080/pdf/USCOURTS-caDC-17-03080-0.pdf, a website which archives federal government documents. What was the substance of Myron Scholberg's hair comparison testimony? How did it contribute to the evidence to convict Butler? Were there errors in Scholberg's testimony? What were the root causes of the errors? Do you believe Butler was innocent? Make sure to read the dissent starting on page 26 of the PDF as you consider your answer.
2. The influence of contextual information was evident in many wrongful convictions related to hair comparison and serology. Humans are susceptible to cognitive bias in many forms (Dror, 2020). Itiel Dror and others have discussed the impact on the reliability of forensic evidence. How did cognitive bias manifest in the police investigation, forensic analysis, and trials in the cases reviewed in this chapter? What reforms will be most

effective to improve the reliability of forensic analysis in this regard?

3. Hair comparison and serology had very different scientific foundations. The scientific differences led to differences in how the techniques contributed to wrongful convictions. Compare and contrast the two disciplines and how they were used in wrongful conviction prosecutions. How did DNA analysis address the scientific limitations of the two techniques?

FURTHER READING

John Roman and his research team at the Urban Institute conducted the study of the Mary Jane Burton cases and a set of postconviction reviews in Arizona (Roman, Walsh, Lachman, & Yahner, 2012). Their report, *Post-Conviction DNA Testing and Wrongful Conviction*, provides a unique opportunity to study a large set of cases to determine the etiology of wrongful convictions. Their work has been important in the assessment of causative factors in wrongful convictions and the prioritization of cases for postconviction review.

As mentioned in the discussion of root cause analysis, the ABS Group analysis of hair comparison errors at the FBI Laboratory highlights important challenges in the management of forensic science units and the enforcement of testimony standards (ABS Group, 2018). The 1985 FBI symposium on hair comparison provides an important bookend to the topic showing the ways that the forensic science community grappled with the problem at the time (The Laboratory Division, Federal Bureau of Investigation, 1985).

The Garrett–Neufeld paper remains an important reference substantiating the importance of forensic science errors in wrongful convictions (Garrett & Neufeld, 2009). The paper should be interpreted in light of the substantive objections that have been raised in response by LaPorte and other authors (LaPorte, 2018). For those interested in diving deeper into the fascinating history of serological typing, the works of Culliford and Gaennslen remain insightful and scientifically valid (Culliford, 1971; Gaennslen, 2000; Gaensslen, 1983).

There are useful official reviews of particular cases, examiners, or organizations that contributed to wrongful convictions. Three deserve highlighting here. The ASCLD/LAB review of Fred Zain demonstrates the value of quality assurance and independent technical reviews to limit the risk of fraudulent or incompetent testimony (McNamara & Linhart, 1993). Morgenthau's report on the Central Park 5 is a model of thorough and objective analysis of a complex case (Morgenthau, 2002). It is far superior to the many, biased accounts that have been promulgated in the mass media about the case. Finally, the Bromwich report on the Houston laboratory details the many deficiencies that arose there in serological analysis and the early years of DNA analysis (Bromwich, 2007). The Bromwich report is discussed in detail in the chapter on organizational dysfunction.

REFERENCES

ABS Group. (2018). *Root Cause Analysis of Microscopic Hair Comparison Analysis*. Federal Bureau of Investigation.

Associated Press. (1994, July 13). Serologist Falsified Evidence in Rape Case. *El Paso Times*, p. 17.

Becka, H., & Swindle, H. (2000, May 7). One in an Occasional Series. *Dallas Morning News*.

Bromwich, M. R. (2007). *Final Report of the Independent Investigator for the Houston Police Department Crime Laboratory and Property Room*. Washington, DC: Fried, Frank, Harris, Shriver & Jacobson LLP. Retrieved from http://www.hpdlabinvestigation.org/

Champod, C., Biedermann, A., Vuille, J., Willis, S., & De Kinder, J. (2016, March 12). ENFSI Guideline for Evaluative Reporting in Forensic Science, A Primer for Legal Practitioners. *Criminal Law & Justice Weekly*, *180*, 189–193.

Culliford, B. J. (1971). *The Examination and Typing of Bloodstains in the Crime Laboratory*. Washington, DC: National Institute of Law Enforcement and Criminal Justice.

Department of Justice. (2018). *Supporting Documentation for Department of Justice Proposed Uniform Lanugage for Testimony and Reports for the Forensic Hair Examination Discipline*. Washington, DC: Department of Justice.

District of Columbia Department of Forensic Sciences. (2014). *FBS07 - Microscopic Examination of Spermatozoa by Christmas Tree Stain*.

Dror, I. E. (2020). Cognitive and Human Factors in Expert Decision Making: Six Fallacies and the Eight Sources of Bias. *Analytical Chemistry*, *92*(12), 7998–8004.

European Network of Forensic Science Institutes. (2015). *ENFSI guideline for evaluative reporting in forensic science*.

Federal Bureau of Investigation. (2015, 4, 19). *FBI/DOJ Microscopic Hair Comparison Analysis Review*. Retrieved from Federal Bureau of Investigation: https://www.fbi.gov/services/laboratory/scientific-analysis/fbidoj-microscopic-hair-comparison-analysis-review

Gaensslen, R. E. (1983). *Sourcebook in Forensic Serology, Immunology, and Biochemistry*. Washington, DC: National Criminal Justice Reference Service. Retrieved from https://www.ncjrs.gov/pdffiles1/pr/160880_unit_5.pdf

Gaennslen, R. E. (2000). Forensic Analysis of Biological Evidence. In C. H. Wecht, *Forensic Sciences* (29 ed., Vol. 1). New York: Matthew Bender and Co.

Garrett, B., & Neufeld, P. (2009, March). Invalid Forensic Science Testimony and Wrongful Convictions. *Virginia Law Review*, 1–97.

Gaudette, B. D., & Keeping, E. S. (1974). An Attempt at Determining Probabilities in Human Scalp Hair Comparisons. *Journal of Forensic Sciences*, *19*, 599–606.

Holt, T., Blevins, K., Foran, D., & Smith, R. (2016). *Examination of the Conditions Affecting Forensic Scientists' Workplace Productivity and Occupational Stress*. Washington, DC.: National Institute of Justice.

Houck, M. M., & Budowle, B. (2002). Correlation of Microscopic and Mitochondrial DNA Hair Comparisons. *Journal of Forensic Sciences*, *47*(5), 964–967.

In re Blair, 11–0441 (Supreme Court of Texas August 23, 2013).

Koch, S. L. (2017). Microscopy of Hair Part 1: A Practical Guide and Manual for Human Hairs. *Forensic Science Communications*, *6*(1), 1–44.

Koch, S. L., Tridico, S. R., Bernard, B. A., Shriver, M. D., & Jablonski, N. G. (2019). The Biology of Hair: A Multidisciplinary Review. *American Journal of Human Biology*. https://doi.org/10.1002/ajhb.23316

LaPorte, G. (2018, April). Wrongful Convictions and DNA Exonerations: Understanding the Role of Forensic Science. *NIJ Journal*, *279*, 1–16.

Matta-Ballesteros v. United States, LA CV16-02596 (US District Court for the Central District of California May 22, 2017).

McNamara, J. J., & Linhart, R. R. (1993). *ASCLD/LAB Investigation Report, West Virginia State Police Crime Laboratory, Serology Division*. South Charleston, West Virginia: ASCLD/LAB.

Morgenthau, R. (2002). *Affirmation in Response to Motion to Vacate Judgment of Conviction*. New York City: District Attorney of New York.

Otterbourg, K. (2020, 12, 14). *Elmer Daniels*. Retrieved from National Registry of Exonerations: http://www.law.umich.edu/special/exoneration/Pages/casedetail.aspx?caseid=5470

Robertson, J. (1999). *Forensic Examination of Hair*. London: Taylor & Francis.

Roman, J., Walsh, K., Lachman, P., & Yahner, J. (2012). *Post-Conviction DNA Testing and Wrongful Conviction*. Washington, DC: Urban Institute.
Scheck, B., Neufeld, P., & Dwyer, J. (2003). *Actual innocence: When justice goes wrong and how to*. New York: Signet.
Scientific Working Group on Materials Analysis (SWGMAT). (2005). *Forensic Human Hair Examination Guidelines*. American Society of Trace Evidence Examiners.
State v. Charles, 511 So. 2d 1164 (Louisiana Court of Appeals 1987).
The Laboratory Division, Federal Bureau of Investigation. (1985). Proceedings of the International Symposium on Forensic Hair Comparisons. Washington, DC. Retrieved March 30, 2020, from https://www.ncjrs.gov/pdffiles1/Digitization/116592NCJRS.pdf
Turvey, B. (2013). *Forensic Fraud: Evaluating Law Enforcement and Forensci Science Cultures in the Context of Examiner Misconduct*. New York: Academic Press.
Wilson, J., Hugenberg, K., & Bernstein, M. (2013). The Cross-race Effect and Eyewitness Identification: How to Improve Recognition and Reduce Decision Errors in Eyewitness Situations. *Social Issues and Policy Review*, 7(1), 83–113.

CHAPTER 4

DNA

Forensic DNA analysis developed rapidly and had an outsized impact on the criminal justice system. Kary Mullis first demonstrated the polymerase chain reaction (PCR) in 1985 and won the Nobel Prize for the discovery in 1993 (Figure 4.1). The first forensic DNA test using PCR was introduced in 1991 and soon was used to solve crimes and exonerate wrongfully convicted defendants. In 1998, the National DNA Index System (NDIS) was established by the FBI based on 13, PCR-based, short-tandem-repeat (STR) DNA markers. By 2001, mitochondrial DNA and other advanced techniques were being used to identify thousands of human remains from the World Trade Center bombing. Today, the NDIS system includes 20 STR markers and over 19 million profiles from convicted offenders and arrestees and has helped to solve almost 600,000 cases.

DNA has played a well-known role in the exoneration of over 600 innocent defendants. But DNA is not fool-proof. It is subject to problems related to contamination, poor chain-of-custody, misinterpretation, and discounting of exculpatory evidence—just like other laboratory disciplines. Also, DNA is not just one analytical technique. Current forensic DNA analysis bears little resemblance to the techniques introduced in the 1980s and 1990s. In its initial form, DNA analysis had a probative value similar to serology and was highly subjective. Many observers felt that DNA population statistics were insufficient and could produce misleading testimony. Standards did not exist or were severely lacking.

DNA ANALYSIS IN THE EARLY 1990s

The 1991 Timothy Durham case illustrates the problems encountered in early DNA analysis (Thompson, Taroni, & Aitken, 2003). The case involved a female child who was a victim of sexual assault. DNA pioneer, Dr. Robert Giles of GeneScreen, received samples from a swimsuit worn by the victim and evidence hairs. Giles used PCR to amplify the dqAlpha gene from the biological evidence. Giles did not attempt the older

DOI: 10.4324/9781003202578-4

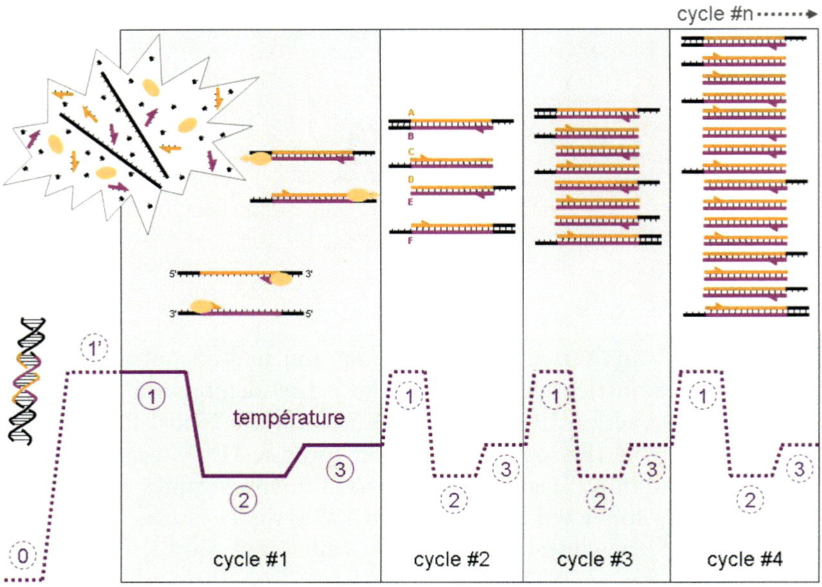

FIGURE 4.1 The polymerase chain reaction (PCR) was recognized for its importance in forensic analysis shortly after its discovery. PCR has been used routinely in forensic DNA laboratories for over 20 years. The reliable use of PCR for DNA analysis required on the development of marker systems, laboratory protocols, and statistical interpretation frameworks. Credit: Wikimedia Commons, Ygonaar, Used per Creative Commons Attribution-Share Alike 2.0 France

technique, based on restriction-fragment-length polymorphism (RFLP), because dqAlpha was much more sensitive, and the amount of genetic material was very limited. At the time, dqAlpha testing could not be automated and ended with a "readout" on an electrophoretic gel. When a particular dqAlpha type was present, a black dot would arise in the corresponding location on the gel. Durham's dqAlpha type was 1.1/1.2, and the victim's type was 1.2/2. The first two attempts to get a dqAlpha profile from the evidence failed. On the third attempt, Giles saw dots at 1.2 and 2, consistent with the victim, and a fainter third spot at 1.1 that was consistent with Durham. He said Durham's 1.1/1.2 type "would be found in the Caucasian population at a frequency of about 5 percent." There were several problems with Giles' work. To begin with, he had not completed a successful differential extraction. In differential extraction, the male and female fractions in a sample are separated, a process which allows separate genetic analysis of the two types of contributors.

Because the female victim's dqAlpha was present, Giles did not know whether the male contributor's dqAlpha type was being masked by the victim's profile. If dots showed at 1.1, 1.2, and 2, then the male contributor could have been a 1.1/1.1, 1.1/1.2, or 1.1/2. The poor differential extraction led to a misleading statement during testimony. Just as many serologists might confuse source and sub-source propositions, Giles confused the population estimate for Durham's dqAlpha profile (1.1/1.2) with the population estimate for the evidence profile (all three combinations that included 1.1). His statement about the population frequency of Durham's profile was misleading at best. Finally, Giles exhibited deep cognitive bias in his laboratory analysis. He kept repeating the test until he got the result he wanted. And when the 1.1 dot was faint, he did not base his "call" on any objective standard for a positive indication on the test result. He may have been motivated by contextual information about the case or the desire to get a result to support his commercial business. More likely, he was motivated by his belief in his own ability, a kind of expert bias sometimes observed in cutting-edge advocates for scientific and technological innovations. He said:

> I can't say that someone could walk in and pick up this particular photograph and make the same call that I would make... I'm making that call based on the fact I've been doing this for several years. I have been involved with gene amplification from its very beginning... I have experience in knowing how to make these particular calls. There is some art involved in that, but that's why I'm trained as a scientist to do what I do.
>
> (Scheck, Neufeld, & Dwyer, 2000)

As a result of Giles' "art," the jury was given the impression that Durham was implicated by the powerful, new science of DNA. Durham was convicted and sentenced to life in prison. He became one of the most prominent, early exonerees of the Innocence Project in 1996, when improved DNA analysis implicated an alternate suspect.

Early DNA analysis had limited probative value that could result in wrongful convictions or failures in postconviction exoneration. Because early DNA could not produce cold hits, investigators would dismiss exculpatory results that didn't fit preexisting case theories. In 1991, Murray Weiner was accused of murdering Robert Evans over a $40,000 debt (Weiner v. San Diego County, 2000). Police found 39 blood stains in Weiner's storage unit and assumed that Weiner had temporarily stored Evans' body there. Four drops of blood were preserved and analyzed using the DNA methods available at the time. Three of them were subject to dqAlpha testing, revealing a 1.1,1.1 characteristic that matched Evans and roughly 3% of the population. The fourth spot was subject to RFLP testing, which excluded Evans. The prosecution held that the fourth spot was not from the same source as the other three, but they had no basis for that claim. Like serology, the dqAlpha test was reliable when used for exclusion or to limit the possible contributors to a sample to a population of sources. The RFLP test was much more selective and probative and should have been considered the more definitive information, even though it was less sensitive (i.e., it required more sample).

Although Weiner was convicted, he was soon granted a new trial on the basis of the testimony of a jailhouse informant who was not considered in the original trial. In the meantime, the public defender took over the case for Weiner and arranged for a dqAlpha test on the fourth spot, which had a 1.1,1.1 characteristic consistent with the other three spots. Further, a blood spatter expert concluded that all four spots came from the same source. Therefore, the prosecutor had no basis to prove that Evans was ever in Weiner's storage shed. The second trial ended in a jury acquittal.

Many postconviction cases in the time period were not overturned on similar exculpatory evidence. If the DNA test did not positively identify an alternative suspect, the prosecutor could argue that the original conviction was valid and should be sustained based on other evidence. This was the case even in sexual assault cases that clearly excluded the defendant as a contributor to the biological evidence. These defendants spent many additional years in prison waiting for DNA technology to "catch up" to their case and prove their innocence by clearly implicating an alternate suspect.

O.J. SIMPSON

O.J. Simpson was not convicted of the murders of his ex-wife, Nicole Brown Simpson, and her partner, Ronald Goldman, but the Simpson case had a profound impact on forensic science and wrongful convictions. Valid and reliable forensic analysis in the Simpson case was compromised by deficiencies in evidence collection, evidence handling, chain-of-custody, and DNA interpretation (Thompson, 1996). The timing of the case coincided with two reports on DNA analysis by the National Research Council (NRC), which had criticized the lack of standards in evidence handling, test procedures, and statistical analysis (National Research Council (US) Committee on DNA Technology in Forensic Science, 1992; National Research Council, 1996).

There were no witnesses to the murders, so investigators relied on the possibility that DNA could be used to reconstruct events and implicate Simpson. Blood samples were collected from the

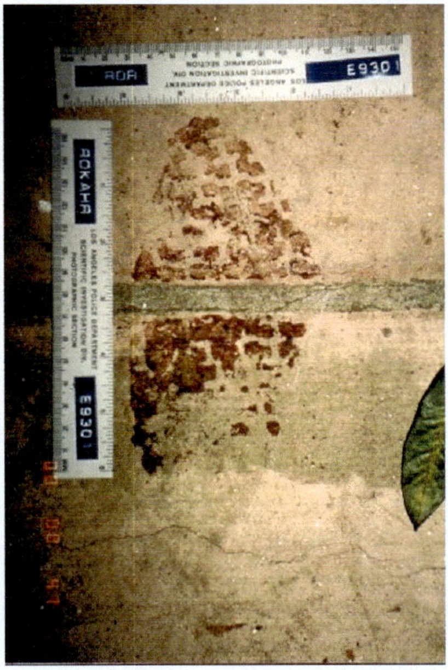

FIGURE 4.2 O.J.'s Bloody shoeprint. Evidence photo from a trial exhibit in the Simpson case. Although DNA may be highly sensitive and selective, other techniques may contribute key information to scene reconstruction. A bloody shoeprint was found near the victims and associated with a rare size 12 Bruno Magli shoe. Simpson denied owning that model of shoe during the criminal trial. During the civil trial, it was established that his ex-wife had bought him a pair of size 12 Bruno Magli shoes and he had worn them to a football event. The evidence was seen to be crucial to the outcome of the civil trial, which was unfavorable to Simpson.

murder scene, Simpson's home, and Simpson's vehicle. The results were clearly inculpatory. Simpson's blood was found at the murder scene. The victims' blood was found at Simpson's residence. Mixtures of Simpson's and victims' blood were found on Simpson's Ford Bronco. The evidence supported the prosecution theory that Simpson had committed the murders and left a bloody trail leading directly to his home (Figure 4.2).

The Los Angeles Police Department (LAPD) collected and documented evidence from the scene, but their training, procedures, and record-keeping were sorely lacking. A nurse collected a blood sample from Simpson the day after the crime but could not remember if 6.5 ml or 8 ml of sample had been taken. Only 6.5 ml was in the vial when it got to the crime laboratory, meaning that some sample may have gone missing in the meantime. The nurse gave the sample to detective Philip Vannatter unsealed, and Vannatter failed to record the evidence collection. He then drove to the Simpson residence and gave the sample to LAPD criminalist Dennis Fung. Noting this odd behavior, the defense demonstrated that police had the opportunity to plant Simpson's blood on evidence swatches or at the crime scene. To counter this claim, samples were sent to the FBI Laboratory to determine if evidence contained EDTA, a preservative used with blood reference samples, including the Simpson sample. The FBI did not have a test method for EDTA in blood but developed one for the case (Miller, McCord, Martz, & Budowle, 1997). They found EDTA in some evidence samples, but FBI examiner Roger Martz testified that the amounts were too small to have originated from a reference standard. EDTA is contained in many food items (such as the Big Mac Simpson had eaten the day before the murders), but there was no research to substantiate that endogenous EDTA could be found in human blood at any concentration. Martz appeared arrogant and dismissive of defense questioning during the trial, and his lack of preparation and poor documentation later led to his public reprimand by the FBI (Bromwich, 1997).

The LAPD crime laboratory was also implicated in poor evidence handling and interpretation. Criminalist Colin Yamauchi spilled some of Simpson's blood while working in the evidence processing room and did not take appropriate steps to mitigate the possibility of cross-contamination. Key samples—including the infamous "bloody glove"—were potentially compromised. The reference samples from the victims were similarly compromised. DNA markers consistent with Simpson were found in reference DNA testing on both vials. This did not prove that the vials were contaminated with Simpson's blood, but it did demonstrate that foreign DNA was present.

At the time, sensitive and selective DNA testing was not available. For example, a blood stain from the steering wheel of Simpson's vehicle was tested using PCR techniques, but the marker systems used could not establish the contribution of any specific individual, i.e., the DNA typing was barely more selective than traditional serology. For example, one victim was characterized for six markers, and the frequency of her profile was about 1 in 2500

(Thompson, 1996). As in serology, that statistic was misleading because it was different from the population of individuals who could be included in the blood stain on the steering wheel. In fact, about half of the population could have been included as a possible contributor to the evidence sample, including O.J. Simpson and Nicole Brown Simpson, with Ronald Goldman being excluded. Various other statistical frameworks were suggested by the prosecution, and it is clear from juror comments after the trial that the statistical discussion was confusing and not impactful for them. They felt that Simpson's lawyers had made the case for contamination or evidence-planting, and the statistical characterization seemed like a smoke screen.

Simpson was acquitted. Afterward, the family of Ronald Goldman sued Simpson successfully for wrongful death, resulting in a $33.5 million award. Legal battles over the matter continue to the present day.

DNA AFTER THE SIMPSON TRIAL

The O.J. Simpson case was a major milestone in the use of DNA. Ironically, although DNA and forensic science would exonerate many defendants, the Simpson acquittal was largely based on the discrediting of the forensic science work done by the Los Angeles Police Department. Barry Scheck's involvement in the case greatly raised the profile of the Innocence Project. As he has stated:

> We did not challenge the underlying reliability of DNA testing methods; we attacked the way that evidence was gathered and processed... Fame is a good thing to have sometimes if you can put it to good use. The Innocence Project benefited from that.
>
> (Morrison, 2014)

The Simpson legal team also challenged the statistical characterization of the DNA results, which were largely based on complex mixtures that were not amenable to simple analysis using the technology available at the time. After the Simpson trial, the second NRC report provided much more clarity on the issue of statistical characterization of DNA, and STR marker systems came along to improve the selectivity and probative value of DNA analysis (National Research Council, 1996). Still, DNA interpretation continued to contribute to wrongful convictions.

The 2002 Kerry Robinson case had some similarities to the O.J. Simpson case with respect to DNA mixture interpretation. A 42-year-old woman was raped in Moultrie, Georgia. The victim said there were three assailants and identified two suspects, Tyrone White and Derrick Smith. In turn, White confessed to his involvement and identified Kerry Robinson and Sedrick Moore as his accomplices, not Smith. The Georgia Bureau of Identification (GBI) conducted a DNA analysis and found that White's DNA was present on 11 of the 13 alleles found. The other two alleles matched the DNA profiles from both Moore and Robinson. At Robinson's trial, the forensic analyst testified that Robinson could not be excluded, although the statistical value of the two matching alleles was very low. In a research study on the case, the interpretation problem was presented to 17 other DNA analysts, 12 of whom excluded Robinson, four of whom settled on "inconclusive," and one of whom agreed with the GBI analyst that Robinson "cannot be excluded" (Dror & Hampikian, 2011). The study authors—one of whom was an advocate for Robinson's innocence—concluded that the case was an example of target bias, in which the examiner was seeking to match the suspect profile to the evidence, no matter how weak the association might have been.

STR ANALYSIS AND MIXTURE INTERPRETATION

The Robinson case illustrated two key issues: the continuing weakness of STR markers for deconvolving mixtures and the inadequacy of analytical software to provide an objective basis for mixture interpretation. These issues have been addressed to a large extent in recent years with the expansion of CODIS STR loci and the development of better software for mixture deconvolution. Nonetheless, agencies have struggled to resolve these problems.

In New York City, the Office of the Chief Medical Examiner (OCME) gained a reputation as a leading DNA analysis laboratory in the aftermath of the World Trade Center attacks on 9/11/2001. They identified many thousands of remains using advanced DNA methods, including very small and degraded samples (Kinship and Data Analysis Panel, 2006). Over the years, OCME continued to be on the cutting edge of DNA analysis, even developing their own system for mixture analysis with small samples.

On December 1, 2013, Taj Patterson was assaulted by approximately 20 Hasidic Jewish men in Brooklyn (People v. Herskovic, 2018). One alleged attacker, Mayer Herskovic, was charged with gang assault and related crimes. Patterson's sneaker had been lost during the attack but was found six days later on a nearby rooftop. The OCME recovered a tiny DNA sample—only 97.9 picograms—from the sneaker. The sample analysis revealed a DNA mixture from two persons. The OCME used their in-house software, Forensic Statistical Tool (FST), to determine that it was 695,000 more probable that the DNA came from Herskovic and an unknown person than from two unknown persons. It also found that it was 133 more likely that the sample was a mixture of Herskovic and Patterson than an unknown person and Patterson. The court opined that "the likelihood ratio result was only 133, a relatively insubstantial number" (People v. Herskovic, 2018). This statement is somewhat ironic, given that such a likelihood ratio would have been the envy of any serologist in the pre-DNA era.

The OCME analysis suffered from several deficiencies. First, the manufacturer of the DNA test kit did not recommend using less than 125 picograms of material for analysis. For a DNA mixture, the required amount would be even greater, perhaps 500–1000 picograms. Second, although OCME had validated FST generally, it did not do so for the Hasidic population. The primary trial issue was whether Herskovic was among the Hasidim who had attacked Patterson, meaning that the relevant analysis would have been to validate and report the population statistics relative to the isolated Hasidic population, not Caucasians or broader populations. OCME did not do this. Third, and most importantly, the OCME analysis did not conform to the standards followed by the rest of the DNA laboratories in the country. The resultant sample profile did not produce an actual match. It was impossible to extract a single DNA sub-source from the biological material on the sneaker. It was not even possible to discern that there were only two sub-sources because one locus showed the presence of five alleles, implying at least three contributors (or an artifact, which was at least as likely). In fact, OCME had discounted nonmatching alleles at several loci. At D7, Mayer's alleles were 10,11 but only 10 was found. At D16, Mayer was 11,12 but the composite profile was 9,11. So, OCME could have interpreted the profile as an exclusion but chose to assume that the nonmatching alleles were the result of dropouts or "flukes." OCME discarded use of FST in 2016 and switched to STRmix, a commercial software for mixture interpretation that had passed FBI validation (Kupferschmid, 2018). Herskovic's conviction was vacated in 2018, and the charges were dismissed.

The Houston Police Department (HPD) laboratory provides a useful case study on the impact of gaps in the management of DNA laboratories. The HPD's wrongful conviction of Josiah Sutton has been detailed by independent reviews by William Thompson (Thompson, 2003) and Michael Bromwich (Bromwich, 2007). According to Bromwich's report, the DNA analysis was compromised by failed differential extractions, failed controls, poor temperature control of the dqAlpha assay, lack of technical review, poor documentation, and statistical misinterpretation.

In the Sutton case, the defense attorney took funds to do independent DNA testing but did not follow through. The HPD experience is an extreme example, but the importance of rigorous and enforced standards and quality assurance persists as a common theme across wrongful conviction case histories.

MISCONDUCT ISSUES

DNA may provide powerful exculpatory evidence. As a result, the findings may be suppressed by police or prosecutors. Such misconduct may relate to investigative tunnel vision or corruption. In the Nathaniel Hatchett case, DNA testing excluded Hatchett as a contributor to semen found in the sexual assault kit. The DNA evidence was discounted because of Hatchett's false confession, and it was theorized that the victim's husband was the source. It was not disclosed to the defense that the husband also did not match the semen DNA (Hatchett v. City of Detroit et al., 2010). Similarly, in the 1997 Keith Cooper case, a partial DNA profile excluded Cooper as a possible contributor, but that fact was not shared with the defense. Postconviction DNA testing was able to produce a complete profile and a cold hit to the source. In the Buncombe Five case, the district attorney suppressed exculpatory DNA evidence after police had elicited several false confessions (State v. Kagonyera/Wilcoxson, 2011). One defendant, Kenneth Kagonyera filed for DNA testing in August of 2001, unaware that lab results had already exculpated him and his four codefendants in March. He provided a false confession in November. The North Carolina Innocence Inquiry Commission formally exonerated the Buncombe Five in 2011 (State v. Kagonyera/Wilcoxson, 2011).

In the 1990s, it was not uncommon for exculpatory DNA to be discounted when it did not identify an alternate suspect. Because dqAlpha, polymarker, and RFLP methods weren't well-suited to complete profiles and cold hits, many wrongfully convicted defendants were exonerated only after the advent of standardized STR markers in the late 1990s. Further, there was reasonable skepticism about DNA reliability in the scientific (National Research Council (US) Committee on DNA Technology in Forensic Science, 1992) and legal (Baird, Neufeld, & Scheck, 1990) communities. These perceptions may have contributed to the discounting of DNA results by law enforcement into the post-2000 period.

Wrongful convictions may be an indicator of deeper dysfunction in a police department or forensic science organization. In many jurisdictions, rape kit backlogs have highlighted these deficiencies (Campbell, et al., 2015). More than 10,000 untested kits were discovered in New

York City in 1999, and more than 12,000 untested kits were found in Los Angeles 10 years later. Other jurisdictions had commensurate problems. In part, the backlogs arose from the limited capacity of labs to conduct DNA analysis. Even when labs had equipment, they did not have trained and qualified staff to run the tests. The backlogs also arose from investigative priorities. Many sexual assault cases involve consent issues. In other words, the assailant is known but asserts that the intercourse was consensual. The failure to do DNA testing in those circumstances meant that serial offenders were not detected. Also, police would not ask for analysis in cases in which they believed that the victim was uncooperative or unreliable. Arguably, the most extreme example arose in Detroit (Figure 4.3). In 2008, wrongful convictions related to ballistic evidence revealed serious deficiencies in the city crime lab. On August 17, 2009, investigators arranged a tour of a

FIGURE 4.3 Abandoned laboratory from a Detroit crime lab. The Detroit Police Crime Lab moved into the closed Foster Elementary School building in 1989. The lab was closed in 2009 in the wake of scandals associated with the ballistics unit and rape kit backlog. The building was not well-guarded, and much equipment and evidence were left behind, including live ammunition and breathalyzers. This picture shows a former lab within the abandoned building, which was eventually demolished in 2015. It is unknown how much evidence was lost or destroyed. Credit: Detroiturbex.com, Foster Elementary School/Detroit Police Crime Lab.

property storage facility and discovered 11,219 unprocessed rape kits. The lab was subsequently shut down. It took many years to process the evidence. Over 2,500 had been submitted for testing but it was unclear how many had been actually analyzed. The vast majority of the cases had been closed after minimal investigation by police who were dismissive of any attempt to perform appropriate case follow-up. Rebecca Campbell and her research team at Michigan State University conducted an "action-research" program to test 1,595 sexual assault kits, which yielded 785 DNA profiles and 455 cold hits. A total of 127 serial sexual assaults were identified in the subset. Interestingly, the cold-hit rates did not correlate with whether the victim knew the offender.

Campbell found that police had negative beliefs and stereotypes about victims. Many victims were presumed to be prostitutes. Younger victims were not considered credible. Victims who knew their assailant were not considered credible. The crime lab had communicated their lack of capacity to police, who interpreted the feedback to mean that the lab did not want to "waste our time on kits from sketchy victims." There was no consistent protocol to determine when investigation would continue or DNA testing performed. Prosecutors reinforced the problem. When they wanted testing, they wanted it right away, leading to a constant crisis mentality. They told police that they would not take any cases if there were questions about the credibility of a victim. Campbell found five primary factors that contributed to the backlog. First, there was no policy or protocol and the decision to have a kit tested was done on a case-by-case basis. Second, there were insufficient personnel to do the work. The Detroit lab had only two DNA analysts, far fewer than comparable jurisdictions. There was no prosecutor unit dedicated to sexual assaults. Third, the Detroit police department had constant leadership turnover—usually a chief lasted about two years in the job. The sex crimes unit had similar changes in its leadership. Fourth, the people collecting the rape kits were not specially trained. The kits were often collected by medical personnel who discounted the importance of the collection or the case. This related closely to the last factor, the lack of local social services or advocates. On average, Detroit had one rape crisis advocate for the entire city. There was no community-based advocacy for the victims and an almost complete absence of trained sexual assault nurse practitioners. These types of deficiencies are not unique to rape kit backlog issues. They bear great similarities to the factors associated with wrongful convictions. The attitudes and dysfunction are commonly observed in jurisdictions which fail to invest in forensic laboratories, enforce best practice protocols, or commit to quality assurance.

CRIME SCENE INVESTIGATION AND EVIDENCE TRACKING

One of the key unresolved issues in forensic science policy relates to the preservation, storage, and tracking of evidence. DNA technology has changed quickly. The method applied at the time of the crime may be very different from the method used at the time of the trial. By the time of postconviction testing many years later, whole new approaches could have been developed. Sometimes, the limitations of older methods are not communicated by the crime lab or understood by investigators.

The Nicholas McGuffin case involved the murder of his girlfriend in 2000. Her body was found far from the murder scene. Her right shoe was found by a garage mechanic in the days after the murder. Her left shoe—which was noticeably bloody—was found the week after the murder about 10 miles away. In 2000, the initial DNA analysis revealed contributions from the victim and a police officer on the bloody shoe but no trace of a contribution from McGuffin. The analyst also observed markers from a possible third contributor, but the levels were so low that they didn't meet guidelines to make a definitive call one way or the other. The extra peaks were described in bench notes only. The case went unsolved for several years, when a new police chief decided to reinvestigate. It took months to reassemble the evidence, some of which was as far away as Scotland Yard in the United Kingdom. The police got the crime lab report, but nothing about the bench notes showing a possible foreign DNA contributor. No new DNA analysis was performed on the shoe, and McGuffin was convicted of manslaughter on the basis of a prosecution theory of a domestic fight based on the victim's possible pregnancy. The jury voted 10 to 2 for conviction on that charge, which didn't require a unanimous verdict. Postconviction, McGuffin was eventually able to get DNA testing on the shoe, which revealed a full profile from a male contributor that was present on the inside and outside of the right shoe and associated with the bloodstains on the left shoe. His conviction was vacated on this basis, and he was not tried again. The DNA was not clearly exculpatory because the evidence handling at the time of the murder had been highly questionable. The DNA could have been contaminated by several different sources. More salient was the fact that the original trial process was inherently unfair to McGuffin because of errors related to the forensic evidence. The original investigation ended without recovery or tracking of the evidence. The reinvestigation never reviewed the forensic evidence in sufficient detail to determine if the DNA analysis could be redone to get better results. The forensic report and testimony didn't address the possibility of the foreign DNA. The bench notes were shared with the defense, but the defense lawyer didn't call in an expert or recognize the importance of the foreign DNA markers. The McGuffin case demonstrates that poor communication and understanding of forensic evidence can lead to errors (or fail to prevent errors).

In some ways, the power of DNA raises the stakes on evidence and reporting issues. Small mistakes can produce unexpected consequences. Dwayne Jackson was wrongfully convicted of a robbery in Las Vegas, Nevada because his DNA had been switched inadvertently with that of his cousin, Howard Grissom. The Las Vegas Metropolitan Police Department (LVMPD) had a chance to find the error when Grissom was arrested for another robbery in 2008. Grissom's DNA was collected, but LVMPD only searched the local DNA index for unsolved, open cases. The previous robbery was a "solved" case so wasn't included in the search. The mistake was discovered when Grissom was implicated in a violent rape in California in 2010. The case implicated poor policy in the Las Vegas Metropolitan Police Department. First, Jackson had pled guilty to the robbery offense, so the DNA was not retested, which is routine when cases go to trial. Also, the failure to conduct a thorough DNA search in 2008 prevented LVMPD from seeing the mistake. Jackson served time for an offense he did not commit, and his cousin committed multiple serious crimes while he was free. LVMPD paid $1.5 million in compensation to Jackson and updated their DNA and database policies. Although the original sample swap was certainly an honest error, policy shortfalls multiplied the consequences of the mistake.

It should be noted that similar sample swaps have contributed to problems in other cases. A similar case in Australia was traced to an error in the recording of a birth date, which led to a mix-up of DNA profiles and a wrongful conviction. The error was also linked to quality assurance failures that were covered up by the DNA laboratory (Holmes & Nedim, 2017). Cross-contamination in a medical examiner's office turned up in 2020 in Newfoundland. That did not lead to a known wrongful conviction but did delay a murder trial. Similar contamination issues have been found in laboratories around the world.

STUDY QUESTIONS

1. There were at least four types of issues in the O.J. case: crime scene collection, crime lab methods, interpretation, and testimony (e.g., on the EDTA issue). Consider the way that LAPD and the FBI responded to the possibility of evidence tampering using the FBI's new method for EDTA detection. Why was there a concern about contamination? How did EDTA factor into the issue? What did the FBI do to elucidate the problem? What went wrong with Roger Martz's testimony? How are these issues similar to issues seen in wrongful convictions?

2. What factors associated with the rape kit backlog in Detroit are also associated with wrongful convictions? How might these factors contribute to wrongful convictions as root causes? What do you think should be done to improve the response to sexual assault? Do forensic scientists have a role to play? (For more information about policy and practice considerations, see https://www.sakitta.org/.)
3. DNA analysis continues to improve, and crime labs are challenged to look at smaller samples and more difficult mixtures. Many labs are considering completely new approaches, such as next-generation sequencing, rapid DNA testing, and familial DNA searches. Just as in the early days of DNA in the 1990s, some work may be compromised by shortfalls in standards and validation. What should be done to mitigate the risk of errors related to these new technologies?

FURTHER READING

There are three insightful publications that detail key elements of the forensic analysis in the Simpson case. William Thompson published a critical paper from a defense point of view (Thompson, 1996). Thompson has challenged the "infallibility" of DNA analysis and made important contributions to the research literature (Thompson, 2013). The FBI scientists published their approach to analysis of EDTA in blood a few years after the trial (Miller, McCord, Martz, & Budowle, 1997). The DOJ Office of Inspector General examined the Martz testimony and related organizational issues in the FBI as part of the broader Bromwich report (Bromwich, 1997).

Campbell's report and other work on rape kit backlogs should be required reading for anyone in police investigation, forensic science, or victim advocacy. Her report is quite long, but the section on causative factors (starting on page 135 of the report) is both highly readable and deeply perceptive (Campbell, et al., 2015).

Much of the history of DNA has yet to be written. The 1996 National Research Council report remains relevant to the problem of population estimates in DNA interpretation (National Research Council, 1996). John Butler's *Fundamentals of Forensic DNA Typing* is the definitive textbook on the subject (2009). He and his (National Institute of Standards and Technology (NIST) colleagues maintain the STRBase website, https://strbase.nist.gov/, which contains background information on all aspects of DNA typing.

REFERENCES

Baird, M., Neufeld, P., & Scheck, B. (1990). DNA Testing-Is Forensic DNA Testing Reliable. *ABA Journal*, 76, 34.

Bromwich, M. (1997). *The FBI Laboratory: An Investigation into Laboratory Practices and Alleged Misconduct in Explosives-Related and Other Cases.* Washington, DC: US Department of Justice Office of Inspector General.

Butler, J. (2009). *Fundamentals of Forensic DNA Typing.* New York: Academic Press.

Campbell, R., Fehler-Cabral, G., Pierce, S., Sharma, D., Bybee, D., Shaw, J., . . . & Feeney, H. (2015). *The Detroit Sexual Assault Kit (SAK) Action Research Project (ARP)*, Final Report. National Institute of Justice.

Dror, I. E., & Hampikian, G. (2011). Subjectivity and bias in forensic DNA mixture interpretation. *Science and Justice*, *51*(4), 204–208.

Hatchett v. City of Detroit et al, 08-CV-11864 (US District Court, Eastern District of Michigan, Southern Division 02 10, 2010).

Holmes, Z., & Nedim, U. (2017, 05, 14). *Innocent Man Convicted After Botched DNA Test.* Retrieved from Sydney Criminal Lawyers: https://www.sydneycriminallawyers.com.au/blog/innocent-man-convicted-after-botched-dna-test/

Kinship and Data Analysis Panel (2006). *Lessons Learned From 9/11: DNA Identification in Mass Fatality Incidents.* Washington, DC: National Institute of Justice, Office of Justice Programs.

Kupferschmid, T. (March 2018). *OCME DNA Report Language Relating to Mixtures of Two or Three Individuals.* New York City: Office of the Chief Medical Examiner.

Miller, M., McCord, B., Martz, R., & Budowle, B. (1997). The Analysis of EDTA in Dried Bloodstains by Electrospray LC-MS-MS and Ion Chromatography. *Journal of Analytical Toxicology*, *21*(November/December), 521–528.

Morrison, P. (2014, June 17). Column: Barry Scheck on the O.J. trial, DNA evidence and the Innocence Project. *Los Angeles Times.*

National Research Council (US) Committee on DNA Technology in Forensic Science (1992). *DNA Technology in Forensic Science.* Washington, DC: National Academies Press.

National Research Council (1996). *The Evaluation of Forensic DNA Evidence.* Washington, DC: National Academies Press.

North Carolina Innocence Inquiry Commission. (2011). State v. Kagonyera/Wilcoxson. Retrieved from North Carolina Innocence Inquiry Commission: https://innocencecommission-nc.gov/cases/state-v-kagonyera-wilcoxson/

People v. Herskovic, 2017-02494 (Supreme Court of New York, Appellate Division, Second Department October 10, 2018).
Scheck, B., Neufeld, P., & Dwyer, J. (2000). *Actual Innocence*. New York: Random House.
Thompson, W. (1996). DNA Evidence in the O.J. Simpson Trial. *University of Colorado Law Review*, *67*(Fall), pp. 827–857.
Thompson, W. (2013). 15 Forensic DNA Evidence. In *Genetic Explanations* (pp. 227–255). Cambridge, MA: Harvard University Press.
Thompson, W., Taroni, F., & Aitken, C. (2003). How the Probability of a False Positive Affects the Value of DNA Evidence. *Journal of Forensic Science*, *48*(1), 1–8.
Weiner v. San Diego County, 98–55752 (United States Court of Appeals for the Ninth Circuit April 27, 2000).

CHAPTER 5

Unvalidated Forensic Science

THE CHALLENGE OF INNOVATION

Dr. Henry Faulds lived in Japan from 1874 to 1886, not far from the modern Ginsa shopping district in Tokyo. You can visit a small memorial to Dr. Faulds in a garden near the Tsukiji subway stop. Very simply, the memorial states that Dr. Faulds, "Pioneer in Fingerprint Identification," lived in the neighborhood. A proper Presbyterian, he had come to Japan to heal the sick as a medical missionary from the Church of Scotland. While there, he participated in excavations to examine ancient shell mounds, which are of interest to researchers in evolutionary biology. He came across 2,000-year-old pottery shards with distinctive swirls and ridges and realized that he was looking at the ancient fingerprints of the potters who had formed the clay. He also realized that he could tell which potter made various pieces by matching their fingerprint impressions. He started recording ink impressions of all ten fingers of every European and Japanese person he could corner. Figure 5.1 shows an early version of his feature classification scheme.

As it happened during this time, Dr. Faulds found that some of the alcohol in his laboratory was "disappearing." On a beaker that had been used by the culprit, he found a nearly perfect set of latent fingerprints. The fingerprints matched those of one of his medical students, who had indeed been stealing the alcohol for personal use. In another case, he exonerated one of his staff accused of a robbery by showing the man's fingerprints did not match the evidence from the crime scene. He realized the power of fingerprint identification very early, though he expressed a

DOI: 10.4324/9781003202578-5

> most depressing sense of moral responsibility and danger. What if someone were wrongly identified and made to suffer innocently through a defective method? It seemed to me that a great deal had to be done before publicly proposing the adoption of such a scheme.
>
> (Faulds, Henry. "Finger prints: A chapter in the history of their use for personal identification." *Sci. Am. Suppl* 1872 (1911): 326-327)

He performed experiments with persistence, rubbing fingerprints raw, then watching the skin grow back to form the ridges exactly as before. He tracked children to see if their fingerprints changed as they grew up. He studied his fingerprint collection to see if there were any fingerprints that looked the same. And, satisfied, he eventually published a complete scientific paper on the individuality and permanence of fingerprints in the prestigious journal, *Nature*, in 1880 (Faulds, 1880). He wrote,

> When bloody finger marks or impressions on clay, glass, etc. exist, they may lead to the scientific identification of criminals. Already I have had experience in two such cases ... There can be no doubt as to the advance of having, besides their photographs, a nature-copy of the forever unchangeable finger furrows of important criminals.

Sadly, he was unsuccessful in convincing police departments to adopt his idea. London, New York, Paris—none of them were interested. Not until

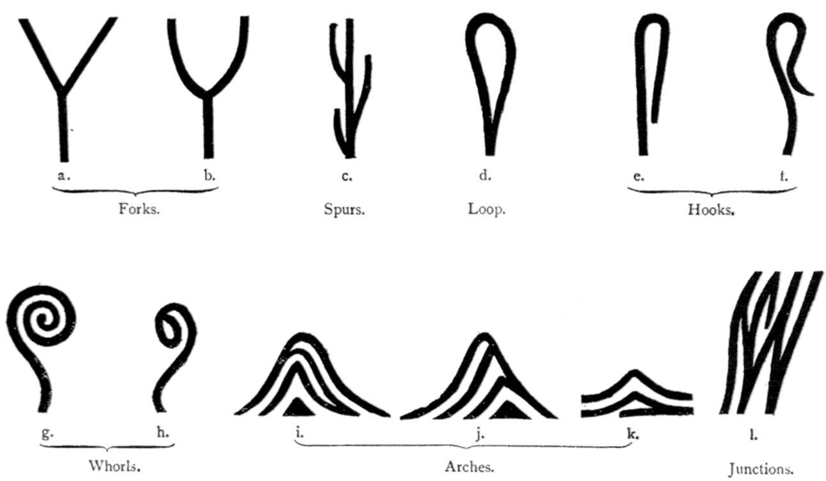

FIGURE 5.1 Faulds classification system. Classification system of patterns, Henry Faulds, 1905. Bifurcations ("forks"), whorls, and arches are reflected in Faulds' system in a manner similar to current practice. From Look and Learn History Picture Archive, Work ID: vxhsnfeb. Source: Wellcome Collection, Creative Commons Attribution (CC BY 4.0).

nearly 20 years later were fingerprints adopted in law enforcement, and that was in British India by Sir Edward Henry.

Forensic science faces a paradox. Innovation has improved the probative value of forensic evidence and contributed to the overall reliability of the criminal justice system. On the other hand, unproven innovations have caused wrongful convictions and undermined public trust in the criminal justice system. Most forensic professionals share Faulds' concern; they do not want to implicate an innocent person by using a faulty method. Even when using a "proven" method, forensic scientists tend to avoid conclusions that implicate a suspect if the evidence does not clearly support that conclusion. For example, fingerprint examiners may make inconclusive, exclusion, or No Value determinations in research studies when given difficult—but matching—print comparisons (Busey et al., 2021). More broadly, forensic science organizations are slow to adopt new science and technology unless it has been proven to be more effective than current practice, hence the reluctance to adopt fingerprints until well into the 20th century. The forensic science community has limited mechanisms for the review or governance of novel forensic methods.

COURT ACCEPTANCE OF UNPROVEN METHODS

Sometimes, advocates are not as careful and introspective as Faulds. They will bring new methods into an investigation without doing the hard work of scientific validation. Advocates will convince police and prosecutors that they have a groundbreaking new way to solve cases. Too often, investigators will grasp at any chance to catch "bad guys." In an age of constant technological change, police and prosecutors have a limited ability to discern the difference between credible methods and incredible claims. Advocates will also take advantage of the often-inadequate court review of novel scientific methods. Courts are supposed to be the gatekeepers who reject unproven or misleading evidence. Even though Frye and Daubert and other mechanisms exist to assist in this task, many invalid forensic methods have been accepted by judges. There is a limited basis to believe that courts are getting better at judging the validity of new methods. Given the increasing complexity and specialization seen in science, it is possible that courts may be more challenged than ever. Notably, courts appear to do a better job in civil cases than in criminal cases. One researcher, Rachel Dioso-Villa, looked at arson cases, which are routinely adjudicated in both civil and criminal courts (Dioso-Villa, 2016). Dioso-Villa found bias in admissibility decisions on arson evidence based on the role of the party that introduces the evidence, even when accounting for confounding factors such as attorney experience and expert qualifications. Overall, the difference may be due to the adversarial deficit in criminal cases—criminal defense attorneys have less training and fewer resources to contest scientific evidence.

The history of court reviews in criminal cases demonstrates the unpredictability and inconsistency of the process. Courts may be highly variable in their acceptance or rejection of a method. For example, voiceprint analysis and polygraph lie detection have each been the focus of key court decisions regarding the admissibility of expert testimony. Prior to the development of digital analysis methods, voiceprint identification was based on the examination of amplitude recordings within frequency bands and comparison of evidence patterns with a possible source (see Figure 5.2). In 1988, voiceprint evidence was reviewed by the dissenting opinion in the appeals court in the David Shawn Pope wrongful conviction for sexual assault (Pope v. State, 1988). The dissent found nine prior decisions in which spectrographic voiceprint analysis was deemed admissible, and two of which limited the admissibility to "corroboration purposes only." It also found nine prior decisions in which spectrographic voiceprint analysis was deemed inadmissible. Such variability is a hallmark of ineffective and unreliable systems.

No court decisions attempted to scope the validity of voiceprint analysis on a technical level, such as the fidelity of the voice recording or the feature elements used in the examination process. In 2003, after additional variability in court reviews, the United States District Court for the Southern District of Texas held that voiceprint analysis was

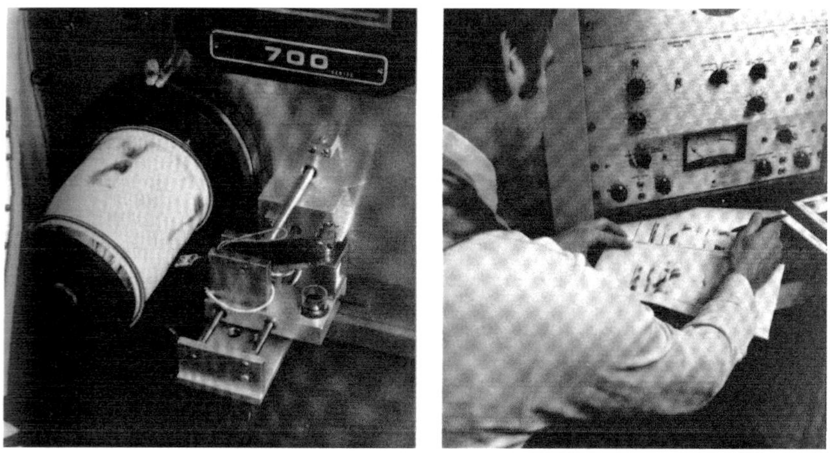

FIGURE 5.2 The 1980 FBI Law Enforcement Bulletin depicted the spectrograph recording and the process of comparison for voiceprint identification. Specific words or diphthongs were compared in recordings from evidence and by a possible source (Koenig, 1980). Source: FBI Law Enforcement Bulletin (Koenig, 1980).

inadmissible under Daubert, and that appears to have settled the matter (United States v. Angleton, 2003). At that time, courts were reviewing a technique that was based on manual examination of amplitude variation in voices in discrete frequency bands related to specific sounds or words. Automated techniques can now analyze voices using a much wider range of variables. Arguably, digital voiceprint analysis is completely distinct from 20th century methods. It should be judged de novo without regard to prior reviews and subject to an appropriate set of studies with regard to its accuracy and reliability (Morrison & Thompson, 2016). It remains to be seen whether the courts will have the capacity to recognize the novelty of digital voiceprint analysis and subject it to consistent and rigorous review. There is a Speaker Recognition Subcommittee of the Organization of Scientific Area Committees that is planning to address this issue (Organization of Scientific Area Committees, 2022). Again, the OSAC review may be the best venue for review of voiceprint *by the scientific community*, but it is not guaranteed to impact the technique's acceptance *by the legal community* and courts.

CUTTING-EDGE ADVOCATES

In general, novel methods are introduced by advocates who have conducted some level of research that may not have established objective, scientific validity. Advocates may believe they are on the "cutting edge" of practice and are introducing important innovations. This attitude is not limited to forensic science. In our dynamic world of ever-changing technology, there is no shortage of experts who claim to be transforming the paradigm of some aspect of human existence (Kuhn, 1962). In many cases, the views of self-appointed experts are not challenged, even if their theories have been discredited. Theoretically, the forensic expert should be in a different position. The forensic community or the courts should provide a check on unvalidated methods. Law enforcement agencies should avoid fraudulent purveyors of "snake oil." In practice, there are so many practitioners, agencies, and jurisdictions, that a persistent advocate can find a niche to introduce a promising idea, especially if it seems to solve a difficult case or reinforce a shaky one.

The Pope voiceprint trial illustrates some of the problems that can occur. Pope was convicted of rape in 1986 based in part on a spectrographic voice identification of a phone conversation. The initial analysis was done by a Houston police officer, Larry Howe Williams, who had done 1000 voiceprint examinations in prior cases. Dr. Henry Truby, who had a Ph.D. in acoustic phonetics and was extensively published on voiceprint identification, also conducted an examination and confirmed Williams' conclusion that Pope was the source of the voice on the evidence recording. The defense called Stuart Ritterman from the University of South Florida. Ritterman disputed the validity of voiceprint spectrography, but the trial judge admitted the evidence under Frye general acceptance test. During the trial, Williams provided significant limiting testimony about his work. Truby, on the other hand, exaggerated the value of his identification, saying,

> I found a sufficient number [of identical patterns] to serve as an identification to convince me, and then take a few more just to reinforce it, that no matter how much you do of these samples, you would continue to get points of similarity every now and then.
>
> (The Pope v State 1988 opinion)

When asked if he could identify a voice down to "one single person in the whole wide world ... like fingerprints," Truby replied, "Exactly." (Pope v. State, 1988) At the time, there was significant research showing the limitations of the technique, including the work of Dr. Oscar Tosi from Michigan State University. Tosi had shown that the method had at least a 2.4% error rate even under ideal conditions. Pope was convicted.

The appeals court majority declined to review the trial court's decision to accept voiceprint testimony, "because the overwhelming evidence against appellant renders this error, if any, harmless." As noted above, the dissenting opinion did not agree with the trial court or the majority in the appeals decision. It applied the Frye test and determined voiceprint to be inadmissible. The opinion cited a scathing 1979 report from the National Research Council (NRC) that eventually led to the abandonment of voiceprint identification by the FBI and many other laboratories (Committee on Evaluation of Sound Spectrograms Assembly of Behavioral and Social Sciences, 1979). At the time of the Pope conviction, the NRC report and Tosi research had already established the weaknesses of voiceprint as it was practiced by Williams and Truby. Oddly, Truby must have been aware of the NRC and Tosi work but his testimony did not reflect that knowledge in any way. He appears to have been convinced that he could perform spectrographic analyses that were more accurate and selective than had ever been observed in a controlled research study. His behavior is reminiscent of Giles' misinterpretation in the Durham case, as described in the chapter on DNA analysis in wrongful convictions. Giles was convinced he could see a pattern in an electrophoresis gel that others couldn't because he was an expert scientist. Truby harbored a similar bias about patterns in voiceprints.

The FBI reviewed 696 voiceprint cases in 1986. Their review uncovered just one false identification and two false eliminations in those cases, but there was no basis at the time to determine the ground truth. There may have been many more errors in the FBI cases that couldn't be discovered without independent knowledge about the actual source of the voices on the evidence recordings. The field itself hadn't been subject to meaningful standards or governance. The International Association for Identification didn't establish standards for voiceprint examinations until 1992, several years after Pope's conviction. Internationally, voiceprint fell out of favor due to high-profile errors. In 1997, Basque separatist Jerome Prieto was jailed for 10 months in connection with a car bombing on the basis of a voiceprint identification, after which the French Acoustical Society called for an end to the use of voiceprint examination in legal proceedings. In the Pope case in 1999, the Dallas County District Attorney got a tip on the case pointing to a different assailant. The prosecutor followed up with a DNA test on the rape kit that excluded Pope. In 2001, Texas Governor Rick Perry pardoned Pope; he received $385,000 in compensation and a $6,500 per month lifetime annuity.

The Pope case was a perfect storm of factors that correlate with unvalidated forensic techniques. It included exaggerated claims about the sensitivity and selectivity of the method. There was a renowned, cutting-edge expert who was willing to testify that his ability far outpaced any research study. There was a trial court judge who accepted a technique that the NRC and the scientific community had already demonstrated was flawed and subject to significant errors. And the standards and governance of the field had not been established to scope the validity and reliability of the method or the appropriate language for testimony. These factors have been repeated in various forms in many other wrongful convictions in other fields.

CANINE DETECTION

Although canine detection is quite different, the experience in wrongful convictions has surprising similarities to that of voiceprint identification. When used to produce investigative leads with an understanding of limitations, dogs and voice recordings can be used with reasonable confidence (Figure 5.3). Like voiceprint, canine detection has been used by practitioners without established standards or governance. In contrast to voiceprint, consensus standards have now been developed to govern canine detection. Also, there are many more people who revere the almost mystical powers that dogs are thought to possess. This starts with the uncommon bonds that humans and dogs have developed over many centuries. On top of that, many people believe that dogs have an incredibly sensitive sense of smell. These two premises lead dog handlers, law enforcement, and the courts to put greater trust in canine detection than is warranted on the basis of scientific validity and reliability.

FIGURE 5.3 National Fire Dog Monument. Canine detection can be reliable when it conforms to standards in practice, training, and reporting. NIST OSAC includes a Dogs & Sensors Subcommittee that produces science-based standards. The figure depicts the National Fire Dog Monument. Dogs have been used to detect accelerants at arson scenes. Some handlers have misrepresented the sensitivity and reliability of dogs in wrongful convictions using statements that reflect a belief in their "almost mystical" sensory powers. Source: Wikimedia Commons, Creative Commons Attribution 2.0 Generic license.

The James Hebshie case provides a clear example of the pitfalls (United States v. Hebshie, 2010). After a fire in Hebshie's store in Taunton, Massachusetts, fire investigators brought in Billy, a dog that had been trained to detect accelerants. Billy alerted after his handler led him directly to the location where it was presumed that the fire had originated. The fire investigators then collected chemical samples from that area but no other place at the fire scene. The chemical analysis concluded that light petroleum distillates were present, but that is a broad term for many substances—such as lighter fluid—that were sold in the store anyway. Because there were no control samples from around the store, the chemical test was not significantly probative. At trial, Sergeant Douglas Lynch, the dog handler, was allowed to go on at great length about his emotional relationship with Billy and his entirely subjective ability to interpret her face, what she thought, intended, and the "strength" of the alert she gave in this case (United States v. Hebshie, 2010). In Hebshie's appeal, Judge Nancy Gertner provided a clear analysis of the issue:

> It is not an understatement to say that Lynch, the dog handler, was permitted to testify to an almost mystical account of Billy's powers and her unique olfactory capabilities. He presented unsubstantiated claims about the dog's accuracy. He was allowed to go on at great length about his emotional relationship with the dog and his entirely subjective ability to interpret her face, what she thought, intended, and the "strength" of the alert she gave in this case. Finally, Lynch was permitted to testify that the dog did not alert to anything else on the premises, as if the dog had been allowed to range widely on the fire scene (she was not), and as if the dog's failure to alert had evidential value (it does not). (United States v. Hebshie, 2010)

Unlike in the Pope case related to voiceprint, Hebshie's lawyer did not "quarrel with" the canine detection evidence or other deficient testimony related to the interpretation of the fire scene. He did present an expert who held that the fire started in the store's basement, but that theory had little weight because of the failure to challenge the dog alert. Hebshie was convicted, but Judge Gertner overturned the conviction on the basis of inadequate defense, saying, "While the cause-and-origin testimony purports to identify where the fire began, the canine evidence and the laboratory results are essential to prove that the fire was an arson, not an accident. Without it, there is simply no crime."

The Hebshie case is not unique. Many dog handlers believe that they have a deep connection with their dog that lets them interpret the dog's signals. They may not recognize the ways that they may influence the detector dog by their speech and actions. In addition, it is common for others to put undue trust in the capabilities of a handler and detector dog team. The most extreme example involved John Preston and his purebred German Shepherd detector dog, Harass II. Preston consulted with many police agencies and was involved in several wrongful convictions. He was among the first dog handlers to use dog scent lineups to implicate suspects. A dog scent lineup is used to associate crime scene evidence with an individual human source and is still in common use, especially in the Netherlands and other parts of Europe (Ferry et al., 2019). That said, the practice is highly variable and unstandardized and has not been proven to be valid and reliable in scientific research studies.

In the Wilton Dedge sexual assault case, Preston used a dog scent lineup. The victim's sheets were lined up with "control" sheets. Harass II sniffed a paper bag with paper towels that had been handled by Dedge. That served as the reference or "known" source. Harass II alerted on the victim's sheets and then was taken to the victim's house, where the dog alerted on several locations where Dedge had presumably been. The dog's performance was impressive, but it was highly questionable because the whole show took place three months after the crime had taken place. The volatile organic compounds associated with individual odors do not persist for that period of time. Any odor patterns would be greatly overwhelmed by background chemicals. Dogs lack sufficient sensitivity or selectivity to overcome fundamental physics and chemistry. Further, the towels had dubious value. Dedge had washed his hands in the bathroom at the county courthouse, after which a police detective grabbed the towels from the trash can and "preserved" them in a paper bag from the courthouse coffee shop Merjian, 2010). Preston's testimony in the Dedge case and others contained many false statements. He said he was a member of professional canine associations, but he was not. He said he and his dog had training that they did not receive. In some trials, he said his dog could detect scents after many months or after the scent had penetrated walls and shoes. In the Dedge case, Preston discounted the possibility that the paper bag had been contaminated by sitting next to the victim's sheets in the evidence locker. The Dedge case also included invalid hair testimony in which the examiner exaggerated the probative value of a hair match and cited his past experience as a basis for the uniqueness of hair morphological characteristics. Seventeen years after Dedge was convicted, mitochondrial DNA showed he was not the source of the hair. Three years after that, Dedge was excluded as a source of the rape kit evidence by Y-STR DNA testing. After his exoneration, the state of Florida gave him $2 million in compensation.

Canine detection can be done in a valid way that meets practice standards. The National Institute of Standards and Technology (NIST) Organization of Scientific Area Committees has a very active Dogs & Sensors Subcommittee (Organization of Scientific Area Committees, 2022). That subcommittee leverages almost two decades of work by the independent Scientific Working Group on Dogs and Orthogonal Detectors (SWGDOG). SWGDOG produced a standard for dog scent lineups in 2010, and OSAC has sought to update and formalize that standard. Nonetheless, the scientific reliability and validity of dog scent lineups has not been established, so it is unclear if the OSAC standards process is sufficient to prevent future wrongful convictions.

SHOEPRINT INDIVIDUALIZATION

As in canine detection, many unvalidated methods are based on the misuse of forensic techniques that would be valid if properly applied. In these cases, an expert will attempt to extend the bounds of an established discipline using a novel detection, laboratory, and interpretation framework. Often, the expert views their work as cutting-edge and innovative and their colleagues and critics as hopelessly behind the times. In shoeprint examination, Dr. Louise Robbins conducted research that attempted to establish a basis for the individualization of shoeprints on the basis of wear patterns. Shoeprint examiners are generally limited to class-level conclusions. For example, they may determine that a particular shoeprint was made by a particular model of shoe.

The shoeprint may have distinctive features related to damage or alteration that permit a speculative conclusion that a particular shoe was likely the source of a particular shoeprint. Many examiners have noted that shoes have distinctive wear patterns that are associated with the gait of the wearer. The patterns may take the form of small ridges on the outsole that will change over time as the shoe is worn (Pawloski, 2019). Robbins used this basic idea to analyze shoeprints and make conclusions that the source of a shoeprint was a specific shoe to the exclusion of all other shoes in the world. She called her technique "Cinderella Evidence" because it relied on insole comparisons. Initially, she was a trusted colleague of leading researchers and practitioners in the field. Over time, her desire to solve cases and exaggerated belief in her personal capabilities led to wrongful convictions.

In the Dale Johnston murder case, FBI examiner William Bodziak examined a muddy impression in a cornfield and could not determine if it had been made by Johnston's boot or bare foot (State v. Johnston, 1986). He sent the case to Robbins, who concluded that a particular left boot of Johnston's had made the impression. The trial court and a subsequent appeals court accepted Robbin's testimony. The appeals court said, "Dr. Robbins was qualified by her knowledge, skill, experience, training, and education to make the comparison." Johnston was convicted and sentenced to death. He was exonerated postconviction by the confession and conviction of an alternate suspect. Bodziak did not refer further cases to Robbins and became a fierce critic of her methods.

Robbins was a certified forensic anthropologist but there was no equivalent certification program for footprint analysis of the type she was advancing. Like Henry Faulds, she based her theories on her understanding of anthropology. There is no evidence that she was any less earnest than Faulds. By all accounts, she believed that she was providing valid forensic analysis. Like Faulds, she collected large amounts of observational data to support her hypothesis that each person's feet have a unique configuration that can be discerned from footprints and shoe impressions (Tuttle, 1986). One critic, Russell Tuttle, said that she fell "into the trap of mindless empiricism, wherein a seeming myriad of traits are enumerated and measured without clearly demonstrating what they mean." She did not establish the independence of the variables she was measuring or their persistence. In applying the ideas to forensic work, she failed to account for distortions related to the medium in which the prints were impressed. She also never conducted sufficient research to show how the impressions were changed by the modern use of shoes. Her anthropological work largely related to paleontology research of ancient humans who appeared to be barefoot, although it appears she exaggerated the value of foot impressions for anthropological research purposes also. In one story, she claimed that an ancient footprint had been made by a female human who was five-and-a-half months pregnant— a stunningly precise and invalid claim. Tuttle quipped about Robbins' textbook on her technique, "I pray that Ms. Robbins will pass peer review, but frankly would not want to be in her shoes should this advice be followed."

By the 1980s, Robbins had become widely known for her "Cinderella Evidence." Unlike Faulds, who struggled to get anyone to notice the value of fingerprints, Robbins found many police investigators who were willing to get her help to solve cases. In part, she failed because her method was fundamentally unsound. Faulds turned out to be right about the individuality of fingerprints and the ability to account for distortions in latent fingerprint impressions. Robbins turned out to be deeply mistaken about those issues for shoeprint analysis. Further, because she became closely identified with Cinderella Evidence, she may have become an advocate instead of an objective scientist. She may have been blind to the limitations of her work that were evident to many other research scientists and forensic scientists.

WINK RESPONSE AND CHILD ABUSE ACCOMMODATION SYNDROME

Expert advocacy bias has played a tragic role in many wrongful convictions. By "expert advocacy bias," it is meant that experts like Robbins become identified with a particular method and develop a personal or financial stake in its acceptance. Another example is Dr. Bruce Woodling, who popularized the "wink response." Woodling maintained that he could determine if a child had been anally assaulted by touching the child's taint with a swab. If there was a reflexive response, Woodling concluded that the child had been assaulted. There is no basis in science for that conclusion. Woodling's testimony was a key factor in several child abuse hysteria cases involving multiple defendants. He testified in the Kern County, California cases against the Kniffen and McCuan families and the notorious McMartin preschool case. Both cases were associated with deep mental and emotional abuse of the alleged child victims by local authorities and the eventual exoneration of the defendants. He also trained hundreds of law enforcement and child protective investigators in his methods. At the time that Woodling was popularizing this invalid method, many physicians were adopting the colposcope and standardized methods for the determination of pediatric sexual abuse. The American Academy of Pediatrics (AAP) has established standards for this work, but there remains significant controversy (Committee on Child Abuse and Neglect, 2013). Woodling's misrepresentations predated AAP standards, but it was clear from the outset that he had not performed sufficient research to validate his method.

Experts in child abuse cases may be affected by moral panic, the understandable tendency to seek justice when our moral sensibilities have been offended (Grometstein, 2008). Moral panic has been observed in child abuse cases in the United States and Canada dating from the 1980s, but the phenomenon spread globally from there. It may manifest in expert opinion in the same manner as in the Woodling example with the introduction of unvalidated methods or testimony.

Another example is testimony related to Child Abuse Accommodation Syndrome (CSAAS), which may relate to physical or sexual abuse cases. Children may be reluctant to report abuse against caregivers until significant time has elapsed after the incidents. Even after discovery, a child may avoid giving inculpatory testimony. A forensic psychologist may conclude that this tendency—often referred to under the CSAAS terminology—may account for changes in victim testimony about abuse. The originator of CSAAS was Dr. Roland Summit, who found five factors that can be associated with CSAAS, including secrecy, helplessness, entrapment/accommodation, delayed disclosure, and retraction. Court acceptance of CSAAS has been variable because Summit's theory has not been generally validated by research. Further, many psychologists have testified about CSAAS without conducting an examination of the child witness or referencing specific indicators of CSAAS as defined by Summit.

In the Roland Tracy case, the child victim retracted an initial accusation of abuse. Psychologist Dr. Hunter Comly testified that the original accusation was more reliable because "there are probably no more than two or three children per thousand who come forth with such a serious allegation who are found later to be dishonest." There is no objective basis for that claim. It also bears no relation to any of Summit's CSAAS work. Tracy was convicted, but an appeals court vacated the conviction because the defense had not objected to the invalid and exaggerated CSAAS testimony. Tracy was acquitted after a second trial, in large part because the victim's sister also recanted her testimony against him.

It should be said that Summit does not support the way that CSAAS has been misapplied in criminal cases. He viewed his work as an opportunity to improve the mental health treatment of child victims and guide investigators facing uncertainty about the interpretation of child victim abuse reports. In 1993, he published a journal article, *Abuse of the Child Sexual Abuse Accommodation Syndrome*, arguing that CSAAS was a useful framework to explain the dynamics of sexual victimization, post-traumatic stress, and secondary trauma associated with a child victim facing disbelief and rejection from adults (Summit, 1993). Unlike some other experts described here, Summit clearly sought to limit any use of his work in a forensic context to those elements that had appropriate research validity. He may have suffered from being ahead of his time. The connections between victim trauma and post-incident behavior have been the subject of substantial research since Summit's original paper. This research has had a positive effect on trauma-informed care in medicine and policing, especially in sexual assault cases. Summit's idea—that traumatized children may exhibit specific behaviors associated with their experiences—was sound. Unfortunately, it has been misapplied in pediatric abuse cases in a way that contributed to wrongful convictions.

POSTMORTEM ARTIFACTS

Unvalidated methods may be used at any point in the processing of forensic evidence. Bite mark examination may be invalid as a discipline—as will be covered in the next chapter—but there has been substantial activity by odontologists and researchers to establish and enforce standards. The biggest challenge for the field has always been the poor performance of human skin as a registration medium for bite mark impressions. Many practitioners have attempted to improve the methods to visualize bite mark impressions, and scientific research continues on the general problem of visualization of bruises (Scafide et al., 2020).

In the 1980s, odontologist Michael West developed a method for bite mark visualization using ultraviolet light (West et al., 1990). West saw himself as a bit of a Renaissance Man, the type of criminalist who could do research or practice in a variety of disciplines. He performed blood spatter analysis, gunshot residue, video enhancement, and many other techniques in criminal cases. He worked closely with Steven Hayne, a forensic pathologist in Mississippi who had performed thousands of autopsies and was himself associated with multiple wrongful convictions. In 1992, Hayne performed an autopsy in a murder case and concluded that the victim had been killed by two stab wounds to the chest (Eddie Lee Howard, Jr. v. State of Mississippi, 2018). The victim was then buried, but Hayne had the body exhumed to look for possible bite marks. He called in West, who used his ultraviolet technique to find three presumed bite marks on the victim. Eddie Lee Howard, who had been arrested on an unrelated sex crime, was then implicated in the murder case based on the bite marks. West testified that the bite marks were "indeed and without doubt inflicted by … Howard" (Eddie Lee Howard, Jr. v. State of Mississippi, 2018) Nobody else could see the bite marks, and West claimed to have lost the photographs he had taken of them. A reviewing odontologist, Dr. Iain Pretty, could not find the bite marks or any skin injury at the places on the body West had supposedly found them. Howard was convicted and sentenced to death, but the conviction was overturned because Howard had attempted to defend himself and was not competent to do so. A second trial also ended in a conviction and death sentence, though by that time West's methods had fallen into disfavor with the general bite mark community. In 2010, DNA testing excluded Howard from all of the evidence in the case, and in 2020, the Mississippi Supreme Court vacated the conviction. West remained defiant throughout the process. When Dr. Richard Souviron—the bite mark examiner who had become famous as a result of the Ted Bundy conviction—said that bite marks could only be used to exclude suspects, West said he was "stunned" and added that "twenty years ago [Dr. Souviron] was the top of the profession … now he's not" (Deposition of Michael Howard West, Howard v. State of Mississippi, Case Nos. 2000-0115-CV1, 2010-DR-01043-SCT, 16 April 2016). He labeled Souviron an "egomaniac" and Howard's postconviction defense attorney Chris Fabricant a "sociopath."

In any case, he was never able to substantiate the scientific basis for his use of ultraviolet light to visualize bite marks nor was anyone else ever able to duplicate his results. As seen in Figure 5.4, ultraviolet light imaging can visualize bruising injuries such as bite marks, but West failed to establish an empirical basis for his claims or limit his analysis to verified patterned injuries. His methods and results were never duplicated by other researchers. His individualization testimony is no longer accepted by the bite mark community, and West stopped doing forensic work in 2006. West is similar to many other "cutting-edge" experts in wrongful convictions. He believed in himself and was convinced that he was right about bite mark comparison and ultraviolet visualization. His dismissive comments about his colleagues are unsurprising in this light. Many wrongful convictions are associated with incompetent and untrained examiners. Invalid science is more commonly associated with examiners like West who may be extraordinarily intelligent but see themselves as being above the mainstream of their professions.

PATTERNED EVIDENCE

Not all cutting-edge experts appear to be arrogant in this way. Some researchers and practitioners advocate for new methods because they

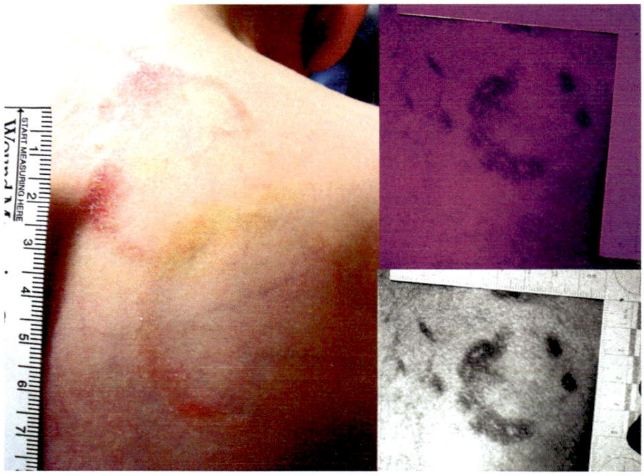

FIGURE 5.4 A child abuse victim with bite marks on the back. A visual-light image was taken two days after the attack (left). An ultraviolet-light image was taken two months after the attack (upper right). An enhanced image is shown in the lower right (Golden & Wright, 2011). Source: Dorion, Robert BJ, ed. ***Bitemark evidence: a color atlas and text.*** CRC Press, 2011.

sincerely want to see advancements in the field, but they fail to recognize the importance of building a scientific foundation and rigorous standards for their work. Two examples come from conceptual extensions of friction ridge examination—lip prints and ear prints.

In 1993, Patrick "Pall Mall" Ferguson was shot and killed in Elgin, Illinois (People v. Davis, 2007). A roll of duct tape was found at the scene, and forensic examiner Leanne Gray found an upper and lower lip print on the first six to eight inches of the duct tape's sticky side. She compared photographs of the lip prints to those of Lavelle Davis, a suspect in the case, but could not make a conclusion. She called in Steven McKasson of the Southern Illinois forensic science lab. McKasson found 13 points of similarity between Davis' lip standard and the photograph using a methodology similar to fingerprint analysis-comparison-evaluation. He testified at Davis' trial that lip prints are as unique as fingerprints. The trial court held a short review of the admissibility of lip print comparison but did not conduct a Frye hearing. They relied on statements from Gray and McKasson that lip print comparison was accepted scientific evidence that was considered a "positive means of identification" by the FBI. In fact, the FBI had never done any lip print work, and very little research had been done on lip prints, with the exception of a small population study in Poland (Reddy, 2011). Lip print comparison had never been subject to a known evidence review in the United States, and no forensic laboratory had ever reported a lip print comparison. Davis' defense lawyer later claimed that he needed an expert to rebut the lip print evidence, but neither the trial court nor the public defender's office provided the necessary resources, and Davis' family couldn't afford it. Davis was convicted in 1997, but the conviction was overturned based on the lip print testimony in 2006. Raymond Mims, who was convicted as Davis' accomplice in the murder, remains in prison serving a 40-year sentence for his alleged role in the shooting. Gary and McKasson exaggerated the value of their lip print comparison, but they appeared to be working honestly to solve a difficult case. They did not seem to appreciate that their statements about lip print reliability would undermine the case in the long term. They could have limited their testimony to a description of the characteristics that the evidence and the Davis reference prints had in common. Such testimony would have been difficult to challenge postconviction and would have been more consistent with the limited scientific knowledge they actually possessed about lip patterns. In addition, it is clear that the trial court and the defense were deficient in their review of the validity of lip prints. The court should have held a Frye hearing and—at minimum—scoped the limitations of the testimony from Gary and McKasson. The defense attorney should have had the resources (or initiative) to consult an independent expert to challenge the validity of the lip print testimony.

Another wrongful conviction used an ear print comparison, which is not technically a friction ridge method but bears close similarities from a practice and morphological perspective. The idea of using ear prints in a forensic context may seem outlandish, but there have been attempts to use ears as a biometric identifier (Abaza et al., 2013). When considering "junk science," it is best to reserve judgment. Validity should be based on a review of the empirical and observational evidence, not initial impressions. After all, DNA analysis would have been considered impossible at one time. As writer Arthur C. Clarke has observed, "Any sufficiently advanced technology is indistinguishable from magic" ("Hazards of Prophecy: The Failure of Imagination" in the collection Profiles of the Future: An Enquiry into the Limits of the Possible (1962, rev. 1973), pp. 14, 21, 36). In that context, lip and ear print comparisons are better described as unvalidated methods than junk science.

During a 1994 burglary and murder, the assailant appeared to leave an ear print on the victim's bedroom door. Washington State Crime Lab criminalist Michael Grubb concluded that the latent "could have been made by David Kunze" based on photographs of Kunze's ear (Fisher, 2018). Later, they obtained exemplar prints of Kunze's left ear by applying hand lotion and placing panes of glass against it using various degrees of pressure. The patterns were then visualized using standard fingerprint powder. Grubb performed a comparison of the Kunze ear print with the questioned evidence and concluded that "David Kunze is the likely source of the ear-print and cheek-print which were lifted from the outside of the bedroom door at the homicide scene" (Fisher, 2018). This formulation—while superior to the lip print individualization presented in the Davis case—was still invalid because it implied a random match probability. Grubb didn't have any population statistics on which to base any likelihood estimate. He had no basis to assess the uniqueness of any ear morphological features. Another analyst, George Miller, declined to make any conclusion, saying that he was a latent fingerprint examiner and therefore not qualified to do an ear print comparison. The trial court did hold a Frye hearing on ear print identification before it was admitted in evidence. Grubb likened the technique to other pattern and impression evidence. He was trained specifically in firearm and tool mark analysis, but his point is valid to an extent; it is possible that ear print impressions could be analyzed and compared in the same way as bullets or fingerprints. Unlike Grubb, two other prosecution witnesses had a personal stake in the acceptance of ear print identification by the court. Alfred Iannarelli had published two books on "ear identification" and told the court that the questioned mark at the scene was an exact match to Kunze's ear (Iannarelli, 1989). Similarly, Dutch police officer Cornelius Van der Lugt weighed in, saying that he had applied ear print comparison in 200 cases in Europe, six of which went to trial in Holland. Van der Lugt also held that Kunze was the source of the evidence impression. He also held that the method was accepted around the world. The defense presented a dozen experts to disagree, including Andre Moenssens, a distinguished forensic researcher from the University of Missouri. Moenssens pointed out that "there has been no investigation in the possible rate of error that comparisons between known and unknown ear samples might produce." The court accepted ear print evidence nonetheless, and Kunze was found guilty and sentenced to life without parole. The conviction was overturned by an appeals court on the basis of the ear print identification. A second trial—this time without the ear print testimony—ended in mistrial, but several jurors indicated that they would have acquitted Kunze. No third trial was ever scheduled, and the murder remains unsolved.

SUMMARY

In the Frye hearing connected to the Kunze case, Moenssens made essentially the same point as Henry Faulds had made about fingerprint comparison a century before. Faulds did foundational work on the uniqueness of fingerprints because he was deeply concerned about the possibility of a wrongful conviction. He never established a system error rate for fingerprints as a methodology, but he and other researchers did demonstrate the persistence and basic population estimates for fingerprint features. Unlike Faulds, many experts in wrongful convictions failed to establish any basis for the error rate of their technique. In such cases, they should have refrained from introducing their idea into forensic practice or limited the language of their conclusions to reflect the uncertainties. Often, they based their conclusions and testimony on an evaluation of their personal abilities and the perceived value of their innovation in the best circumstances. This is an all-too-human tendency, of course. The forensic science community lacks governance mechanisms to develop and enforce standards to prevent the acceptance of unproven methods. Failing that, one would expect the courts to discern the difference between valid and invalid testimony. These mechanisms have not proven as successful as hoped in wrongful conviction cases.

STUDY QUESTIONS

1. Consider one of the cases discussed in this chapter. Imagine that you have been tasked to review the forensic evidence in the case, then determine whether there were errors associated with the forensic evidence and make recommendations for system improvements to prevent similar errors in future cases.
2. There are many fields that rely on innovations that may be put into practice before they're ready. Some examples include: new therapeutic drugs or medical procedures; new government policies; information systems; and new vehicle or energy technologies. Consider an innovation in a non-forensic context that didn't succeed when it was first tried. What did that situation have in common with some of the unvalidated techniques and wrongful convictions discussed in this chapter? Some specific ideas include:

   - Elizabeth Holmes and her blood testing company
   - Palm Pilot and other "smart" phones and portable assistants before the iPhone
   - COVID responses, including anything from hydroxychloroquine to lockdowns

3. This chapter presented information about several proposed forensic techniques. It is possible that these methods may be developed into reliable forensic applications in the future. For example, it was discussed that there is active research to improve the imaging of bruises. Which technique do you believe holds the

most promise? What research and development is needed? What should be done before the forensic science community adopts the method into practice? What would the benefits and risks be?

FURTHER READING

Henry Faulds' original article is available on *Nature*'s website. It has historical value and may be an instructive example of a cutting-edge expert who advocated for "careful study" prior to the adoption of a forensic technique (Faulds, 1880). Ed German maintains the onin.com website, which includes a wealth of current and historical information about latent print analysis. Aspiring forensic scientists should spend a day browsing onin.com to educate themselves about the state of the field.

Many forensic experts and organizations have done important work to improve the scientific foundations of specific disciplines. Calvin Goddard described the development of the "scientific identification of bullets" in his 1926 paper in the *Journal of Criminal Law and Criminology* (Goddard, 1926). Summit gave a history of the misuse of Child Sexual Abuse Accommodation Syndrome that reflects his work to ground the field in scientific observation (Summit, 1993). John Lentini wrote a 2019 paper on the history and development of fire investigation since the 1970s and 1980s (Lentini, 2019). These three histories provide many lessons to the student of forensic science and insights into wrongful convictions related to unvalidated science.

The experience of forensic science may be generalized to other types of experts. Kuhn's discussion of scientific paradigms is relevant (Kuhn, 1962), as is Raymond Nickerson's discussion of confirmation bias among scientists and many other types of experts (Nickerson, 1998). Itiel Dror has contributed an important theoretical perspective on these issues as they apply to forensic science. His paper, *How can Francis Bacon help forensic science? The four idols of human biases*, describes the challenges faced by forensic science as it attempts the difficult task of assessing the reliability and validity of new methods (Dror, 2009).

REFERENCES

Abaza, A., Ross, A., Hebert, C., Harrison, M., & Nixon, M. (2013). A Survey on Ear Biometrics. *ACM Computing Surveys (CSUR)*, *45*(2), 1–35.

Busey, T. A., Heise, N., Hicklin, R. A., Ulery, B. T., & Buscaglia, J. (2021). Characterizing Missed Identifications and Errors in Latent Fingerprint Comparisons Using Eye-tracking Data. *PloS One*, *16*(5), e0251674.

Committee on Child Abuse and Neglect. (2013). The Evaluation of Children in the Primary Care Setting When Sexual Abuse Is Suspected. *Pediatrics*, *132*(2), e558–e567.

Committee on Evaluation of Sound Spectrograms Assembly of Behavioral and Social Sciences. (1979). *On the Theory and Practice of Voice Identification*. Washington, DC: National Research Council, National Academy of Sciences.

Dioso-Villa, R. (2016). Is the Expert Admissibility Game Fixed?: Judicial Gatekeeping of Fire and Arson Evidence. *Law & Policy*, *38*(1), 54–80.

Dror, I. E. (2009). How Can Francis Bacon Help Forensic Science-The Four Idols of Human Biases. *Jurimetrics*, *93*, 93–110.

Eddie Lee Howard, Jr. v. State of Mississippi, 2018-CA-01586-SCT (Supreme Court of Mississippi 2018).

Faulds, H. (1880). On the Skin-furrows of the Hand. *Nature*, *22*(574), 605.

Ferry, B., Ensminger, J., Schoon, A., Bobrovskij, Z., Cant, D., Gawkowski, M., ... & Jezierski, T. (2019). Scent Lineups Compared Across Eleven Countries: Looking for the Future of a Controversial Forensic Technique. *Forensic Science International* (September), *302*. https://doi.org/10.1016/j.forsciint.2019.109895

Fisher, J. (2018, October 2). *Earmark Identification in the David Wayne Kunze Case*. Retrieved from Jim Fisher True Crime: http://jimfishertruecrime.blogspot.com/2012/04/earmark-identification-in-david-wayne.html

Goddard, C. (1926). Scientific Identification of Firearms and Bullets. *Journal of Criminal Law and Criminology*, *17*(2, August), 254–263.

Golden, G., & Wright, F. (2011). Photography. In R. Dorion (Ed.), *Bitemark Evidence: A Color Atlas and Text* (pp. 74–102). Boca Raton: CRC Press.

Grometstein, R. (2008). Wrongful Conviction and Moral Panic: National and International Perspectives on Organized Child Sexual Abuse. In C. R. Huff, & M. Killias (Eds.), *Wrongful Conviction: International Perspectives on Miscarriages of Justice* (pp. 11–32). Philadelphia, PA: Temple University Press. Retrieved from https://www.ncjrs.gov/App/publications/Abstract.aspx?id=247359

Iannarelli, A. (1989). *Ear Identification*. Freemont, CA: Paramount Publishing.

Koenig, B. E. (1980). Speaker Identification (Part 1) Three Methods--Listening, Machine, and Aural-Visual. *FBI Law Enforcement Bulletin* (January), 1–4.

Kuhn, T. (1962). *The Structure of Scientific Revolutions*. Chicago: University of Chicago.

Lentini, J. (2019). Fire investigation: Historical perspective and recent developments. *Forensic Science Reviews*, *31*, 37–44.

Merjian, A. (2010). Anatomy of a Wrongful Conviction: State v. Dedge and What It Tells Us About Our Flawed Criminal Justice System. *University of Pennsylvania Journal of Law and Social Change*, *13*, 137–148.

Morrison, G., & Thompson, W. (2016). Assessing the Admissibility of a New Generation of Forensic Voice Comparison Testimony. *The Columbia Science and Technology Law Review*, *18*, 326.

Nickerson, R. S. (1998). Confirmation Bias: A Ubiquitous Phenomenon in Many Guises. *Review of General Psychology*, *2*(2), 175–220.

Organization of Scientific Area Committees. (2022, January 25). Speaker Recognition Subcommittee. Retrieved from National Institute of Standards and Technology: https://www.nist.gov/osac/speaker-recognition-subcommittee

Organization of Scientific Area Committees. (2022, January 27). Dogs & Sensors Subcommittee. Retrieved from National Instiute of Standards and Technology: https://www.nist.gov/osac/dogs-sensors-subcommittee

Pawloski, S. (2019, 5, 16). The Accumulation of Wear on Footwear Pattern Analysis. *Themis: Research Journal of Justice Studies and Forensic Science*, *7*(1), 1–18.

People v. Davis, 2-06-0319 (Appellate Court of Illinois, Second District November 20, 2007).

Pope v. State, 756 W. S. 2d 401 (Court of Appeals of Texas, Dallas August 4, 1988).

Reddy, L. (2011). Lip Prints: An Overview in Forensic Dentistry. *Journal of Advanced Dental Research*, *3*(1), 18–21.

Scafide, K., Sheridan, D., Downing, N., & Hayat, M. (2020). Detection of Inflicted Bruises by Alternate Light: Results of a Randomized Controlled Trial. *Journal of Forensic Science*, *65*(4), 1191–1198.

State v. Johnston, 412 (Court of Appeals of Ohio, Fourth Appellate District, Hocking County August 6, 1986).

Summit, R. (1993). Abuse of the Child Sexual Abuse Accommodation Syndrome. *Journal of Child Sexual Abuse*, *1*(4), 153–164.

Tuttle, R. (1986). Footprints: Collection, Analysis, and Interpretation. Louise Robbins [review]. *American Anthropologist*, *88*, 1000–1002.

United States v. Angleton, 269 F. Supp. 2d 892 (Southern District of Texas 2003).

United States v. Hebshie, 02cr10185-NG (United States District Court for the District of Massachusetts November 15, 2010).

West, M., Barsley, R., Frair, J., & Hall, F. (1990). Reflective Ultraviolet Imagining System (RUVIS) and the Detection of Trace Evidence and Wounds on Human Skin. *Journal of Forensic Identification*, *40*(5), 249–255.

CHAPTER 6

Bite Mark Comparison

Physical and sexual assaults may produce visible bodily injuries, including bruises that may be associated with a biting injury. The dentition of the biter may produce three levels of injury. A bite may produce minor bruising, bruising with penetration of the teeth into the skin, and maceration of the flesh under the skin. If only minor bruising is observed, it is unlikely that the injury can be associated with biting or be forensically useful to the bite mark examiner. If maceration of the flesh occurs, the level of injury may be so severe that the injury cannot be associated with patterns in the biter's dentition. A forensic comparison may be possible when the biter's teeth cut the skin to a limited extent. In this situation, the bite mark "impression" is supported by clear indications of the relative position of the teeth. In general, the bite mark will include only anterior teeth. The bite mark examiner will seek to determine if the anterior positions of a reference dentition align with the skin pattern from the victim. There are many variables associated with the process, including the extent of unusual features in a suspect dentition, the clarity of bite mark impressions, distortions associated with the pliability of human skin, distortions associated with variations in human biting patterns, distortions associated with healing (or postmortem artifacts), and the limitations of subjective interpretations. These variables have been studied by researchers and practitioners, but it is evident that it is difficult to account for them in real-world scenarios. For example, researchers cannot produce realistic human bite marks without violating human-subjects protocols. Also, human skin is a poor registration medium for bite mark impressions due to its pliability and the inevitable changes that occur soon after an injury. The scientific consensus now holds that bite mark comparison lacks sufficient foundation and is unreliable (Saks et al., 2016).

Historically, odontologists limited their work to identification of remains based on comparisons of dentition with dental records. A famous case involved the identification of the remains of Adolf Hitler at the end of World War II (Sognnae & Strom, 1973). Bite mark comparison was used in criminal cases in England in the postwar period

DOI: 10.4324/9781003202578-6

and was accepted into American courts in the 1970s. The technique was popularized during the trial of serial killer, Ted Bundy, in Florida in 1984. Bundy's dentition was considered unusual, with many chips and canted teeth, as can be easily observed in Figure 6.1. At least one victim had injuries that appeared to be bite marks, and four separate odontologists—Dr. Richard Souviron, Dr. Lowell Levine, Dr. Homer Campbell, and Dr. Norman Sperber—agreed that Bundy was likely to be the biter who produced the marks. The comparison was based on a photograph of the victim at autopsy that included a ruler that permitted a comparison. The flesh around the mark had been excised and was also used in the comparison process, although the process of excision undoubtedly produced distortions that would not have permitted a reliable conclusion. Regardless, the case led to the acceptance of bite mark comparison in Florida courts, the conviction of a notorious serial killer, and the widespread popularization of bite mark comparison in the United States and around the world.

Three of the four examiners in the Bundy case became Presidents of the American Board of Forensic Odontology (ABFO). All four produced bite mark comparisons that contributed to wrongful convictions. Similarly, the premier forensic science association in the United States, the American Academy of Forensic Sciences (AAFS), has had five Presidents who were odontologists. Of the five, three (Campbell, Sperber, and Robert Barsley) produced bite mark comparisons that contributed

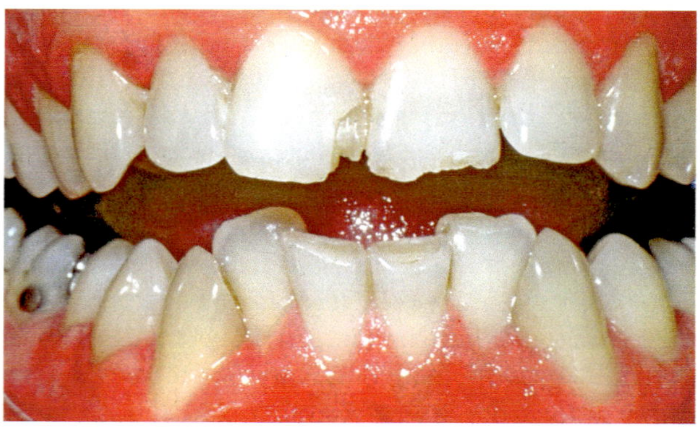

FIGURE 6.1 The anterior (front) teeth of Ted Bundy in 1979. The features of Bundy's dentition were considered unusual and facilitated a match conclusion to evidence. Many wrongful convictions include bite marks and presumed sources that appeared to have unusual characteristics of a similar type. The fundamental limitations of bite mark evidence produced false positives nonetheless. Source: Senn, ***History of Bitemark Evidence,*** 2011.

to wrongful convictions. No other AAFS President has conducted a forensic examination that contributed to a known wrongful conviction. The influence of the ABFO within the forensic science community has been maintained despite the record of wrongful convictions. In part, this is due to the widely respected role that odontologists have played in the resolution of cases involving the unidentified dead, particularly in mass disasters and human rights abuses. For example, Levine participated in the investigation of human rights violations in Argentina and the identification of remains of American soldiers from Vietnam. Further, ABFO established practice standards that are reasonably reflected in forensic practice. In many wrongful convictions, the bite mark examiner followed ABFO guidelines on the collection, analysis, and interpretation of bite marks. With the exception of Michael West, very few bite mark examiners have been accused of fraudulent work.

ABFO AND STANDARDS OF PRACTICE

ABFO has limited its membership to practicing dental professionals. There is no research basis for this requirement. Dental experts may have some specialized knowledge, but the practice of bite mark comparison could be conducted by anyone with skills in pattern recognition and configural processing. The ABFO requirement has had two key consequences. ABFO membership has been composed of educated professionals with doctoral degrees, which has engendered a level of respect among other forensic professionals. Also, most certified bite mark examiners have been independent consultants working on a part-time basis. Bite mark examiners have often been retained by law enforcement or prosecutors and seldom subject to the requirements, quality assurance mechanisms, or governance that cover other forensic professionals. In essence, ABFO has averted AAFS oversight while bite mark examiners have avoided governance from traditional forensic science organizations.

To be fair, ABFO has significantly altered its standards in response to wrongful convictions and research studies demonstrating the limitations of the validity of the method as applied in practice (American Board of Forensic Odontology, 1995; 2018). ABFO has participated in some research work to elucidate the accuracy and reliability of certified examiners. For example, 32 certified bite mark examiners at the 1999 ABFO meeting were found to have an accuracy rate of 86% (Arheart & Pretty, 2001). Current standards permit only three types of conclusions concerning the association of a bite mark with a source: Excluded as Having Made the Bite mark; Not Excluded as Having Made the Bite mark, and Inconclusive. Under prior standards, the examiner was allowed to make more definitive conclusions, including individualizations. In past reports and testimony, the language used by examiners has included a very wide range of conclusion types that may have misled investigators, officers of the court, and juries to place more weight on bite mark evidence than was warranted. It should be noted that many examiners used photographs and exhibits that showed victim injuries and may have elicited emotional and prejudicial responses from fact-finders.

It should also be noted that many observers, including the Texas Forensic Science Commission—hold that the entire field of bite mark examination must be abandoned because examiners cannot reliably distinguish bite marks from other injuries or indications on human skin, let alone determine whether a particular individual biter may have been the source of the mark (Texas Forensic Science Commission, 2016). Wrongful convictions may demonstrate that the scientific limitations of bite mark comparison may be so severe that it cannot be reliably performed under any circumstances. This contention is supported by the fact that many wrongful convictions are associated with the most experienced leaders in the field. If the examiners who develop and enforce the standards of the discipline produce mistakes, it may be an indication that the underlying basis for the technique is fundamentally flawed. In other disciplines, many errors are associated with the failure to follow best practices or establish enforceable standards. In bite mark comparison, errors have occurred *despite* the use of best practices and ABFO standards. For example, most bite mark examiners in wrongful convictions followed ABFO guidelines for the photography and documentation of presumed bite marks, as reflected in Figure 6.2.

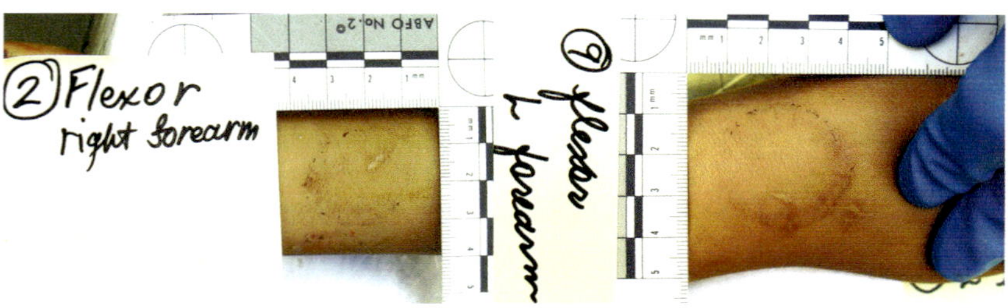

FIGURE 6.2 ABFO standards are very specific concerning the photographic documentation of bite marks. In part, this is due to the need to account for distortions associated with bite mark impressions in human skin. This orientation-type photograph shows information about the injury, anatomical location, and photographic scale. The examiner used the ABFO number 2 scale, which is officially endorsed by the ABFO. Source: Delattre, "The Team Approach in Bitemark Investigation," 2011.

Dr. Homer Campbell, who was one of the examiners in the Bundy case and also an AAFS President, may be the most interesting example in this regard. Campbell limited his testimony as clearly as any certified bite mark examiner. He used only three conclusions: exclusion, consistent with, and "reasonable degree of dental certainty that those teeth did in fact make that mark." These conclusions are more expansive than current standards but also less expansive than most other examiners in wrongful conviction cases. Campbell testified in the trial of Calvin Washington and Joe Sidney Williams that Williams dentition was "consistent with the injury found on the decedent" (Hall, 2015). That formulation has a similar semantic meaning to the ABFO's "not excluded" conclusion. Arguably, Campbell's testimony was acceptably limited in scope, but his conclusion was incorrect. Williams was exonerated by postconviction DNA testing. Campbell was also one of four forensic scientists who contributed mistaken testimony related to bite marks in the conviction of Steven Chaney.

STEVEN CHANEY

John and Sally Sweek were stabbed to death in Dallas, Texas on June 20, 1987. Steven Chaney was arrested for the murders a month later. The forensic evidence appeared to be compelling (Texas Forensic Science Commission, 2016; Ex parte Steven Mark Chaney, Applicant, 2018). A fingerprint from the kitchen wall matched Chaney, and the case investigator testified that it had been recently left. Throughout the house, bloody shoeprints were observed of at least two different types. The shoeprint examiner said Chaney's sneakers were of the same sole design as one of the types of shoeprints at the scene. During the trial, the defense called a Footlocker employee as a shoe expert who said the pattern appeared on 50% to 80% of shoes based on his personal experience. A forensic serologist said that she found traces of blood on Chaney's shoes, but they could not be typed. Another analyst couldn't find any blood on Chaney's shoes.

Three different bite mark examiners testified. All three were ABFO-certified. Dr. Jim Hales, a consultant for the Dallas County Medical Examiner's Office, said Chaney's dentition "matched" the bite mark and provided a statistical interpretation of "one to a million." He recanted this statistical interpretation in 2015 during postconviction proceedings. Dr. Homer Campbell "concluded that to a reasonable degree of dental certainty, [Chaney] made the bite marks on Sweek's body." Defense expert Dr. John McDowell said Chaney "could have made the bite marks" and that he "could not be wholly excluded from making the marks." Although McDowell said that he was not certain, his testimony would conform to the highest level of source attribution allowed under current ABFO guidelines. It is likely that the jury interpreted McDowell's testimony as inculpatory. The prosecutor said the bite mark testimony was "better than eyewitness testimony."

The victim's autopsy report was signed by the medical examiner and three other forensic pathologists, who noted that the bite mark was "crusted and contused." They initially concluded that the evidence of healing implied that the wound had been inflicted two to three days before death. Their view changed by the time of trial. Two forensic pathologists testified that the bite mark occurred at or about the time of death and supplemented the autopsy report to reflect the change. At trial, the medical examiner, James Weiner, testified that he observed bite marks on John Sweek's arm and opined that the injuries were inflicted "at or about the time of Mr. Sweek's death." He did not clarify the basis for the changed conclusion, though he did say postconviction that he may have confused "crusting" from healing with "serum drying." It is possible that the forensic pathologists were influenced by the conclusions of the bite mark examiners and police investigators to make an invalid change based on contextual bias, not medical or scientific data.

The other forensic testimony included several errors. The fingerprint examiner had no scientific basis to make a conclusion about the time when the print had been deposited. The defense "expert" from Footlocker had no scientific basis for a population estimate about sole designs. The language of the bite mark examiners' testimony was highly variable. Although they could be seen to agree on some level, Hales testified to an individualization, Campbell to some lesser version of individualization, and McDowell to a classification of possible sources. Postconviction, some reviewers stated that it was not even clear that the mark was a human bite mark and may have been caused by a belt buckle or other weapon.

In 2015, DNA testing excluded Chaney from the evidence at the scene and three male profiles were identified from Sally Sweek's fingernails. The conviction was vacated in part on the basis of the Texas "junk science" statute because of the issues with the bite mark evidence. It also was the subject of an extensive review by the Texas Forensic Science Commission, which led to the abandonment of bite mark comparison as evidence in criminal cases in Texas. The Texas Court of Criminal Appeals issued a finding of actual innocence for Chaney in 2018, who received $2.26 million in compensation. Chaney died in 2021.

EXAMINER VARIABILITY AND BIAS

The Chaney case demonstrates variability in the language of bite mark interpretation and testimony. In the Roy Brown case, the variability related to the conclusions, not the language of interpretation. Edward Mofson, Lowell Levine, and Homer Campbell all provided bite mark comparisons (Santos, 2006). Like Campbell, Levine served as President of the AAFS. In fact, Campbell's 1991–92 term coincided with the Brown case, which went to trial in January of 1992. In the Brown case, both Levine and Campbell concluded that Brown was excluded as a source of the bite mark. Levine's exclusion was suppressed by the prosecution and not disclosed to the defense. Mofson testified five different times during the trial and postconviction phases of the case, four times implicating Brown and once excluding him. Mofson was an ABFO-certified examiner following the standards of the discipline, although some accounts have stated incorrectly that he was not certified. (Pretty & Bowers, 2011). Nonetheless, he dismissed clear evidence that Brown was not the source of the bite marks because Brown was missing two front incisors. Mofson testified that the marks were "inconsistent but explainably so in my opinion ... there are inconsistencies that are explainable and there are inconsistencies that are not explainable." (Santos, 2006)

Mofson's statement is reminiscent of issues in hair comparison. In both disciplines, the variability in evidence may exceed the differences among possible sources. In hair comparison, the examiner must sample many reference hairs from an individual to determine the variability of that person's hair morphology. The comparison seeks to determine if the evidence hair falls within the range of variability observed in the reference samples. Hair comparison examiners are able to do this analysis separately for the evidence and source and attach semi-quantitative metrics to their feature extraction. Bite mark examiners also face variability, but the variability relates to the manner in which the biter made the impression, not source variability. They cannot sample the ways that a possible source dentition may manifest in impression evidence, so they cannot reliably determine whether a particular impression was within the range of possible impressions that a source dentition could have produced. Instead, bite mark examiners produce photographic or digital overlays that compare a mark with a possible source dentition, as seen in Figure 6.2. To account for distortion (i.e., variability in the manner of impression), they will adjust the tooth images in the overlay to align them with patterns in the skin impression. This subjective process has always meant that bite marks were dubious for individualization at best. The Mofson testimony in the Brown case demonstrates that the process can lead the examiner to discount mismatches of almost any type—even when the suspect was missing teeth that should have corresponded to patterns observed in evidence. The variability in bite mark impressions leads to variability in source conclusions. There is no research to establish whether bite mark variability can be accounted for in an objective manner to mitigate the possibility of examiner variability.

Wrongful convictions demonstrate the uncertainties in the use of human skin as a registration medium for bite mark impressions and may suggest that the technique is untenable for any level of individual or class association. This may be true even when a suspect's dentition is unusual or the bite mark appears to have been made by an individual with unusual dentition. In many wrongful convictions, it is difficult to determine the level of difficulty of comparisons. Bite mark examiners do not have objective metrics that define the forensic value of a bite mark impression or the difficulty of a comparison. When discovered, exonerations are generally the result of DNA testing of biological evidence. In fact, many bite mark examiners now limit their findings to identification of areas that may be most useful for swabbing for biological evidence and subsequent DNA testing. This approach assumes that a biter will leave saliva or other biological fluids behind at a bite mark location and that it is therefore useful to distinguish bite marks from other skin injuries.

KEITH HARWARD

Two years after he served as AAFS President in 1980/81, Lowell Levine made a bite mark examination error in a Newport News, Virginia murder/sexual assault case (Harward v. Commonwealth, 1988). Levine's testimony was the key evidence against defendant Keith Harward. The case involved a home invasion in the small community adjacent to the Newport News shipyards, where the aircraft carrier USS Carl Vinson was being outfit. Jesse Perron was a civilian welder working on the ship. Harward and Jerry Crotty were sailors on the ship. On the night of September 14, 1982, Crotty entered the back of the Perron house, killed Jesse Perron with a crowbar, and sexually assaulted Teresa Perron while the couple's three children slept in other rooms (Figure 6.3). Crotty bit her several times on the legs during the assault. Crotty and Teresa Perron each smoked at least one cigarette, and three cigarette butts were recovered later from the scene. After Crotty left, he was observed going through the shipyard gate by a security guard. The guard noted that Crotty's uniform was bloody but did not stop him. Teresa Perron went to the hospital, where a rape kit was collected and pictures of the bite marks were taken. Police dogs tracked a scent from the house to the shipyard gate.

FIGURE 6.3 Newport News street. The Newport News shipyard is less than a half-mile from the Perron family home in 1982. The neighborhood remains deeply connected to the shipyard but is also subject to serious crime. Shortly after taking this picture, the author witnessed a hit-and-run automobile collision on this street, which the assailant also traveled before and after the rape/murder. Source: Photograph by the author, John Morgan.

The police then conducted a highly unusual "bite mark dragnet." A local dentist and a dentist from the USS Carl Vinson collected dental records from sailors for comparison to the evidence bite marks. The dentists were not ABFO-certified. This extraordinary step was inherently invalid. It was likely that they would find some match—perhaps several—to the evidence dentition given the hundreds of men whose dentition was collected. Harward's dentition was noted as a possible match, but the dentists did not implicate him or any other sailor in the initial dragnet.

A few months later, Harward's girlfriend complained to police that he had bitten her during a fight. Police investigators then called in Levine, who said that Harward's dentition matched the evidence bite marks. At the trial, he said, "[W]ith reasonable medical certainty, Mr. Harward caused the bite marks on the leg" (Harward v. Commonwealth, 1988). He demonstrated to the jury distinctive individual characteristics of Harward's teeth and features visible in the photographs which had led to his conclusion. One of Harward's teeth "canted sideways" and another had a "hook type area." These features aligned with features visible in the photographs of the bite marks. Levine also explained and displayed a "chipped area" and "breakage" that were present and distinctive in both the photo and his wax impression of Harward's teeth. Another ABFO-certified examiner, Dr. A.W. Kagey, confirmed Levine's findings. Kagey was aware of Levine's conclusions. Such "non-blind" verifications are subject to confirmation bias and are not recommended practice for any forensic discipline.

The case also included questionable serological typing. Crotty was likely a non-secretor but his actual type is unknown. Harward was an A secretor, Jesse Perron an O secretor, and Teresa Perron was a B secretor. As noted, three cigarette butts were recovered from the scene. Two had B and H antigens and presumably were from Teresa Perron. One had no antigens and may have come from Crotty if he wasn't a secretor. The rape kit swabs had H antigens associated with O secretor. The possibility that the rape kit antigens came from Jesse Perron was discounted by police at the time of the trial. In any case, Harward's A blood group substances were not observed in any evidence—a fact which should have exculpated him as the rapist. It is possible the testing wasn't sensitive enough to pick up the male fraction in the rape kit. More likely, the serology was simply exculpatory and should have been given more weight than the bite marks. Levine was a well-spoken and prominent forensic scientist; he had been AAFS president just two years before the Harward case. This may have led police and prosecutors to weigh Levine's match conclusion too heavily against Harward, who was convicted of the rape and murder.

In 2016, the rape kit was subject to DNA testing which exonerated Harward and identified Crotty, who had died in an Ohio prison ten years before. Levine had erred by testifying to an invalid individualization. Even more importantly, he had identified features in the bite mark that should have made the comparison very straightforward and reliable. As a leader in the field, Levine should have been in a perfect position to identify the features and make an accurate source attribution. His clear error demonstrates fundamental weaknesses in the use of bite mark identification.

ERRORS BY PROMINENT EXAMINERS

Campbell and Levine were not outliers as prominent bite mark examiners who were involved in wrongful convictions. Richard Souviron, who had popularized bite mark comparison in the Bundy case, has been associated with at least one wrongful conviction and has recanted identifications in several other cases. In the wrongful conviction of Robert DuBoise, he relied on Polaroid photographs and excised tissue from a decedent in much the same manner as he had done in the Bundy case (Office of the State Attorney 13th Judicial Circuit, 2020). He testified at trial that "within a reasonable degree of dental certainty appellant had bitten the victim." Dr. Norman Sperber, who had worked with Souviron on the Bundy case, testified for the defense that there were too many inconsistencies between the marks on the victim and DuBoise's dentition. DuBoise was convicted and received a death sentence. He was exonerated postconviction by DNA analysis that identified an alternate suspect who by then was in prison for a similar offense. The conviction was vacated and charges dismissed in 2020. Souviron said, "Today, I would say I could not eliminate him. There could have been a million other people whose teeth fit ... I played a part in his conviction. There's no question I feel terrible." (Office of the State Attorney 13th Judicial Circuit, 2020).

The AAFS has named an award after Sperber, the Norman D. Sperber Award for Forensic Dental Excellence. Sperber has also produced an erroneous bite mark examination in a detected wrongful conviction. That error raises fundamental questions about the challenge of distinguishing between bite marks and other injuries. William Richards was implicated in the 1993 murder of his wife, Pamela Richards, in California. The first three trials ended in mistrial, but he was convicted of first-degree murder in the fourth trial and sentenced to 25 years to life in prison (In re Richards, 2016). The victim had a crescent-shaped lesion on her right hand. Sperber said the injury was a bite mark and that he "could not exclude" the defendant as the biter. William Richards had an under-erupted canine tooth, which Sperber stated that he observed in "one or two or less" out of 100 people. Sperber did note that he relied on a photograph that had significant angular distortion, a problem which led him to limit the strength of his conclusion. Postconviction, two other examiners, Dr. Charles Bowers and Dr. Raymond Johansen, used a digital processing technique to remove the angular distortion and demonstrate that William Richards could not be included as a possible source of the bite mark. In 2016, Bowers, Johansen, and Sperber agreed that there was doubt as to whether the injury was even a bite mark. It should be noted that the digital processing technique used by Bowers and Johansen remains unvalidated and may not be more reliable than the overlay techniques used by other forensic odontologists. More importantly, if the field cannot reliably distinguish between bite marks and other injuries, it certainly cannot be used reliably to include or exclude an individual from having made a bite mark. No digital enhancement technology or other interpretation method can mitigate that fundamental issue.

RAY KRONE

Sperber gave exculpatory testimony in the Ray Krone case, which was a landmark wrongful conviction in the state of Arizona in 1991. His colleagues, Raymond Rawson and John Piakis, implicated Krone with an individualization based on presumed bite marks on the victim's neck and left breast (State v. Krone, 1995). The only other evidence was circumstantial; Krone was slated to help the victim close the bar where the murdered occurred. Rawson testified that a tooth could be in about 150 different positions, which he maintained could be discerned from bite mark impressions. If there were two teeth, he testified that the 150 positions of the second tooth would be an independent variable, saying the random match probability of a match "would be 150 times 150, whatever that is, maybe 1200 or something like that." (State v. Krone, 1995) Based on the faulty bite mark evidence, the media called Krone the Snaggletooth killer. Sperber pointed out that Krone had two higher teeth than his incisors, but the bite mark patterns did not reflect that unusual aspect of his dentition. At a retrial, Homer Campbell also testified that the mark was an exclusion, agreeing with Sperber. The case also included a hair comparison error involving poorly communicated and invalid testimony. The examiner said he "could not exclude" Krone as a source of an evidence hair that was actually not suitable for comparison. In other words, the examiner had not done a valid comparison and could not exclude any person but testified as if Krone was in a subpopulation of possible sources. Some early DNA testing was done in the case and could have been interpreted as exculpatory, but it was dismissed as unimportant by the prosecution. Krone was convicted and sentenced to life in prison. In 2002, DNA testing exonerated Krone and identified an alternate suspect who was then in prison for a sexual assault. That man, Kenneth Phillips, had been living near the scene of the murder. Krone received $4.4 million in settlements in connection with his wrongful conviction. He has become an important advocate for DNA testing and innocence organizations.

There are several interesting aspects of the Krone case. First, Rawson's statistical characterization was clearly invalid. The features of dentition are not independent variables. The features are not represented in bite mark impressions in sufficient detail to characterize 150 positions or anything remotely close to that figure. And 150 multiplied by 150 is a lot more than 1200. The testimony was "transparent" in that Rawson provided a clear basis for his belief, but it was clearly incorrect and should not have been provided by Rawson or admitted in court. The mischaracterization is similar to that of Arnold Melnikoff, who provided a similar set of estimates for the uniqueness of hair morphological features in his testimony in several Montana wrongful convictions. It should be noted that Sperber's statistical estimate in the William Richards case was also invalid, even though Sperber's characterization was not as glaringly mistaken. Many observers may place undue weight on statistical characterizations and have very little basis to judge the validity of such estimates. They may believe that a quantitative characterization is inherently more reliable or "powerful" than a qualitative characterization. As a result, invalid statistical interpretations have an especially pernicious impact in wrongful convictions.

Further, the Krone case demonstrates the problem of investigational tunnel vision. Police had sufficient leads to identify Phillips at the time of the original investigation. Further, they had exculpatory DNA and bite mark results but were unwilling to change their view of the case based on the contradictory information. They relied on invalid hair and bite mark reports and continued to press a weak case that had almost no other supporting evidence. In many wrongful convictions, this "continuation bias" effect prevents police or prosecutors from properly considering exculpatory forensic evidence.

UNUSUAL DENTITIONS

In the 1984 Robert Lee Stinson case, ABFO-certified odontologists Raymond Rawson and Lowell Johnson found eight bite marks on the body of a rape/murder victim (Robert Lee Stinson v. James Gauger, Lowell Johnson, and Raymond Rawson, 2015). The bite marks showed a distinctive pattern associated with a missing upper lateral tooth. Stinson was missing his right-center incisor. Those two tooth positions are close but are not the same. Johnson seemed to confuse the positions in his reports and testimony. The bite mark impressions were very distinctive and even had some three-dimensional details, meaning that the relative position of the missing tooth should have been straightforward to determine and interpret. Stinson was missing the wrong tooth, so he should have been excluded. Nonetheless, Johnson concluded that the bite marks were made by Stinson "to a reasonable degree of scientific certainty." Rawson conducted his review in a hotel room and clearly knew Johnson's conclusions. His review was perfunctory. He said, "We can say that there is no other set of dentitions like that." (Robert Lee Stinson v. James Gauger, Lowell Johnson, and Raymond Rawson, 2015) It is unclear if the error was due to confirmation bias by Johnson and Rawson, their failure to adhere to the standards of the field, or merely the limitations of bite mark comparison as a discipline (or all three). Stinson was exonerated by DNA testing in 2005. A DNA cold hit in 2012 identified an alternate suspect, who pled guilty and was sentenced to 19 years in prison. Stinson settled his lawsuit against the city of Milwaukee for $7.5 million in 2019.

Robert Barsley was the last bite mark examiner to be President of the AAFS, serving from 2012 to 2013. He provided erroneous testimony in the Willie Jackson wrongful conviction for sexual assault in Jefferson Parish, Louisiana in 1989. Like defendants in the other cases described above, Jackson had unusual features in his dentition. Barsley noted a tooth with a gold crown, two false teeth with gold covering, and a chip in a front tooth. The crown had worn down over the years and seemed to correspond to a feature in the presumed bite mark. Barsley said he was "convinced … a hundred percent" that Jackson was the biter. He gave contradictory testimony about the value of bite mark examination, saying at one point that he doesn't use the word "identical" and at another that the photographs of the bite mark and Jackson's dentition were "identical." The bite mark was critical evidence because the victim could not make a positive identification of Jackson. He was convicted and sentenced to 40 years in prison. A few days later, his brother Milton Jackson came forward and confessed to the crime. The appeals court rejected Willie Jackson's appeal on the basis of the new confession because it was felt the bite mark identification was clearly inculpatory and dispositive. Fourteen years later, DNA testing excluded Willie Jackson from the evidence in the case. Two years after that, DNA testing was able to link Milton Jackson to the evidence. Milton Jackson was already in prison for a 1998 rape. Willie Jackson was officially exonerated and received $330,000 in state compensation.

STUDY QUESTIONS

1. How does the ABFO limit bite mark testimony today? How does it differ from prior standards? Are the changes a sufficient response to the problems of wrongful convictions? What are the appropriate limits on bite mark testimony?
2. There are many other wrongful convictions associated with bite mark evidence, such as cases involving David Kunze, Juan Ramos, and Kennedy Brewer. (Brewer v. Steven Timothy Hayne

& Michael H. W., 2015) The National Registry of Exonerations (NRE) and other public documents provide background information on these cases. Consider a case from this chapter or one of the three suggested cases. Review the forensic evidence, determine whether there were errors associated with the forensic evidence, and make recommendations for system improvement to prevent similar errors in future cases.

3. What types of research could be done to improve the scientific foundations of bite mark evidence? Consider issues related to the uniqueness of dentition, human skin as an impression medium, and the effects of healing or postmortem changes. How could such research mitigate the possibility of future wrongful convictions?

FURTHER READING

The Texas Forensic Science Commission produced a report on the Chaney case and bite mark evidence (Texas Forensic Science Commission, 2016). The report includes a wide range of supporting information about bite mark evidence and relevant scientific research. Innocence Project lawyer Chris Fabricant represented Chaney and is undoubtedly the fiercest critic of bite mark evidence. He wrote a 2016 law review article on bite marks and other discredited evidence (Fabricant & Carrington, 2016). In 2022, he published a critique of "junk science" and wrongful convictions (Fabricant, 2022). He highlighted the Harvard case, among others, in which he has been involved.

Two bite mark examiners, Iain Pretty and David Sweet, collaborated on a 2010 paper, "*A paradigm shift in the analysis of bitemarks*," that describes the issues surrounding wrongful convictions and how the field has attempted to respond (Pretty & Sweet, 2010). David Senn has provided the most in-depth defense of the field in his writings and presentations. His article, "*Bitemark Analysis: The Good, the Bad, and the Ugly*", was published in the newsletter of the American Society of Forensic Odontology (ASFO), but that publication is available to ASFO members only. Senn gave a presentation to the NRC committee that issued the 2009 report on forensic science, and the slides are available from the NRC website (Senn, 2007).

REFERENCES

American Board of Forensic Odontology. (1995). *ABFO Bite Mark Methodology Guidelines*. American Academy of Forensic Sciences.

American Board of Forensic Odontology. (2018). *Standards and Guidelines for Evaluating Bitemarks*. American Board of Forensic Odontology. Retrieved from http://abfo.org/wp-content/uploads/2012/08/ABFO-Standards-Guidelines-for-Evaluating-Bitemarks-Feb-2018.pdf

Arheart, K., & Pretty, I. (2001). Results of the 4th ABFO Bitemark Workshop—1999. *Forensic Science International*, *124*(2–3), 104–111.

Brewer v. Steven Timothy Hayne & Michael H. W., 3:13-cv-898-HTW-LRA (United States District Court for the Southern District of Mississippi, Northern Division April 16, 2015).

Delattre, V. (2011). The Team Approach in Bitemark Investigation. In R. Dorion (Ed.), *Bitemark Evidence: A Color Atlas and Text* (pp. 43–49). Boca Raton: CRC Press.

Ex parte Steven Mark Chaney, Applicant, WR-84,091-01 (Court of Criminal Appeals of Texas December 19, 2018).

Fabricant, M. (2022). *Junk Science and the American Criminal Justice System*. New York, NY: Akashic Books.

Fabricant, M., & Carrington, T. (2016). The Shifted Paradigm: Forensic Science's Overdue Evolution from Magic to Law. *Virginia Journal of Criminal Law*, *4*, 1.

Hall, M. (2015, October 20). Another Texas Exoneration Calls Bite Mark Evidence into Question. *Texas Monthly*.

Harward v. Commonwealth, 0323–86 (Court of Appeals of Virginia January 19, 1988).

In re Richards, S223651 (Supreme Court of California May 26, 2016).

Office of the State Attorney 13th Judicial Circuit. (2020, September 15). *State Attorney's Office Launches Review of Convictions Based on Bite Mark Evidence Following Discovery of DuBoise's Wrongful Conviction*. Retrieved from Office of the State Attorney 13th Judicial Circuit Hillsborough: https://www.sao13th.com/2020/09/15/

Pretty, I., & Bowers, C. (2011). Wrongful Convictions and Errneous Bitemark Opinions. In R. Dorion. *Bitemark Evidence: A Color Atlas and Text* (pp. 577–583). Boca Raton: CRC Press.

Pretty, I., & Sweet, D. (2010). A Paradigm Shift in the Analysis of Bitemarks. *Forensic Science International*, *201*(1–3), 38–44.

Robert Lee Stinson v. James Gauger, Lowell Johnson, and Raymond Rawson, 13-3343 (United States Court of Appeals, Seventh Circuit August 25, 2015).

Saks, M. J., et al. (2016). Forensic Bitemark Identification: Weak Foundations, Exaggerated Claims. *Journal of Law and the Biosciences*, 538–575.

Santos, F. (2006, December 21). In Quest for a Killer, an Inmate Finds Vindication. *New York Times*.

Senn, D. (2007, April 23). *Forensic Odontology Bite Marks*. Retrieved from National Academy of Sciences: https://www.nationalacademies.org/event/04-23-2007/docs/DCE28C1630A25BCE2CDC2D6D4AF1150422F385D384B8

Senn, D. (2011). History of Bitemark Evidence. In R. Dorion (Ed.), *Bitemark Evidence: A Color Atlas and Text* (pp. 3–24). Boca Raton: CRC Press.

Sognnae, R., & Strom, F. (1973). The Odonotological Identification of Adolf Hitler. *Acta Odontologica Scandinavica*, *31*(1), 43–69.

State v. Krone, CR-92–0480-AP (Supreme Court of Arizona June 22, 1995).

Texas Forensic Science Commission. (2016). *Forensic Bitemark Comparison Complaint Filed by National Innocence Project on Behalf of Steven Mark Chaney - Final Report*. Austin: Texas Forensic Science Commission.

Texas Forensic Science Commission. (2016). *Forensic Bitemark Comparison Complaint Filed by National Innocence Project on Bhealf of Steven Mark Chaney - Final Report*. Austin: Texas Forensic Science Commission.

CHAPTER 7

Fingerprints and Friction Ridge Examination

Friction ridge skin can be found on human fingers, palms, and feet (National Institute of Justice, 2011). Friction ridge patterns are largely formed by 10 weeks of gestational age and persist for the lifetime of the individual. The patterns grow larger as the person grows to adulthood, but the shapes and configuration remain the same. Friction ridge patterns are unique to each individual, a proposition that has been exhaustively tested. For example, the federal US government maintains fingerprint databases of over 200 million individuals through the FBI and Department of Homeland Security. The FBI's Next Generation Identification (formerly known as IAFIS, or International Automated Fingerprint Identification System) holds over 162 million ten-print exemplars and produces millions of accurate and reliable matches each year (Federal Bureau of Identification, 2021). Over 97% of matches are fully automated and returned within 15 seconds. Because environmental factors *in utero* affect friction ridge formation, identical twins can be distinguished by their fingerprints (Jain et al., 2002). Friction ridge detail may be broken down into three types. Level 1 detail classifies prints by overall pattern, such as whorl, loop, or arch, and the thickness, separation, and depth of ridges. Level 1 detail is largely genetically determined and may be the same among twins or siblings. Level 2 detail includes minutiae, such as ridge endings, bifurcations, and other anomalies. Most biometric and forensic analyses rely on Level 2 detail. Level 3 detail includes the location of sweat pores.

Millions of fingerprints have been examined, enrolled in databases, and used for criminal identification. Thus far, no two persons have had matching prints, not even among twins. So, naturally, many people believe that fingerprints are just about infallible as a forensic technique. If you want to compare one finger to another, that's pretty much the case. But latent prints found at crime scenes do not contain the same level of information as exemplars from fingerprint databases. When someone leaves

DOI: 10.4324/9781003202578-7

a fingerprint impression, they seldom leave the nice, neat mark you may see in a television drama. People smudge the print, grab objects with a corner of the finger, leave prints on impossibly rough surfaces, or even leave impressions only from the palm or side of the hand. Latent fingerprints are formed from the oils, sweat, proteins, and salt left by human touch. Most of the time, usable fingerprints are not visibly apparent on a particular object. Even the slightest handling of an object by another individual may render other fingerprints completely unusable. Many prints will evaporate within hours, certainly days, so they may disappear before they are discovered and collected. The prints can even be smudged by rubber gloves or the sides of the evidence bags in which they are transmitted. The success of any comparison is largely dependent on the quality of the print, as seen in Figure 7.1. Assuming a usable print is present, crime scene investigators will "develop" the print using powders or fumes or other methods. One of the primary innovations since the introduction of fingerprinting has been the development of these methods. For example, many labs expose evidence to super glue, or cyanoacrylate, which was developed by Japanese police official Masato Soba and his colleagues in the 1970s. In 1979, American fingerprint expert Ed German visited the

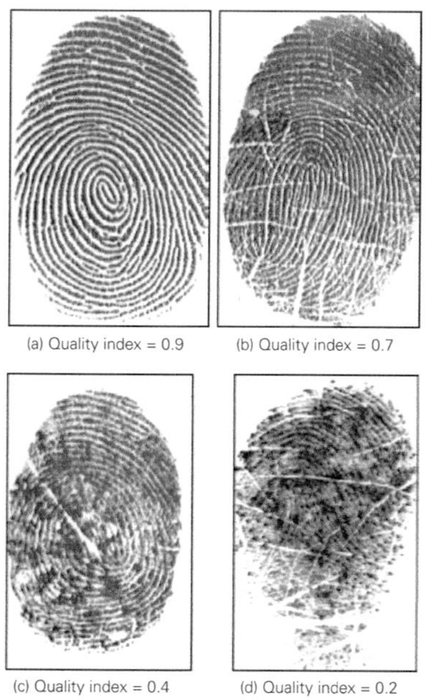

FIGURE 7.1 Four fingerprints of varying quality. The print in the lower right contains significant noise but may be suitable for some purposes if reliable feature extraction is performed during the analysis stage. Source: ***The Fingerprint Sourcebook*** (McRoberts, 2010).

National Police Agency of Japan in Tokyo to learn about Japanese forensic techniques. For whatever reason, although the Japanese were anxious to show off many impression evidence techniques, they were unwilling to tell German what materials they were actually using. German, unbeknownst to the Japanese, could read the katakana letters on the bottle phonetically, which spelled "aron-arufa." German scoured Japanese stores for this little chemical until coming across a bottle of "aron-arufa," which turned out to smell just like the chemical used in the NPA lab. And that turned out to be super glue (German, 2022).

As with other impression evidence, the forensic utility of friction ridge examination depends on the fidelity of latent patterns in evidence. The latent prints will not include the level of information that is collected in biometric repositories. Latent prints will include only partial sections and usually be distorted by effects in the impression or collection process. Therefore, distinctive friction ridge details may not be observed in the evidence. For example, Level 3 features cannot be reliably exploited in latent prints. Latent print examiners are trained to apply a methodical process in latent print examination called Analysis-Comparison-Evaluation-Verification (ACE-V) (Friction Ridge Subcommittee of the Organization of Scientific Area Committees, 2013). The process begins with an assessment of the forensic utility of a print to address the fundamental question of whether a print has sufficient information for comparison, database search, or exclusion. The examiner then extracts features from the print and makes a judgment concerning the orientation of the print and the likely source (e.g., a particular finger or palmar region). The print may be compared to an exemplar from a suspect or a set of exemplars from a database search. The examiner makes a subjective conclusion concerning whether a particular reference print came from the same source as the evidence. An independent examination is then performed to verify the first examiner's conclusion.

The process requires subjective determinations at every stage. Therefore, many observers have argued that latent print examination is inherently unscientific and unreliable. The examiner may be influenced by contextual bias from case information, or the verification process may be compromised by knowledge of the prior examiner's conclusions (Dror, 2018). The most notable case example was not a wrongful conviction: the Brandon Mayfield case.

BRANDON MAYFIELD

On March 11, 2004, ten bombs on four trains killed 191 people and injured more than 1000 in Madrid, Spain (Office of the Inspector General, 2006). Although initially blamed on Basque separatists, it was established that al Qaeda was responsible and had intended to use the bombings to influence Spain to withdraw its forces from the war in Iraq. The Spanish National Police (SNP) recovered a backpack with an unexploded device and developed latent prints from the evidence. The SNP sent eight, low-resolution latent print images to the FBI to determine if they could develop a suspect. On March 15 and 16, an FBI supervisory fingerprint examiner extracted seven minutiae from the latent print and ran a search in the IAFIS database. The examiner matched the fourth candidate in the IAFIS search to the latent print. A retired FBI examiner working as a contractor verified the match. The Unit Chief of the Latent Print Unit (LPU) reported the match to Interpol but did not complete a thorough review of the work. The examiners did not know it at the time, but the name of "candidate 4" was Brandon Mayfield, who had worked as a lawyer for Muslim clients in domestic disputes. FBI investigators put Mayfield under surveillance, believing that he was connected to the Madrid bombings (Figure 7.2).

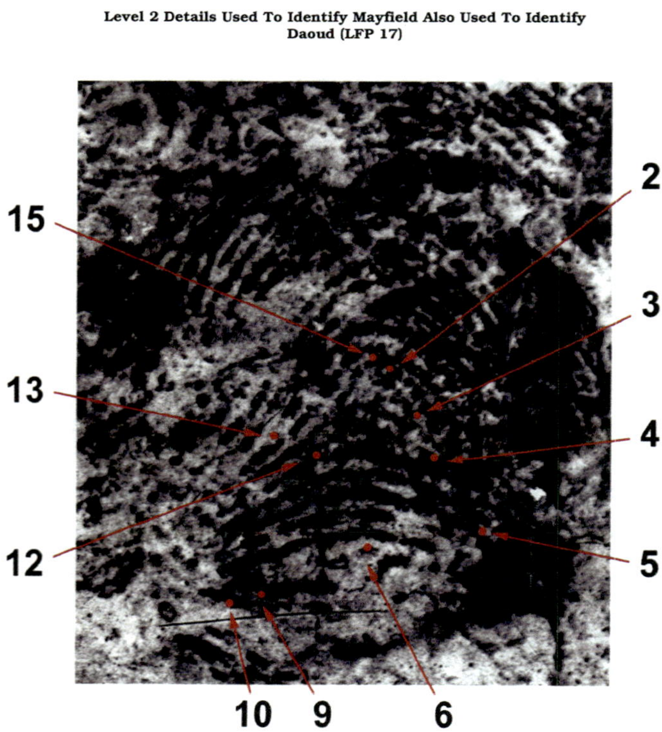

FIGURE 7.2 The FBI developed 15 points of comparison to associate Brandon Mayfield with the latent print from the SNP. The figures show the 10 points of comparison that were closely aligned in the Mayfield and Daoud exemplar prints. This level of agreement indicates that Mayfield was a close nonmatch to the evidence. Further, note the overall quality of the latent image. The poor quality was not a sufficient reason for the misidentification, though it may have contributed to the difficulties in feature extraction and comparison in the case. Source: Department of Justice, Office of the Inspector General, 2006.

Level 2 Details Used To Identify Mayfield Also Used To Identify Daoud (Mayfield Exemplar)

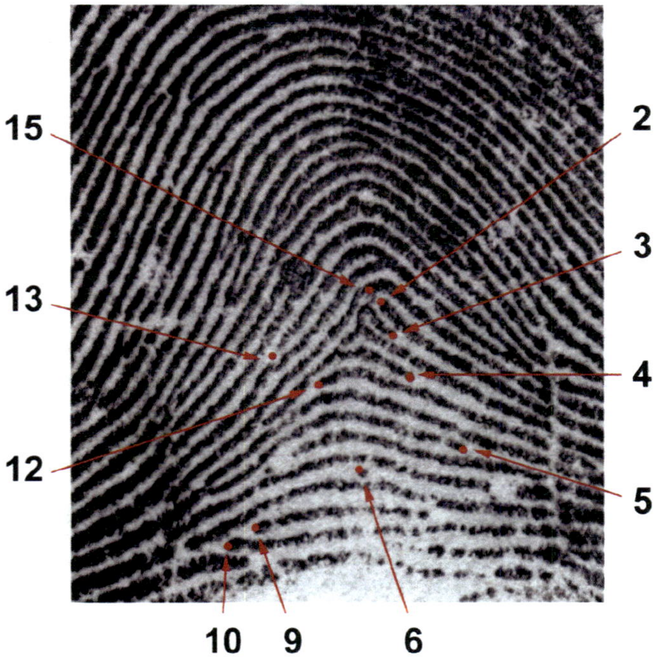

Level 2 Details Used To Identify Mayfield Also Used To Identify Daoud (Daoud Exemplar)

FIGURE 7.2 (Continued)

In April, the SNP clarified that the print had been taken from a plastic bag and provided better images to the FBI. The FBI provided Mayfield's reference exemplars to the SNP, but the SNP disagreed about the FBI's conclusions. They said the comparison was inconclusive and were unwilling to agree that Mayfield was implicated in the bombings. In response, the FBI prepared a three-page exhibit and briefing, detailing the basis for their identification. In effect, the FBI discounted the SNP's objections and failed to consider that they had made a major mistake.

In May, the FBI arrested Mayfield as a "material witness." On May 17, a federal judge ordered an independent examination of the print. That independent examiner verified the FBI's identification of Mayfield. Meanwhile, on May 19, the SNP informed the FBI that the print actually belonged to Algerian national Ouhnane Daoud. On May 23, FBI examiner Steve Meagher demonstrated the error and concluded that Mayfield was not the source of the Madrid print. Meagher was closely identified with the contention that latent print examination had a zero-error rate, saying at a Daubert hearing in 2002, "The methodology has an error rate of zero where practitioner error rate is whatever practitioner error rates for that individual or group of individuals" (United States v. Llera Plaza, 188 F. Supp. 2d 549 (E.D. Pa. 2002)). In the Mayfield case, Meagher amply demonstrated that the practitioner error rate and methodological error rate are not distinguishable. Methodologies must be applied by practitioners.

In July, the FBI issued a report agreeing with SNP findings and initiating a review of the error (Stacey, 2004). They found that the comparison was difficult because the latent print shared many characteristics with the Mayfield print. Although the original image was poor and lacked a scale for context, that was not considered a sufficient reason for the error. More importantly, there was poor communication about the image issue, a failure to follow established standards on image quality and forensic utility, and an environment in which the examiners felt the need to rush under the stress of a high-profile case.

The Mayfield identification error implicated a complex set of human and algorithmic deficiencies that may be unavoidable, especially as biometric databases get bigger and more close nonmatches provide confounding challenges to the forensic examiner. In the Mayfield case, the error began with the statistical model used in the IAFIS search. Fingerprint search algorithms provide a basis to characterize the statistical uniqueness of reference prints and latent prints. Some have suggested that fingerprint matching should be exclusively computer-based because algorithms are seen as more "objective" than human examiners. Unfortunately, statistical models also have inherent biases and limitations that are not easily removed or accounted for. As noted, Mayfield was the fourth "hit" on the IAFIS search list. It is unknown whether the Daoud print would have ranked higher. It is common for close non-matches to outrank actual matches in score-based searches (Neumann & Saunders, 2019). Although the Mayfield case is a clear example of the effects of human bias, it also demonstrated that computer algorithms have their own limitations.

The comparison also implicated the concept of target bias, in which the examiner assumed there was a match and sought to discover the features of a known exemplar in the evidence. Although only seven features were identified in the original analysis of the latent, examiners "found" 12 or 13 matching characteristics while looking for features from Mayfield's prints in the latent. This was not intentional, but it did demonstrate the problem of target bias, which is the most common form of bias observed in latent print comparisons in wrongful convictions. Today, some laboratories—particularly in Europe—have instituted a version of linear sequential unmasking (LSU), a practice in which recursive feature extraction is limited or prohibited. In other words, controls are implemented to establish the features of the unknown before any suspect prints are examined and to determine the extent to which an examiner can look back and extract more features from the latent print after looking at a reference print from a suspect. At minimum, LSU policies require documentation when the examiner "teases the points," as it is sometimes called. In the Mayfield case, there were discrepancies related to documentation and charting of the latent prints and exemplars, even under the standards at the FBI Laboratory at the time.

Also, the FBI review noted that 12 Level 2 characteristics were generally required for making a match conclusion. The LPU supervisor failed to note that the standard was not met during the original analysis. In other words, the FBI did not maintain its quality assurance standards and policies, perhaps because of the high-profile or high-pressure nature of the case. The FBI went on to institute a policy of independent supervisory verifications in high-profile cases. That policy does not reflect the experience of wrongful convictions, which most often occur in routine cases with very little public notoriety at the time of the original investigation.

In general, the FBI examiners were convinced of their own expertise and dismissive of the SNP. They did not pay attention to the issues raised by the SNP about the print comparison. This tendency may have impacted the verification process, which is designed to catch errors. Instead, the internal FBI verifier and the independent court-appointed verifier both deferred to the original analyst. Increasingly, labs now have a policy of blind verification in which the reviewing examiner is unaware of the original conclusion or other contextual information.

After the SNP identified Daoud, Mayfield was released after having been detained for about three weeks. He was later awarded a $2 million settlement and given an apology by the US government.

SUITABILITY DECISIONS

Contextual bias rarely contributes to a fingerprint error in a wrongful conviction. First, actual identification errors are rare. Research has established that trained and certified latent fingerprint examiners are highly reliable when making identifications (Ulery et al., 2011). More commonly, examiners vary in their decisions about the suitability of prints for comparison or default to an inconclusive finding when an identification was possible (Busey et al., 2021). These research results are supported by the experience of wrongful convictions. Examiners may make errors when they use prints that were unsuitable for forensic analysis. They may also fail to recognize and report exculpatory prints at the time of trial. At other times, examiners will report an exculpatory print that is discounted by investigators or the trial court. Because there are usually foreign prints at most crime scenes, the relevance of exculpatory prints may not be recognized or may be too easily explained away. This leads to an underutilization of latent print evidence and contributes to avoidable wrongful convictions.

Several cases demonstrate challenges related to suitability decisions. In a 2004 double murder case in Florida, defendant Clemente Aguirre-Jarquin was implicated by a latent palm print found on a knife found near the victims' home. A similar knife was missing from Aguirre-Jarquin's workplace. Aguirre-Jarquin had discovered the bodies, telling police that he was in the house looking for beer. Police found 67 bloody shoe impressions, 64 of which were consistent with Aguirre-Jarquin's shoes. His underwear, socks, T-shirt, and shorts also contained blood and DNA from one of the victims. He was convicted and sentenced to death. Postconviction, the latent print examiner's work on the case was questioned when it was discovered that the print on the knife was not suitable for comparison. In fact, examiner Donna Birks had relied on only seven points of comparison (Clemente Javier Aquirre-Jarquin v. State of Florida, 2008). A second examiner, Christina Barber with the Florida Department of Law Enforcement, found that Birks had used unsuitable prints in the Aguirre-Jarquin case and five others, including one other known incorrect identification. Barber concluded that four of the seven points of comparison used by Birks did not even align with features in Aguirre-Jarquin's print. Nonetheless, Aguirre-Jarquin's conviction was upheld after discovery of the error. Additional DNA analysis found that an alternate suspect—the daughter of one victim—left DNA in eight locations that were consistent with her being the assailant and that Aguirre-Jarquin's DNA could not be found on any evidence from the victims' home. The Florida Supreme Court then ordered a new trial, which was ended after a witness came forward with information that implicated the daughter as having the opportunity to commit the murders. Aguirre-Jarquin has not received an official exoneration but has filed for state compensation and a federal lawsuit for his wrongful conviction. The case remains unsolved.

At least two other cases involved the use of insufficient points of comparison. In the 2002 Lana Canen case in Elkhart, Indiana, examiner Dennis Chapman had been trained to compare ten-prints, not latent prints (Lana Canen v. Dennis Chapman, 2017). Chapman made a misidentification based on only seven points of comparison. The latent print was of sufficient quality to extract more features but the examiner did not do so. A defense examiner—who was also untrained and uncertified—agreed with Chapman's conclusion. Although the Level 1 configuration of the evidence and Canen's print were similar, the Level 2 features did not actually line up with each other. Canen was convicted of murder and sentenced to 55 years in prison. Postconviction, a new lawyer for Canen hired a certified latent print examiner, Kathleen Bright-Birnbaum, to conduct an independent examination. Bright-Birnbaum excluded Canen. The prosecutor then blocked a reexamination by the Indiana State Police, so the defense attorney filed for an evidentiary hearing. At this point, the prosecutor showed Bright-Birnbaum's analysis to Chapman, who then realized his mistake. At the evidentiary hearing, Chapman testified that he had made a misidentification and that he was influenced by the pressure of trying to help the police department solve the case. It appears that he was also aware of case information implicating Canen in the murder as a possible accomplice. Afterward, the Indiana State Police conducted their own reexamination and agreed that Canen should have been excluded. The Canen conviction was vacated. Her wrongful conviction lawsuit was dismissed without a settlement. Like the filings in the civil lawsuit, some observers have focused on Chapman and complained that he was not fired by the police department after the Canen wrongful conviction was discovered. Chapman was responsible for the misidentification and had exaggerated his credentials for latent print examination in court. That said, the case implicates much broader causative factors. First, the Elkhart police failed to train Chapman or get him certified. They did not establish minimal standards for latent print comparison. Police investigators clearly influenced Chapman to provide a positive identification to support a weak case against Canen. Chapman was put into an impossible situation that was partly his own doing but mostly the responsibility of the leadership in the Elkhart County Sheriff's Department. At some level, Chapman's analysis failed because he used too few points of comparison, was untrained, and was subject to confirmation bias. More fundamentally, the error was the result of organizational factors that devalued the importance of latent print comparison and the practice and professional standards that are required for reliable forensic analysis.

A similar case occurred in Monroe County, New York, in the 1997 conviction of Douglas Warney for murder. Three latent prints were found on pornographic videotape boxes at the crime scene, two of which were linked to the victim. The third was unidentified, but examiner Robert Garland concluded that Warney was "a possible source of the print" (Warney v. Monroe County, 2009). Garland found three points of comparison that appeared to align with Warney's reference print. The association of the print at any level with Warney was mistaken. In 1979, the International Association for Identification (IAI) had passed a resolution making it professional misconduct for any latent print examiner to provide courtroom testimony that labeled an identification "possible, probable, or likely," rather than "certain." Postconviction, DNA testing excluded Warney as the murderer and identified alternate suspect Eldred Johnson. As it happens, Johnson was in the state fingerprint database and might have been identified in the original investigation if a fingerprint database search had been attempted. It should be noted that this is speculative because latent print searching has improved substantially since 1997, so there is no guarantee that Johnson would have been identified at that time. In any case, a postconviction reanalysis of the latent print by Ron Smith & Associates found that Warney should have been excluded based on an "absence of feature correlation." In other words, the latent print didn't match Warney. Also, serological analysis at the time of trial was exculpatory. Many blood stains were subjected to serological analysis. Many matched the victim, none matched Warney, and several came from an unknown source—presumably Eldred Johnson. The case does implicate confirmation bias, but the issue was much broader than the forensic examiners. The investigators and prosecutors had identified Warney as a suspect after Warney had called to provide a tip about the case. Warney had an IQ of 68 and wound up making a false confession. The exculpatory print and serology evidence was then discounted or molded to fit the prosecution theory of the case. Their tunnel vision prevented a more thorough investigation that could have identified the actual perpetrator and exculpated Warney well before the case went to trial. Investigative tunnel vision is a common—almost universal—feature of wrongful convictions. It can even extend to the discounting of exculpatory forensic evidence, such as observed in the Warney case. Warney received over $4 million from state compensation and a civil suit settlement.

It is highly unusual for a latent print examiner to report a class-level association as occurred in the Warney case, but it does happen. The untrained examiner in the Glenn Ford wrongful conviction said that 35% of the population would share the Level 1 whorl pattern shared by Ford and the source of an evidence print. The crime occurred in 1983. The trial was delayed until 1994, so the entire case postdated the IAI policy on class-level associations. Ford's murder conviction was later overturned, although he was not exonerated as actually innocent because of evidence pointing to his involvement in an associated armed robbery.

ADVERSARIAL DEFICIT

In many wrongful convictions, defendants did not have access to trained and certified defense experts to counter inculpatory friction ridge evidence. Research indicates that juries place great weight on latent prints and may only question its value if another expert provides a countervailing conclusion (Rairden et al., 2018). Two cases demonstrate the value and limitations of defense expert testimony. The 1996 conviction of Beniah Dandridge for murder was based in part on a latent print identification. Bloody fingerprints at the scene were matched to Dandridge by examiner Carol Curlee. As it happens, the latent actually belonged to Dandridge's son (Double Loop Podcast, 2021). The two men shared many Level 1 and Level 2 characteristics, making the comparison difficult. Curlee had hurried her analysis and relied on too few points of comparison to make her conclusion. The defense hired a retired FBI examiner, Mervin Smith, who testified that the prints were not made by Dandridge. The prosecutor made inflammatory statements about the expert, calling him a "prostitute" for the defense. Dandridge was convicted and sentenced to life in prison. The fingerprint misidentification was confirmed two decades later, and a reanalysis by the Alabama Bureau of Investigation agreed that the prints were actually left by Dandridge's son. Dandridge was then exonerated. He died in a traffic accident two years after his release (Possley, 2015).

The Richard Jackson case implicates a broader set of concerns with regard to the use of latent print evidence (Jackson v. Paparo, 2002). Three prosecution examiners produced erroneous identifications. In a situation reminiscent of the Mayfield case, the two concurring examiners were aware of the conclusion of the first examiner and may have been unduly influenced by that information. Only one of the three examiners was certified, but they were all trained and experienced latent print examiners. Two defense examiners—both retired FBI agents—testified that the prints were exclusions. After Jackson was convicted, the misidentifications were brought to the attention of the IAI, which convened a panel of seven fingerprint experts to review the prints. They agreed that Jackson should have been excluded. An FBI review made the same conclusion, and Jackson was exonerated. An appeals court in the ensuing civil lawsuit found that the misidentifications were honest mistakes, not fraudulent. Clearly, the examiners should have made an exclusion, but the difficult comparison was outside the scope of their expertise. Fortunately, Jackson had access to defense experts who could challenge the work of the prosecution examiners.

The case demonstrates three key ideas. First, there is a difference between the reliability of latent print examination in principle and the reliability of latent print examination as applied. Errors can and do occur, especially with difficult comparisons. It had taken Anthony Paparo, the first examiner, two days of examination to find 11 points of similarity between the bloody evidence prints and Jackson's exemplar. It is likely that Paparo was subject to target bias and was searching for features from Jackson's prints in the evidence to justify a match conclusion. Second, the case demonstrates the value of blind verification. The two other prosecution experts were influenced by Paparo's initial conclusion. If they had made a truly independent analysis, it is much less likely that they would have concurred with his error. Finally, trial disagreements about latent print comparisons are very rare. The disagreement in the Jackson case should have been a "red flag" that motivated a reconsideration of the prints and a blind review or an independent technical review. In many wrongful convictions, such a review would have revealed substantial failures to follow best practices or document feature comparisons. Given that many poorly trained and uncertified examiners have been responsible for errors, a thorough technical review could have prevented some wrongful convictions.

FRAUDULENT FRICTION RIDGE COMPARISONS

The perceived value of latent prints can also lead to fraudulent misrepresentations and evidence planting. The most notorious case was a scandal involving the New York State Police in the 1980s and 1990s that involved three known wrongful convictions (Roth, 1997). In the Shirley Kinge case, uncertified examiner David Harding and his colleague Robert Lishansky planted prints on gasoline cans. Kinge's prints were collected from a glass after a meeting with her at a restaurant and then planted on a gasoline can from the crime scene. In addition, the victim's prints were planted on a gasoline can from Kinge's home. Harding and Lishansky shared the "glory" by each taking credit for one of the print comparisons. The lead investigator David McElligott and prosecutor on the case were aware that there may have been issues with the authenticity of the prints. Two experienced latent print examiners from another state police unit were at the original crime scene but were not used. One of them, Linus Rautenstrauch, refused to testify on the case due to his belief that Harding and Lishasky were incompetent. He pointed out poor documentation, poor evidence preservation, and professional deficiencies. His concerns were dismissed as "arrogant" by McElligott. After the misconduct came to light, a governor's investigating commission supported Rautenstrauch's claims, including failure to photograph the prints, enter them into evidence, or preserve the evidence. Harding kept prints at his personal residence and wiped the gasoline can clean after his examination. The issue might never have come to light except that Harding bragged about planting evidence and committing perjury during a job interview with the US Central Intelligence Agency. The NYSP scandal is covered in more detail in Chapter 12 on organizational dysfunction.

Other examiners have falsified or suppressed evidence. Examiner James Bakken falsified prints using a photocopy machine in the 1968 wrongful conviction of William DePalma. As in the NYSP scandal, Bakken was partly motivated by the prestige of solving cases. He had received an Award of Merit from the local American Legion for his portable crime laboratory for the back of a police vehicle. Like Rautenstrauch in the NYSP scandal, Bakken's colleague, David Nelson, was aware of Bakken's practice of falsifying evidence and tried to blow the whistle on him. Also like Rautenstrauch, Nelson's concerns were dismissed. He quit the department and moved out of state. Later, an Aerospace Corporation analysis demonstrated that the evidence prints used by Bakken contained elements associated with printer toner, including titanium, aluminum, and iron.

BOSTON POLICE DEPARTMENT

One of the most noted misidentifications started as an honest mistake and escalated to evidence suppression. Stephan Cowans was implicated in the shooting of a police officer in Boston, Massachusetts in 1997. Two Boston Police Department (BPD) examiners, Dennis LeBlanc and Rosemary McLaughlin, linked a thumbprint to Cowans. The examiners had not been properly trained and did not follow the standards of the discipline (Smith, 2004). Two defense examiners confirmed the match. But the match was actually in error. LeBlanc appeared to shortcut procedures after he learned that Cowans was a primary suspect in the murder investigation. McLaughlin's review was cursory at best. A post-conviction review revealed that LeBlanc discovered his mistake and concealed it all the way through the trial. It also revealed long-standing deficiencies in the BPD latent print unit, which had become a "dumping ground" for incompetent officers (Cole, 2006). LeBlanc was largely blamed for the misidentification and certainly shared some culpability in the matter. His defense was based on the management of the latent print unit by BPD. He said, "The system failed me. And the system failed Cowans." BPD proficiency tests support LeBlanc's claim. Six BPD examiners scored between 47% and 65% on a written knowledge assessment. Examiners produced false positives and false negatives on both the "easy" Level I and the harder Level II comparisons in proficiency testing (Cole, 2006). The unit was reorganized and achieved accreditation in 2009. Cowans was exonerated and received $3.7 million from compensation and a civil lawsuit settlement. He was murdered in his home in 2007.

In the wake of the Cowans case, BPD was involved in two other cases that relied on the use of simultaneous impressions, which occurs when two or more friction ridge impressions are deposited on a surface at the same time. For example, the examiner uses points of comparison from more than one finger to support a source conclusion (Scientific Working Group on Friction Ridge Analysis, Study and Technology, 2008). The Boston case related to the 1993 murder of an off-duty police officer, John Mulligan. Examiner Robert Foilb used simultaneous impressions to identify Terry Patterson. Another suspect, Sean Ellis, was identified by an eyewitness. Patterson gave a partial confession and was sentenced to life in prison. Ellis was only convicted after the Patterson match was introduced in his third trial. Patterson's conviction was eventually vacated on the basis of inadequate defense. A 2005 appeal decision in the Patterson case included an extended consideration of the scientific validity of simultaneous impressions (Commonwealth v. Patterson, 2005). The court held that simultaneous impression analysis was not the same technique as ACE-V friction ridge comparison of individual fingers and was not generally accepted by the fingerprint examiner community. Patterson then pled guilty to manslaughter and was released for time served. Later, it was revealed that Mulligan had been deeply involved in police corruption and may have been killed by a corrections officer who was upset that Mulligan was sexually harassing his daughter. The Ellis conviction was vacated largely on the basis of that new evidence. There is now a standard for the analysis of simultaneous impressions by latent print examiners (Friction Ridge Subcommittee of the Organization of Scientific Area Committees, 2013).

RELEVANCE TO POLICE INVESTIGATION

Almost all friction ridge misidentifications have been committed by examiners who lacked training and certification. In agencies that apply reforms related to target bias and blind verification, certified examiners applying the standards of the discipline should be considered highly reliable. This claim is supported by extensive research (Ulery et al., 2011). Contexual bias may impact some friction ridge examinations. More importantly, wrongful convictions may occur when latent prints are underutilized by police departments who discount or ignore exculpatory prints. As seen in the Douglas Warney case, latent prints may exculpate an innocent suspect.

There are other examples in wrongful convictions. Michael Seri was misidentified by latent palm prints on library books by an examiner who said he "couldn't rule out the possibility" that Seri was the source of the prints (Martineau, 2003). The examiner explained that police hadn't taken enough of his handprint for comparison. Postconviction, an alternate suspect was matched to the prints and Seri exonerated, but the actual perpetrator could have been found using AFIS or a more thorough investigation before Seri's conviction.

In recent years, the capabilities of automated latent fingerprint databases have improved significantly, enabling more "cold hits" of the type that DNA has produced for many years. The value of these cold hits may not be immediately recognized. Donald Nash was convicted of the murder of his girlfriend in 2009 *after* two alternate suspects had been identified by AFIS searches of prints from the victim's car (Nash v. State, 2016). The first alternate suspect, Anthony Feldman, had a long criminal record consistent with the circumstantial evidence around the murder. Police investigators discounted the presence of Feldman's prints even though he had no connection to the victim that could have explained the presence of his prints. The prints of Alfred Heyer were also found on victim's car. He admitted that he may have "gone and looked inside" an abandoned car at the time but refused to provide a DNA sample for testing without a court order. When the issue was raised to prosecutor Jessica Sparks, she said it was too late because she had already charged Nash with the murder. The trial judge did not permit testimony about alternate suspects. The judge did permit testimony from DNA examiner Ruth Montgomery that Nash's DNA wasn't present in the biological material found under the victim's fingernails. Montgomery speculated that the victim had washed her hair before the murder and removed Nash's DNA in the process. Nash's conviction was overturned in part on the basis of the invalid Montgomery testimony. A new prosecutor dismissed the charges citing reasonable doubt about Nash's guilt. He has filed a federal lawsuit regarding his wrongful conviction.

Some wrongful convictions arise from interpretation errors, not misidentifications. The 1987 conviction of Steven Chaney for a double homicide was based in part on the presence of his left thumbprint on the wall of the victim's apartment (Ex parte Steven Mark Chaney, Applicant, 2018). Chaney claimed that he had known the victims and had visited their home but was not present at the time of the murders. Investigator James Vineyard said the print had been left recently and was indicative of Chaney squatting or kneeling near the victims. Vineyard's testimony was speculative at best. He could not determine the age of the print because no scientific research has successfully validated any method to do so. The print supported an invalid bite mark identification, as detailed in that chapter.

SHIRLEY MCKIE

Shirley McKie served as a police detective in Scotland in the late 1990s (Campbell, 2011). In 1997, her thumbprint was found on the bathroom door frame at a murder scene. Examiners used 16 points of comparison to associate McKie with the latent print, as seen in Figure 7.3. Suspect David Asbury's prints were also found at the scene, and he was convicted after McKie testified that she had not been inside the home. She was later charged but acquitted of perjury, based on the idea that fingerprint examiners cannot make mistakes. Two American examiners testified that the print did not belong to McKie, but no United Kingdom examiner was willing to do so. A 2011 government inquiry determined that the identification was in fact an error and found another misidentification in the same case. They made 86 recommendations to improve the practice and interpretation of latent print examination.

The McKie case had several challenging aspects. She was ostracized by her colleagues and even her father gave her "a hard time." Police leaders showed systemic bias against McKie and failed to recognize the possibility that an error had been made. Other examiners were clearly pressured to align with their colleagues against McKie. Behind the scenes, examiners had highlighted the complexity of the mark and the possible inconsistencies in the comparison. McKie was consistent in maintaining that she could not have made the mark, but the authorities displayed deep tunnel vision in discounting her statements. Most troubling were the years between her acquittal for perjury and the appointment of the fingerprint inquiry in 2008. Government authorities clearly felt McKie was lying and had little interest in resolving the issue in a transparent way. Eventually, the latent print examiners who made the identification were suspended, transferred, or forcibly

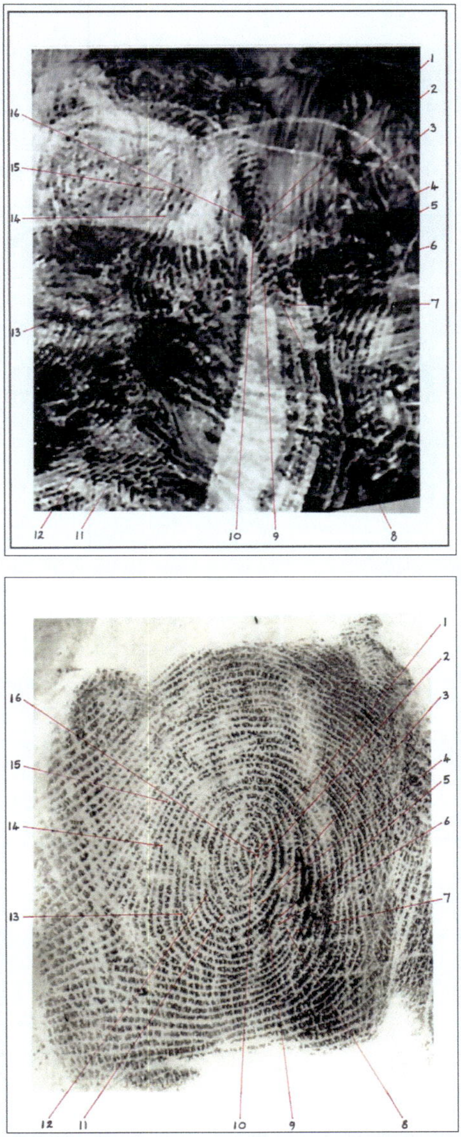

FIGURE 7.3 McKie fingerprint inquiry. The latent (left) and McKie reference print, as published in the Fingerprint Inquiry Report. Note that the 16 points of comparison are indicated. Source: The Fingerprint Inquiry Report (Campbell, 2011).

retired. That was clearly inappropriate as well. At least two of the examiners were convinced that they were right (perhaps to this day) and had made an honest mistake. The primary errors in the case had little to do with the examiners and a great deal to do with the attitudes of police officials and the policies and procedures for latent print examination. In some respects, it was easier to blame the examiners than the authorities. It was easier to say they were fraudulent or incompetent than it would be to acknowledge that errors are inevitable. It was easier to blame McKie or the examiners and label them as "bad apples" than to do the hard work of root cause analysis and organizational improvement. Eventually, the 2011 inquiry report did accomplish those goals, but only after the passage of time and substantial quantities of venality and personal suffering.

BRIAN ROSE

In some cases, valid latent print identifications have been rejected by a court. In 2006, Brian Rose was arrested for attempted carjacking and murder in Baltimore County, Maryland after a police chase (United States v. Rose, 2009). Two latent prints were recovered from the vehicle and were matched to Rose. A Baltimore County judge ruled that fingerprint identification testimony was unreliable, making the case difficult to try in state court. A federal indictment was then brought in 2008, leading to his conviction. The federal district court reviewed the reliability of latent prints in case law and the Rose case and found

> [F]ingerprint identification evidence based on the ACE-V methodology is generally accepted in the relevant scientific community, has a very low incidence of erroneous misidentifications, and is sufficiently reliable to be admissible under Fed. R. Ev. 702 generally and specifically in this case.
>
> (United States v. Rose, 2009)

The Rose case is notable on several counts. It has been cited as a basis for the unreliability of latent prints (Cooley & Oberfield, 2007). This claim is not sustainable because the Rose prints were supported by witnesses of the police pursuit and its aftermath and by DNA testing. The defense also claimed that the Mayfield misidentification and subsequent human factors research undermine the reliability of latent print evidence (Dror & Charlton, Why Experts Make Errors, 2006). The federal court recognized that fingerprint identification must have a non-zero-error rate.

Also, the court recognized the importance of independent verification and the value of giving the defendant an opportunity to have an independent expert examine the prints. These considerations do not form a basis to assume that friction ridge identification is unreliable. They do support the idea that friction ridge identification is unreliable in the absence of training, competency testing, practice standards, and organizational support. The experience of wrongful convictions is in accord with the ruling of the federal court accepting the reliability of friction ridge identification when properly applied.

CONTRAST WITH BITE MARK COMPARISON

Bite mark and fingerprint comparison are both limited by the distortions and limitations of the impressions collected from evidence. Nonetheless, the experience of wrongful convictions has been radically different in the two disciplines. The limitations of human skin as a registration medium for bite mark impressions have led to misidentifications by the leading experts in the field, many of whom have been associated with wrongful convictions. In contrast, there are no wrongful convictions associated with leading figures in the friction ridge community, such as leaders of the IAI or participants in standards working groups. Almost all misidentifications have been committed by untrained individuals from organizations with poor oversight of their latent print units.

There are several reasons for the differences between the disciplines. Latent friction ridge prints are often available at crime scenes. Latent prints can be developed and visualized using well-established, scientific techniques. Also, examiners are trained to reject latent prints of poor quality. They make suitability decisions that govern how a print may be used, such as whether the print is suitable for AFIS searches or for comparison. The friction ridge community has developed a set of training, practice, and interpretation standards that—when applied—lead to extremely reliable identification conclusions.

This experience suggests that the friction ridge community should focus reform efforts on improvements in training, certification, quality assurance, context management, and governance. Further, continued research to improve the objectivity and reliability of latent print utility decisions may help to prevent the use of distorted or low-value prints. Finally, the community should consider the problem of the underutilization of exculpatory prints. This final issue relates to the inherent conservatism of examiners who make inconclusive findings when a positive association would be possible. It also relates to the tunnel vision of investigators who may discount exculpatory print evidence that contradicts the prevailing theory of a case. Police and prosecutors should recognize the importance of exculpatory forensic evidence and conduct appropriate follow-up investigation to ensure that alternative theories are fully considered.

STUDY QUESTIONS

1. The OSAC Friction Ridge Subcommittee has developed a detailed process map for friction ridge examination. It covers Administrative Assessment, Technical Assessment, Latent Analysis, Known Analysis, Comparison/Evaluation, and Reporting/Verification (OSAC Friction Ridge Subcommittee, 2019). A web link can be found in the References section below. Consider the first element, Case Screening, which includes:

    - Approval received?
    - Analysis timeframe appropriate?
    - Technically feasible?
    - Sufficient quality?
    - Sufficient quantity?
    - Knowns collected properly?
    - Analysis requested appropriate?
    - Resources available to address bias?
    - Forensic Service Provider agency-specific requirements

    These questions relate to issues that are observed in wrongful convictions. Pick any task from Case Screening (or one of the other elements of the process map) and consider the possible errors that may arise in that step. Could that error lead to a wrongful conviction? How could the organization mitigate the risk of error?
2. Ed German quotes a Japanese proverb that says, "Even monkeys fall from trees." In other words, even the best experts can make mistakes or become too prideful. On his website, German discusses "Problem Idents" in real cases (see https://onin.com/fp/problemidents.html). He provides several examples of difficult comparisons that resulted in identification errors. Some examples relate to wrongful convictions discussed in this chapter. Consider his review of the prints from the Lana Canen case. Can you distinguish the latent print from Canen's inked print? Is there sufficient detail to support a match? How would an organization prevent errors related to close nonmatches?
3. Many latent print units are organized as part of a law enforcement agency, not an independent crime laboratory. Can this

produce biases among latent print examiners? Do some wrongful conviction errors reflect a close relationship between police and latent print units? Will police be more or less likely to rely on latent print examinations from internal units? Discuss some organizational strategies that would improve the effectiveness and reliability of latent print identification.

FURTHER READING

Friction ridge identification has been the subject of substantial criticism and research since the Madrid bombing case. Simon Cole has written extensively on the history of the field and the issues related to the "zero error rate" problem (Cole, 2005). The President's Council on Applied Science and Technology issued a critical report calling for black-box studies of latent print identification and other pattern-evidence disciplines (PCAST Working Group, 2016). Itiel Dror has done extensive research on cognitive bias (Dror, 2020). Thomas Busey and other researchers have examined the cognitive abilities and processes used by latent print examiners (Busey et al., 2021).

The DOJ Office of Inspector General report on the Madrid bombing remains relevant to current practice (Office of the Inspector General, 2006). Robert Stacey's paper is much shorter and addresses particular issues in the examination process that the field is still grappling with (Stacey, 2004). The final report of the McKie investigation is both exhaustive and informative (Campbell, 2011).

The field of fingerprint identification has a long history. As noted, the www.onin.com website covers that history and is updated regularly on current issues. The Double Loop podcast is used by many examiners to stay abreast of current developments in research, practice, and law (available at www.doublelooppodcast.com). The Fingerprint Sourcebook collects the fundamental aspects of friction ridge identification as a field (National Institute of Justice, 2011). As always, the Organization of Scientific Area Committees is a useful resource on particular topics and standards (OSAC Friction Ridge Subcommittee, 2019).

REFERENCES

Busey, T. A., Heise, N., Hicklin, R. A., Ulery, B. T., & Buscaglia, J. (2021). Characterizing Missed Identifications and Errors in Latent Fingerprint Comparisons Using Eye-tracking Data. *PloS One*, *16*(5), e0251674.

Campbell, A. (2011). *The Fingerprint Inquiry Report*. Edinborough: APS Group Scotland.

Clemente Javier Aquirre Jarquin v. State of Florida, SC06-1550 (Supreme Court of Florida February 7, 2008).

Cole, S. A. (2005). More Than Zero: Accounting for Error in Latent Print Identification. *Journal of Criminal Law and Criminology*, *95*, 985–1078.

Cole, S. A. (2006). The Prevalence and Potential Causes of Wrongful Conviction by Fingerprint Evidence. *Golden Gate University Law Review*, *37*, 39.

Commonwealth v. Patterson, SJC-09478 (Supreme Judicial Court of Massachusetts December 27, 2005).

Cooley, C. M., & Oberfield, G. S. (2007). Increasing Forensic Evidence's Reliability and Minimizing Wrongful Convictions: Applying Daubert Isn't the Only Problem. *Tulsa Law Review*, *43*(2), 285–380.

Double Loop Podcast. (2021, April). *Double Loop Podcast Compares Fingerprints*. http://doublelooppodcast.com/.

Dror, I.E. (2018). Biases in Forensic Experts. *Science*, *360*(6386), 243.

Dror, I. E. (2020). Cognitive and Human Factors in Expert Decision Making: Six Fallacies and the Eight Sources of Bias. *Analytical Chemistry*, *92*(12), 7998–8004.

Dror, I.E., & Charlton, D. (2006). Why Experts Make Errors. *Journal of Forensic Identification*, *56*(4), 600–616.

Ex parte Steven Mark Chaney, Applicant, WR-84,091-01 (Court of Criminal Appeals of Texas December 19, 2018).

Federal Bureau of Identification. (2021). *NGI Fact Sheet*. Retrieved from https://www.fbi.gov/file-repository/ngi-monthly-fact-sheet/view

Friction Ridge Subcommittee of the Organization of Scientific Area Committees. (2013). *Guideline for the Articulation of the Decision-Making Process Leading to an Expert Opinion of Source Identification in Friction Ridge Examinations*. National Institute of Standards and Technology.

German, E. (2022). *Latent Print Examination*. Retrieved from Onin .com: https://onin.com/fp/index.htm

Jackson v. Paparo, 00-3413 (United States District Court for the Eastern District of Pennsylvania October 25, 2002).

Jain, A., Prabhakar, S., & Pankanti, S. (2002). On the Similarity of Identical Twin Fingerprints. *Pattern Recognition*, *35*, 2653–2663.

Lana Canen v. Dennis Chapman, 16-1621 (United States Court of Appeals, Seventh Circuit January 27, 2017).

Martineau, K. (2003, July 22). He Paid for Police Mistake. *Hartford Courant*, 75.

McRoberts, A. (2010). *The Fingerprint Sourcebook*. Washington, DC: National Institute of Justice.

Nash v. State, 504 S. W. 3d 831 (Missouri Court of Appeals 2016).

National Institute of Justice. (2011). *The Fingerprint Sourcebook*. Washington, DC: National Criminal Justice Reference Service. Retrieved from https://www.ncjrs.gov/pdffiles1/nij/225320.pdf

Neumann, C., & Saunders, C. P. (2019). *Foundational Research Into the Quantification of the Value of Forensic Evidence for Complex Evidential Forms Arising from Impression and Pattern Evidence: Final Summary Overview Report*. National Institute of Justice.

Office of the Inspector General. (2006). *Review of the FBI's Handling of the Brandon Mayfield Case*. Washington, DC: Office of the Inspector General, Oversight and Review Division, US Department of Justice.

OSAC Friction Ridge Subcommittee. (2019). *Friction Ridge Process Map (Current Practice)*. National Institute of Standards and Technology. Retrieved from https://www.nist.gov/document/friction-ridge-process-map-december-2019

PCAST Working Group. (2016). *Report to the President: Forensic Science in Criminal Courts, Ensuring Scientific Validity of Feature Comparison Methods*. Washington, DC: President's Council of Advisors on Science and Technology.

Possley, M. (2015, 10, 12). *Beniah Alton Dandridge*. Retrieved from National Registry of Exonerations: https://www.law.umich.edu/special/exoneration/Pages/casedetail.aspx?caseid=4768

Rairden, A., Garrett, B., Kelley, S., Murrie, D., & Castillo, A. (2018). Resolving Latent Conflict: What Happens When Latent Print Examiners Enter the Cage? *Forensic Science International*, *289*, 215–222.

Roth, N. (1997). *The New York State Police Evidence Tampering Investigation Report to the Honorable George Pataki*. Ithaca.

Scientific Working Group on Friction Ridge Analysis, Study and Technology. (2008). *Standard for Simultaneous Impression Examination*. http://clpex.com/swgfast/.

Smith, R. (2004). *Request for Latent Print Consultation Services*. Meridian: Ron Smith & Associates.

Stacey, R. A. (2004). A Report on the Erroneous Fingerprint Individualization in the Madrid Train Bombing Case. *Journal of Forensic Identification*, *706*, https://archives.fbi.gov/archives/about-us/lab/forensic-science-communications/fsc/jan2005/special_report/2005_special_report.htm.

State ex rel. Schmitt v. Green, WD83688 (Court of Appeals of Missouri, Western District, Writ Division April 28, 2020).

Ulery, B. T., Hicklin, R. A., Buscaglia, J., & Roberts, M. A. (2011). Accuracy and Reliability of Forensic Latent Fingerprint Decisions. *Proceedings of the National Academy of Sciences*, *108*(19), 7733–7738.

United States v. Rose, CCB-08-0149 (US District Court, D. Maryland December 8, 2009).

Warney v. Monroe County, 08–0947 (US Court of Appeals for the Second Circuit November 13, 2009).

CHAPTER 8

Firearms and Toolmarks

Firearms are commonly used in connection with crime. Forensic science can answer key questions to establish facts concerning the use of a firearm. What was the type of firearm used? What was the specific firearm that fired a bullet or discharged a cartridge casing? Who could have shot the firearm? What was the trajectory of a bullet at the crime scene or through a victim? These questions implicate multiple forensic disciplines. A firearm and toolmark examiner may characterize the marks made on bullets or casings during the firing of a weapon (Figure 8.1). A chemist may characterize the residue left behind by the firing of a round of ammunition. A crime scene reconstruction expert or forensic pathologist may determine the path of a bullet. Each determination has its own scientific and practical limitations. This chapter will examine the use of toolmark examination, especially as it relates to "ballistics," the association of a firearm with evidence based on impression evidence analysis of the toolmarks left by the firing action of a gun.

The potential value of ballistics has been recognized for a long time and led to the early adoption of techniques prior to the full development of scientific research and practice standards. As described previously (in Chapter 1, Context of Wrongful Convictions ...), the wrongful conviction of Charles Stielow and Nelson Green motivated key researchers to implement new technologies for firearms identification with a more rigorous foundation. First, Calvin Goddard and collaborators developed the comparison microscope, which permits side-by-side viewing of evidence and exemplar bullets and casings. Second, researchers examined the variability of weapons, manufacturing methods, and ammunition types to establish the types of markings that could be used to differentiate among possible sources of evidence. The markings on cartridge casings provide the most useful forensic information because the patterns tend to be reproducible from round to round and are not distorted by environmental conditions. Casings are easily collected at a crime scene and preserved for later analysis. In contrast, the markings of evidence bullets vary from round to round, especially in cheaply made firearms. Bullets are usually deformed when they strike bodies or other objects,

DOI: 10.4324/9781003202578-8

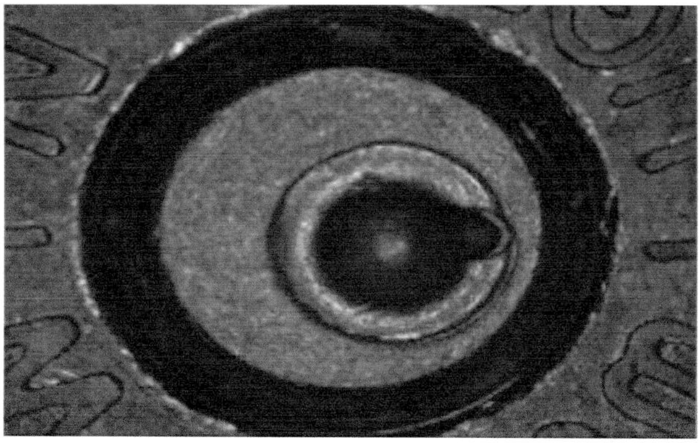

FIGURE 8.1 The image shows the breech face impression on a cartridge casing using two-dimensional reflectance microscopy with ring-light illumination. When a gun is fired, the breech face is imprinted on the back of the cartridge casing, making distinctive marks. The firing pin also makes an impression mark on the casing either at a rim or center position, depending on the design of the firearm. Source: National Institute of Standards and Technology (NIST).

creating distortions that can compromise the comparison process. Figure 8.2 shows a deformed bullet from the Kennedy assassination that was imaged using modern, three-dimensional scanning techniques (Press, 2019). The recovery of bullets from a victim or crime scene may be difficult. In recent years, manufacturing methods have made it more difficult to differentiate among consecutively manufactured barrels. Some models—such as Glock handguns—have always been challenging due to the geometry of their rifling. As a result of these limitations, firearms examiners may make a source identification conclusion even when there are toolmarks on an evidence bullet that aren't seen in an exemplar. They may rely on the number of consecutive matching striae (CMS), the scratches made by a barrel on a bullet, or other criteria to make that identification. As yet, there is an insufficient research basis to relate CMS and other criteria to the statistical characterization of a firearm association.

Toolmark examiners have the advantage that they examine variations in physical or mechanical phenomena, which are inherently more replicable than biological phenomena (like fingerprints or handwriting). This advantage has enabled the development of ballistics databases that have contributed many cold hits in firearms cases. Ballistics databases are dependent on the quality of images in the system and the strength of the searching algorithm, making interjurisdictional cold hits extremely difficult to obtain, even when limiting the search to only

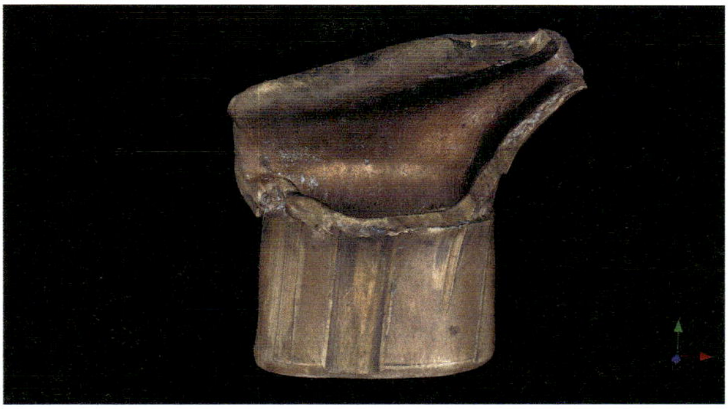

FIGURE 8.2 Kennedy assassination bullet image. The image shows a fragment of the bullet that fatally wounded President John F. Kennedy on November 22, 1963. The bullet morphology was captured using modern, three-dimensional scanning techniques. The bullet was significantly deformed, but the lands and grooves remain visible at the base for comparison to test fires. Source: National Institute of Standards and Technology (Press, 2019).

crime guns. Technological improvements promise to ameliorate this problem and extend the use of ballistics to a wider range of crimes (Morgan J. S., 2016).

THEORY OF IDENTIFICATION

There are few forensic disciplines that are as reliant on subjective interpretations and the discounting of nonmatching features as the firearms examiner comparing bullets. The Association of Firearm and Toolmark Examiners (AFTE) theory of identification allows examiners to conclude that evidence and exemplar toolmarks have a common origin "when the unique surface contours of two toolmarks are in sufficient agreement." (Scientific Working Group for Firearms and Toolmarks, 2017). The Department of Justice's Uniform Language for Testimony and Reports (ULTR) (US Department of Justice, 2020) clarified this issue. "A 'source identification' is not based upon a statistically derived or verified measurement or an actual comparison to all firearms or toolmarks in the world." Although the ULTR permits "source identification" testimony, it also states, "An examiner shall not assert that two toolmarks originated from the same source to the exclusion of all other sources."

Defense attorneys and other critics recognize that a defendant is severely disadvantaged when an examiner testifies that "the toolmarks were made by the same gun" instead of "the toolmarks are consistent with each other." Some have called for examiners to use the latter formulation because the discipline has not established its reliability sufficiently to justify individualization conclusions. Most notably, the President's Council of Advisors on Science and Technology (PCAST) has recommended that black-box studies be conducted (PCAST Working Group, 2016). A black-box study would measure the reliability of firearms examination as applied end-to-end. Technically, separate black-box studies would be required for a very wide range of firearm and ammunition types because the selectivity of firearms identification varies substantially based on class and subclass characteristics. For example, a black-box study on polygonally rifled firearms would not be relevant to other firearm types.

The problems of shot-to-shot variation and shared subclass characteristics provide a more difficult challenge to the examiner. For example, consecutively fired bullets from the same firearm usually have observable differences under the comparison microscope. It is also true that examiners cannot conclude that a particular bullet or cartridge case originated from a particular firearm to the exclusion of all other possible sources.

To account for the uncertainties in the examination process, ballistics examiners do not attempt to match a crime scene bullet or cartridge case to a particular firearm to the exclusion of all other firearms. First, it would be an impossible task because there is no database of all firearms and such a database is not feasible for a variety of policy and technical issues (Committee to Assess the Feasibility, 2008). Also, the examiner uses a comparison microscope to compare one closed set of a pair of items at a time, such as a crime scene cartridge case and a reference cartridge case from a test fire in the laboratory. The examiner can only perform a limited number of pairwise comparisons to reach a conclusion in a case. Due to these practical limitations, the examiner uses class and subclass characteristics to narrow the scope of possible comparisons to consider in a case. In very broad terms, class characteristics pertain to the model of firearm and subclass characteristics pertain to a set of firearms of a particular model that share common manufacturing history (such as consecutively manufactured barrels). In addition, the examiner uses whatever case information is available to limit the number of firearms that must be considered for comparison. For example, the set may be limited to firearms associated with the case, firearms of the same type that have been associated with linked crimes, or firearms of the same type that are found from a NIBIN database search of crime guns from the local jurisdiction. Most firearms examiners do not consciously pursue closed-set designs for their comparison work. Instead, closed-set design is a necessary result of the conditions under which they conduct their examination process.

The closed-set approach is necessitated by the practical and scientific considerations of firearms examination. Many observers have criticized forensic disciplines for this approach, which is starkly different from nuclear DNA analysis. In DNA examination, a biological sample is collected and fully characterized prior to comparison. It is possible to build population statistics that permit individualization of a sample against the entire human population. Because of the ability to perform such open-set analysis, DNA analysis lends itself to sophisticated statistical analysis and complete separation of the analyst from law enforcement investigation to limit confirmation bias. If firearms examiners were forced to compare an evidence bullet or cartridge case to the open set of all possible firearms in the world, the discipline would be impractical. If the examiner could never use case information to limit the closed set of possible comparison candidates, then many investigations would be abandoned because of cost and time limitations. At minimum, the examiner must be able to limit the comparison set through the consideration of class and subclass characteristics.

Because of the fundamental nature of firearms investigation, research has focused on issues that clarify the difficulties of closed-set analyses at the subclass level. For example, the landmark 1998 Brundage study considered ten consecutively manufactured rifled barrels from Ruger P85 pistols (Brundage, 1998; Brundage, 1998). The study has been extended and repeated in various forms (Hamby et al., 2009). The methodology is chosen to represent the most difficult problem faced by the firearms examiner. The 2009 paper states, "It would be expected that the greatest potential for similarity of striations would be encountered with firearm barrels that are consecutively rifled using the same rifling tool." The paper states its conclusion as follows:

> A long term internationally administered validity test using consecutively rifled barrels, a condition widely considered the most likely to produce errors, was completed by 507 different participants (502 examiners, 5 using instrumentation) and resulted in 7,597 correct identification conclusions and no false positive conclusions.

PCAST dismissed the Hamby paper and all others like it, comparing them to an elaborate Sudoku puzzle because of their closed-set design. Their reasoning went as follows:

> This "closed-set" design is simpler than the problem encountered in casework because the correct answer is always present in the collection. In such studies, examiners can perform perfectly if they simply match each bullet to the standard that is closest. By contrast, in an open-set study (as in casework), there is no guarantee that the correct

> source is present—and thus no guarantee that the closest match is correct. Closed-set comparisons would thus be expected to underestimate the false positive rate.
>
> (PCAST Working Group, 2016)

PCAST did not address the reasoning behind research designs that use consecutively manufactured barrels. PCAST recognized only one black-box study in ballistics examination that met its criteria for research validity, a study from the University of Iowa at Ames. The level of difficulty of comparisons in the Ames study may have been easier or more difficult than what is observed in casework. There are limited objective metrics by which to gauge the difficulty of firearms comparisons. In summary, there is insufficient research basis to make definitive determinations about the systemic reliability of firearms identification.

WRONGFUL CONVICTIONS

The experience of wrongful convictions may be valuable to provide insight into the general reliability of ballistics identification. Of course, it is impossible to determine the error rate of a discipline based on wrongful convictions because many errors may never be detected.

Mistaken firearms identifications rarely lead to known wrongful convictions in the modern era. Most known wrongful convictions arose in the early 20th century before the development of the comparison microscope. When misidentifications have occurred more recently, they are more often associated with insufficient training, poor evidence handling, or lack of adherence to standards.

Patrick Pursley was convicted of a murder in Winnebago County, Illinois in 1993 and acquitted in a retrial in 2019. The murder had taken place during a vehicle robbery (People v. Pursley, 2018). The victim was shot in the head twice. One bullet was recovered from the car dashboard and another at autopsy. Deformation had caused damage to the bullets but still permitted some level of comparison. Two shell casings were also recovered. A 9 mm Taurus pistol was found in Pursley's apartment. Illinois State Police (ISP) firearms examiner Daniel Gunnell made two test fires from the Taurus. He said the evidence bullets and test fires had been made by the same gun "to the exclusion of all others." He said the cartridges from the test fires and the shell casings in evidence were fired by the Taurus "to the exclusion of all others." On cross-examination, Gunnell revealed flaws in his methodology, including failure to make a firing pin comparison test on the cartridge casings and failure to take photographs of the evidence. Defense examiner Mark Boese did his own test fires and concluded that the evidence bullets had been fired by a

Taurus but did not feel he had sufficient correspondence of impression features to declare a match to the Pursley firearm specifically. Boese found three or four striations that were similar in the evidence bullets and test fires but also found several differences that he felt prevented a definitive conclusion. The ballistics comparison was the key evidence in the case, and Pursley was convicted and sentenced to life without parole.

In 2008 and 2009, the Northwestern University Center on Wrongful Convictions helped Pursley file for new ballistics testing, which was granted by the Illinois Appellate Court in 2011. ISP examiner Russell McLain performed new test fires and reexamined the evidence. He generally agreed with Gunnell's conclusions. In 2012, ISP examiner Beth Patty performed another reexamination. She agreed with Gunnell on the cartridge casings but reached an inconclusive determination on the bullets. Gunnell then reexamined the evidence and came to the same conclusion as Patty but attributed the difference to handling or degradation of the evidence. Pursley was then able to retain his own expert, John Murdock, an experienced examiner with research experience. Murdock had access to a microscope that could image details at a finer scale than any ISP equipment. While Gunnell's original examination had been performed at a magnification of 40X, Murdock used a magnification of 120X to find new feature details. Murdock excluded the Pursley weapon as the source of the evidence bullets and casings, though he clarified that his exclusion was only possible using higher magnification microscopy. A fifth examiner, Chris Coleman, performed a verification of Murdock's conclusions. Coleman knew that Murdock had performed the comparisons but was not aware of Murdock's results. Coleman agreed with Murdock's findings. Afterward, he performed an open, technical review of Murdock's notes and comparisons. At an evidentiary hearing, Gunnell stated that Murdock's observations supported an inconclusive finding, not an elimination. The conviction was overturned on the basis that Murdock's reanalysis constituted newly discovered evidence (People v. Pursley, 2018).

The six examiners in the Pursley case largely conformed to consensus standards, though Gunnell overstated the statistical weight of his conclusion at trial and made a significant error in his failure to examine the firing pin impressions in the casings. Murdock was able to access new microscope technology, which constituted "newly discovered evidence," although there is limited research to support Murdock's use of fine morphological details in his comparison. It is possible that he was observing a fine level of detail that is not as persistent as coarser morphological information. Degradation due to oxidation or handling may alter these features over time. Ongoing research should elucidate those issues.

The Pursley case also demonstrated significant variability among the examiners. Gunnell and Boese differed in their conclusions because of the inherent subjectivity of interpretation in firearms examiners. Both examiners observed nonmatching bullet features—which is common—but the two examiners placed different weight on the importance of the nonmatching striae. Subjectivity remains an issue in the field, although researchers are making progress on the development of mathematical frameworks for ballistics toolmark comparisons (Zheng, 2022).

ANTHONY HINTON

The 1986 Anthony Hinton case may have also implicated forensic examiner variability in ballistic examination, although practice failures were a more important issue (Hinton v. Alabama, 2014). Hinton was convicted and given a death sentence in connection with a series of murders and store robberies. Bullets were recovered from two murder victims and a third robbery scene. The victim at the third robbery survived and identified Hinton as his assailant, as did another witness. A .38 caliber revolver was recovered from the mattress of his mother, who lived with him. The Alabama Department of Forensic Sciences (ADFS) concluded that the revolver had fired all six bullets. The judge provided $1000 to Hinton to hire an independent expert, saying that "as far as I know" that was the limit under state law. In fact, the statute had been changed to permit any figure deemed reasonable by the judge. The defense expert was Andrew Payne, who was trained as a civil engineer, not ballistics expert. Payne received his degree in 1933, a half-century before the trial. His expertise related to military ordnance, not firearms and toolmark identification. Payne had only one eye so he could not properly use a comparison microscope as intended. Payne testified that the Hinton revolver was so corroded that it could not produce identifiable marks on bullets. The revolver had probably been used with chlorate primers, which were more common in the 1930s and 1940s but tended to deposit corrosive salts in gun barrels and obliterate the rifling associated with bullet toolmarks. Payne also said the bullets from the crime scenes did not match one another. Although Payne did an excellent job considering his lack of credentials, Hinton was convicted.

Postconviction, Hinton was able to hire John Dillon, a former FBI examiner, and two other experts. They agreed with Payne that the bullets could not be matched to the Hinton revolver. One evidence bullet was extruded, meaning it was produced from a severely out-of-time revolver. In other words, the chamber in the gun's cylinder was not aligned with the gun bore when it was shot. The Hinton revolver could not produce the extrusion observed in the evidence bullets even when it was deliberately manipulated by the postconviction examiners. The ADFS examiner, Lawden Yates, refused to cooperate with the new experts or show them the basis for his conclusion that the bullets matched the revolver. Another ADFS examiner, John Davidson, reexamined the evidence and agreed with Yates' conclusions. Eventually, the notes of the ADFS examiners were provided, showing that they had not followed proper procedures, did not record any land and groove information, and had noted many inconsistencies in the comparisons. Hinton's conviction was overturned based on inadequate defense, in particular the failure to retain a qualified expert. The prosecution dismissed the charges after the reexamination of the ballistics evidence.

The Hinton case suggests several possible problems. Clearly, the defense examiner was not qualified. Although Payne contributed useful insights, he was neither trained nor qualified to conduct a ballistic examination, especially one with the level of complexity presented. The judge should have provided additional resources to retain an appropriate expert in a capital murder case. Yates and Davidson may have been influenced by contextual information from the case. They may have concluded that Hinton had hidden the revolver in his mother's room to evade police recovery of the weapon. Even in Alabama in the 1980s, the revolver was an unusual weapon. Given that the crimes had been committed with a revolver—which is clearly the case given the extrusion observed in the evidence bullets—they may have "rushed to judgment" to make a match to the recovered weapon from Hinton's mother. The safest report would have said the comparison was inconclusive because of the condition of the revolver and bullets. They could have testified that the murder weapon was of a similar type to the Hinton revolver but could not be matched specifically. Instead, they chose to make a match conclusion to support a case that must have seemed a foregone conclusion at the time. In this case, forensic variability and contextual bias may have been implicated, but they were closely tied to work that did not conform to analysis and interpretation standards in firearm examination.

DETROIT POLICE DEPARTMENT

The most extreme failures in ballistic examination in the modern era involved the Detroit Police Department (DPD) Forensic Services

Laboratory (FSL). DPD was also implicated in egregious rape kit backlogs. The lab was closed in 2008 for multiple issues, including failures in ballistics comparison (Ricks v. Pauch, 2020; Anderson, 2018). The Michigan State Police (MSP) conducted an independent audit of 200 cases from the Detroit lab, of which 10% were found to have identification errors (Michigan State Police, 2008). Many problems were Class I failures, which include any type of misidentification. Additional information on the problems in Detroit are detailed in Chapter 12's treatment of organizational dysfunction.

Two wrongful convictions have been identified as a result of the DPD failures in firearms identification. Desmond Ricks was convicted of murder in 1992 and exonerated in 2017, receiving $1 million in compensation from the state of Michigan. It appears that test fires were substituted for evidence bullets at some point during the investigation of the case. Reviewing examiner David Townshend said that the evidence bullets he received were in pristine condition when provided to him in an unsealed envelope, but the original DPD examiner had noted that the evidence bullets were heavily damaged. Postconviction, an MSP analyst found that the evidence bullets were fired from a .38 caliber gun with a 5R twist, meaning the barrel produced five striations with a right-hand twist on the bullets. The seized handgun was a .38 caliber gun with a 6R twist, meaning that it did not match the evidence. Another examiner, David Balash, confirmed the 5R subclass designation on the evidence bullets and the exclusion. Balash testified that the match was "exceptionally unbelievable" and could only have been the result of gross incompetence or fraud. Given that it appears that manufactured evidence had been sent to Townshend, the case facts appear to demonstrate that the DPD lab's failure to conform to standards was at times elevated to include false and deliberate attempts to cover up possible misidentifications.

LEE HARVEY OSWALD AND JOSEPH BROWN

The ballistics examiner requires a deep understanding of firearms, their manufacturing history, and the variations that may arise in their use (Siegel, 1987). Although it would be ideal to avoid contextual information in ballistics examination, that is not always possible or advisable. This challenge may be demonstrated by two very different crimes, the 1963 assassination of President John Kennedy and the 1973 murder of Earlene Barksdale.

Lee Harvey Oswald carried a Smith & Wesson .38 Special revolver which he used to kill Dallas police officer J.D. Tippit 45 minutes after the Kennedy assassination, as seen in Figure 8.3 (Testimony of Courtland Cunningham and Joseph D. Nicol, 1964). The gun had a long history and was not always a .38 Special. It was originally a .38-200 British

FIGURE 8.3 Oswald used this .38 caliber handgun to shoot a Dallas police officer and was found with five rounds of .38 Special ammunition when arrested. The gun was originally a .38 Regular handgun, which would have accepted a tapered round that was 1.24" long. It had been modified to accept .38 Special ammunition, which is about 1.55" long. Source: Records of the President's Commission on the Assassination of President Kennedy, National Archives.

service revolver, originally manufactured in the United States. The .38 "regular" was common in the early 20th century but had fallen into disuse after the introduction of .38 Specials. The .38 Regular ammunition is shorter and wider at the base than .38 Special ammunition, so .38 Regular firearms would be modified to take the more widely available .38 Special ammunition. This is exactly what had happened to the Oswald weapon. Oswald shot Tippit with a mix of Remington-Peters and Winchester-Western rounds. The modified gun did not leave reproducible marks on the bullets recovered at Tippit's autopsy, but cartridge cases at the scene of the shooting were matched to the Oswald weapon. The lead FBI ballistics examiner on the case, Courtland Cunningham, explained these details to the Warren Commission when they investigated the circumstances of the Kennedy assassination.

A decade later, Cunningham was brought in to review the ballistics evidence from the Barksdale murder. The bullets recovered from the victim were .38 Specials. Joseph Brown became a suspect in the Barksdale case when he turned himself in for a hotel robbery that occurred the day after the Barksdale murder. Brown had used a .38 caliber Smith & Wesson handgun in the hotel robbery. Cunningham examined the autopsy bullets but did not exclude the possibility that Brown's weapon might have fired the rounds. Although the victim was shot with .38 Special ammunition, it was possible—even likely—that Brown's weapon had been modified like many other .38 Regulars to accommodate .38 Special ammunition. Cunningham said he would need to inspect the Brown weapon and issued an inconclusive report (Joseph Green Brown, Petitioner appellant, v. Louie L. Wainwright, Secretary Florida Department of Corrections, 1986). Many media and other accounts of the case have mistakenly asserted that the examination was a clear exclusion, which it was not (Siegel, 1987). The gun should have been inspected so that a definitive conclusion could have been attempted, but that never happened. The prosecution listed Cunningham on the witness list for the trial. The defense expected to cross-examine Cunningham and have him attempt to chamber a .38 Special round in the gun, believing that it would be impossible to do so in a .38 Regular revolver. At the last minute, the prosecution withdrew Cunningham from the witness list. The defense attorney frantically contacted Cunningham, who was fishing on a boat in the ocean. The judge did not grant a continuance to allow Cunningham to testify for the defense, which was forced to rely on the inconclusive, written report. The prosecutor took full advantage of the uncertainty in his closing, saying, "They say it's a .38-caliber pistol, .38-caliber bullet. We have a .38-caliber pistol." (Siegel, 1987).

Due to his involvement in the Kennedy assassination, Cunningham was the recognized world expert on the ballistics of .38 Special and .38 Regular revolvers. The case background shows that he was aware of the context of the weapon. That information would have influenced him to consider the possibility that the weapon had been modified. In that sense, the contextual information should have helped to produce a more reliable result. He should have insisted on a personal inspection of the weapon prior to issuing his report. He did not do so. He also should have been available for the trial and addressed the revolver modification issue directly. The defense attorney should have subpoenaed Cunningham. The judge should have allowed a continuance. And, most clearly, the prosecutor should not have deliberately mischaracterized the evidence and undermined the ability of the court to resolve the ballistics definitively. Brown was convicted and sentenced to death. His accomplice in the hotel robbery recanted his testimony against Brown postconviction. On that basis, the conviction was vacated. Prosecutors dropped the charges. In 2013, Brown was convicted of murdering his wife.

COMPOSITIONAL BULLET LEAD ANALYSIS

Compositional bullet lead analysis (CBLA) has also been used to identify the provenance of bullets recovered from crime scenes. The chemical composition of bullets, cartridge casings, primer, and powder will vary depending on the source materials and processes used in their manufacture. For bullets, the FBI developed an analytical methodology that used inductively coupled-plasma (ICP) optical emission spectroscopy (OES) to characterize levels of arsenic, antimony, tin, copper, bismuth, silver, and cadmium in evidence bullets. They developed a statistical methodology called "chaining" that determined the statistical standard deviation of evidence bullets and potential sources. If the compositional range of crime scene bullets and bullet fragments fell within a range consistent with a suspect's bullets, the two sources were stated to be "analytically indistinguishable." ICP-OES is a valid method for chemical analysis that has been used to produce valid work in a wide variety of fields. The FBI methodology produced reliable compositional profiles of bullets. Unfortunately, there was only limited data on the variability of bullet composition among sources, so the interpretation framework was speculative at best. In 2004, the National Research Council (NRC) reviewed CBLA and concluded, "Variations among and within lead bullet manufacturers make any modeling of the general manufacturing process unreliable and potentially misleading in [CBLA] comparisons" (National Research Council, 2004). The report did not state that CBLA was completely invalid, especially given the reliability of ICP-OES, but it did note that CBLA could not be used to connect the composition of a bullet to a specific source of ammunition. The FBI abandoned CBLA shortly after the NRC report was released.

The weakness of CBLA was known to the FBI as early as 1991, when Special Agent Ernest Peele issued a memorandum detailing its limitations. Several years later, Peele would provide testimony against Jason Krause in a murder trial in Arizona (State v. Krause, 2015). The case arose after an incident in which four young people were four-wheeling on back roads. The driver was purposefully causing the vehicle to backfire. As the jeep passed Krause's home, the driver was shot, lost control of the vehicle, and crashed it into a parked truck. He had been killed by a gunshot wound to the head. Two .22 caliber bullets were recovered from the jeep. Peele—following the well-established FBI methodology—testified that the bullets from the jeep and the bullet that killed the driver were "analytically indistinguishable" from ammunition owned by Krause. Krause was convicted of manslaughter and served a decade in prison. Postconviction, trajectory analysis and witness statements supported an alternative hypothesis that the shot that killed the driver came from inside the vehicle. The FBI issued a letter stating that Peele's testimony "exceeds the limits of the science and cannot be supported by the FBI." Of course, that letter contradicted the official FBI view of CBLA at the time of the Krause trial. Nonetheless, the FBI letter was important because Krause's defense lawyer had conceded that Krause had fired the fatal round on the basis of the CBLA. Instead, the defense had pursued a "third party culpability" defense maintaining that the shooting was accidental, an approach that did not impress the jury. In 2015, the Arizona Court of Appeals reversed the conviction. In 2017, the charges were dismissed. In 2019, Krause filed a civil lawsuit for his wrongful conviction. Arguably, the main problem was the failure of the FBI to acknowledge the limitations of CBLA. Had the defense—or law enforcement—known of the FBI's reservations about CBLA, they might have investigated alternative theories of the case. Instead, they believed that the CBLA was definitive proof of Krause's culpability.

By 2000, most forensic professionals were well aware of the problems with CBLA. That year, Philip Cannon was convicted in an Oregon triple murder case (Cannon v. Polk County/Polk County Sheriff, 2014). The Oregon state crime laboratory declined to perform CBLA to support the case. Michael Conrady, an Oregon State University researcher, did the analysis and presented his findings. In keeping with the FBI approach, he said the evidence bullets and bullets from Cannon's home were "analytically indistinguishable." He also said the technique had a 1 in 400 error rate without any valid scientific or statistical basis. Cannon's conviction was overturned in 2009 because his defense attorney had failed to challenge the CBLA evidence. Charges were dismissed because the original evidence had gone missing. Meanwhile, the original case prosecutor resigned due to allegations of spousal assault. It was later discovered that she had stored the evidence in her filing cabinet. A new trial was never held, although there was some basis to believe that Cannon may have been the actual assailant in the case. The flawed forensics and prosecutorial misconduct had undermined any chance to bring him or any other suspect to trial for the murders.

GUNSHOT RESIDUE

Gunshot residue (GSR) may also be used to associate an individual with a shooting. A fired weapon exposes the shooter and bystanders to a cloud of GSR that may be detected on their skin or clothing for a period of time after the event. Inorganic GSR constituents include lead, barium, and antimony. Typically, a suspect's hands are swabbed according to a protocol that minimizes contamination and maximizes the amount of GSR that is collected. Early GSR analysis depended on the use of atomic absorption spectroscopy (AAS), which was highly reliable for the detection of the chemical constituents but was subject to interpretation difficulties similar to those that undermined the use of CBLA (Dalby et al., 2010). Environmental contamination could produce results that were chemically similar to GSR. For example, auto mechanics may be exposed to lead, barium, or antimony from brake pads and lubricants. Even today, GSR field tests are subject to the same limitations as AAS and require laboratory confirmation prior to their use in a court proceeding.

GSR analysis improved considerably with the introduction of more advanced analytical methods, including secondary electron microscopy (SEM) and energy dispersive spectroscopy (EDS). SEM or optical microscopy can be used to examine the distinctive morphology of inorganic GSR particles. EDS, which looks at characteristic x-rays that are emitted by materials exposed to the electron flux from an SEM, can be used to determine the chemical composition of individual particles to determine if they are consistent with possible GSR. Even when using a sophisticated technique like SEM-EDS, there are uncertainties. Some particles may not have all three elemental constituents. GSR may be found on bystanders. Crime scenes and police vehicles may have sufficient GSR present to transfer onto an individual who was nowhere close to a shooting. GSR cannot be used to limit the time at which a person was exposed to a shooting. The interpretation and communication of inorganic GSR analysis requires careful consideration of these factors.

Many wrongful convictions have included GSR analysis in which examiners used inadequate analytical methods or poor sampling protocols. Misinterpretations and miscommunications have also contributed to wrongful convictions by failing to convey the appropriate limitations of GSR analysis. For example, an analyst may associate a particle with GSR even if contains only lead, a conclusion that is not supported by science or current standards (Gunshot Residue Subcommittee Chemistry Scientific Area Committee Organization of Scientific Area Committees for Forensic Science, 2020).

In 1998, Tyrone Jones was implicated in a murder in Baltimore City after two particles of presumed GSR were found on swabs from his left hand (Hanes, 2005). One particle had all three characteristic elements, but the other one had only two. As prosecution expert Daniel Van Gelder testified, between 500 and 2500 particles of GSR may be deposited when a person fires a weapon, so many laboratories (including the FBI) will not permit a positive GSR conclusion without a finding of three particles and a detection of all three primary inorganic constituents in each presumed GSR particle (Jones v. State, 2000). Jones' defense claimed that the testimony mischaracterized the probative value of the GSR and failed to account for the possibility of secondary transfer. For example, a police firing range was located near the location where the GSR sampling occurred in the Jones case. The appeals court upheld Jones' conviction after his direct appeal. Maryland courts later became more skeptical of GSR evidence, and the Jones case was reopened after issues arose with eyewitness testimony and evidence suppression. The conviction was vacated, and the prosecution dismissed the charges. In part, court skepticism was related to the variability in interpretation thresholds. The Maryland State Police had purportedly relied on as little as one GSR particle, Baltimore on two, and the FBI on three.

GSR USING ATOMIC ABSORPTION SPECTROSCOPY

In the 1995 Glover/Johnson/Wheatt murder conviction in Ohio, analysts used AAS to determine that there was a large amount of GSR on Wheatt's left hand and the left side of his jacket but none on Glover. Some amount of GSR was found on Johnson's left glove (State v. Glover, 2016). The sampling took place eight hours after the shooting, which increased the possibility of secondary transfer. The suspects had been transported in a police vehicle. Police cars are an abundant source of GSR and a likely location for secondary transfer of GSR particles onto an individual (Berk et al., 2007). Police also found "lead particles" inside and outside of a black Chevy Blazer that was used by the shooter to leave the scene. The suspects had confirmed that they were in the Blazer at the scene of the shooting but said they only witnessed the shooting. Given that the only eyewitness was a significant distance away from the scene and provided a questionable identification of Johnson, the GSR results were key evidence to implicate the three men in the shooting (Transcript of Evidentiary Hearing, 2008). They were convicted, but the eyewitness later recanted.

She said the police had provided an unduly suggestive photo array to her that led her to make a mistaken identification. The convictions were later overturned due to the failure to share exculpatory witness statements with the defense. In part, the appeals court recognized that the GSR evidence should be given less inculpatory weight due to the recognition of the limitations of AAS as a definitive method to identify inorganic GSR.

In this respect, CBLA using ICP-OES and GSR using AAS shared a common problem. Both methods used reliable chemical analysis equipment to produce accurate chemical compositions of the samples. Nonetheless, the interpretation of CBLA and AAS/GSR results are compromised by the uncertainties in the underlying physical phenomena. In CBLA, the uncertainties relate to the overlap of intra-lot and inter-lot variability. In AAS/GSR, the uncertainties relate to environmental contaminants, secondary transfer, and the exposure of bystanders to GSR. These concerns are largely addressed by the use of SEM/EDS for GSR analysis and may be further ameliorated by the adoption of organic GSR analysis in coming years. Nonetheless, field sampling of GSR has the same limitations as AAS and is still employed. In some instances, investigators and the courts may rely on field sampling to implicate a suspect without doing appropriate confirmatory testing in the crime lab. As in the Glover/Johnson/Wheatt case, this practice may lead to wrongful convictions or unnecessary uncertainties in the adjudication of a case.

The Glover/Johnson/Wheatt case raised another issue worthy of closer examination: that of contextual information and cognitive bias (State v. Glover, 2016) The original examiner, Dr. Sharon Rosenberg with the Cuyahoga County Coroner's Office, had testified:

> I have no knowledge of the situation. I normally do not make any attempt to be involved with the police examinations or the reports until after all facts are in. This is not something I care to have any influence from outside sources on. (State v. Glover, 2016)

Postconviction defense expert John Kilty, formerly with the FBI laboratory, criticized Rosenberg's view, saying that the contextual information concerning the sampling delay should have been used to conclude that any GSR testing would be "inherently flawed." He stated, "We had the biggest phone bill in the FBI laboratory because we'd call the contributors … to get verifiable information about the case … because it's our obligation to interpret the results after we do the exam" (State v. Glover, 2016). Kilty argued that contextual information is necessary for the forensic analyst to produce a reliable interpretation of forensic results. In the case of GSR analysis, the argument would relate to the activity-level propositions relating to the various possibilities leading to GSR exposure. The individual may have been the shooter, a bystander, or the recipient of secondary transfer. Kilty argued that Rosenberg should have conducted a criminalistic analysis based on the contextual information to support the GSR chemical analysis. In some sense, Kilty is correct because the interpretation of the GSR results is a type of forensic investigation. The levels of particles, their constituents, and crime scene reconstruction can all be used to provide scientific insights into the activity-level propositions about the GSR results. However, this criminalistic analysis is distinct from the chemical analysis of GSR. The two types of analyses should not be confused or conflated. The criminalistic analysis should be done separately and after the chemical analysis is complete. The chemist and the criminalist may be the same person working through a sequence of operations, though the skill sets for the two types of work are wholly distinct. In an ideal situation, the two analyses would be performed by two different professionals working in a sequence under appropriate workflow protocols.

THE SAVANNAH THREE

The various limitations of GSR were amply demonstrated in the 1992 murder case involving "The Savannah Three" in Georgia (Gardiner v. State, 1994). The defendants were Kenneth Gardiner, Mark Jones, Dominic Lucci, who were soldiers from nearby Fort Stewart. They were visiting Savannah to hold a bachelor party for Jones. Around the same time, three men in a 1992 Chevrolet Cavalier fired AK-47-like weapons and killed Stanley Jackson. Gardiner, Jones, and Lucci were driving a similar car and were found at a nearby topless bar. The men claimed that they were at Jones' wedding rehearsal 50 minutes away at the time of the shooting. An eyewitness identified Jones and Gardiner as the shooters. The men agreed to be swabbed for GSR, and Jones' hand tested positive. The person who took the sample from Jones did not "thoroughly wash and dry" his hands, did not wear gloves, and cartridge cases from the scene of the shooting were not included with the swab sample sent to the laboratory. No comparison test was done between the gunshot residue from Jones's hand and the residue from the cartridge cases. There was also evidence that Jones had handled clothing that had been worn during a machine gun range exercise the previous day, and that a transfer of gunshot residue could have occurred at that time (Jones v. Medlin, 2017). The car and clothing were also tested for GSR but none was found. No confirmatory chemical testing was done on the positive field test from Jones' hand. No murder weapon was ever recovered.

The case was complicated by racial overtones. The victim was African American and the defendants were white. Jones had made an incriminating statement to another soldier that he intended to shoot "a black guy up there I got to get." Gardiner and Lucci played Dungeons and Dragons, which was characterized by the prosecution as a fantasy game involving teams of assassins who plot to kill people. Lucci kept throwing knives in his car. Unbeknownst to the defendants, there was another incident in the town involving soldiers with automatic weapons who were threatening to shoot black people on street corners. That incident occurred three hours after the arrest of Gardiner, Jones, and Lucci. The incident report was never shared with the defense. Postconviction, the key eyewitness—a local pastor who identified Jones and Gardiner on the day of shooting—recanted and became an advocate for their exoneration. Centurion Ministries—an innocence organization which has been involved in many successful exonerations that don't involve DNA—took the case in 2009. Their convictions were reversed by the Georgia Supreme Court in 2017 based primarily on the failure to share the evidence that other persons were "ready to engage in racially motivated violence" on the night of Stanley Jackson's death. The prosecution subsequently dismissed the charges.

STUDY QUESTIONS

1. One of the founders of forensic science, Edmond Locard, said that "every contact leaves a trace." How might this be relevant to the interpretation of gunshot residue evidence?
2. The markings on the bullet that killed President Kennedy may be observed in Figure 8.2. These markings match test fires from the Mannlicher-Carcano 6.5x52 mm rifle purchased by Lee Harvey Oswald under the alias A. Hidell. Oswald's palmprint was found on the rifle. Oswald's wife said she was told by him that he had attempted and failed to assassinate an Army general with the rifle. Trajectory analysis indicates that the shot came from the Texas Book Repository where Oswald worked. Although Oswald was killed before any trial, he has been "convicted" by authorities and public opinion as the individual responsible for killing Kennedy. What forensic errors—if they were discovered—could support Oswald's innocence? Could the evidence be interpreted to support alternative theories?
3. Researchers are working on new technologies that may improve the reliability of certain ballistics tests. New three-dimensional microscope systems permit much more detailed imaging of bullets and cartridge casings (Morgan, 2016). Organic gunshot residue has been explored to replace or supplement inorganic gunshot residue (Morgan & Ropero Miller, 2015; Ignitable Liquids, Explosives, & Gunshot Residue Subcommittee, 2021). These technologies may result in more reliable verdicts in the

future. How might their adoption be associated with wrongful convictions? What scientific research and validation should be performed to mitigate the risk of errors with the new techniques?

FURTHER READING

Robert Thompson has written a practical introduction to firearms identification that is useful for both the novice and the experienced professional (Thompson, 2010). Advances in microscopy and database searching have already revolutionized the use of firearms investigation. The National Integrated Ballistic Information Network (NIBIN). has established a website with useful information, including data from their Crime Gun Intelligence Centers. See https://www.atf.gov/firearms/national-integrated-ballistic-information-network-nibin. The future of ballistics identification may be seen by a review of the NIST Ballistic Toolmark Research Database (Zheng, 2022) and the expanding set of research data based on optical topography of bullets and cartridge casings (Morgan, 2016).

The Patrick Pursley case is the most important ballistics-related exoneration in the modern era. The 2018 Illinois Appellate Court decision provides a clear and thorough summary of the firearms identification work by ISP and John Murdock (People v. Pursley, 2018). The case is important because many defense attorneys now believe that firearms identification is vulnerable to challenge based on the subjectivity of its interpretation framework. Adina Schwartz provides a useful introduction to challenges of firearms and toolmark evidence (Schwartz, 2008)

CBLA is an interesting cautionary tale for the consideration of forensic techniques that lacked sufficient scientific foundation. The most important reference document is the National Research Council report, *Forensic Analysis: Weighing Bullet Lead Evidence* (National Research Council, 2004). The report did generate some substantive responses, such as a critical scientific and statistical review of the committee's work (Finkelstein & Levin, 2005). Interestingly, CBLA was used to associate the Kennedy assassination bullets with Oswald. That work received a critical review after the NRC report (Randich & Grant, 2006).

REFERENCES

Anderson, E. (2018, August 13). After 34 Years Behind Bars, Man Gets New Trial in Detroit. *Detroit Free Press*.

Berk, R., Rochowicz, S., Wong, M., & Kopina, M. (2007). Gunshot Residue in Chicago police vehicles and facilities: an empirical study. *Journal of forensic sciences*, *52*(4), 838–841.

Brundage, J. (1998). The Identification of Consecutively Manufactured Gun Barrels. *AFTE Journal*, *30*(1), 438–444.
Cannon v. Polk County/Polk County Sheriff, 3:10–cv–00224–HA (United States District Court, D. Oregon. December 18, 2014).
Committee to Assess the Feasibility, A. a. (2008). *Ballistic Imaging*. Washington, DC: National Academies Press.
Dalby, O., Butler, D., & Birkett, J. (2010). Analysis of Gunshot Residue and Associated Materials: A Review. *Journal of Forensic Sciences*, *55*(4), 924–943.
Finkelstein, M., & Levin, B. (2005). Compositional Analysis of Bullet Lead as Forensic Evidence. *Journal of Law and Policy*, *13*(1), 119–142.
Gardiner v. State, S94A0285, S94A0286, S94A0287 (Supreme Court of Georgia June 13, 1994).
Gunshot Residue Subcommittee Chemistry Scientific Area Committee Organization of Scientific Area Committees for Forensic Science (2020). *Standard Practice for Expert Opinions on the Interpretation of Primer Gunshot Residue (pGSR) Analysis by Scanning Electron Microscopy/Energy Dispersive X-Ray Spectrometry*. National Institute of Standards and Technology.
Hamby, J. E., Brundage, D. J., & Thorpe, J. W. (2009). The Identification of Bullets Fired from 10 Consecutively Rifled 9mm Ruger Pistol Barrels: A Research Project Involving 507 Participants from 20 Countries. *AFTE Journal*, *41*(2) Spring 2009, 99–110.
Hanes, S. (2005, January 23). Evidence under Suspicion. *Baltimore Sun*, A1, A12-13.
Hinton v. Alabama, 13-6440 (Supreme Court of the United States February 24, 2014).
Ignitable Liquids, Explosives, & Gunshot Residue Subcommittee (2021). *Standard Practice for the Collection and Preservation of Organic Gunshot Residue*. Gaithersburg, MD: Organization of Scientific Area Committees.
Jones v. Medlin, S17A1291. S17A1292. S17A1293 (Supreme Court of Georgia November 2, 2017).
Jones v. State, Number 1962, September Term, 1999 (Court of Special Appeals of Maryland June 9, 2000).
Joseph Green Brown, Petitioner appellant, v. Louie L. Wainwright, Secretary Florida Department of Corrections, 785 F. 2d 1457 (U.S. Court of Appeals for the Eleventh Circuit March 17, 1986).
Michigan State Police (2008). *Detroit Police Department Firearms Unit Preliminary Audit Findings*.
Morgan, J. S. (2016). *Forensic Optical Topography: A Landscape Study*. Washington, DC: National Institute of Justice.

Morgan, J., & Ropero Miller, J. (2015). *Organic Gunshot Residue Analysis for Potential Shooter Determination*. National Institute of Justice.

National Research Council (2004). *Forensic Analysis: Weighing Bullet Lead Evidence*. National Academies Press.

PCAST Working Group (2016). *Report to the President: Forensic Science in Criminal Courts, Ensuring Scientific Validity of Feature Comparison Methods*. Washington, DC: President's Council of Advisors on Science and Technology.

People v. Pursley, 2-17-0227 (Appellate Court of Illinois, Second District May 2, 2018).

Press, R. (2019, December 5). *Kennedy Assassination Bullets Preserved in Digital Form*. Retrieved from National Institute of Standards and Technology: https://www.nist.gov/news-events/news/2019/12/kennedy-assassination-bullets-preserved-digital-form

Randich, E., & Grant, P. (2006). Proper Assessment of the JFK Assassination Bullet Lead Evidence from Metallurgical and Statistical Perspectives. *Journal of Forensic Sciences*, *51*(4), 717–728.

Ricks v. Pauch, 17–12784 (United States District Court for the Eastern District of Michigan, Southern Division March 23, 2020).

Schwartz, A. (2008). Challenging Firearms and Toolmarks Identification–Part One. *The Champion*, 32.

Scientific Working Group for Firearms and Toomarks (2017). Association of Firearm and Toolmark Examiners Theory of Identification. https://afte.org/about-us/what-is-afte/afte-theory-of-identification

Siegel, B. (1987, May 10). A System on Trial: Sentencing the Wrong Man to Die. *Los Angeles Times*.

State v. Glover, 102828, 102829, and 102831 (Court of Appeals of Ohio, Eighth Appellate District, Cuyahoga County May 5, 2016).

State v. Krause, 2 CA-CR 2015–0326-PR (Court of Appeals of Arizona, Division Two November 19, 2015).

Testimony of Courtland Cunningham and Joseph D. Nicol (1964, April 1). *Warren Commission Report and Hearings*. Washington, DC.

Thompson, R. (2010). *Firearm Identification in the Forensic Science Laboratory*. Alexandria: National District Attorneys Association.

Transcript of the Evidentary Hearing, Eugene Johnson v. Rich Gansheimer, 1: 06-CV-2816 (US District Court Northern District of Ohio Western Division November 11, 2008).

Zheng, X. (2022). *NIST Ballistics Toolmark Research Database*. Retrieved from National Institute of Standards and Technology: https://tsapps.nist.gov/NRBTD

CHAPTER 9

Fire Debris Investigation

Fire debris investigation errors have contributed to over 60 known wrongful convictions. It is likely that many more defendants were wrongfully convicted on the basis of flawed analyses than will ever be detected and exonerated. For many years, the field relied on unvalidated methods of interpretation. Investigators assumed that many features found commonly at fire scenes were evidence of an incendiary cause (i.e., arson). In 1980, the National Bureau of Standards (NBS) published the *Fire Investigation Handbook* (Brannigan et al., 1980). NBS, which later became the National Institute of Standards and Technology (NIST), housed a widely respected fire research laboratory. For whatever reason, the NBS handbook included unreliable, unvalidated information about the interpretation of fire scenes. In particular, the handbook contained sparse information about the interpretation of compartment fires (see Figure 9.1). The handbook was used to train fire investigators and was trusted due to the respect accorded to NBS by the forensic science community. Many of the statements in the handbook were not based on adequate empirical studies. The NBS guide extensively cited the National Fire Protection Association's Fire Protection Handbook, which shared similar deficiencies (National Fire Protection Association, 1976). An entire generation of examiners adopted invalid methods of interpretation that they believed were sound and scientific.

Many scientific gaps had not been addressed by adequate funding of independent, scientific research. A 1974 survey of fire investigators highlighted several priorities for scientific research that would later contribute to known wrongful convictions, including methods to diagnose electrical fires, reliability of burn indicators, and the burning characteristics of cigarettes (Boudreau et al., 1974). The chemical analysis methods used to analyze fire debris lacked specificity. Flame-ionization detection gas chromatography was very sensitive but had poor selectivity, especially in comparison with mass spectrometry detection. As a result, many fire investigators "filled in the blanks" by making invalid assumptions about the presence of accelerants or using detection dogs who lacked sufficient training or reliability. The problems associated with canine detection

DOI: 10.4324/9781003202578-9

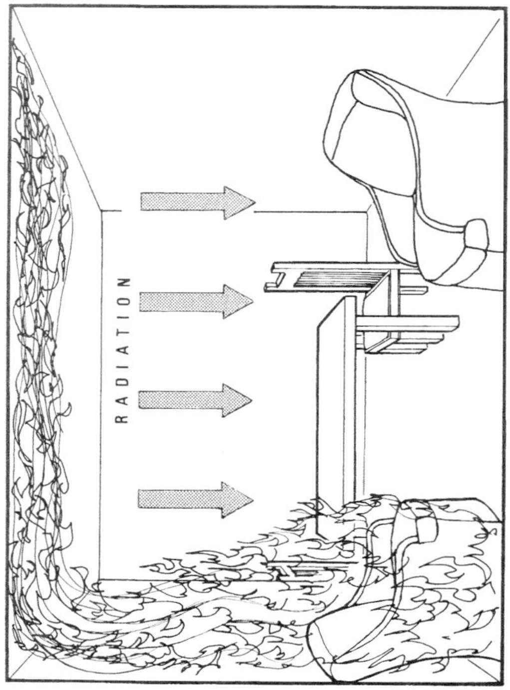

FIGURE 9.1 The *Fire Investigation Handbook* provided an illustration of a compartment fire and did recognize phenomena such as flashover. Flashover occurs when a fire spreads very rapidly due to the intensity of the heat and decomposition of organic materials into flammable gases, such as may happen inside an enclosed space. However, it lacked information about drop fires or similar phenomena that are commonly observed and may be confused with signs of incendiary origin, especially in compartment fire situations. Source: ***Fire Investigation Handbook*** (Brannigan, Bright, & Jason, 1980).

in fire investigation are covered in Chapter 5 on unvalidated forensic techniques.

In 1992, the National Fire Protection Association (NFPA) introduced NFPA 921, a Guide for Fire and Explosion Investigations (National Fire Protection Association, 1992). NFPA 921 addressed many of the shortcomings found in the NBS guide, but many investigators trained in the old methods dismissed the NFPA standard and continued to interpret scenes in the way they had been trained beforehand. Further, NFPA 921 had its own scientific limitations because there remained insufficient empirical work to validate key issues within the discipline. The current iteration, NFPA 921-2017, has incorporated a generation of new knowledge in fire science and provides a much more solid foundation for the interpretation of fire scenes (National Fire Protection Association, 2017). That said, additional research is needed to elucidate key issues in the field (Almirall et al., 2017).

GAPS IN FIRE INTERPRETATION

Several specific issues contributed to wrongful convictions. First, NFPA 921 permitted the use of *negative corpus* until 2011. Negative corpus, or process of elimination, was popularized by Arthur Conan Doyle in connection with his Sherlock Holmes character. Doyle wrote, "When you have eliminated all which is impossible, then whatever remains, however improbable, must be the truth." The forensic community adopted this maxim too readily. The idea is unsound and unscientific. First and foremost, it is inherently unfalsifiable. One cannot prove the negative. Fundamentally, empirical data includes significant uncertainties. In real-world scenarios, these uncertainties are multiplied by the inherently retrospective nature of forensic examination. You can't reliably eliminate a cause altogether. Nor can you provide an objective basis for the relative likelihood of the eliminated cause and your "improbable" truth. Fire debris investigators used the negative corpus approach to eliminate accidental, electrical, or other non-incendiary causes. Once they had eliminated those other possibilities, they assumed a fire was arson even if they had no actual evidence to support that conclusion. NFPA 921 and other standards did require that the investigator determine the point of origin of a fire prior to applying a negative corpus interpretation. It was thought that this requirement would discipline the investigator's logic and constrain the possible fire scenarios. Unfortunately, many investigators relied on invalid methods to determine point of origin, so there was no valid basis to constrain logic or inform the application of negative corpus. Many examiners mistakenly concluded that fires were arson based on negative corpus.

Investigators often misinterpreted burn patterns at scenes. For example, a V-pattern may be observed over a fire's point of origin. In the case of "simple" fires, such as those associated with an electrical outlet, the V-pattern is easily observed, and the point of origin will be readily found at the vertex of the V-pattern. In more complex scenarios, the fire may travel along the ceiling of a compartment fire. This travel may produce drop fires caused by falling debris. The burning of that debris may also cause a V-pattern that is unrelated to the original source of the fire. Further, inverted V-patterns and hourglass patterns may be caused by accelerants or complex convection or radiation effects. Many investigators made unreliable assumptions about these patterns. For example, they assumed that hotter fires were associated with V-patterns with sharper sides (i.e., more acute V's). Because they assumed that hotter fires had to be produced from the use of accelerants, they would conclude a fire was arson on the basis of their observations of the angles of V-patterns. Although V-patterns are still used by fire investigators, current methods emphasize that there are many explanations for the patterns. The investigator must have objective evidence to inform the interpretation of the patterns, not just assume that all V-patterns point to the origin of the fire or imply an incendiary cause.

Investigators used unreliable features to determine the intensity of a fire. Again, this was critical in many investigations because they assumed a hot, intense fire was necessarily an arson fire. Concrete spalling and crazed glass were seen as indicators of an intense, high-temperature fire. These are not always reliable indicators. In many fires, glass is crazed by the sudden change in temperature that occurs when water is directed onto a hot glass surface. This is an indication of fire response, not fire origin. Also, investigators often misinterpreted features that looked like pour patterns but were actually the result of involved fires in compartments. In other words, when a fire spreads to involve an entire room or building, the fire will be intense on all surfaces. Flooring and furniture will burn at very hot temperatures and may produce unusual melting patterns. One of the most common mistakes in wrongful convictions was the misinterpretation of these types of indications. Investigators routinely assumed that any low burning was a sign of arson. Low burning includes any scenario in which an intense, high-temperature fire was observed near the floor. It was assumed that the ceiling would always burn hotter than the floor. Thus, if the floor burned hot, then there must have been accelerants poured on the floor, and the fire was arson. This did not take into account the fact that fully involved compartment fires would engulf every surface, whether it was a floor, wall, or ceiling.

The overall effect of these faulty assumptions was to provide ample justification for an arson finding in almost any fire scenario. If the investigation pointed to a suspect fire, then the fire investigator could easily support that theory. Tunnel vision and invalid science combined to produce miscarriages of justice.

CAMERON TODD WILLINGHAM

The wrongfully convicted defendant may show grace in the face of injustice or inspire pathos in the heart of the observer. Those who contributed to the wrongful conviction may appear callous or grossly incompetent. The aftermath may change the way that forensic science is practiced in fundamental ways. The Cameron Todd Willingham case has all of these aspects. Willingham was executed in 2004 for the murder of his three children. Five years later, Texas Governor Rick Perry issued a posthumous pardon. The Texas Forensic Science Commission (TFSC) issued a report about the Willingham case and the similar Ernest Ray Willis case in 2011 (Texas Forensic Science Commission, 2011). The report detailed severe deficiencies in the fire investigations in the two cases and made numerous recommendations for reform. For at least two decades, fire investigation had lagged fire science and not just in Texas. Changes happened too late for Cameron Todd Willingham (Figure 9.2).

Willingham's nightmare began on the night of December 23, 1991 when a fire started in the family home in Corsicana, Texas. Witnesses said that Willingham refused to enter the smoldering house to rescue his children and seemed more worried about his car and belongings than his family. The next day, neighbors said Willingham and his wife played music and laughed as they sifted through the debris. Later, a state forensic psychiatrist would testify that Willingham was a severe sociopath who lacked conscience and was beyond rehabilitation. The psychiatrist, Dr. James Grigson, would later be expelled from the American Psychiatric Association for ethics violations (Trial by Fire). The lead fire investigator, Manuel Vasquez, said that Willingham had spread accelerant along the floors, front threshold, and front concrete porch in a manner "typically employed to impede firemen in their rescue attempts" (Willingham v. State, 1995). Vasquez had investigated over 1200 fires, and by his own account, "most all of them" were arson. Vasquez conducted a typical fire investigation for the time, which is to say an investigation that was based on his experience and training—not fire science. A week after

FIGURE 9.2 Cameron Todd Willingham. Mug shot of Cameron Todd Willingham, who was wrongfully executed for the murder of his children based on a flawed fire debris investigation. Source: Wikipedia, originally from Texas Department of Criminal Justice.

the fire, Vasquez met Willingham, who denied setting the fire. Vasquez didn't like Willingham, saying, "He just talked and he talked and all he did was lie." Vasquez said that Willingham lied about experiencing smoke inhalation because he didn't show signs of throat damage during the interview. He stated that Willingham's extensive burn injuries were self-inflicted, not the result of attempts to save the children, as Willingham maintained. Vasquez opined, "The fire itself tells me that it's a very aggressive fire; and therefore the fire was not a planned fire. It was a spur-of-the-moment fire." None of these statements or conclusions were valid.

The toll of errors by Vasquez is astounding in retrospect. They were detailed by fire expert Craig Beyler for the TFSC (Beyler, 2009). Vasquez conducted his fire investigation four days after the fire and after the scene had been cleared. He concluded that space heaters in the home couldn't have started the fire because they were turned off when he looked at them. He made estimates of the temperature of the floor and ceiling and other locations without any valid basis and concluded—incorrectly—that areas of high temperature were points of origin where the fire had been deliberately set. He concluded that the fire started on the porch in direct contradiction of eyewitnesses who reported the exact opposite. He associated burning patterns in a hallway with "pooling" of poured accelerant. This contradicted both fire science and witness statements about the fire. Chemical testing found a possible accelerant in only one location that was near a grill and bottle of lighter fluid that were sitting on the front porch of the home. Vasquez did not note the presence of the grill or lighter fluid, and his fire interpretation did not reflect the failure to find accelerant residue anywhere else in the home. He did not note that the children's room had no door and then made the mistaken conclusion that the fire was so hot that it had completely consumed the door. He found crazed glass in the home and concluded that it was evidence of a very hot fire that must have been deliberately set. That conclusion was invalid and incorrect. He assumed that latex paint was not normally flammable because it is water-based but failed to understand that the water is no longer present after the paint dries. Vasquez painted a false picture of Willingham as a man who murdered his three small children in a horrifying way.

In reality, Willingham had searched the home after the fire woke him up and only left the structure after his hair caught fire and because he thought he was about to pass out. Willingham had to be physically restrained from reentering the home to save his children and even gave one firefighter a black eye in the struggle to do so. Willingham's public defender found an independent fire expert, but that individual agreed with Vasquez's conclusions. In the end, the only defense witness was a babysitter who testified to Willingham's love for his children. After his conviction, Willingham hovered between despair and introspection. He wrote some poems and letters. He befriended some inmates and avoided others who preyed on the weak in prison. Willingham met one inmate, Ernest Ray Willis, whose case was eerily similar to his own.

In January, 2004, fire scientist Dr. Gerald Hurst reviewed the evidence in the Willingham case. Hurst had become an influential advocate for improvements in fire investigation, many of which had been incorporated into standards of the National Fire Protection Association (NFPA). NFPA 921—first promulgated in 1992 before the Willingham trial—governs fire investigation and interpretation and directly contradicts much of Vasquez's testimony in the Willingham case. Hurst quickly found many of the errors in the Willingham fire investigation and concluded that the fire was a classic example of flashover, not arson. Hurst concluded that "not a single item of physical evidence ... supports a finding of arson" (Beyler, 2009). The report arrived in the officer of the Governor days before Willingham's scheduled execution. The Governor's office and the Board of Pardons and Paroles apparently ignored the Hurst report. Willingham was denied clemency. He was executed on February 17. Before his execution, he said:

> The only statement I want to make is that I am an innocent man convicted of a crime I did not commit. I have been persecuted for twelve years for something I did not do. From God's dust I came and to dust I will return, so the Earth shall become my throne.
>
> (Texas Forensic Science Commission, 2011)

The TFSC was established the following year. Willingham would receive a posthumous pardon from the Governor of Texas in 2009.

Hurst also reviewed the conviction of Willingham's friend, Ernest Ray Willis, and found very similar errors in that case. Willis, received a grant of habeas corpus from a federal court a few months after Willingham's execution (Willis v. Cockrell, 2004). The Willis case also included failures by fire investigators who relied on outdated methods without a scientific foundation. Fire investigators based their finding of an incendiary cause (i.e., arson) on the presence of burn patterns on the floor and a sofa that they associated with pour patterns of accelerants. No accelerant was ever found inside the house. Willis claimed that he was asleep on the sofa when he noticed the fire, but that story didn't agree with the theory that the fire had been started there. Willis said he survived because the fire was not completely out of control when he escaped, but fire investigators said the fire developed rapidly. Willis suffered no apparent injuries, though he claimed to have a burn mark on his shoulder two days after the fire. A garden hose outside the home smelled of gasoline and a crime lab test found "volatile components" on Willis' pants but no accelerants. Willis' brother, Billy Willis, had escaped the home out of a bedroom window, suffering gash wounds from broken glass and coughing up black, sooty phlegm for hours afterward. Two women died in the blaze. Fire investigators said the fire was set in a way that prevented their escape. Willis was convicted and sentenced to death. Postconviction, another man confessed to starting the fire, though later TFSC analysis concluded that the fire origin was likely electrical in nature. All experts agreed that the "pour patterns" were due to flashover and that the fire had smoldered for some time before it overtook the house, a sequence of events consistent with Willis' story of that night. Without a positive finding of accelerant, current NFPA guidelines would not permit an investigator to conclude an incendiary cause, though some experts have maintained that an "inconclusive" finding would have been most appropriate.

TEXAS FORENSIC SCIENCE COMMISSION REVIEW

Several years later, the TFSC reviewed the Willis and Willingham cases and issued a scathing report of the poor fire debris investigation work that led to the two wrongful convictions. Their root-cause analysis provides unique insight into problems in fire investigation during the period. Throughout the 1980s, many observers had noted that fire science contradicted many of the interpretative approaches used by fire investigators. The National Fire Protection Association (NFPA) adopted new standards in the 1990s to address the gap between science and practice. Most notably, NFPA 921 (National Fire Protection Association, 1992) provided consensus guidance on the best practices for evidence collection and scene interpretation for the determination of the cause of a fire. The 1992 version of NFPA 921 was a major advance for the field, though it had significant deficiencies that led to changes in later versions of the standard (National Fire Protection Association, 2017). Had the investigators in the Willis and Willingham cases followed the NFPA 921-1992 standard, it is unlikely that they would have concluded that the fires were deliberately set. Many investigators—and many jurisdictions—ignored the NFPA 921 standard and continued to follow the guidelines on which they had been trained in the 1970s and 1980s. The TFSC review found that NFPA 921 and related standards were not being applied in Texas, although the Texas State Fire Marshal's Office (SFMO) laboratory had been accredited by the American Society of Crime Laboratory Directors—Laboratory Accreditation Board (ASCLD-LAB), the leading forensic science accreditation body. The ASCLD-LAB accreditation was limited to the SFMO's chemical analysis of fire debris, but there was no evidence that faulty lab work contributed to the Willis or Willingham convictions. In fact, Vasquez and his colleagues dismissed exculpatory lab results that did not fit with their arson interpretation. Fire investigators did not (and still do not generally) reside with a forensic science organization so the ASCLD-LAB accreditation did not cover fire investigators. The Texas SFMO did not enforce scientific standards for the investigators. In fact, SFMO investigators were deeply involved in the erroneous interpretations in the Willis and Willingham cases. SFMO leaders failed to recognize the importance of consensus standards, rigorous training on those standards, and review mechanisms to discern the reliability of Texas fire investigators. To be fair, no national standards existed prior to the release of NFPA 921 in 1992. Investigators learned fire interpretation in apprenticeship training, which emphasized the "art" and nuance of reading a fire scene to determine cause and origin. The publication of NFPA 921 was not greeted by immediate and universal adoption. As the TFSC noted, the Texas SFMO had only one copy in each of its regional offices until the late 1990s. There was a perceived gap between fire scientists and fire investigators, which persists to the present day. In the course of the Willis/Willingham review, SFMO stated, "In reviewing documents and standards in place then and now, we stand by the original investigator's report and conclusions." TFSC found this position "untenable," which was a charitable response given the gross errors perpetrated in the Willingham case in particular.

As outlined in the accompanying table, TFSC recommendations focused on the need to apply scientific methodology to the investigation and interpretation of fire scenes. The commission felt that SFMO and other fire investigators should adopt the NFPA and related standards, train investigators in the application of those standards, and ensure the continuing reliability of practitioners with certification and case reviews. SFMO did adopt the TSFC recommendations. Among other items, they established a Science Advisory Group consisting of independent professionals in fire investigation to conduct case reviews (Table 9.1).

The Texas case reviews led to the exoneration of Sonia Cacy, who was convicted in 1993 of murder related to a house fire in 1991 (Ex parte Cacy, 2016). Cacy's uncle, Bill Richardson, died in the blaze. Cacy's palmprint was found on Richardson's will, which was written shortly before his death. It was unlikely that Cacy would have had much financial motive to kill Richardson because the house and property were almost worthless. Oddly, Richardson had been responsible for accidental fires shortly before the fire that killed him. The first fire started on the house's back porch but was not reported to authorities. An electrical fire in Richardson's home office was extinguished by the police using a garden hose. A third fire started in the garage on the same day as the electrical fire. The fatal fire occurred eight days later. One forensic pathologist concluded that he had died of burns in the fire,

TABLE 9.1 Recommendations of the Texas Forensic Science Commission in the Willis-Willingham Report.

Recommendations of the Texas Forensic Science Commission in the Willis-Willingham Report
1. Adoption of national standards
2. Retroactive review: re-examination of cases when scientific knowledge produces material changes in the probative value of forensic evidence
3. Enhanced certification, including conformance with NFPA 1033, a standard for training of fire investigators released in 2009
4. Collaborative training on incendiary indicators, such as postmortem reviews by active fire investigators
5. Tools for analyzing ignition sources, such as the Ignition Matrix approach to ensure conformance with NFPA 921
6. Periodic curriculum review
7. State Fire Marshall involvement in local investigations involving loss of life
8. Peer review group or multidisciplinary team for review of pending and completed arson cases
9. Testimony standards based on NFPA 1033 and related guidelines
10. Daubert/Kelly hearings in all arson cases to ensure testimony is reliable and relevant
11. Testimony evaluation to ensure compliance with standards
12. Minimum report standards
13. Preservation of documentation
14. Dissemination of new research on fire science
15. Code of conduct/ethics
16. Training for lawyers and judges
17. Funding to support compliance with NFPA standards and TFSC recommendations

Source: Texas Forensic Science Commission (2011).

while a second pathologist noted few signs of carbon monoxide poisoning or smoke inhalation. That pathologist concluded that Richardson had likely set his bed on fire with a dropped cigarette and died of a heart attack. Richardson smoked three packs of cigarettes a day. That theory was undermined when Bexar County toxicologist Joe Castorena concluded that Richardson's clothing tested positive for gasoline. The gasoline finding was sufficient to establish the possibility that he had been killed by a deliberately set fire. Cacy was convicted and sentenced to 55 years in prison but was paroled five years later. Postconviction, Gerald Hurst reviewed Castorena's gas chromotograph mass spectrometry results and found that "many gasoline hydrocarbon peaks were missing." Other experts could not confirm the finding of ignitable liquids. An expert review panel split on the original findings. Five rejected the arson finding, two said it did not meet current standards, and two said there was insufficient data. The habeas court vacated the Cacy conviction on the basis of the shift in fire science and inadequate defense in her original trial. The court noted that the evidence did not establish that Cacy was "actually innocent" but did establish that a reasonable jury would not have convicted her on the basis of the updated scientific review.

THE ROLE OF THE FIRE INVESTIGATOR

The experience in Texas is unique only to the extent that the TFSC established the nature and extent of practice deficiencies in that state. The execution of an innocent person in the Willingham case may have motivated a stronger reaction and impetus for reform. Nonetheless, the issues in Texas were reflected across the United States and the world. It is likely that substantial numbers of wrongful convictions remain to be discovered in old arson cases. It is also likely that many will never be discovered due to the passage of time.

In many cases, the organizational deficiencies of police and fire units combined to produce unjust outcomes. In 1984 in Chicago, a house fire killed a mother and her five children. The official bomb and arson unit report made an inconclusive finding due to the extreme extent of the burning and collapse of the building. A police report concluded that the fire was accidental. The Chicago Fire Department (CFD) Office of Fire Investigation (OFI) would be established a week after the fire. The new OFI commander, Captain Francis Burns, took a training class to the scene to investigate the fire (Transcript of Evidentiary Hearing, 2015). Given that it was not an official investigation, Burns did not document his findings at the time and later relied on the individual reports of his trainees to reconstruct his thinking. The trainee reports were later discarded and weren't available for review at the time of the trial. Burns would testify that the fire was arson based on his discovery of alligator charring, burn-through of the floor, V-patterns on the walls of an adjacent structure, and the elimination of all accidental causes (also referred to as "negative corpus"). Each basis was scientifically invalid. In addition, Burns had not assessed a possible electrical cause related to faulty wiring or flooding in the basement of the building. James Kluppelberg was identified as a possible suspect by his boarder, Duane Glassco. Chicago police detective Jon Burge, who was later implicated in a pattern of police coercion and torture, supervised the investigation. A false confession soon followed (Wrice v. Burge, 2020). Kluppelberg was convicted and sentenced to life without parole. In 2012, after review of the invalid arson testimony and police misconduct in the case, Kluppelberg's conviction was vacated. He received over $9 million in lawsuit settlement and compensation.

In retrospect, Burns' motivation and role remain uncertain. It strains credulity to imagine that he was generally unaware of police misconduct in Chicago at the time. In the Kluppelberg case, he may have only been aware of the confession and sought to support a case he believed was rightly judged to be arson. Cognitive bias in fire debris investigation has contributed to many wrongful convictions (Bieber, 2014). In his paper on this issue, Bieber derived root causes for 27 arson wrongful convictions. He described the invalid use of suspicious burn patterns in the Willingham case, misidentified origin locations, invalid use of accelerant detecting canines, use of negative corpus, and failure to recognize possible electrical origins for a fire. In several cases, he was able to document specific examples of cognitive bias effects. For example, he noted that many secondary reviewers are aware of the conclusions of the primary investigator. Like other disciplines, fire investigation benefits when secondary analysis is blind to the original conclusion and cannot be unduly influenced by it. Bieber held that fire investigators may adopt role bias and view themselves as criminal investigators. Role bias is implicated when an individual is overly influenced by the stress or expectations of their social or professional position. Role bias is a form of continuation bias, which occurs when an individual assumes a hypothesis and fails to consider alternative theories or discordant evidence. Detectives often demonstrate continuation bias in wrongful conviction cases, and fire investigators appear to show similar tendencies. As a forensic science professional, the fire investigator should be fundamentally different from the detective. The fire investigator's role is not to solve a case but rather to elucidate the cause and progress of a fire. In many wrongful convictions, the fire investigators failed to see this distinction and became advocates for the hypothesis that an arson had occurred, and the suspect was guilty of the crime. As in the Kluppelberg case, the fire investigator may proceed on the basis of a hypothesis supported by other case information, such as Kluppelberg's false confession. It is certainly possible that Burns failed to consider alternative hypotheses or information that would have contradicted a conclusion of incendiary origin. Given the limitations of the building fire, the original "inconclusive" finding of the arson unit may have been the most valid interpretation of the scene.

It is impossible to remove contextual information from consideration in fire investigation, and many investigators will purposely take such information into account in their analysis. For example, many insurance investigators will consider the value of insurance policies and the financial situation of a claimant when they assess fire cause and origin. Fire investigation is also inherently subjective and therefore directly susceptible to the unconscious biases human investigators will inevitably exhibit. The use of scientific standards can limit this issue by providing an objective basis for the assessment of the elements associated with fire cause and origin. Training may also ameliorate the issue because an untrained investigator is much more likely to lack the scientific knowledge to make an objective fire assessment.

UNCERTAINTIES IN INTERPRETATION

Fire investigators may be faced with situations with such inherent uncertainty that multiple, valid interpretations may be possible in a case. Trained investigators may credibly disagree about cause and origin even when examining the same set of evidence. In such cases, investigators may be reluctant to make a valid, inconclusive finding or testify concerning the limitations of their findings. Report and testimony standards continue to evolve to provide a framework for appropriate calibration of language when a fire investigator communicates the results of a cause and origin analysis.

Wrongful convictions have arisen in these situations when examiners applied a negative corpus interpretation. As discussed above, the general concept of negative corpus was made famous by Arthur Conan Doyle, the creator of Sherlock Holmes, the fictional "scientific" detective who maintained, "When you have eliminated all which is impossible, then whatever remains, however improbable, must be the truth." (Conan Doyle, 1927). In fire investigation, negative corpus was used to eliminate all accidental causes to justify a conclusion of arson. If all non-arson causes are eliminated, the thinking went, then the only remaining possibility is that the fire was an arson. Negative corpus interpretation fails to take into account the inherent limitations of human knowledge and real-world conditions. Fire scenes—as in the Kluppelberg case—are often so heavily damaged that no reliable conclusion can be drawn. Sometimes, the answer is "I don't know." The logical leap from negative corpus to incendiary cause may be reasonable for fictional characters who have perfect knowledge; it is not applicable in real-world forensic analysis. More fundamentally, the assertion of an incendiary cause is only valid if it is based on positive evidence and is therefore falsifiable. Negative corpus is based on the *absence* of evidence and is therefore not falsifiable and not scientific.

In his root-cause paper, Bieber describes the Joseph Awe case to demonstrate the pitfalls of negative corpus (Bieber, 2014). In 2006 in Harrisville, Wisconsin, Awe's bar burned down and he was accused of having set the fire for insurance purposes (State v. Awe, 2010). Wisconsin Division of Criminal Investigation's Arson Bureau investigator James Sielehr testified to a classic negative corpus determination.

> The only way that we, as investigators, have to classify a fire as arson or incendiary is if we can eliminate all of the rest of those causes. It's like a simple mathematical equation. Matter of deduction. One by one we try to address every single potential accidental ignition source in our area of origin. And once we are able to eliminate them all, there's absolutely nothing left that could have caused the fire except human involvement and that's the only way that we're able to do that. ... And only when you can eliminate each and every one of those can you refer to this as an incendiary fire. That's how we do it. (State v. Awe, 2010)

The insurance company had hired a local electrical engineer to investigate a possible electrical cause for the fire. He concluded that there was no basis to determine an electrical origin. The defense hired an expert with no experience in arson investigation, no familiarity with NFPA 921, and no access to the electrical panel that may have been the source of the fire. The trial occurred the year before NFPA changed the 921 standard to limit the use of negative corpus. The new NFPA 921 standard required the identification of a "competent ignition source at the hypothesized origin" and examining all possible alternate hypotheses. Awe's conviction was overturned on the basis of the updated NFPA standards. Postconviction, John Lentini and colleague Mark Svare held that the fire started in the electrical service panel discounted by the prosecution expert during the original trial (Hall, 2013).

A distinction should be drawn between unvalidated science and failure to follow practice standards. Some scholars have grouped all fire-debris-related wrongful convictions into an overarching category of "junk science" (Giannelli, 2013). In many cases, wrongful convictions were due to failures in documentation or evidence collection, not scientific underpinnings. In 2008, a fire in Victor Caminata's home resulted in $273,000 in damages. Caminata had purchased a wood stove a few weeks before the fire. He said he had tried to extinguish the fire with a chem stick, a flare-like device that is often used to extinguish chimney fires. Caminata claimed that he had not set the fire purposely. It appears that he had installed the wood stove improperly and had several code violations in the chimney and walls around the chimney that contributed to the spread of the fire and damage to the home. An insurance company investigator noted what appeared to be blowtorch marks in the basement rafters of the home (Plaintiff's Reply Brief, 2016). Fire investigator Michael Jenkinson produced a flawed and incomplete scene reconstruction and did not photograph key locations around the woodstove chimney. He would later admit that his work in the case represented what he teaches students not to do. The investigators had not followed NFPA 921 guidelines and failed to conduct appropriate tests to support their theories of the fire cause and origin. They did not consider alternative explanations for the patterns they observed, showing tunnel vision and continuation bias. In the end, they concluded that the fire was arson based on negative corpus because they did not have a clear basis to determine the source of the fire (Caminata v. Cnty. of Wexford, 2016). Caminata's conviction was vacated on the basis of inadequate defense; he didn't have access to an expert to counter the flawed fire debris investigation. He settled a civil lawsuit related to his wrongful conviction for $1.1 million in 2014.

ORGANIZATIONAL DEFICIENCIES

In some cases, problems may arise that are not forensic science errors but are related to organizational issues. In Connecticut, Martina Jackson and Speciale Rose Morris pled guilty to arson after the Connecticut State Police Fire and Explosion Investigation Unit concluded that a house fire had an incendiary cause (Shugarts, 2018). A gasoline can had been found at the scene and petroleum distillates were found in the fire debris. They were never sentenced, and alternate suspects were identified but never charged. After court delays, the state lab was asked to send an examiner to testify concerning the chemical testing. The original examiner had retired, and the new examiner refused to testify on the basis of his predecessor's work. The samples were retested, and no accelerants were found. The charges were dropped. The original test and retest may both have been accurate. Volatile organic compounds evaporate and leak from containers after prolonged shelf storage (Hsieh et al., 2003). The convictions had to be vacated because of delays in the investigation and court adjudication combined with expected staff turnover in the state laboratory.

In 1989, a house fire in the home of Roger and Jacqueline Latta resulted in the tragic death of their two-year-old son, Brad (Latta v. Chapala, 2005). The local prosecutor, Walter Chapala, responded to the scene the morning after the fire. He noted burn patterns on the floor and decided the fire was arson. At the time, fire investigators believed any fire that burned close to the floor should be presumed to be arson. Chapala called it "an obvious arson" although he had never had any arson training. The chief detective on the case, Mike Mollenhauer of the LaPorte County Sheriff's Department, had 17 years of experience but the Latta case was his first involving a death. He concluded that several holes in the floor of the child's bedroom were caused by accelerant. He was aware that an electrical fire had occurred in the attic the prior month and discounted a space heater as a potential source of the fire. When he interviewed the Lattas, he had already decided the fire was arson. He became angry with Jacquelilne Latta because she didn't show sufficient emotion about the death of her son. Barker Herbert Labs supported the prosecution during the investigation and trial. They supported the "finding" by the prosecutor that the low burn patterns proved the fire was arson. The prosecutor withheld key supporting documentation from the chemical analysis of the fire debris, including chromatograms and reference standards. The defense attorney's request for funds for an independent expert were denied. The Latta's were convicted and each sentenced to 50 years in prison. Postconviction, the issues of inadequate defense, suppressed evidence, and out-of-date interpretation were raised on their behalf. They were released on that basis in 2001 and the charges dismissed. Because so much time had lapsed and much of the evidence was no longer available, they have not been fully exonerated. Noted fire investigator John De Haan has reviewed the evidence and concluded that the fire had been caused by a space heater that ignited the curtains in the child's room. It is clear that Chapala's actions played an outsized role in the wrongful conviction. He took it upon himself to be forensic scientist, investigator, prosecutor, and judge and jury. The other professionals went along with his misrepresentations and unscientific analysis.

INADEQUATE DEFENSE

The problem of inadequate defense arises in many wrongful convictions related to fire debris investigation. Defense attorneys seldom consult an independent expert or conduct a thorough cross-examination of prosecution experts. Almost all cases include state experts who testify for the prosecution because an arson trial can't proceed without an official finding that a fire had an incendiary cause. This puts the defense in an impossible situation if they don't have an expert who can question the original findings. Many defense attorneys do not appreciate the subjectivity of fire debris analysis or the extent of changes in fire debris analysis since the introduction of NFPA 921 in 1992. They will default to a strategy that inculpates an alternate suspect who may have committed the arson, thus avoiding the need to challenge the fire investigation. As in the Latta case, the courts also do not appreciate the importance of independent review by a defense expert.

Another example is the 2007 conviction of Daniel Carnevale, who was accused of burning apartment buildings in Pittsburgh in 1993 to cover for his theft of checks from residents' mailboxes (Commonwealth v. Carnevale, 2012). The federal bureau of Alcohol, Tobacco, and Firearms (ATF) assisted in the fire investigation. ATF agent William Petraitis concluded that the fire was an arson based on low burn patterns in the basement mechanical room. An accelerant-sniffing dog was brought in by Petraitis and alerted to the presence of accelerants. Fourteen samples were sent to the ATF lab. Two samples tested positive for gas and lacquer thinner. The accelerant was not found in the area where Petraitis had theorized the fire had originated. He eliminated accidental or electrical causes and based his conclusion of arson on negative corpus. The case went cold for 14 years. Carnevale was arrested for a violent crime in California in 2006, and a jailhouse informant said Carnevale confessed to the Pittsburgh fire in his jail cell. In the meantime, per policy, the ATF had destroyed all of the evidence in the case. Petraitis testified from memory about his findings, including the results of the ATF lab testing. The Carnevale defense did not call or consult any independent expert or call any witnesses. It may have been a waste of time in any case because there was no evidence to review. Carnevale was convicted and sentenced to life in prison without parole. His 2012 appeal was based in part on his lack of access to an independent expert. The court dismissed the concern and said the expert would have had to rely on photographs and the ATF report because the evidence had been destroyed eight years earlier. The court said there was no basis to assume

> that this phantom expert would have changed the outcome of the trial. ... Defendant has utterly failed to provide even the slightest bit of supporting evidence in support of his claim that counsel was ineffective for failing to call an expert arson witness.
>
> (Commonwealth v. Carnevale, 2012)

That judgment was incorrect. In 2019, Carnevale's defense team—assisted by the Innocence Project—discovered a note from the ATF files noting that the accelerant findings were meaningless because the amounts were very low and below standard arson thresholds. Douglas Carpenter of Combustion Science and Engineering concluded that the ATF investigation was based on a flawed, out-of-date interpretation of the fire scene and the cause of the fire was likely the boiler/heating system in the old apartment building. Carnevale's convictions were dismissed in 2019 with the support of prosecutors at that time. The charges were dismissed, and he was released. He filed a federal lawsuit related to his wrongful conviction in early 2022.

STUDY QUESTIONS

1. Arthur Conan Doyle believed that negative corpus was at the heart of the "science of deduction" practiced by the hero of his books, Sherlock Holmes. He used the idea repeatedly in the Holmes stories, most explicitly in *The Sign of Four* and most famously in *The Hound of the Baskervilles*. He also used the idea to advocate for the existence of fairies in his 1922 book, *The Coming of the Fairies*, just as some have used it more

recently to prove the existence of aliens. In the two Sherlock Holmes stories, the detective elicited a confession or caught the murderer in the act. Read the stories and consider the challenge of taking the cases to trial in the absence of proof other than negative corpus. Would you convict the suspect? What alternative theories might still be possible based on the uncertainties in the case? How likely (or unlikely) are Holmes' solutions?

2. Name and describe three ways that the science of fire investigation has changed since the 1980s (Lentini, 2012). Name and describe three remaining scientific issues that are gaps for fire debris investigation (Almirall et al., 2017). Which scientific gaps contributed to the Willingham wrongful conviction?
3. Consider the case of Terri Hinson, whose child was killed in a 1996 house fire. See https://www.newyorker.com/magazine/2009/09/07/trial-by-fire for information about her case. There were V-shaped burn patterns in her child's closet that were determined to be the point of origin of the fire. Because there was nothing in the closet that could ignite the fire by itself, investigators concluded that it had been deliberately set. Later, it was established that the fire was set in the house's attic. What factors led to the error? You might reference a presentation on the case by Robert Blackledge: https://www.nist.gov/system/files/documents/2016/11/22/six_thinking_hats_method_of-removing_bias_from_case_review.blackledge.humanfact.pdf.

FURTHER READING

The Texas Forensic Science Commission report on Willingham and Willis is required reading for anyone interested in wrongful convictions (Texas Forensic Science Commission, 2011). A useful summary presentation at the North Carolina Association of Arson Investigators is available online at https://www.nciaai.com/conferences/documents/2016-conference-class-materials/104-texas-ipot-presentation-pdf/file.

The fire investigation community continues to improve its methods and scientific foundations. The American Association for the Advancement of Science (AAAS) report on remaining research gaps was developed by a group that consisted of interdisciplinary scientists and researchers (Almirall et al., 2017). The OSAC Fire and Explosion Subcommittee has developed two major documents that address issues raised by wrongful convictions: a strategic vision document (Fire & Explosion Investigation Subcommittee, 2021) and a standard for the organization of fire investigation units (Fire & Explosion Investigation Subcommittee, 2019).

John Lentini's work on fire science provides the most balanced and thorough analysis of wrongful convictions in any field of forensic science to date, The Evolution of Fire Investigation and Its Impact on Arson Cases (Lentini, 2012). He maintains a website, https://www.firescientist.com/, and has written a definitive text on fire investigation, Scientific Protocols for Fire Investigation, Third Edition, (Lentini, 2018).

REFERENCES

Almirall, J., Arkes, H., Lentini, J., Mowrer, F., & Pawliszyn, J. (2017). *Forensic Science Assessments: A Quality and Gap Analysis. Report 1: Fire Investigation.* Washington, DC: American Association for the Advancement of Science.

Beyler, C. L. (2009). *Analysis of the Fire Investigation Methods and Procedures Used in the Criminal Arson Cases Against Ernest Ray Willis and Cameron Todd Willingham.* Huntsville: Texas Forensic Science Commission.

Bieber, P. (2014). Anatomy of a Wrongful Arson Conviction: Sentinel Event Analysis in Fire Investigation. International Symposium on Fire Investigation, Science and Technology (pp. 1–17), College Park.

Boudreau, J., Kwan, Q., Faragher, W., & Densult, G. (1974). *Arson and Arson Investigation: Survey and Assessment.* Washington, DC: National Institute of Justice.

Brannigan, F., Bright, R., & Jason, N. (1980). *Fire Investigation Handbook.* Gaithersburg, MD: US Department of Commerce, National Bureau of Standards.

Caminata v. Cnty. of Wexford, 16-1451 (United States Court of Appeals for the Sixth Circuit November 16, 2016).

Commonwealth v. Carnevale, 200615299 (Common Pleas Court of Allegheny County, Pennsylvania, Criminal Division January 26, 2012).

Conan Doyle, A. (1927). The Case Book of Sherlock Holmes. *Strand Magazine.*

DeHaan, J., & Icove, D. (2011). *Kirk's Fire Investigation.* New York, NY: Pearson Higher Ed.

Ex parte Cacy, WR-85, 420–01 (Court of Criminal Appeals of Texas November 2, 2016).

Fire & Explosion Investigation Subcommittee. (2019). *Standard for the Organization and Operation of Fire Investigation Units.* Organization of Scientific Area Committees. Retrieved from https://www.nist.gov/system/files/documents/2020/04/06/Draft%20FIU%20Standard%20AUG%202019_OSAC%20Proposed.pdf

Fire & Explosion Investigation Subcommitee. (2021). *Strengthening Fire and Explosion Investigation in the United States: A Strategic Vision for Moving Forward*. Organization of Scientific Area Committees. Retrieved from https://www.nist.gov/system/files/documents/2021/07/28/Technical%20Guidance%20Document_Strengthening%20Fire%20and%20Explosion%20Investigation%20in%20the%20U.S._A%20Strategic%20Vision%20for%20Moving%20Forward_April%202021.pdf

Giannelli, P. (2013). Junk Science and the Execution of an Innocent Man. *New York University Journal of Law & Liberty*, *7*(2), 221.

Hall, d. (2013, March 26). After 6-year Ordeal and Nearly 3 Years in Prison, Joseph Awe Is a Free Man. *Wisconsin State Journal*.

Hsieh, C., Horng, S., & Liao, P. (2003). Stability of Trace-level VOLatile Organic Compounds Stored in Canisters and Tedlar Bags. *Aerosol and Air Quality Research*, *3*, 17–28. https://doi.org/10.4209/aaqr.2003.06.0003

James Kluppelberg vs. Jon Burge et al, 13 CV 3963 (US District Court for the Northern District of Illinois Eastern Division November 5, 2015).

Latta v. Chapala, 2:03-CV-41 (United States District Court, N.D. Indiana, Hammond Division October 25, 2005).

Lentini, J. (2012). The Evolution of Fire Investigation and Its Impact on Arson Cases. *Criminal Justice*, *27*, 12–18.

Lentini, J. (2018). *Scientific Protocols for Fire Investigation*, 3rd ed. Taylor & Francis Books.

National Fire Protection Association. (1976). *Fire Protection Handbook*, 14th ed. Boston: National Fire Protection Association.

National Fire Protection Association. (1992). *Guide for Fire and Explosion Investigations (NFPA 921–92)*. Quincy: NFPA.

National Fire Protection Association. (2017). *NFPA 921, Guide for Fire and Explosion Investigations*. Quincy: NFPA.

People v. Willis, A139858, A 154925 (Court of Appeal of California, First Appellate District, Division Four April 29, 2019).

Shugarts, J. (2018, July 20). State Police Arrest Fourth Suspect in Oxford Arson. *Republican American Archives*.

State of Wisconsin v. Joseph Awe, 07 CF 54 (State of Wisconsin Circuit Court Marquette County March 21, 2013).

State v. Awe, 2009AP633-CR (Court of Appeals of Wisconsin, District 4 March 4, 2010).

Texas Forensic Science Commission. (2011). *Willingham/Willis Investigation*.

Trial by Fire. (2009). *New Yorker*.

Victor Caminata v. Michael Jenkinson, 16-1451 (US Court of Appeals for the Sixth Circuit August 26, 2016).

Willingham v. State, 71,544 (Court of Criminal Appeals of Texas March 22, 1995).
Willis v. Cockrell, P-01-CA-20 CAPITAL HABEAS (United States District Court for the Western District of Texas, Pecos Division August 9, 2004).
Wrice v. Burge, 14 C 5934 (United States District Court for the Northern District of Illinois, Eastern Division January 27, 2020).

CHAPTER 10

Forensic Medicine and Pediatric Abuse

The abuse of a child is an especially heinous crime. The child victim is innocent and inherently vulnerable, lacking in power and agency. The child victim may not be able to report the crime because they are too young to articulate what has happened, too isolated, or too much in fear. They are generally victimized by those who are close to them or an authority figure. The child victim carries the psychological and physical burdens of abuse with them long after an incident of victimization has occurred.

The detection, investigation, and prosecution of child abuse occurs within this context of factors. The investigator faces a terrible dilemma. The uncertainties mean that it is very difficult to prove a case beyond a reasonable doubt. After all, the child victim may not be able to provide a reliable witness account, and no other witnesses are likely to have been present. There may even be doubt as to whether a crime has even occurred. The serious nature of the possible crime may motivate the investigator to pursue a weak case that would be abandoned in any other context. The investigator may follow a lower standard of proof or use less reliable evidence. In other contexts, it is common for detectives and prosecutors to demonstrate tunnel vision and continuation bias. They are susceptible to the human tendency to follow an initial hypothesis and discount alternative theories or contradictory evidence (sometimes referred to as "choice supportive bias"). Child abuse investigators are likely to be more vulnerable to these biases. They have less objective evidence on which to rely and more motivation to see justice done on behalf of the child victim.

MORAL PANIC

In extreme cases, investigators have come to believe that organized child abuse is widespread, leading to a "moral panic" (Grometstein, 2006). In general, moral panics are associated with multiple factors, including

DOI: 10.4324/9781003202578-10

the presumption that deviant people are committing acts that affront deeply held beliefs of society at large. There are calls for urgent action by those who claim to be experts in detecting and dealing with the danger. Advocates claim that the danger has been hidden from view due to a conspiracy, lack of leadership, or lack of expertise and insight, among others. In the minds of advocates, the danger can justify the modification of other social norms, including the fair administration of justice. Sociologists have described moral panics in a variety of sociocultural contexts, and it is likely that social media has exacerbated the general likelihood of moral panics. Within a criminal justice framework, moral panics have been associated with claims of organized child abuse networks from the 1970s and afterward. The most famous case involved the McMartin preschool in the early 1980s (see Figure 10.1). These cases have led to the arrest of dozens of suspected abusers who were alleged to

FIGURE 10.1 Virginia Mcmartin, pictured, founded the McMartin Preschool in Manhattan Beach, which was implicated in a child sexual abuse scandal that lasted for seven years but resulted in no convictions. Investigators alleged that 360 children had been abused, but the case depended on suggestive interviews, dubious medical findings, and bizarre ritual abuse claims. Pediatric abuse cases of the period reflected a moral panic reminiscent of the Salem witch trials. Source: Mel Melcon, Los Angeles Times, Creative Commons Attribution 4.0 International License. Image cropped.

have victimized large numbers of children. The incidents were not confined to specific countries, and organized abuse cases were filed in every US state and most Western countries. The prevalence of organized abuse claims has declined substantially since that time.

The indicators of moral panic may also be observed in individual cases in which pediatric sexual and physical abuse has been alleged. Investigators may feel that they are the only voices to support a victimized child. They may have real concerns that an abused child will be returned to be victimized again or that an abuser will go free and reoffend. Under such an impression, it is possible that they may exhibit tunnel vision, ignore exculpatory evidence, misrepresent evidence, or misuse their authority. By necessity, they will call on medical experts to support a prosecution due to the inherent limitations of juvenile witnesses. In particular, it may not even be clear if a crime has taken place, especially in infant head trauma or sexual abuse cases. The conclusions of a medical specialist will be needed to determine if the child has been abused and therefore may have an outsized impact on the case outcome.

In this context, the medical specialist is no longer a clinician who is only concerned with the well-being of the child and the best medical interventions to heal physical or emotional wounds. They also become a forensic examiner, a role with very different demands and constraints. The medical specialist may not have training in forensic reporting or testimony. In clinical practice, they may rely on past experience or medical guesswork, but those approaches provide an insufficient foundation for a finding of guilt beyond a reasonable doubt in a criminal court. Medical experts are seldom affiliated with a forensic science organization. Their licensing and certification depend on their medical training and performance, not the quality of their forensic work. Meanwhile, they may be the primary source of reliable and objective information to support or undermine a child abuse case. If the medical specialist fails in this role, innocent caregivers may be unjustly convicted of heinous crimes.

The physician or medical expert is not immune from the possibility that their revulsion over the abuse of a child may bias their interpretation of a case. Unlike other forensic professionals, they cannot be easily walled off from contextual information. More commonly, they seek out contextual information to improve the reliability of their clinical diagnosis. This context will also impact their forensic reports and testimony. In some wrongful convictions, the medical findings may have been in error because of the lack of information about the medical background of a victim or the other records in a case. Unfortunately, this information may also bias the examiner and produce an unreliable forensic interpretation. The problem of cognitive bias in forensic medicine deserves additional research attention.

SHAKEN BABY SYNDROME

The American Academy of Pediatrics (AAP) provides standards for the assessment of pediatric abuse. The standards have been modified considerably since the 1990s. In part, this was in response to wrongful convictions which demonstrated that standards lacked specificity and empirical foundations. Pediatric abuse is inherently difficult for the researcher because it cannot be studied in traditional empirical frameworks. Most research has been based on clinical reports, especially those relating to confessed abusers (De Leeuw, Beuls, Parizel, Jorens, & Jacobs, 2013).

In 2019, AAP issued the *Consensus statement on abusive head trauma in infants and young children*, which sought to clarify the assessment of pediatric head injuries (Choudhary et al., 2018). The term, abusive head trauma (AHT), was promoted in the 2000s to replace the term shaken baby syndrome (SBS). In theory, AHT could relate to situations in which the injury was the result of many factors other than shaking. Previously, SBS was diagnosed on the basis of a "triad" of observations: subdural brain hemorrhage, retinal bleeding, and hypoxic encephalopathy (i.e., brain damage due to a shortage of blood flow to the brain). Figure 10.2 provides a guide to the various types of brain hemorrhage, any of which may be observed in alleged pediatric abuse cases.

The theory of SBS is based on the vulnerability of infants to brain and spinal injury even in the absence of external physical trauma. When the triad of symptoms was observed, the infant was presumed to have been violently shaken. The shaking was assumed to produce internal injuries that were often diagnosed postmortem. It was further assumed that the injuries were so severe that the child could not survive for an extended period after shaking, so the last caregiver was often presumed to have inflicted the injuries. Thus, SBS was sometimes called a "diagnosis of murder" because the medical finding was sufficient to implicate the last caregiver as the murderer of the child. AAP's 2019 statement on AHT diverged from this view and held that "no single injury is diagnostic of AHT" and emphasized the need for a differential diagnosis based on all factors available to the diagnostician. It also argued that some claims made by defense lawyers to argue against an AHT finding were invalid, including cerebral venous sinus thrombosis (CVST, a blood clot in the veins that drain the brain) and lumbar puncture (a medical diagnostic test used to assess spinal injuries). Innocence advocates have argued that the AAP statement undermines legitimate medical defenses and therefore represents a false consensus that is not supported by medical research, clinical evidence, or legal case histories (Findley et al., 2019; Papetti et al., 2019). If there is a consensus among legal and medical professionals, it is the need for a thorough differential diagnosis that considers all possible causes of pediatric injuries or conditions.

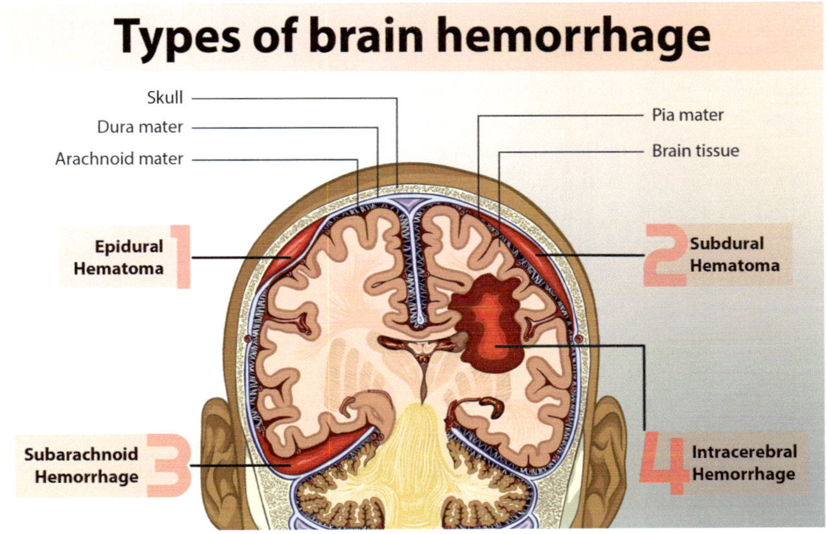

FIGURE 10.2 An illustration of the different types of brain hemorrhage. The four primary types of brain hemorrhage. While the subdural hematoma is most often associated with shaken baby syndrome, the other types of hemorrhage are also observed in pediatric abuse cases. Any hemorrhage may lead to hypoxic encephalopathy, depending on its severity. Source https://www.myupchar.com/en/disease/brain-hemorrhage Creative Commons license from Wikimedia.

JULIE BAUMER

The AAP may have felt the need to respond to the wrongful conviction case of Julie Baumer, who took responsibility for the care of her nephew due to his mother's incapacity. The baby required intensive neonatal care but was able to go home with Baumer at two weeks of age. She took him to the pediatrician twice, and he appeared healthy. On October 3, 2003, she took him to the emergency room when he became "very fussy" and unwilling to eat. The emergency room physician said the baby was severely dehydrated, hypoglycemic, anemic, and in kidney failure. The pediatric intensive care unit found severe brain trauma and a skull fracture that were said to have been inflicted in the last 12–24 hours based on CT and MRI scans. The pediatric radiologist concluded that the baby's injuries were best explained by blunt force trauma and shaking, though the radiologist and the Chief of Pediatric Neurosurgery agreed that the injuries were consistent with a fall.

The baby survived. Baumer filed to adopt the child, but she was charged with first-degree child abuse four months later. At trial, prosecution witnesses gave conflicting testimony about the nature and age of the child's injuries, but Baumer's lawyer called only one expert on her behalf. That individual was found to be unqualified to read CT scans and therefore was unable to provide any testimony that countered prosecution arguments. Baumer was convicted and sentenced to 10–15 years in prison.

The Michigan Innocence Clinic intervened on her behalf and were able to overturn the conviction on the basis of inadequate defense. A second trial was then held. Prosecution experts held that the child was a victim of abusive head trauma. Defense experts held that the child was suffering from CVST, one of the conditions dismissed by the 2019 AAP consensus statement. They claimed that fetal monitoring strips that had not been introduced in the first trial were evidence in support of the CVST diagnosis. In response, the prosecution argued that CVST is very rare and affects only 5 people in 1 million each year. The risk is greatest for newborns such as Baumer's nephew. The defense was supported by a wide range of medical experts, including physicians who had testified for the prosecution in the first trial. Among other issues, the diagnosis of the radiologist concerning the child's head injuries was called into question by the possibility that their assessment was influenced by contextual information from other medical professionals. Once the emergency room physician suspected abuse, it is possible that the other medical practitioners exercised professional deference and made conclusions that aligned with that view. In summary, prosecutors could not overcome the many uncertainties in the case. Baumer was acquitted by the second jury and awarded $204,389 for her wrongful conviction by the state of Michigan.

LUCID INTERVAL

As the Baumer case demonstrates, there are inherent uncertainties in infant AHT cases. The diagnostic confidence level required for medical intervention may be much lower than that required to support a forensic conclusion in a court of law. Pediatric abuse cases have greater inherent uncertainty due to the inability to conduct empirical studies to improve the understanding of the phenomenology of injuries. Case variability complicates analysis even further. These issues are similar to those faced by bite mark examination, which is characterized by lack of empirical data, variations and distortions in latent evidence, and association with clinical medicine (i.e., dentists). Over the years, the AAP has addressed the problems in pediatric abuse by emphasizing the need for rigorous evidence collection, documentation, differential diagnosis, and limiting language concerning the level of confidence in forensic conclusions. In particular, pediatric abuse cases require careful consideration of medical history, which may directly relate to considerations in differential diagnosis. Also, research has improved some understanding of key issues. For example, the AAP now recognizes that children with fatal head injuries may "have altered mental status immediately after the injury" but does not accept that an asymptomatic lucid interval may occur prior to neurologic collapse. The word, "asymptomatic," does much work here because AHT cases often include victims with extensive symptoms of head trauma but some level of lucidity prior to death.

The 1995 Audrey Edmunds conviction is a famous example of a shaken baby syndrome case involving lucid interval issues (State of Wisconsin v. Audrey Edmunds, 2008). The victim's injuries provided substantial evidence for sustained and severe physical trauma. The question in the case revolved around whether the injuries were sustained while the child—Natalie, a seven-month-old baby—was in Edmund's care. During prior visits to the pediatrician, the baby had shown lethargy and vomiting. The parents appeared to be caring and loving and testified that they had never shaken or hit Natalie. For her part, Edmunds said the baby appeared normal when she was dropped off at her home day care but soon began to cry and refused her bottle. After tending to other children, Edmunds said she found Natalie had stopped crying and was limp. Liquid was coming out of her nose and mouth. She called 911 but the child was pronounced dead later that night at the hospital.

Under the understanding of SBS in 1995, Edmunds must have been responsible for "reckless homicide" and have shaken the baby to death. One defense expert did testify that a lucid interval after shaking was possible, but there was no scientific research to support that claim. By 2008, six experts were willing to state that a lucid interval was possible in Natalie's case, while four maintained that the 1990s understanding was still valid. The research concerning abusive head trauma and lucid interval has advanced considerably in recent years, now supporting lucid intervals up to 72 hours (De Leeuw et al., 2013a). The 2008 appeals court vacated the Edmunds conviction on the basis of "newly discovered evidence" relating to the emergence of a medical debate concerning lucid interval in AHT cases. The charges against Edmunds were then dismissed. She has steadfastly maintained her innocence and even written a book about the case.

PROSECUTION VIEWS

One prosecutor, Milwaukee County Deputy District Attorney Matthew Torbenson, views the Edmunds case as an example of the use of false defenses in AHT cases (Torbenson, 2019). Torbenson notes that forensic pathologists still hold that the lucid interval is unlikely (or impossible) after lethal AHT and that defense experts and attorneys are producing a false courtroom controversy about the issue. One expert whose work has been cited in multiple exonerations, Dr. Jennian Geddes, has asserted that hypoxia—low oxygen levels—can cause the brain to swell and produce subdural hematomas of the type observed in AHT cases. In actual testimony, Geddes says that this was only a theory and should not be a basis for overturning convictions. To Torbenson's point, the 2016 appeals decision in the Edmunds case refers to the Geddes theory as a "finding" and failed to appreciate the distinction between a scientific hypothesis and an empirical observation. Torbenson details "irresponsible" testimony by medical experts in postconviction hearings. For example, he noted the case of biomechanics expert John Lloyd, whose work was widely cited in the Drayton Witt exoneration. Lloyd misrepresented his credentials as a professor at University of South Florida and subsequently entered a provisional plea of no contest to felony counts of perjury. Torbenson has claimed that many defense experts are biased by financial rewards in AHT cases. He advises prosecutors to be aware of the overall context of a case, the possible non-abuse causes that may be raised by the defense, and the need for a trial strategy that fully counters common defense strategies.

It is clear that reliable child abuse prosecution requires diligence among the medical professionals involved in the case. Communication and documentation failures can lead to unreliable verdicts. In 2002 in Illinois, Randy Liebech was arrested and charged with the death of three-year-old Steven Quinn, the son of his girlfriend, Kenyatta Brown. Brown's possible involvement in the death was discounted by critical care pediatrician Dr. Paul Severin, who held that Steven's injuries were inflicted four to six hours prior to hospital admission. The child had been in Liebich's care throughout the day, so Severin's conclusion implicated Liebich in the crime and exculpated Brown. Nonetheless, there was substantial evidence that Brown had abused the child previously and that Liebich and Brown used PCP, marijuana, and heroin around the child.

Forensic pathologist Dr. Darinka Mileusnic-Polchan documented more than 40 bruises and other marks at autopsy, including some that appeared to be healing (People v. Liebich, 2016). A CT scan showed a large subdural hemorrhage. Mileusnic-Polchan and her colleague, Dr. Shaku Teas, agreed that the injuries that led to Steven's death occurred at least five days before his death. Unknown to Mileusnic-Polchan and Teas, the CT scan was contradicted by hospital records showing that the subdural hemorrhage was not found when hospital doctors opened the child's skull to relieve pressure on the brain. The child also had pancreatitis from a healing hematoma that was 10–21 days old and myocarditis. Mileusnic-Polchan also never saw lab reports showing that the pancreatitis was at least ten days old and that the child had sustained a traumatic event five days before removal of life support. As detailed in the 2016 appeal decision that led to the vacating of Liebich's conviction, there was poor communication among the doctors and forensic pathologists in the case. Mileusnic-Polchan did not have access to the full medical record, which put her in an impossible position in attempting to analyze the case.

Mileusnic-Polchan, Teas, and Severin did not put great weight on the relevance of the emerging research concerning extended lucid intervals after abuse, although there were uncertainties concerning AHT and subdural hemorrhage in the case. During the postconviction proceedings, Mileusnic-Polchan clearly indicated that the head injury was "closer to five days old than to three days old." She also noted that Steven's myocarditis was at least a week old and could have been coded as the cause of death in the absence of the other findings. In deciding not to pursue a second trial after Liebich's conviction was overturned, the State's Attorney noted that Steven was a "chronically mistreated child" but relied on Mileusnic-Polchan's analysis to conclude that the child had died from abdominal injuries inflicted at least two days before hospital admission. The decision did not absolve Liebich in the case, but it did recognize the uncertainties about the timing of the injuries and the possibility that Kenyatta Brown or another individual may have inflicted the injuries that led to Steven's death.

EFFECTIVE DEFENSE

Given the diagnostic difficulties, an effective defense in a child abuse case requires access to competent medical experts. Many defendants cannot afford to retain experts. This problem may be getting worse due to the increasing complexity of medical and scientific knowledge. A clear example is the 2015 conviction of Dane Kurkowski and Codie Lynn Stevens for the death of their baby. The child suffered bruising as the result of a difficult birth but appeared to thrive over the first two months of life, though he was fussy and irritable. Krukowski dropped the baby while bathing him, but it appeared the child only received a "dime-sized bruise." The baby was acting normal the next day. Two days later, the bump was not visible during a pediatrician visit. The pediatrician, Dr.

Elvira Dawes, recommended they take the child to a chiropractor in the hopes of reducing his fussiness. The chiropractor, Michael Dense, "adjusted" the baby by suspending him by the feet. The baby's grandmother reported that she heard the child's back crack at least twice. They took the child to two more chiropractic appointments with another practitioner, Dr. Jason Barrigar, over the next two weeks.

On February 21, two weeks after the bathtub incident, the baby appeared to be having a seizure and was taken to the emergency room. The hospital physicians could find no signs of trauma and administered intravenous Ativan, an anti-seizure medication. A CAT scan revealed brain bleeding. He was then transferred to the pediatric intensive care unit, where his condition deteriorated. He was put on a ventilator and feeding tube and a catheter was used to relieve intracranial pressure. Multiple rib fractures and retinal hemorrhages were found, which doctors concluded were so severe that they must have resulted from "non-accidental trauma and shaking" that was likely 36–48 hours old.

The child survived, but Krukowski and Stevens were arrested and charged with second degree child abuse. At trial, nine physicians testified to various aspects of the baby's medical history. The defense received $1000 from the court for an independent expert but none actually testified, presumably because this amount was grossly insufficient. They were convicted largely on the basis that they failed to obtain the medical care the baby needed and were not honest with the hospital doctors about the bathtub fall. The Michigan Court of Appeals overturned the conviction in 2019 because the evidence was insufficient to support a theory of "abandonment," which presupposes the withdrawal of parental protection and support. The court did not address the defendants' inadequate defense claim because the conviction was overturned on the insufficient evidence issue. That said, postconviction experts criticized the work of the medical experts in the original trial and claimed that they failed to conform to AAP guidelines in differential diagnosis. In particular, Dr. Karl Williams, chief medical examiner in Allegheny County, Pennsylvania, said the baby's injuries were not consistent with a shaken baby or AHT finding, and the medical experts had failed to account for the possibility that birth injuries or chiropractic manipulation could have caused the injuries. It is reasonable to assume that Krukowski and Stevens would not have been convicted if they had access to a defense expert during the original trial.

EXPERT VARIABILITY

The variability of medical experts is a general feature of AHT cases. Physician interpretations may vary based on the amount of information available to them, their training, or their biases. Usually, the medical expert is providing a reasonable diagnostic analysis even when disagreements arise. In pediatric sexual abuse cases, this type of variability is less common. This may be due to fundamental differences in the cases. Sexual abuse victims tend to be old enough to report abuse. As a result, medical examinations are used to support the credibility of victim testimony, not supplant it altogether. Also, medical findings in sexual abuse cases may not provide a clear indication of abuse. For over 20 years, the AAP has maintained that abuse may not produce physical findings in every case (Committee on Child Abuse and Neglect, 1999). Nonetheless, some medical practitioners may report or testify to a very high level of confidence that abuse occurred or about the circumstances of the abuse. Those conclusions are simply invalid if they are not based on clear medical evidence and provided within an appropriate context of the scientific limitations.

Practitioners may become advocates for victims and exaggerate their ability to discern the indications of sexual abuse. The Bruce Woodling "wink response" history—discussed in Chapter 5 on unvalidated methods—is a salient example. The misapplication of Child Abuse Accommodation Syndrome (CSAAS), also covered in the same chapter, provides a similar lesson. The wink response and CSAAS methods were very different from a phenomenological perspective. The wink response was based on a theory about the physiological response to anal penetration. CSAAS was based on a theory about the psychological response among children to sexual abuse. Of the two, CSAAS retains validity if applied in a clinical setting to improve the treatment of traumatized children. Both approaches have been used in child sexual abuse trials to support the reliability of child victim reports when the child's statements have been variable or even absent. The CSAAS theory has even been used to support the conclusion that abuse has occurred when there were no physical findings whatsoever. In these cases, the medical practitioner may make a conclusion of abuse based on the report of a child during a medical examination. AAP standards do allow for a medical practitioner to testify that abuse was possible but not substantiated in the absence of medical findings. In these cases, the absence of medical findings does not prove or disprove anything about the case. It just means that abuse, if it occurred, did not produce a physiological indication that a medical practitioner can detect. This distinction has led to some confusion in pediatric sexual abuse cases, including wrongful convictions, because investigators or fact-finders may not appreciate the meaning when a forensic report produces a non-probative result. Prosecutors and investigators may misinterpret the report or testimony to imply that the possibility of abuse is the same as a conclusion that abuse occurred. Defense lawyers may misinterpret the report or testimony of unsubstantiated abuse as proof that abuse definitely did not occur. Judges and juries may make similar mistakes.

DANIEL AND FRANCES KELLER

In 1991 Daniel and Frances Keller were accused of child sex abuse in Travis County, Texas. At the time, there were many cases of moral panic in which prosecutors and the public believed that child sex rings were victimizing large numbers of children. In many instances, the investigation would envelop additional suspects. The Keller case was no exception, and three other suspects were accused, including one who signed a confession. The cases also involved suggestive interviews with the presumed child victims, who would often report extreme and sensational behavior associated with the abuse. In the Keller case, a child reported that the Kellers had taken her to a cemetery, where they had dug up a grave. The child said that Daniel Keller had thrown a man dressed as a policeman into a hole, shot him, and cut the body up with a chainsaw while the children helped (Ex parte Keller, 2015). Police supported this testimony using infrared images showing disturbed ground in the cemetery. The owners of the cemetery later reported that the questioned graves were associated with normal maintenance at the site (Smith, 2009).

Emergency room doctor Dr. Michael Mouw performed a physical examination of a four-year-old female who was alleged to have been victimized. Mouw was not trained to examine children for sexual abuse. He testified that he found vaginal deformities that could have been signs of abuse, including redness and two lacerations. Two weeks later, pediatrician Dr. Beth Nauert did not find these indications, which she concluded had occurred soon before the Mouw exam and had healed in the meantime. In late 1992, the Kellers were convicted at a trial in which their defense lawyer did not present any independent child abuse experts. A CSAAS expert did testify concerning the variability in the reports from the alleged child victims. Essentially, Mouw's original diagnosis was given unquestioned force by other medical experts and the court. The jury could only conclude that serious abuse had occurred and that the Kellers were the only ones in a position to inflict it (Ex parte Keller, 2015).

In 2001, the state of Texas modified its standards for the determination of pediatric abuse to provide clearer guidance to medical professionals in the interpretation of anogenital findings in suspected pediatric abuse cases. Mouw also received training in such analysis after the 1992 trial. Although he did not recant his observations, he did recant his conclusion. In 2009, he told the media and later testified at an evidentiary hearing that the observed trauma "was actually a normal variation in the [child's] anatomy." Under the Texas and AAP standards, Mouw's trial and postconviction testimony could both be called into question. The observations were consistent with normal variation or with abuse but could not be definitively categorized either way. The Kellers's convictions were vacated on the basis of the Mouw recantation. A court later made an actual innocence finding, and they were awarded $3.4 million in compensation by the state of Texas and a $27,000/month lifetime annuity. It should be noted that some alleged child victims—now grown adults—remain convinced that the Kellers committed abuse.

BRIAN FRANKLIN

In 1994, a 13-year-old girl, "BR," accused Brian Franklin of sexually assaulting her. Examining physician Dr. Jan Lamb testified that "that there was a rupture in a certain area of the hymen indicative of blunt force trauma and that the injury observed on BR would be consistent with her bleeding at the time of the offense." (Ex parte Franklin, 2002). Lamb had performed the examination over a month after the alleged assault. Lamb said that she found bright red blood that she associated with ruptured capillaries as opposed to the darker color associated with menstrual blood. At trial, Lamb admitted on cross-examination that she could not distinguish whether the observations were associated with a sexual assault or first intercourse. A forensic serologist testified for the defense that blood stains found on BR's clothing were bright red and an indication of more recent abuse. Given the time frames and uncertainties involved, this testimony was highly speculative and invalid. Franklin was convicted and sentenced to life in prison.

Postconviction, the victim came forward to report that she had been repeatedly sexually assaulted by her stepfather, who later pled guilty to injuring a child. The stepfather had accompanied BR on visits to counselors and was present at the Lamb medical examination. She did not recant her testimony against Franklin. Franklin's conviction was overturned on the basis of BR's false trial testimony. The county prosecutor did elect to retry Franklin. Lamb clarified that her observations and conclusions were consistent with assault by Franklin, BR's stepfather, or both men. She was not aware of the possibility of another abuser at the time of the original trial and said she would have testified differently had she been aware of other abuse. Arguably, Lamb's testimony was valid in both trials, although she did not provide appropriate limiting testimony in the first trial until she was challenged by the defense on cross-examination. Franklin was acquitted by the jury at the second trial.

OTHER SEXUAL ABUSE CASES

In the 1991 trial of Andrew Anthony Taylor, the associate medical examiner of Miami-Dade County, Dr. Valerie Rao, testified concerning bruises on the victim and colposcope-based observations of injuries consistent with sexual abuse. The victim recanted as an adult, attributing the false allegation to physical abuse from her mother (Andrew Anthony Taylor vs. State of Florida, 2017). As detailed in the decision concerning Taylor's petition for postconviction compensation, Dr. Rao "persuasively and credibly testified" concerning the victim's injuries and the context and limitations of her findings. Rao had limited her testimony to descriptive analysis and statements about the possibility—not certainty—that the injuries were the result of sexual abuse. One may argue whether the language misled the jury. A statement that the injuries were "consistent with sexual abuse" may be interpreted by a juror to mean that abuse was a certainty. Members of the public may believe that experts may condition their answers to "cover" for the possibility that their interpretation is mistaken. Jurors in the Taylor case may have been favorably impressed by Rao, trusted her opinion, and interpreted her language as a definitive finding of abuse. AAP guidelines have been updated to allow more subtlety in the confidence level that is expressed by medical experts, but it is unclear if these changes would prevent confusion among fact-finders.

In the 1985 Harold Snowden case, the key issue was the detection of vaginal Gardnerella vaginitis (GV) in an alleged female victim and gonorrhea in the throat of an alleged male victim. All three alleged victims were under six years old. At the time, GV was considered a sexually transmitted disease, but a 1992 paper established that it could be found in the absence of abuse (Ingram, et al., 1992). Also, the gonorrhea test can have false positives, an issue possibly evidenced in the case when a subsequent test of the alleged male victim was negative (although it is unclear if this was due to the treatment of the infection). The AAP still considers gonorrhea to be a reliable indicator of a sexually transmitted disease. The defense presented an expert who raised the issue of the reliability of gonorrhea tests for consideration during the Snowden trial. A child psychologist testified during the trial that "99.5% of children tell the truth" about abuse, which was a misleading CSAAS-based interpretation (Snowden v. Singletary, 1998). Snowden's conviction was overturned in 1998 on the basis that the CSAAS testimony was improper and the 99.5% figure without basis.

HANNAH OVERTON

One final, noteworthy case is the 2007 conviction of Hannah Overton for the alleged murder of four-year-old Andrew Burd, in Corpus Christi, Texas (Ex parte Overton, 2014). Overton and her husband were in the process of adopting Andrew. In October 2006, they brought the child to an urgent care center. He was not breathing but was revived using chest compressions. He then vomited excessively, and the attending nurse said the vomit smelled and looked like chili. Andrew died the next day at a local children's hospital. His blood tests had shown a sodium level of 242 or more, nearly twice normal levels and considered acutely lethal. The medical examiner determined the death was a homicide. He claimed that Overton had poisoned the child with toxic levels of sodium and failed to provide him with adequate or timely medical care. The trial was held a year later, and she was convicted of capital murder and sentenced to life without parole. The jury held that the conviction was based on her failure to obtain timely medical care for Andrew, not on a finding that she had poisoned him.

Andrew had a history of unusual eating habits. He would eat off the floor, get into the trash, and even eat cat food. Overton said the child would throw tantrums if he was not allowed to eat whatever he wanted and whenever he wanted. He was obsessed with salty foods. On the day of his death, he had eaten chili with Zatarian's seasoning added to it. Overton had also given him water with Zatarian's. The child then insisted on getting more chili, but his tantrum caused him to throw up his food. The child calmed down, but his body temperature appeared to be very low. Overton wrapped him in a blanket and heating pad and became concerned he might be "in some sort of shock."

Before the trial, the defense team consulted Dr. Michael Moritz, a leading expert on hypernatremia (sodium intoxication). Overton had an extensive defense team, but none of the lawyers attended the Moritz deposition in its entirety. Moritz was not called to testify, and his deposition was not entered into evidence. One defense counsel said the deposition was "messed up" and full of interruptions and invalid objections from the prosecution. In addition, the trial had two postponements, and the defense did not want to inconvenience the court or the doctor. Moritz had said that Andrew exhibited classic signs of emotional deprivation syndrome, which was preexisting and not a result of the care he received in Overton's household during the foster-care period. He said Andrew most likely consumed the lethal dose of sodium voluntarily—even deliberately—and there was very little Overton could have done to prevent the death. Moritz explained that extreme hypernatremia has a mortality rate of at least 30–50%. He further said that hospitals often exacerbate the condition by the routine administration of saline intravenous fluids or the use of salt to induce vomiting in suspected poisonings. Further, the signs of hypernatremia are often difficult for a parent to differentiate. In Andrew's case, Overton thought he might have a lung infection based on prior experience. The symptoms of hypernatremia—vomiting, confusion, lethargy—may be subtle for a parent without prior experience of salt poisoning. In the hospital, it took hours for the blood test results to come back and be confirmed, a delay which was also significant in Andrew's outcome. Moritz said that he has treated hypernatremia and used supportive care and dialysis, but the ultimate outcome is based on luck "to a large degree." Even if Andrew had lived, he would likely have had "irreversible neurological injury."

Overton was not well-served by her defense team. The failure to present Moritz's testimony was not based on a trial strategy. The decision was based on the difficulty of presenting the deposition or dealing with court delays. The habeas court found that the testimony could have changed the outcome of the trial and vacated the conviction on the basis of inadequate defense. A concurring opinion also noted that the lead prosecutor admitted to being an alcoholic and prescription drug abuser at the time of trial. She didn't remember case details or documents when asked during postconviction proceedings. The prosecutor had sent a "spy" to Overton's church group to learn the defense strategy in the case. The prosecutor also suppressed evidence that some samples of Andrew's vomit had been preserved. That fact might have allowed Moritz or another medical expert to test the vomit to make a more definitive finding about the nature of the hypernatremia. It might have supported the defense theory that Andrew had ingested salt earlier in the day without Overton's permission or knowledge. The concurrence noted that Overton was six-months pregnant at the time of the incident and had fallen asleep with her two-year-old son and Andrew while watching cartoons. When she woke, Andrew had left. She found him in the pantry. The child threw a tantrum when she interrupted him, and he proceeded to demand more salt. He could have ingested salt without her knowledge while she had been asleep. Further, the prosecution had insisted that Andrew had no preexisting conditions or emotional issues despite extensive evidence to the contrary. A previous foster parent had told Andrew's pediatrician about his behavior and had taken him to a neurologist. That pediatrician altered his view of the case between the trial and postconviction review and held that Andrew had likely ingested a great deal of salt on his own in addition to the Zatarian's he was given by Overton.

A dissent noted that the defense did call an expert, Dr. Judy Melinek. Melinek's testimony was similar to Moritz's testimony. It also noted interviews with two of Overton's older children, who claimed that Overton used pepper as a punishment. They said Overton punished Andrew in this way but that it was limited to "sprinkles." The dissent noted that the defense was apparently trying to prevent this information from being entered into consideration during the trial, and that was the reason why they didn't include Moritz's testimony. The defense attorneys did not admit that this was their strategy, but the habeas dissent made the inference from the sequence of events in the trial. Moritz had speculated about the likelihood that Andrew would have died regardless of when Overton had taken the child to urgent care or the hospital. The defense did succeed in this regard. The children's interviews were not introduced during the trial. Moritz was unaware of the children's statements and said during the postconviction review that the possibility could change his opinion about Overton's culpability. Thus, the dissent held that the defense counsel was competent and Overton had received a fair trial.

The majority opinion overturned Overton's conviction. A year later, the district court attorney dismissed the charge. In 2017, Overton received a finding of actual innocence. She received $573,333 in compensation and an annuity from the state of Texas.

The Overton case is an extraordinary combination of the factors that arise in pediatric abuse cases. Andrew was a child, and his thoughts and actions are wholly unknown to us. He may or may not have been poisoned. He may or may not have survived with faster medical attention. He may have had intellectual or emotional issues that resulted from poor care as a baby or toddler. The opinions do not speculate about the actions of the urgent care facility or hospital, but they may not have reacted correctly to Andrew's case when they had the opportunity. Further, there were problems with communication among the medical providers, forensic pathologist, and trial experts. At minimum, miscommunication had prevented the consideration of important medical details. At worst, the prosecutor committed misconduct that prevented a fair trial. Based on the points in the trial dissent, it is not even clear if the defense counsel had served Overton poorly or had cleverly avoided the introduction of incriminating evidence.

How does one judge the Overton case? Officially, she was an innocent person who was wrongfully convicted. Unofficially, the facts paint an ambiguous picture. The only certainty is that the Overton case is a failure of the criminal justice system. The experts did not have the full picture of the medical and contextual issues in the case. Dr. Moritz's expertise was not represented at the trial. The prosecution and defense failed to give the jury a complete and thorough picture of the considerations. The issues may have their root cause in the inherent uncertainties and subjectivity of forensic medicine and in the inability of the criminal court system to use complex forensic science in a consistently reliable manner.

STUDY QUESTIONS

1. The Michigan Supreme Court hearing in the Krukowski/Stevens case is available on YouTube at https://youtu.be/uQIaNU545Ec. The Supreme Court denied the appeal after that hearing, upholding the lower court ruling that exonerated the couple. The decision can be found online at https://law.justia.com/cases/michigan

/court-of-appeals-unpublished/2019/334320.html. In your view, were they guilty of child abuse in the second degree? How does the forensic medical testimony support or refute your view of the case?
2. Many pediatric abuse cases rely on a medical finding that a crime occurred. For example, the medical expert must conclude that the evidence supports a finding of abusive head trauma. Therefore, a prosecution-friendly medical interpretation will always be presented at trial, even if the medical data may support a defense-friendly interpretation as well. What does this imply about the need for the defense to have access to adequate medical expertise? Are lawyers well-trained to understand medical science so that they can represent their clients properly?
3. Consider the Hannah Overton case. What forms of cognitive bias were present among the medical professionals? Is it possible that the child's medical care was inadequate? How would this possibility influence medical testimony? What can be done to limit cognitive bias among those who give forensic medical testimony?

FURTHER READING

Grometstein contributed an important essay on the international spread of pediatric abuse allegations and accompanying moral panic in the Huff and Kilias book on wrongful convictions in the international context (Grometstein, 2006). The other essays in that book provide a clear basis that wrongful convictions are by no means an exclusive phenomenon of one country or structure of government.

Papetti, Kaneb, and Herf provide a substantive critique of the American Academy of Pediatrics' approach to abusive head trauma in their 2019 paper (Papetti, Kaneb, & Herf, 2019). Papetti has also contributed a book on shaken baby syndrome (Papetti, 2018). One should review the various American Academy of Pediatrics standards provided in the references prior to reading the paper by Papetti et al. It is clear that the standards have improved a great deal, but the issues are far from fully resolved. For those who wish to learn more about the general topic, Johnson's book, *Physical Abusers and Sexual Offenders*, encompasses cases relating to adult and child victims (Johnson, 2007).

There are countless books written about wrongful convictions in child abuse cases. Many of them are poorly written and hopelessly biased. One exception is *Witch Hunt* by Kathryn Lyon (Lyon, 1998). Dozens of individuals were convicted in connection with the Wenatchee, Washington case. Several defendants were arrested after criticizing the conduct of the investigation. Almost all of the convictions were eventually overturned.

REFERENCES

Andrew Anthony Taylor vs. State of Florida, 17–002295VWI (Division of Administrative Hearings, Florida November 28, 2017).

Choudhary, A., Servaes, S., Slovis, T., Palusci, V., Hedlund, G., Narang, S., ... Offiah, A. (2018). Consensus Statement on Abusive Head Trauma in Infants. *Pediatic Radiology*, 1048–1065.

Committee on Child Abuse and Neglect. (1999). Guidelines for the Evaluation of Sexual Abuse of Children: Subject Review. *Pediatrics*, *103*, 186–191. https://doi.org/10.1542/peds.103.1.186

Committee on Child Abuse and Neglect. (2013). The Evaluation of Children in the Primary Care Setting When Sexual Abuse Is Suspected. *Pediatrics*, *132*(2), e558–e567.

De Leeuw, M., Beuls, E., Jorens, P., Parizel, P., & Jacobs, W. (2013a). History of an Abusive Head Trauma Including a Lucid Interval and a Retinal Hemorrhage Is Most Likely False. *The American Journal of Forensic Medicine and Pathology*, *34*(3), 271–276.

De Leeuw, M., Beuls, E., Parizel, P., Jorens, P., & Jacobs, W. (2013b). Confessed Abusive Blunt Head Trauma. *The American Journal of Forensic Medicine and Pathology*, *34*(2), 130–132.

Ex parte Franklin, 72 S.W.3d 671 (Court of Criminal Appeals of Texas April 10, 2002).

Ex parte Keller, WR-36, 232–02 (Court of Criminal Appeals of Texas May 20, 2015).

Ex parte Overton, WR-75,804-02 (Court of Criminal Appeals of Texas September 17, 2014).

Findley, K., Risinger, D., Barnes, P., Mack, J., Moran, D., Scheck, B., & Bohan, T. (2019). Feigned Consensus: Usurping the Law in Shaken Baby Syndrome/Abusive Head Trauma Prosecutions. *SSRN Electronic Journal* (January), 1–64.

Grometstein, R. (2006). Wrongful Conviction and the Moral Panic About Organized Child Abuse: National and International Perspectives. In C. Huff, & M. Kilias (Eds.), *Wrongful Conviction: International Perspectives on Miscarriages of Justice*. Philadelphia, PA: Temple University Press.

Ingram, D., White, S., Lyna, P., Crews, K., Schmid, J., Everett, V., & Koch, G. (1992). Gardnerella vaginalis infection and sexual contact in female children. *Child Abuse & Neglect*, *16*(6), 847–853. https://doi.org/10.1016/0145-2134(92)90086-7

Johnson, S. (2007). *Physical Abusers and Sexual Offenders: Forensic and Clinical Strategies*. Boca Raton, FL: CRC Press.

Lyon, K. (1998). *Witch Hunt: A True Story of Social Hysteria and Abused Justice*. New York, NY: Avon Books.

Papetti, Randy. (2018) *The Forensic Unreliability of the Shaken Baby Syndrome*. La Jolla, CA: Academic Forensic Pathology International.

Papetti, R., Kaneb, P., & Herf, L. (2019). Outside the Echo Chamber: A Response to the "Consensus Statement on Abusive Head Trauma in Infants and Young Children. *Santa Clara Law Review*, *59*, 299–366.

People v. Liebich, 2-13-0894 (Appellate Court of Illinois, Second District March 28, 2016).

Smith, J. (2009, March 27). Believing the Children. *Austin Chronicle*.

Snowden v. Singletary, 94-4303 (US Court of Appeals, Eleventh Circuit February 18, 1998).

State of Wisconsin v. Audrey Edmunds, 2007AP933 (Court of Appeals of Wisconsin January 31, 2008).

Summit, R. (1992). Abuse of the Child Sexual Abuse Accommodation Syndrome. *Journal of Child Sexual Abuse*, *1*(4), 153–164.

Torbenson, M. (2019). Overcoming Untrue Defenses in Abusive Head Trauma. In Lurie Children's Hospital Child Maltreatment Symposium.

CHAPTER 11

Forensic Pathology

While the clinical pathologist examines the causes of disease and injury, the forensic pathologist is concerned with the examination of causes of death. Inevitably, forensic pathology has been an element of every wrongful conviction involving a decedent. That does not imply that the forensic pathologist contributed to the wrongful conviction in each case. The cause and manner of death determination may have been correct, and other evidence or circumstances may have influenced the conviction. But it is likely that the case depended on the forensic pathologist at some level. For example, if the death is not ruled a homicide, it is unlikely that a prosecutor can pursue a homicide case, and it may never see a trial court. If the death is ruled a homicide, then the forensic pathologist will be "on the side" of the prosecution to support the case. Therefore, the forensic pathologist is much more likely to support a prosecution theory of a case than a defense theory of a case.

The forensic pathologist may provide a diverse set of conclusions about a death. First, the manner of death may be classified as homicide, suicide, accident, natural, or undetermined. These classifications are essentially oriented around the public health system and do not necessarily correspond to legal definitions. For example, the manner of death may be homicide because the determination is based on the condition that the death was caused by action of another person, even if that person did not deliberately cause the death. So, the manner of death in murders is homicide. But not all deaths coded as homicide by a forensic pathologist are murders. The cause of death relates to the medical reasons for the death and may include a wide variety of proximate and ultimate causes. For example, an individual's death may be caused by a heart attack (the proximate cause) but have been ultimately caused by coronary artery disease. In wrongful convictions, the forensic pathologist may contribute many other types of analysis, including an assessment of injuries, time of death, and toxicological analysis. As observed in bite mark analysis, injury assessment of a decedent may produce errors if a postmortem artifact is misinterpreted. In some cases, the autopsy may include an analysis of the type of weapon, such as a particular knife, that may have caused

DOI: 10.4324/9781003202578-11

an injury. Also, the autopsy may include an analysis of the trajectory of a bullet that struck the decedent. The time of death or postmortem interval may be estimated from the condition of the body and aspects of the environment in which the body was found. These determinations may have a profound influence on the outcome of a case because they may support or refute a case theory or defendant's alibi. Postmortem interval estimates are also highly variable and subjective, as outlined in Figure 11.2. Postmortem toxicology may provide support for a theory of homicide if poisons are found. Modern biochemical analysis permits more detailed examination of the metabolism of drugs and poisons and their effects on various organs. As a result, the forensic toxicologist may play the critical role in the assessment of the cause and manner of death.

MEDICAL EXAMINERS AND CORONERS

Death investigation systems are highly variable. Many jurisdictions rely on coroners. Historically, coroners were a representative of the crown and played a role in tax and revenue collection. Their role in death investigation arose from the fact that the proceeds from a wrongful death would often become the property of the king. Eventually, such determinations were their primary stock in trade. In the 20th century, some governments replaced coroner systems with medical examiners. In New York City in 1914, a reform mayor, John Purroy Mitchell, discovered severe corruption among appointed coroners (Helpern & Knight, 1977). In one case involving the death of a friend of the mayor, the coroner would not issue a death certificate unless the deceased was taken to a particular undertaker favored by the coroner. Famously, Mitchell called on Leonard Wallstein to conduct an investigation. Wallstein found that coroners would issue death certificates on a small card with the name of the deceased and the cause of death and no other information. Often, the cause of death would be meaningless because the coroners had no medical training whatsoever. District attorneys would routinely ignore the coroner's conclusions and hire their own physicians and pathologists to perform an autopsy and investigation. In 1915, the state legislature established the New York City Office of the Chief Medical Examiner (OCME), which remains the primary forensic laboratory serving the city to this day. The OCME was directed and staffed by skilled pathologists and microscopists, transforming death investigations in the city and serving as a model for many other jurisdictions.

Nonetheless, many coroners remain, including appointed and elected coroners without medical training, as seen in Figure 11.1. In general, coroner systems now rely on trained forensic pathologists to conduct autopsies and issue death certificates. Many observers have complained

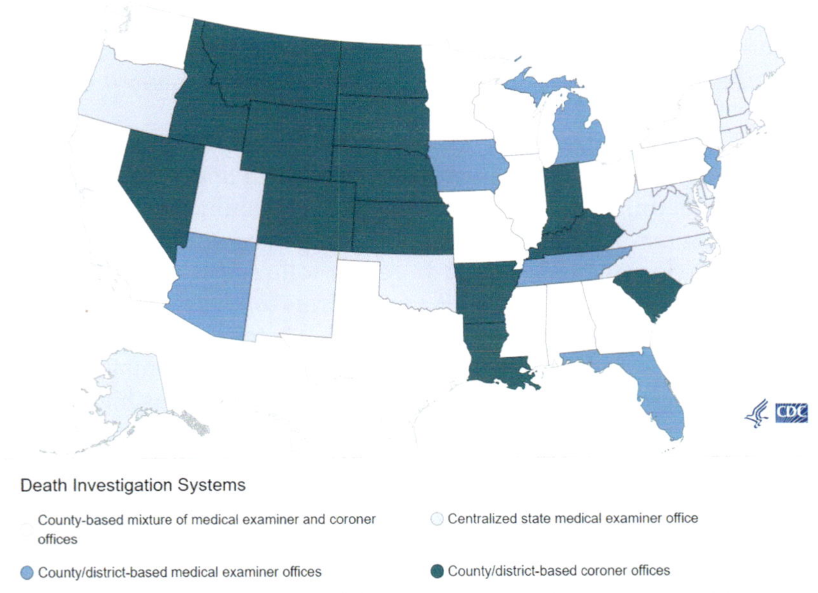

FIGURE 11.1 Death Investigation Systems by State. The organization of death investigation systems varies widely by state. Although 22 states and Washington, DC use medical examiners exclusively, many other states use coroner systems or a mix of coroners and medical examiners. Coroner systems rely on forensic pathologists to make cause and manner of death determinations. A shortage of certified forensic pathologists continues to engender significant risk of unreliability in death investigation regardless of organizational context. Source: Centers for Disease Control and Prevention.

that coroner systems may contribute to wrongful convictions and other miscarriages of justice. The 2009 National Academy of Sciences (NAS) report on forensic science recommended that coroner systems be phased out because they lacked the staff and resources to meet accreditation standards,

> which inhibit their ability to perform a competent physical examination, make and/or exclude medical diagnoses on dead bodies, and make determinations of the cause and manner of death. The historic role of the coroner is insufficient to accurately perform the medicolegal and public health functions related to sudden, unexpected, or violent death.
>
> (Committee on Identifying the Needs of the Forensic Sciences Community, National Research Council, 2009)

However, there is minimal evidence that coroners contribute to a disproportionate share of wrongful convictions, especially if they follow medical and scientific standards and retain trained and board-certified forensic pathologists.

The 2009 report was not the first time that the NAS had weighed in on medicolegal death investigation in the United States. In 1928, they issued a bulletin, The Coroner and Medical Examiner, which recommended that coroner systems be abolished and proposed other reforms (Schultz & Morgan, 1928). A 1932 report followed with more recommendations (Woods, 1933). Significant reforms followed that required a board-certified forensic pathologist to opine on unexpected or suspicious deaths. Regardless of organizational structure and the recommendations of legal and scientific scholars, death investigation remains highly variable. Some findings may lack transparency or sound scientific and medical standards to inform cause and manner determinations. Resources tend to limit the number of autopsies that can be performed or the time that a forensic pathologist can allot to a case. There is a chronic shortage of certified forensic pathologists trained in death investigation and autopsies. In a typical year, only 30–40 individuals receive board certification. And, although the demand is believed to justify about 1000, only 400–500 forensic pathologists are in practice (Hanzlick, Death Investigation Systems and Procedures, 2017).

VARIABILITY IN FORENSIC PATHOLOGY

The Centers for Disease Control, National Institute of Justice, National Association of Medical Examiners, and other bodies have established some standards that guide death investigation. These documents tend to be guidelines that delineate the documentation and considerations in death investigation and do not preclude more speculative interpretations by the forensic pathologist. This is due to the deference that is accorded to the pathologist's education, training, and expertise. It is assumed that the forensic pathologist will encounter unique circumstances and must have discretion to make judgments "within reasonable medical certainty" in the interpretation of cause and manner of death (Figure 11.2).

There are several problems with this approach that have arisen in wrongful convictions. First, the forensic pathologist's views may depend more on training and prior experience, which could bias interpretation. Even the language used to describe cause of death may vary from one expert to another. Second, the forensic pathologist is exposed to contextual information about the case. It is inevitable that this case context will also bias the pathologist's interpretations. There is no accepted standard for the forensic pathologist to consider only medical information, so it

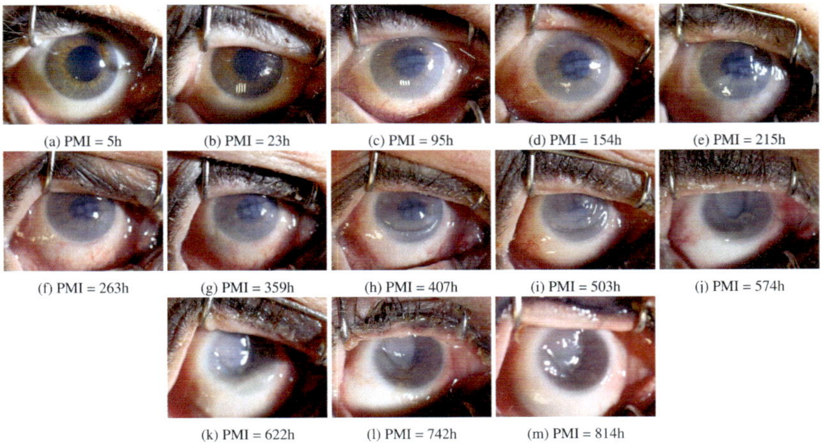

FIGURE 11.2 Postmortem changes of the eye. There are many methods to estimate the postmortem interval (PMI), including the apparent condition of the eye. Many researchers are conducting research to improve the accuracy and reliability of PMI estimates, but the field remains challenged by the extensive number of variables that may impact estimates, including the environment and antemortem factors. (Boyd) Source: (Boyd) Creative Commons Attribution 4.0 License.

is common for the expert to rely on subjective case information outside of the strict limits of forensic pathology (Dror et al., 2021). These biases can relate to pressure from outside sources, such as case investigators or even commercial interests (Oliver, 2011). Forensic pathologists contribute to the understanding of public health. Their work must be seen primarily through that lens, not a legal one. Their biases mirror those of clinical medicine, an area of expertise that has been more widely studied than forensic science (Croskerry et al., 2013).

Finally, the forensic pathologist seldom has perfect information on which to rely to make cause and manner determinations. There may be substantial and valid disagreement among forensic pathologists concerning the interpretation of the evidence in a case. Interpretative variability may relate to case uncertainties or scientific limitations. For example, postmortem interval estimates will vary depending on analytical method and the scope of contextual information that may be considered. The forensic pathologist may communicate these uncertainties to investigators, lawyers, or fact-finders, but the interpretative variability may not be self-evident to non-experts. Many defendants in wrongful conviction cases did not have access to an independent expert to review their case and determine if alternative interpretations were possible that aligned with the defense theory of the case. As in other forensic domains, the complexity of biomedical knowledge has only increased, further exacerbating the adversarial deficit faced by defendants.

STEVEN HAYNE

The fundamental problems in medicolegal death investigation may produce extreme outcomes. In Mississippi, uncertified pathologist Steven Hayne performed almost all criminal autopsies for decades. It is estimated he conducted over 1,500 each year, far in excess of the recommendations of the National Association of Medical Examiners. He was paid $550 for each autopsy through his business, Pathology Consultation Incorporated. Hayne was involved in many wrongful convictions. In the Tyler Edmonds case, he said he could determine that two people had pulled the trigger of the murder weapon at the same time. By not-coincidental happenstance, that finding confirmed Edmonds' false confession. In the Levon Brooks and Kennedy Brewer cases, he found what he thought were bite marks on the victims. As he did in many cases, he called in Michael West to do the analysis. In fact, Hayne was responsible for continuing to use West for bite mark analysis for years after West had been discredited for his unorthodox and inaccurate comparisons. West had been decertified by the American Board of Forensic Odontology at the time of the Brewer trial. He made invalid (and incorrect) individualizations in both Brooks and Brewer cases. Hayne contributed directly to the Brewer misidentification in his assessment of wounds on the victim's body. He dismissed the possibility that the marks were from decomposition, slippage, or insect bites despite the body having been in water for several days. Certified odontologist Richard Souviron testified that the marks were not human and were likely the result of insect bites. In the even more egregious Eddie Lee Howard case, Hayne had a body exhumed to allow West to "find" bite marks on the victim. Hayne practiced for over 20 years before he was barred from conducting autopsies in Mississippi. Even at that point, many elected coroners in the state tried to bring him back (unsuccessfully). The gaps in governance, quality assurance, certification, and the forensic pathology profession that allowed Hayne to operate for so long persist to this day.

ROBERT BAYARDO

A more interesting example is Dr. Robert Bayardo, although there is little or no evidence Bayardo purposely misrepresented his findings. In the Anthony Graves murder case, a family was killed and their house burned. Robert Carter, father of one of the children, confessed to shooting a teenaged victim but said Graves killed the other five victims. The victims were stabbed to death, and two of them were stabbed in the head through the skull. Graves' former boss, Roy Allen Rueter, testified that he had given Graves a switchblade knife. Rueter had made the knife from a kit and made a similar one for himself. He would later say that the knives "were so flimsy that I had to keep a rubber band wrapped around it so it would stay shut. … I'm around metal all day, and I knew that thing couldn't kill a rabbit" (Colloff, 2010). Graves said he didn't get any knife from Rueter and denied any involvement in the murder. Police never found Graves' knife or the murder weapon. Bayardo used Rueter's knife to compare the blade to the wounds on the victims, including the holes through the skulls of two of the victims (Graves v. Cockrell, 2003). He testified that the incisions "fit like a glove" and provide a "perfect fit" to the wounds. He did admit on cross-examination that many other knives would also fit the wounds. Graves did have a medical expert, Dr. Robert Bux, who testified on his behalf about the uncertainties in the wound assessment. Graves was convicted and sentenced to death largely on the basis of the Carter allegations and the supporting knife testimony. Postconviction, Dr. Harrell Gill-King reviewed the Bayardo findings and pointed out that the wound assessment was based on a physical insertion of the Rueter blade into the wound. In other words, Bayardo had actually inserted the blade into the wounds, which is not a reliable examination method because the blade could be too easily manipulated during insertion and the act of insertion altered the evidence to make subsequent examination impossible. Unfortunately, Bux, the original defense expert, had failed to point out the unorthodox Bayardo methodology during the trial. Carter recanted his testimony against Graves and took responsibility for the murders just before his own execution. It was later discovered that Carter had given contradictory statements about Graves' involvement that were clearly exculpatory but never shared with the defense. Graves' conviction was vacated based on the prosecutorial misconduct. The new district attorney's subsequent review determined that Graves was innocent. Graves received $1,457,000 in state compensation, and the original prosecutor was disbarred.

Bayardo was involved in several other wrongful convictions and erroneous statements. The most famous was likely the Cathy Lynn Henderson case. Henderson was convicted of murdering a three-month-old child and was set to be executed. She had maintained that she accidently dropped the child but later panicked, buried the body, and fled the state. She also gave a murder confession that she later recanted. In 1995 at the original trial, Bayardo had testified that the child's injuries could not have been caused by an accidental fall and instead were from the child being violently swung against a hard surface (Ex parte Henderson, 2012). He recanted just before Henderson's execution and said the medical evidence was ambiguous. He based his change of view on the changing scientific assessment of pediatric injuries. Several other experts then weighed in on various sides of the case during evidentiary hearings. The case—like many others involving pediatric abuse—included extreme variability among forensic pathologists and medical experts about the likelihood that the injuries were the result of an accident or intentional abuse. Henderson's conviction was eventually vacated. She then pled guilty to first-degree murder rather than face a retrial. She died shortly afterward in 2016.

In the 1996 Lacresha Murray case, Bayardo was among four competing experts who opined on matters relating to whether Murray inflicted lethal injuries on a 2-year-old toddler (Murray v. Earle, 2005). The autopsy revealed that the child had suffered four broken ribs and her liver was split in two. As the medical examiner on the case, Bayardo testified that the child had died within five to fifteen minutes after these injuries were inflicted and within one to two hours before arriving at the hospital. He did not take into account evidence of preexisting injuries or the possibility that resuscitation efforts had contributed to the observed injuries. In fact, responders had worked very hard to attempt to revive the child, including a large number of chest presses that contributed to the injuries observed at autopsy. Another medical examiner, Vincent DeMaio, testified that the tread pattern on Murray's shoes matched bruises on the body of the child, calling it a "perfect match." DiMaio was describing two parallel lines of bruises that could have matched a very wide variety of causes. A forensic shoe examiner looked at the pattern and did not agree with DeMaio's conclusion. DiMaio, author of a textbook on forensic pathology and widely respected in the field, later clarified that he had limited his analysis to "class characteristics" and that the bruises could have had other origins. In 1996, Murray's original conviction was set aside due to issues related to inadequate defense. In 1999, Murray's second conviction was set aside due to procedural issues relating to a confession that violated protective rights for minors under Texas law.

In 1987, Michael Morton was convicted of murdering his wife, Christine Norwood. Bayardo testified that the time of death was no later than 1:15 am based on the partially digested contents of her stomach and restaurant records showing that the couple had finished eating by 9:30 pm the previous evening (In re Morton, 2010). Bayardo based this estimate on a stomach-emptying time of four hours. Current scientific research at the time of trial indicated that a large meal—such as the last meal of the deceased—could take as long eight hours to digest and could be slowed by alcohol or low stomach acid (Suzuki, 1987). The time of death estimate was a key element of the case because Morton argued that his wife was alive when he left for work at 5:30 am the next morning and was killed by a stranger in the house after that time. If she was killed earlier, then Morton was lying and was the only person who could have killed his wife. Morton had left a note for his wife, saying,

> Chris—I know you didn't mean to—but you made me feel really unwanted, last night. After a good meal, we came home; you binged on the rest of the cookies. Then with your nightgown around your waist and while I was rubbing your hands and arms—you farted and fell asleep.
>
> (In re Morton, 2010)

The prosecution used the note as evidence that Morton had killed his wife "in a sexual rage" while Morton held that it was evidence that she had eaten even later than the restaurant dinner. There was significant evidence of an intruder, including a blood-stained bandana found near the house and a foreign footprint in the backyard. Fifteen latent fingerprints were found at the scene that did not match any known person, but no attempt was made to associate those prints to other suspects or similar crimes. In 2011, DNA testing found that the blood on the bandana was a mixture from Morton's wife and an unknown male. The DNA profile was uploaded to the national DNA index and hit to Mark Norwood, who had a long and violent criminal record and had been convicted of another murder in the intervening years. Morton was exonerated and awarded $1.9 million in compensation. Bayardo's time of death estimate was grossly incorrect. The evidence indicates that Christine Morton had been raped and killed by a violent drifter after 5:30 am on that day in 1987. By the time of the exoneration, the case prosecutor had become a judge. He was found to have withheld exculpatory evidence in the case, was forced to resign his judgeship, and was sentenced to 10 days in jail. Norwood was convicted of the Morton murder and sentenced to life in prison.

This history is not an indication that Bayardo was an especially incompetent or corrupt medical examiner. Bayardo is, in fact, a trained and respected forensic pathologist who has racked up 63 years of experience in the profession, dating all the way back to the Eisenhower administration. Each of his mistakes have been made by other forensic pathologists in other jurisdictions in similar cases. In the Morton case, his error may have been compounded by the deference generally given to him and other forensic pathologists and medical professionals. As seen in the Murray case, another respected medical examiner, Vincent DiMaio, also contributed to the wrongful conviction. DiMaio has hardly been a prosecution-only witness. For example, DiMaio was instrumental in uncovering Fred Zain's misconduct in DNA analysis in the Gilbert Alejandro wrongful conviction case. Bayardo has demonstrated similar impartiality.

In some respects, this means that Bayardo's missteps are more troubling. His experience may be relevant more broadly to the profession of forensic pathology. The uncertainties in many forensic pathological analyses are not well-understood by the courts. Report and testimony standards do not address the importance of uncertainties in many analyses. For example, postmortem interval estimates are notoriously poor but often presented with undue and invalid confidence. Bayardo continued to practice long after he would have retired from a different profession, in part due to the shortage of forensic pathologists. At the Norwood trial for the murder of Christine Morton, Bayardo admitted that his memory had begun to fail and he was forced to rely solely on his old notes. It is not unusual for retired forensic experts to testify in trials involving analyses they performed while they were professionally active. They also play an important role as independent consultants after retirement. In other disciplines, there is generally an adequate supply of younger professionals to assume the workload of retiring examiners. In forensic pathology, examiners are in short supply so older practitioners may continue to work well into their senior years.

DEATH SCENE INVESTIGATION

One may get the impression that forensic pathology errors are limited to certain states or contexts. That is not the case. There are many ways that a cause and manner determination may be compromised. Like other forensic analysis, forensic pathology may be undermined by poor crime scene work. Investigators may assume a case is a suicide and fail to preserve and collect evidence at the crime scene. Alternatively, investigators may compromise a crime scene and undermine reliable interpretation of the postmortem indications.

The 1992 murder of "wealthy art collector and notorious philanderer Roger de la Burde" is a useful example (Monroe v. Angelone, 2003). Burde's longtime partner, Beverly Monroe, was convicted of his murder. The case was undermined by poor crime scene investigation, suppression of evidence, and the bizarre circumstances surrounding Burde's life and death. Burde and Monroe had worked as chemists for Philip Morris. After leaving the company, Burde came to style himself as a Polish count. He had a reasonable fortune and maintained a horse farm that came to be known as "Windsor." Monroe had attempted to purchase an untraceable handgun in the months before Burde's death. She was aware of his philandering but had maintained her relationship with him for 13 years. During the trial and afterward, she claimed that many people would have had reason to kill Burde. For example, one woman was pregnant with Burde's child at the time of his death.

Burde died from a single gunshot wound to the forehead fired from his own handgun. Police initially believed Burde had committed suicide, so very little evidence was collected from the scene. They failed to collect cigarette butts or material from the fireplace ash. They didn't search for a suicide note or other papers. They didn't preserve Burde's clothes or the sofa where he died. These items became central issues when gunshot residue tests later suggested the possibility of murder. Medical examiner David Brown did attend the death at the Windsor scene and concluded that Burde's death was a suicide. Later, an autopsy confirmed the conclusion. A ballistics expert, Ann Jones, found gunshot residue (GSR) patterns that suggested Burde had been shot between the third and fourth fingers of his right hand, which was covering Burde's forehead when the weapon discharged. Although she was forced to rely on photographs (not chemical analysis) for some of her analysis, Jones concluded that suicide was highly unlikely.

At this point, Marcella Fierro—later the inspiration for heroine Kay Scarpetta in the Patricia Cornwell crime novels—became involved in the case and concluded that suicide was unlikely. She did not rule out suicide completely but her testimony was key support for the prosecution's theory that Monroe had killed Burde. The federal habeas court in 2002 faulted Fierro's testimony in the case for failure to describe the GSR evidence or the GSR patterns on Burde's hands. The court said, "Given the confusing questions and the unresponsive answers, there is little chance that the jury understood that there were several types of residue evidence and the implications of each." Monroe's federal habeas claim was ultimately successful, but she did not receive compensation for a wrongful conviction from Virginia. In hindsight, the forensic pathologists seemed to be unduly influenced by case context. When investigators felt Burde had committed suicide, the forensic pathologists used that interpretation for the cause and manner determination. When the GSR tests seemed to indicate murder, Fierro aligned with that interpretation. The investigative and forensic rush to judgment undermined the case from the beginning and may have prevented a reliable analysis. Crime scene investigation mistakes—primarily the responsibility of the local police—remained a challenge that eventually and inevitably led to the successful habeas petition.

MICHAEL SKAKEL

The sensational case of Michael Skakel is one clear example that demonstrates the sheer breadth and reach of issues in the court system (Skakel v. Commissioner of Correction, 2018). The case started with the murder of 15-year-old Martha Moxley in Greenwich,

Connecticut in 1975. It ended in 2020 when prosecutors chose not to retry Skakel for the murder due to the passage of time. From 1975 to 2000, Skakel had been under suspicion for the murder but was not prosecuted. What followed was a trial that became a media circus. Skakel, a nephew of Robert and Ethel Kennedy, was represented by a defense team that rivaled the O.J. Simpson "dream team" in size but not in competence. One lawyer, Mickey Sherman, reportedly billed the Skakel family for $1.5 million for the trial defense and was later sentenced to a year in prison for tax evasion. At one point in 2013, Skakel's conviction was vacated on the basis of inadequate defense related to Sherman's work, but that ruling was overturned by the Connecticut Supreme Court in 2016 on a 4 to 3 vote. The court then reversed itself two years later and vacated the conviction.

The victim was last seen with Skakel's older brother, Thomas Skakel, at 9:30 pm on the night before Halloween. At some point in the night, she was beaten and stabbed to death with a golf club that belonged to the Skakel family. The body was not found until 12:30 in the afternoon on Halloween. The body was not turned over for autopsy until five or six hours later, and the autopsy itself did not occur until November 1. The events of that night were later reconstructed to some degree. Thomas Skakel admitted that he had had "minor sexual contact" with Moxley. Michael Skakel admitted he had masturbated outside her house that night. Dogs were heard barking around 10 pm—this will be important to note. The Moxley family noticed her missing and began to look for her around 1 am. The time of death became the central issue in the trial. The defense held that she died between 9:30 and 10 pm, when Michael Skakel had an alibi. The prosecution held that she could have been killed any time before 1 am, when the family noticed her missing.

The state's chief medical examiner in 1975, Elliott Gross, considered the condition of the body and concluded that he could not narrow the time of death much further than police investigators. Moxley had died some hours before she was found based on the level of rigor mortis of the body, but it was unclear if she was killed the previous night or even in the morning of Halloween. The state's new chief medical examiner at the time of trial in 2002, Harold Wayne Carver, considered lividity, rigor mortis, and digestion in his estimate of time of death. Because the autopsy did not occur until November 1, Carver could not make a definitive conclusion concerning time of death on the basis of lividity (postmortem discoloration due to blood pooling). Police investigator Thomas Keegan had observed the body at 1:15 pm on Halloween and said that the body was in rigor mortis at that time. Carver said that finding generally limited the time of death to before 5 am on Halloween. Moxley had last eaten between 6 and 6:30 pm on October 30. The stomach was empty at autopsy. Given the conditions, Carver concluded that she died after 8:30 pm on October 30, a conclusion of minor value given that she was seen alive after that time. A defense expert, Joseph Jachimczyk, agreed with the medical findings with the exception of the digestion issue. He did point out that the stomach would empty after four hours on average, not one or two as his colleagues had said. The research literature does support longer times for stomach emptying. If Jachimczyk were correct, Moxley's death could have to have occurred around 10 pm. Less rigorously, Jachimczyk said his time of death was also based on contextual factors. He noted the barking dogs around 10 pm and Moxley's 10:30 pm curfew. He concluded the death must have occurred at 10 pm and had upset the dogs. As the dissent in the 2018 opinion summarized,

> Although Jachimczyk was, of course, free to consider nonmedical evidence such as curfews and barking dogs in forming his opinion as to the likely time of death, there was no suggestion that he had any special expertise in the fields of teenage or canine behavior.
>
> (Skakel v. Commissioner of Correction, 2018)

The majority did not agree and interpreted the variability among the experts to indicate that the time of death was consistent only with the defense theory of the case. Ironically, it appears that the trial jury had concluded that the time of death was consistent only with the prosecution theory of the case, which was also an incorrect interpretation of the dueling experts. Jachimczyk and the other forensic pathologists were clear about the uncertainties of the estimates for time of death, but the lawyers and fact-finders tended to interpret the opinions to be consistent with their own preconceived ideas about the case. Jachimczyk did make a fundamental error himself when he used nonmedical factors to imply that he could pinpoint the time of death. In doing so, he was playing the role of the police investigator or judge or jury, not a forensic practitioner. The Skakel case clearly demonstrates that the uncertainties in forensic interpretation—especially those in subjective disciplines—may not be represented accurately by prosecutors and defense attorneys. Skakel had plenty of money to ensure his point of view was represented, but that money appears to have muddied the waters more than helped his case. After all, both state experts provided interpretations that were consistent with a broad range of times of death, including both the prosecution and defense theories of the case.

BIAS AND VARIABILITY

The variability of scientific opinions is reflected in the forensic pathology conclusions in wrongful conviction cases. The Neal Robbins case involved the death of a 17-month-old girl who sustained significant injuries while in Robbins' care. The child's mother testified that Robbins had previously hurt the child by inflicting a black eye on one occasion, an injured leg on another, and head bruises during a third (Robbins v. State, 2002). Robbins said he did not hurt the child and said the death was due to sudden infant death syndrome (SIDS). His defense maintained that the injuries found at autopsy were due to resuscitation efforts. Five different forensic pathologists gave varying conclusions about the death. Assistant medical examiner Patricia Moore concluded death was by "suffocation by compression." Postconviction, she changed her conclusion to "undetermined" and said the resuscitation efforts could have caused the injuries. Forensic pathologists Robert Bux and Dwayne Wolf both concluded "undetermined" and said the suffocation conclusion was not supported by evidence. Postconviction, Thomas Wheeler agreed with Bux and Wolf. Linda Norton, who succeeded Moore on the case in an official capacity, concluded postconviction that the death was homicide by suffocation and changed the death certificate to match her conclusion. Initially, Robbins' conviction was upheld on appeal, but in 2013 Texas passed a law allowing a new trial when scientific testimony is contradicted postconviction. In 2016, Robbins was granted a new trial, but he was never given a certificate of actual innocence or compensation (Ex parte Robbins, 2014). The case result raises significant questions about the legal standards associated with improved science. The alternative hypotheses were presented at the original Robbins trial. The Moore/Norton conclusions were reasonable interpretations of the evidence given the history of the case. They suffered from the fact that signs of suffocation in a small child may be difficult to find. They further were undermined by the possibility that the resuscitation efforts had inflicted some injuries to the child. These concerns do not necessarily disprove suffocation or vindicate Robbins. It is significant that no forensic pathologist chose to conclude that the child died by SIDS or natural causes. In other words, no forensic pathologist was willing to state that Robbins was clearly innocent. It is likely, however, that the prosecution would have been reluctant to go to trial based on an "undetermined" manner of death. This conclusion would have forced the prosecutor to rely on other evidence to convince the jury that Robbins had inflicted lethal injuries or—at the least—inflicted significant harm to the child. Meanwhile, the defense could claim that there was no conclusive evidence that a crime had even occurred because the death certificate was ambiguous on that point. In effect, Moore was the judge and jury in the Robbins case. Most forensic pathologists would not want to be put into that position, but the dynamics of the court system demand it. Unfortunately, science does not provide definitive answers in many, real-world scenarios. It may be that "undetermined" was the most scientifically valid conclusion in the Robbins case.

In each example discussed thus far, one could argue that cognitive bias may have played a role in the misinterpretation of evidence by the forensic pathologist. Usually, this concern relates to contextual bias in which case information influences the examiner's analysis. In forensic pathology, professional courtesy or pressure may influence the examiner also. An excellent example is the case of Larry Souter. The case began with a victim, Kristy Ringler, who was killed by two blows to the head and found on a roadside in Newaygo County, Michigan. The autopsy was performed by Dr. Steven Bauserman, who found large lacerations on Ringler's head and theorized that the "death could have been either a homicide or the result of being hit by a car" (Larry Pat Souter, Petitioner-Appellant, v. Kurt Jones, Warden, Respondent-Appellee, 2005). Glass was recovered from the body. In addition, a discarded, broken, brown, Canadian Club whiskey bottle with blood stains was found nearby. Souter was the last person seen with the victim when she was alive and admitted that the bottle was his. Blood on the bottle was type A, and both Souter and Ringler had type A blood. The state police crime laboratory analysis analyzed the particles from the victim and concluded that they were inconsistent with automobile headlight glass and the whiskey bottle. In fact, they were not even brown in color like the bottle. Police investigators came to believe that the injuries were inflicted by an automobile's sideview mirror that had sideswiped the victim. A second forensic pathologist, Lawrence Simpson, was also consulted by the police. Simpson said the injuries were "consistent with being struck by a car rather than homicide." The case was set aside until 1983, when a new medical examiner, Dr. Ronald Graeser, reviewed the autopsy slides and concluded that the "bottle matched the shape of the wounds" and issued a report that said the whiskey bottle "may well have" been the murder weapon. His colleague, Dr. Stephen Cohle, agreed with this opinion. The prosecutor again chose not to proceed with charges against Souter. In 1991, Graeser revised his report. This time, he said Ringler's injuries were caused by the bottle and that it was "virtually impossible" that they came from an automobile accident or rearview mirror. The prosecutor then went to trial. As it happens, Graeser had been apprenticed to Cohle and Bauserman, two of the other forensic pathologists who worked on the case. At trial, Graeser gave speculative testimony about the victim's wounds and opined that the bottle had lost its sharp edges in the dozen years since Ringler's death. Bauserman and Cohle supported Graeser's testimony and said the injuries were consistent with being struck by the bottle. Simpson—the forensic pathologist called in by the police for a second opinion in 1979—testified for the defense and said the bottle always lacked a sharp edge and that a car accident was the most likely cause of death.

Postconviction, Bauserman and Cohle both retracted their testimony and said the bottle was not the likely murder weapon. In fact, Cohle said he was "strongly influenced in 1992" by Graeser and relied on Graeser's unsupported contention that the bottle had lost its sharp edge over the years. In fact, the bottle was made using a manufacturing process that prevented the creation of sharp spurs or edges. A review by a forensic expert demonstrated that the bottle never had a sharp edge in 1979 or afterward and could not have made the wounds. Cohle admitted that he had not done a thorough review of the autopsy data and said the wounds didn't match the whiskey bottle anyway. Postconviction, Bauserman said that his views about the injuries were based on speculation and deferred to Cohle. Cohle and Bauserman may have been unduly influenced by Graeser. Or perhaps they were being protective of a colleague they had mentored. The main problem was one that forensic pathologists routinely face—the analysis was inherently subjective. There was no way to definitively determine at autopsy whether Ringler was killed by the bottle or an automobile accident. Bauserman's initial inconclusive determination was in fact the most valid determination. In addition, the case demonstrates the endemic problem of the shortage of board-certified forensic pathologists. Cohle was board-certified, but Graeser and Bauserman were not. It may be that Newaygo County simply couldn't recruit a board-certified forensic pathologist due to availability or cost. Whatever the reason, the criminal case relied on the work of uncertified examiners. Finally, it is interesting that the state crime lab's glass analysis was not credited by Graeser or the other forensic pathologists. The glass from the victim could not have come from the bottle. It wasn't even the same color. It is unclear why this information was not taken into account in the analysis by the forensic pathologists.

Souter's conviction was eventually overturned in 2005. In an unusual twist, a woman came forward to claim that her father had committed a possible hit and run at the time of Ringler's death. Her father had reported the possibility to the police and even noted a resulting, broken sideview mirror on his motor home. Souter was actually innocent. His conviction was vacated, and he was released in 2005.

CONTEXTUAL INFORMATION

The problem of contextual information management is not straightforward for the forensic pathologist. In the Souter case, the results of other forensic analyses were relevant to wound determinations on the victim. In other cases, contextual information may be important in ways that may at first appear to be irrelevant to the forensic pathologist. The more recent Robert Weitzel case is an interesting example. Weitzel was convicted of five counts of manslaughter or misdemeanor homicide of elderly patients (Park, 2002). The case seemed to encompass issues regarding end-of-life care. Weitzel had prescribed large amounts of psychotropic drugs and morphine to his patients. Ostensibly, this was justified to ease their suffering at the end of their lives. The case revolved around prosecution and defense theories concerning the standard of care Weitzel owed his patients. In a "battle of experts," medical opinions were offered by the defense that he had provided appropriate pain relief to dying patients. Medical opinions were offered by the prosecution that the doses were lethal and the patients' conditions were treatable and their wishes for end-of-life care were not followed. In fact, they were both wrong because they were unaware of key context. The Drug Enforcement Administration was investigating Weitzel for prescription drug abuse. Weitzel had not poisoned his elderly patients with psychotropic drugs. He was overprescribing so that he could take some of their medications to support his own drug addiction. Later, US District Judge Dee Benson stated, "This is a case of a doctor addicted to narcotics who was defrauding his patients and pharmacies to get it for himself. It's as simple as that." (Deseret News, 2002). Within the context of their knowledge, the trial medical experts may have provided appropriate interpretations. Had they known the full context, they would likely have altered their interpretations of the deaths of the patients. Clearly, the case demonstrates that the forensic pathologist may require a wide range of contextual information that may not appear to be task-relevant at first glance. The field may face serious difficulties in solving the problem of cognitive bias and context management.

It is likely that forensic pathology will continue to contribute to wrongful convictions. The fundamental issues are still there—the shortage of board-certified forensic pathologists, the inherently subjective nature of many interpretations, as well as the gaps in interpretation, reporting, and testimony standards. Although improvements have been made, much work remains to be done.

ANTHONY COPPOLINO

The 1966 case of Carl Anthony Coppolino was not a wrongful conviction. It was, however, a landmark in forensic pathology and the use of forensic evidence. The case reflects many issues that would later arise in wrongful convictions and the response of the legal community to changes in forensic science.

The key forensic pathologist was Milton Helpern, who was only the third chief of the New York OCME in its 50-year history to that point. The lead defense attorney was F. Lee Bailey, who would also serve on the OJ Simpson defense team. Bailey popularized the rhetoric that has come to characterize much critical discourse about forensic evidence. Even to this day, many accounts of the case deem the forensic evidence "contradictory" (Evans, 2022) or invalid. The case itself was on the cusp of the old and the new, the traditional way that forensic pathology was performed and the new methods in toxicology and interpretation that took hold in the late 20th century (Helpern & Knight, 1977).

Coppolino had a degree as a Doctor of Medicine. His wife, Carmela Musetto, also had a medical degree and worked as a researcher for Hoffman-La Roche. They set up house in Red Bank, New Jersey in the greater New York metro area. Coppolino worked as an anesthesiologist at a local hospital. In 1961, a nurse-anesthetist at the hospital received four anonymous, typewritten letters threatening her with mutilation if she didn't quit her job. Coppolino admitted to the FBI that he had written the letters to protect his position as an anesthesiologist at the hospital and wanted to get rid of his competition. The hospital let him resign quietly. As it turned out, he had taken out a disability policy and claimed that he had coronary artery disease and was unable to work. Later, some observers speculated that Coppolino had used his knowledge of anesthetic drugs to produce temporary heart palpitations that showed up on an electrocardiogram. Regardless, he did receive a $20,000 disability award.

Not being able to work, he took up hypnosis and soon began to visit a married neighbor, Marjorie Farber, who needed help to quit smoking. By 1963, they had commenced an affair. They even went to Florida and Puerto Rico for vacations together. Farber's husband, Colonel Bill Farber, became suspicious and demanded that the relationship end. According to Marjorie Farber, Coppolino gave her a syringe and a white powder, succinylcholine. Succinylcholine is a drug that paralyzes the subject. In small doses, it induces muscle relaxation for surgery. In large doses, it has been used as part of lethal injection cocktails. In 1963, it was considered an undetectable poison because it quickly metabolizes to choline and succinic acid, which are found normally in the body.

According to Marjorie Farber's account, Coppolino instructed her to dissolve the powder in water and inject it in her husband while he slept. At her first attempt, she jabbed the needle in her husband's leg but didn't press the plunger. He woke up complaining of a charley horse in his leg and fell very ill but survived. Later that night, Marjorie Farber called Coppolino, who came over and tried to suffocate Colonel Farber with a plastic bag. That attempt also failed when the colonel vomited, and Marjorie told Coppolino to stop. Coppolino returned the next afternoon and gave the colonel an injection of a sedative, presumably more succinylcholine. This apparently was still insufficient because Coppolino then told her, "He's a hard one to kill; he's taking a long time to die." Coppolino then allegedly finished the job by suffocating the colonel with a pillow. They put a note on the bedroom door that said, "Daddy is sleeping---do not disturb" to keep the Farber children out of the room. Coppolino prevailed on his wife, Carmela, to produce and sign the death certificate with a cause of death of a heart attack. Legally, this was improper in a case in which the decedent died unexpectedly and was not under a physician's care. Nonetheless, the certificate went unquestioned and the colonel was buried at Arlington National Cemetery.

In 1965, the Coppolinos moved to Sarasota, Florida. The affair between Carl Coppolino and Marjorie Farber had continued in the intervening two years. Farber actually bought land next to the Coppolinos. In the meantime, Coppolino had begun an affair with a rich divorcee in Sarasota. This time, he asked Carmela for a divorce, but she refused. A few weeks earlier, he had obtained succinylcholine from a friend under the pretense of doing animal research. It is believed that he injected his wife with the poison and killed her. He called a doctor, a friend of Carmela's, who came over and found her friend's body. Coppolino told the doctor that Carmela had had a heart attack. The doctor did consult with the county medical examiner, who shrugged the case off because the sheriff hadn't called him in to do an autopsy. For his part, the police chief came to the scene but did not investigate because Coppolino and his wife's friend were both doctors who seemed satisfied that everything was in order. The police chief should have ordered an autopsy for the death of a healthy, 32-year-old woman. Even if there had been no murder, it was extremely unusual for a young person to die so suddenly. Carmela's father was distraught over his daughter's death, but Coppolino told him that an autopsy had been done and a heart attack was confirmed. Five weeks later, Coppolino married the rich divorcee.

It was at this point that he miscalculated. Marjorie Farber went to the police with her suspicions about Carmela's death. She told them about the murder of her own husband and her view that Coppolino had probably murdered his wife also. The police called in Helpern and the New York OCME to determine if they could help with the case. By that point, Colonel Farber had been dead and buried for two years and Carmela for over three months. They disinterred Carmela and performed an autopsy. They found no coronary artery disease whatsoever. They found a puncture wound on her buttocks. They pulled a section of flesh from the site and found a 1.5-inch, red streak of hemorrhage that had been preserved in the embalming process. The OCME chief toxicologist, Dr. Charles Umberger, found elevated levels of succinic acid in the body, with unusually elevated levels in her brain. That didn't necessarily prove that she had been poisoned with succinylcholine. They then recruited Dr. Bert LaDu, the chair of the Department of Pharmacology at New York University. Today, there is a Bert LaDu Professor of Anesthesiology Research at the University of Michigan, reflecting LaDu's overall contributions to the field. LaDu would go on to perform groundbreaking research on how different individuals react to succinylcholine based on their genetic traits. LaDu recognized that succinylcholine does not break down directly into succinic acid. There is an intermediate molecule, succinylmonocholine, that is stable in fat (such as will be found in the buttocks). As it happens, the metabolism of succinylmonocholine is directly related to the variability of individual reactions to succinylcholine anesthetic (Davis et al., 1997). LaDu found traces of succinylmonocholine in Carmela Coppolino along the track mark found by Helpern at autopsy. Afterward, Colonel Farber was also disinterred but no succinylcholine or its metabolites were discovered. Helpern did find a double fracture of the colonel's cricoid cartilage near the larynx, a common finding in strangulation cases.

Coppolino went on trial in New Jersey for the murder of Colonel Farber in late 1996. His defense lawyer was F. Lee Bailey. Bailey had just gained notoriety as the man who had cleared Sam Sheppard following his wrongful conviction in 1954 and had also defended Albert DeSalvo, the Boston Strangler. Bailey pursued a scorched-earth approach to the forensic evidence. He sought to paint Helpern as a corrupt bureaucrat who had made up his mind that Coppolino was guilty and made the medicolegal findings fit his preconceived theories. During cross-examination, he repeatedly implied that Helpern had directed his staff to find evidence to inculpate Coppolino. In Bailey's view, if the forensic team didn't find inculpatory evidence, Helpern made sure to shoehorn the data to fit the "right" conclusion. This strategy may have backfired on Bailey to some extent. Helpern was no Fred Zain. His colleagues were ordinary scientists and were clearly excited by the technical challenges of the case, not the chance to inculpate Coppolino. Bailey claimed that Farber's fractured cricoid was caused when the coffin lid fell on the body during exhumation, though that did not actually occur. He claimed Helpern's choline tests were invalid because they could not be related to a quantitative level of choline in the samples. Helpern and Bailey had a fundamental disagreement on a key point—the standard of evidence in a capital case versus a "normal" case. Helpern felt the standards should be the same in all cases and claimed that he had maintained a consistent—and therefore trustworthy—approach in the Coppolino investigation. Bailey was incensed by this attitude, which he took to be dismissive of the gravity of the charges and the need for greater assurance on the validity of the evidence.

The trial was undermined by the testimony of Marjorie Farber, who was accused by Bailey of fabricating "a cock-and-bull story" about the death of her husband. The New Jersey trial ended with Coppolino's acquittal for the murder of Colonel Farber.

The trial for his wife's murder occurred in Florida in early 1967. The proof available in the Florida case was much more substantial because the needle track and succinylmonocholine analysis could be used to determine the definitive cause and manner of Carmela's death. Both deaths had initially been attributed to heart attacks, and Helpern did detect artherosclerosis in Colonel Farber's coronary arteries, though he considered the level to be insufficient to cause a heart attack. In contrast, Carmela simply could not have died of any type of heart attack. The evidence of succinylcholine poisoning was clear, if LaDu's testimony was accepted. His technique was completely novel and had in fact been developed for the Coppolino case. Bailey, of course, demanded a Frye hearing on the matter but the trial judge declined. The jury returned a verdict of guilty for second degree murder, which implied death without prior intent. The verdict was not technically in keeping with a poisoning death but may have been motivated by the uncertainties of the novel toxicological analysis. Coppolino served 12 years before being paroled and lived until 2017. On appeal, the 2nd District Court of Appeal in Florida held, "The trial court listened to the testimony of the expert witnesses and, in an exercise of his discretion, ruled that the tests in question were sufficiently reliable to justify their admission" (Coppolino v. State, 1968).

Coppolino wrote a book about his case, *The Crime That Never Was*. Bailey was outraged by the verdict. He said Helpern's OCME was "a scandal and the source of some peremptory and sloppy opinions." He alleged that "any verdict based on evidence coming the New York Office of the Chief Medical Examiner should be scrutinized by defense lawyers." This would be good advice in any circumstance. Bailey would later be suspended from practicing law in New Jersey over another murder trial and disbarred in Massachusetts and Florida for misconduct in which he transferred assets from a defendant into his own accounts. Helpern provided a reliable version of the Coppolino case in his memoirs (Helpern & Knight, 1977).

The case included the best and the worst of the death investigation system in the United States. There were two failures to investigate unexpected deaths. There were instances in which close associates of decedents signed or influenced death certificates. Coppolino's defense team showed more bluster than competence in their opposition to the forensic evidence. Bailey's tactics provide an interesting comparison to the OJ Simpson case. Bailey was marginalized in that case by Barry Scheck and Peter Neufeld. While Scheck and Neufeld are hardly immune from aggressive tactics, their strategy in the Simpson case differed from

Bailey's approach. They impugned the motives of the police—particularly Mark Fuhrman—but their attacks on the forensic evidence were far deeper and more substantive than Bailey's strategy in the Coppolino case. They focused on chain of custody, contamination, interpretation standards, competence, and quality assurance. Scheck commented that the actual forensic analysis in the Simpson case was generally accurate and reliable, but the systems around that analysis were wanting. In contrast, Bailey cast a wide net of aspersion against everyone involved in the prosecution and investigation of Coppolino. He continued to do so well after the trials were over and done. While he did question the scientific methods, his primary strategy was to discredit the forensic science by discrediting Milton Helpern. This strategy succeeded in New Jersey due to the age of the exhumed body and the need to rely on Marjorie Farber's testimony. In fact, the forensic evidence could not support the New Jersey case because the body was just too decomposed to perform reliable analysis. On the other hand, the Florida case was based on an autopsy for a death that was much more recent. In the Florida prosecution, the OCME established that toxicology could prove key facts in uncertain cases, even when difficult analyses were required to detect unusual metabolites. Arguably, the court should have held a Frye hearing on the LaDu approach, but subsequent events have demonstrated the validity of his ideas. Today, succinylcholine can be detected and quantified by standard mass spectrometric methods. It is much harder for a potential murderer to find an undetectable poison than it was in 1966. One may speculate concerning the viability of the Bailey trial strategy in today's courts.

STUDY QUESTIONS

1. Consider the Coppolino case. Was Coppolino wrongfully convicted? In other words, did he get a fair trial? Do you think he was innocent or guilty of the murders? How was the case compromised by the work done by the scene investigators who attended the deaths of the two alleged victims? You might refer to the current standard for death investigation (National Medicolegal Review Panel, 2011). Was the toxicology used by the New York OCME valid? Were the forensic pathologists biased in this case? You might refer to the Dror work on this topic (Dror et al., 2021). There were several medical professionals who issued death certificates. What is your view of their professionalism and the reliability of their findings?
2. What is the task-relevant information for a forensic pathologist to consider when determining cause and manner of death? In

the Skakel case, was it appropriate to consider the barking of dogs in the assessment of time of death? What problems might occur if the forensic pathologist is strictly limited to medical interpretations?

3. Consider the possibility that tasers may contribute to the death of an individual during a police use of force. Some medical examiners have reported that they were reluctant to list tasers on a death certificate due to concerns about civil liability (Oliver, 2011). Nonetheless, a thorough investigation of the issue by the Department of Justice has determined that tasers—although generally safe—can contribute to death in some circumstances (Study Panel of Death Following Electro-Muscular Disruption, 2011). What considerations should a forensic pathologist use when determining whether a taser exposure contributed to a death? Is it possible that public pressure or civil liability could exert undue influence on the findings? What should be done to ensure justice for the decedent, police officer, and others involved in such a case?

FURTHER READING

The Centers for Disease Control and Prevention, National Institute of Justice, and other professional organizations have begun the long, slow process of developing appropriate standards across the incredibly complex field of forensic pathology. The National Association for Medical Examiners Forensic Autopsy Performance Standards (Peterson & Clark, 2020) and OSAC *Organizational and Foundational Standard for Medicolegal Death Investigation* (Organization of Scientific Area Committees, 2018) are notable examples. The United Kingdom *Code of Practice and Performance Standards for Forensic Pathology in England, Wales and Northern Ireland* (Home Office, The Forensic Science Regulator, Department of Justice and The Royal College of Pathologists, 2021) is an important example in the international space.

There is surprising little scholarly research about the forensic pathology discipline. Georgia medical examiner Randy Hanzlick contributed a significant perspective to the issues surrounding the medical examiner/coroner debate. A good place to start on that issue is his review article, Coroner versus medical examiner systems: Can we end the debate? (Hanzlick & Fudenberg, 2014). His text on death investigation, *Death Investigation Systems and Procedures*, also remains a useful reference (Hanzlick, 2017). Bill Oliver has written several research papers on bias in forensic pathology determination and the need for independent and objective cause and manner determinations. See, for example, the NAME position paper on the latter topic (Melinek et al., 2013). For historical perspective, Milton Helpern's autobiography discusses the Coppolino case and his personal experience as a 20th century forensic pathologist and leader in the field (Helpern & Knight, 1977).

REFERENCES

Boyd, A. (n.d.). Post-Mortem Iris Recognition: A Survey and Assessment of the State of the Art. *IEEE Access*, 136570–136593. https://doi.org/10.1109/access.2020.3011364

Colloff, P. (2010, October). Innocence Lost. *Texas Monthly*.

Committee on Identifying the Needs of the Forensic Sciences Community, National Research Council. (2009). *Strengthening Forensic Science in the United States: A Path Forward*. Washington, DC: National Academies Press.

Coppolino v. State, 223 So. 2d 68 (2nd District Court of Appeal November 8, 1968).

Croskerry, P., Singhal, G., & Mamede, S. (2013). Cognitive debiasing 1: origins of bias and theory of debiasing. *BMJ quality & safety*, *22*(Suppl 2), ii58–ii64.

Davis, L., Britten, J., & Morgan, M. (1997). Cholinesterase Its Significance in Anaesthetic Practice. *Anaesthesia*, *52*, 244–260.

Deseret News. (2002, September 12). Weitzel Gets Year in Jail Cell for Fraud. *Deseret News*.

Dror, I., Melinek, J., Arden, J., Kukucka, J., Hawkins, S., Carter, J., & Atherton, D. (2021). Cognitive Bias in Forensic Pathology Decisions. *Journal of Forensic Sciences*, *66*(5), 1751–1757.

Evans, C. (2022). *Carl Anthony Coppolino Trials: 1966 & 1967*. Retrieved March 7, 2022, from Encyclopedia.com: https://www.encyclopedia.com/law/law-magazines/carl-anthony-coppolino-trials-1966-1967#:~:text=On%20April%2028%2C%201967%2C%20they,poisoning%20is%20hard%20to%20imagine.

Ex parte Henderson, AP-76,925 (Court of Criminal Appeals of Texas December 5, 2012).

Ex parte Robbins, WR-73, 484–02 (Court of Criminal Appeals of Texas November 26, 2014).

Graves v. Cockrell, 02–41416 (United States Court of Appeals for the Fifth Circuit August 15, 2003).

Hanzlick, R. (2017). *Death Investigation Systems and Procedures*. Boca Raton: CRC Press.

Hanzlick, R., & Fudenberg, J. (2014). Coroner versus Medical Examiner Systems: Can We End the Debate? *Academic Forensic Pathology*, *4*(1), 10–17.

Helpern, M., & Knight, B. (1977). *The Memoirs of Milton Helpern.* New York: St. Martin's Press.

Home Office, The Forensic Science Regulator, Department of Justice and The Royal College of Pathologists. (2021). *Code of Practice and Performance Standards for Forensic Pathology in England, Wales and Northern Ireland.* London, UK: Home Office, The Forensic Science Regulator, Department of Justice and The Royal College of Pathologists.

In re Morton, 03-08-00585-CR (Court of Appeals of Texas, Third District, Austin January 8, 2010).

Larry Pat Souter, Petitioner-Appellant, v. Kurt Jones, Warden, Respondent-Appellee, 03–1528 (United States Court of Appeals,Sixth Circuit January 18, 2005).

Melinek, J., Thomas, L., & Oliver, W. (2013). National Association of Medical Examiners Position Paper: Medical Examiner, Coroner, and Forensic Pathologist Independence. *Academic Forensic Pathology, 3*(1), 93–98.

Monroe v. Angelone, 02-6548, 02,6625 (United States Court of Appeals, Fourth Circuit March 26, 2003).

Murray v. Earle, 03–51379 (United States Court of Appeals for the Fifth Circuit March 31, 2005).

National Medicolegal Review Panel. (2011). *Death Investigation: A Guide for the Scene Investigator, Technical Update.* Washington, DC: US Department of Justice, Office of Justice Programs, National Institute of Justice.

Oliver, W. (2011). The Effect of Threat of Litigation on Forensic Pathologist Diagnostic Decision Making. *The American Journal of Forensic Medicine and Pathology, 32*(4), 383–386.

Organization of Scientific Area Committees. (2018). *Organizational and Foundational Standard for Medicolegal Death Investigation.* Academy Standards Board.

Park, L. (2002, November 23). Jury Clears Dr. Weitzel after Two Hours of Deliberation. *Standard-Examiner Davis Bureau.*

Peterson, G., & Clark, S. (2020). *Forensic Autopsy Performance Standards.* National Association of Medical Examiners.

Robbins v. State, 1939-00 (Court of Criminal Appeals of Texas October 23, 2002).

Schultz, O., & Morgan, E. (1928). *The Coroner and the Medical Examiner, Issued Under the Auspices of the Committee on Medicolegal Problems.* Gaithersburg, MD: National Research Council of the National Academy of Sciences.

Skakel v. Commissioner of Correction, SC 19251 (Supreme Court of Connecticut May 4, 2018).

Study Panel of Death Following Electro-Muscular Disruption. (2011). *Study of Deaths Following Electro Muscular Disruption*. National Institute of Justice.

Suzuki, S. (1987). Experimental Studies on the Presumption of the Time after Foodintake from Stomach Contents. *Forensic Science International*, *35*(2–3), 83–117.

Woods, A. (1933). Possibilities and Need for the Development of Legal Medicine in the United States. *West Virginia Law Review*, *39*, 1–5.

CHAPTER 12

Organizational Dysfunction

There may be many root causes that contribute to a wrongful conviction. The examiner may not have the training or ability to perform the analysis. The scientific foundation for a method may not be established by research or standards. There may be miscommunications, failures to collect or track evidence, or misconduct. At some level, however, all root causes are system errors and all system errors relate to organizational deficiencies. The forensic science organization that produces forensic results may be dysfunctional in a way that undermines the reliability of the examiner's work. The examiner may maintain a high standard of professional work while other criminal justice system actors misuse forensic evidence. Alternatively, the examiner may produce negligent or fraudulent work, but the organization lacks sufficient quality assurance and accountability mechanisms. In some instances, forensic errors may not relate to organizational deficiencies in a forensic science organization because the examiner may not even be associated with a crime laboratory. Independent consultants have produced many forensic errors in wrongful conviction cases.

Any organization can produce errors. Forensic science organizations are no exception. A crime lab may have contributed to a wrongful conviction and may need to examine its structure, policies, and procedures to mitigate the possibility of future errors. Importantly, the organization can only mitigate the risk of error, not eliminate it. Many critics of forensic science have held that errors are a symptom of deep systemic flaws in labs or the forensic science community. Ironically, the demand that labs must eliminate errors altogether may produce more problems. When a lab or forensic stakeholder advocates for a zero-error policy, they may contribute to a culture of finger-pointing and recrimination that increases the likelihood of serious errors. Laboratories that follow a high-reliability-organization model will emphasize the inevitability of errors and develop systems that identify potential problems before they

DOI: 10.4324/9781003202578-12

result in catastrophic consequences. In this context, wrongful convictions represent the most catastrophic consequence that may be produced by organizational deficiency in a crime laboratory. The study of wrongful convictions may contribute to a reduction in the risk of future errors of all types.

Independent investigations have produced useful insights into some situations involving wrongful convictions associated with severely dysfunctional forensic organizations. We may categorize these situations broadly as "laboratory scandals." This term does not imply that fraud or negligence was present in every case. In fact, only individuals—not organizations—are able to commit fraud or negligence. Organizations may provide an environment in which fraud or negligence continues and may contribute to catastrophic failures. The organizational environment may foster a lack of accountability, transparency, or quality assurance. By organization in this context, one may refer to a variety of organizational structures ranging from the unit level to the broader interagency context (e.g., a statewide laboratory system). In other parts of this text, the organizational level of interest has been at the level of the forensic discipline, which constitutes a community of professionals. They may organize themselves strictly or loosely, but they are an organization. In this chapter, we will consider the forensic science organization, which may include multiple disciplines and may be organized as a public or private entity. Public forensic science organizations may be traditional crime laboratories, medical examiner or coroner's offices, forensic units within law enforcement agencies, or small units within other organizational contexts. Private forensic science organizations may be contract laboratories, universities, research institutions, or independent consultants. Each type of organization has its own strengths and weaknesses that may lead to forensic errors. When an organization fails to correct its errors or contributes to catastrophic errors (such as wrongful convictions), the organization may be judged dysfunctional by the community of its stakeholders. In general, this situation is often called a laboratory scandal.

ANALYTIC APPROACH

Novelist Leo Tolstoy wrote, "Happy families are all alike; every unhappy family is unhappy in its own way." Similarly, broken organizations may manifest their dysfunction in ways that may not be generalizable. The issues that cause problems in one crime laboratory may not translate to the analyses of other situations. Many outside observers of laboratory scandals tend to jump to invalid conclusions that paint a broad brush about the forensic science community. They conclude that all forensic science is woefully inadequate or corrupt on the basis of the fraud or negligence seen in individual instances. On the other hand, forensic science advocates may attribute all problems to "bad apples" that are not representative of the rest of the forensic science community. They prematurely dismiss any claim that laboratory scandals may reveal systemic flaws in other organizations. In analyzing the influence of organizational dysfunction on wrongful convictions, a middle ground may be the best option. One should examine each situation to determine the systemic issues that contributed to the organizational dysfunction in that situation. When similar issues arise in multiple contexts, then it is appropriate to attempt to generalize the causes and correlates associated with forensic errors. When attempting retrospective analysis, it is difficult to make firm conclusions. One is not conducting controlled experiments, but rather making careful observations linked to systemic analysis. Just as forensic scientists should be careful when drawing conclusions, observers of forensic science should take similar care to draw reliable but well-calibrated inferences from the experiences of organizational dysfunction.

This chapter relies on the analysis of independent investigations of laboratory scandals. In many cases, official reviews were conducted in the aftermath of public revelations of serious misconduct. The reviews may have been conducted by investigators in any branch of government or by independent entities such as accreditation bodies. Generally, media investigations are not a reliable source of information about these situations on their own but may provide additional insights to supplement official investigations.

FBI LABORATORY

The most widely investigated forensic science organization is the FBI Laboratory (Figure 12.1). The FBI lab has been in operation for over 90 years and has been involved in almost every field of forensic science. For many years, the FBI was a "backstop" for state and local labs to handle difficult forensic work in key cases. That role has diminished since 2001, when the agency mission was redirected to emphasize federal and terrorism investigations and de-emphasize work with state and local law enforcement. The Department of Justice (DOJ) Office of Inspector General (OIG) has conducted several reviews of the FBI lab when potential problems were identified. The FBI itself has also sponsored some reviews of its past casework.

In 1997, then DOJ Inspector General Michael Bromwich issued a landmark review, *The FBI Laboratory: An Investigation into Laboratory Practices and Alleged Misconduct in Explosives-Related*

FIGURE 12.1 FBI Laboratory. The FBI Laboratory has grown from a single room in 1932 to a state-of-the-art facility (sometimes likened to a battleship) housing over 500 staff in Quantico, Virginia. For most of its history, the FBI Laboratory was housed in cramped quarters in the Justice Department Building in downtown Washington, DC. The proximity of the lab enabled close collaboration between investigators and lab scientists. Source: Federal Bureau of Investigation.

and Other Cases. After leaving the federal government, Bromwich would be retained to review the troubled Houston police laboratory. The two Bromwich reports remain the gold standard for clear and thorough reviews of forensic science organizations.

The 1997 Bromwich review was precipitated by complaints from FBI Supervisory Special Agent Frederic Whitehurst, who started work in the FBI Laboratory in 1986 as a chemist in the analysis of explosives and explosives residue. Whitehurst, a Ph.D. chemist, arrived in the laboratory at a time when most analysts outside the latent fingerprint section were required to be FBI agents. Staff who weren't agents were not viewed on par with "special agents." Civilian staff were called "professional support examiners." Their reports would often be given to agent-supervisors, who could change their reports and put their own names on the findings. Whitehurst worked under Terry Rudolph, who himself had a doctorate in chemistry and was the lab's senior examiner in explosives residue analysis. Whitehurst was appalled by what he viewed as Rudolph's sloppy documentation, indifference to contamination, and unscientific interpretations.

In a case against Steven Psinakis for alleged smuggling of explosives to the Philippines, Whitehurst approached a defense expert and told him that he believed Rudolph's identification of pentaerythritol tetranitrate (PETN) was due to contamination and therefore invalid. He did not share his misgivings with the prosecutor or FBI leadership until he returned from the trial. Afterward, Whitehurst was suspended for one week without pay and placed on six months of probation. The prosecutor in the Psinakis trial, Assistant United States Attorney Charles Burch, wrote a letter to Laboratory Director John Hicks about the matter in July 1989. He agreed that Rudolph's work was deficient. Materials Analysis Unit (MAU) chief Jerry Butler reviewed 200 of Rudolph's cases and found only "administrative shortcomings." The Counter-Terrorism Unit (CTU) chief, Roger Martz, did a technical review of 95 of Rudolph's case files and found no technical errors. A few years later, Martz would provide important but flawed testimony in the O.J. Simpson trial, as detailed previously in the DNA section. Martz's review of the Rudolph cases was similarly deficient and failed to put the issue to rest.

The next year, Whitehurst complained to lab leadership about Rudolph's work. He claimed Rudolph was racist, had abused annual leave, had perjured himself, and had lied to a prosecutor. A new investigation was launched. This time, a new MAU chief, James Corby, reviewed 200 of Rudolph's cases and found errors in 57. Although Corby and other management recommended a severe reprimand for Rudolph, lab director Hicks only gave him an oral admonition. Astonishingly, at the same meeting he provided the oral reprimand, he also gave Rudolph a $500 bonus. No subordinate staff, including Whitehurst, were aware of the review or its outcome.

Whitehurst came to believe that his complaints were ignored and that he was the subject of unfair employment discrimination as a whistleblower. He would send dozens of complaints to the OIG amounting to over 1000 pages of documentation. His allegations covered a wide range of cases, criticisms, and colleagues. The OIG followed up on all of his allegations, although Whitehurst was apparently unaware of the full scope of their work until the release of the 1997 Bromwich report. That report credited some of Whitehurst's claims but harshly criticized the man himself. Bromwich recommended that Whitehurst be reassigned because he could no longer work effectively inside the laboratory. He had made many inflammatory and unsubstantiated allegations against innocent colleagues. The report, The FBI Laboratory: An Investigation into Laboratory Practices and Alleged Misconduct in Explosives-Related and Other Cases, said Whitehurst may lack:

> the requisite common sense and judgment to serve as a forensic examiner. ... Any decision about Whitehurst must involve a careful weighing

> of the substantial contribution he made in bringing to light issues in the Laboratory that needed to be addressed against the considerable harm he has caused to the reputations of innocent persons and the fact that his frequently overstated and incendiary way of criticizing Laboratory personnel will make it extremely difficult if not impossible for him to work effectively within the Laboratory.
>
> (Bromwich, 1997)

Whitehurst—and many outside observers—continued to maintain that he was punished for his whistleblower activities. The OIG rejected those claims. Although his working relationships were strained, the FBI did not retaliate against Whitehurst for his whistleblower actions. He was referred to psychotherapy under the FBI Health Care Program Unit and Employee Assistance Program, but the OIG did not conclude that this constituted evidence for retaliation.

The OIG report detailed significant misconduct and deficiencies inside the FBI Laboratory. Examiners produced invalid, inaccurate testimony in several cases, including testimony that was outside the scope of the expertise of the examiner. The management of the lab should have established and enforced testimony standards that prevented invalid testimony, but this reform would not take hold for many years after the Bromwich investigation. For example, the OIG investigation found that Michael Malone had testified falsely in a matter involving the removal of Alcee Hastings from the federal judiciary. Unbeknownst to the OIG, Malone had already given false hair and trace testimony in at least four wrongful convictions. There are more than a dozen other wrongful convictions in which an FBI examiner provided exaggerated hair comparison testimony, though none of those instances were as extreme as Malone's misrepresentations. The FBI's own review of old hair cases in the 2010s found that the large majority of cases included testimony errors that exaggerated the probative value of hair comparisons (ABS Group, 2018). The primary finding of that review was that FBI managers had failed to establish and enforce testimony standards in hair comparison cases—a finding that was completely consistent with the Bromwich report almost 20 years before. The Bromwich report was issued near the end of the time period in which hair comparisons were presented without supporting DNA analysis. The FBI Laboratory did not respond effectively to root-cause findings in the Bromwich report on testimony standards.

The OIG report also faulted other management failures, including the failures by Butler and Martz to follow up on the initial complaint from AUSA Burch related to the Psinakis case. Managers failed to perform adequate technical reviews or ensure full documentation of tests and test reports. Among other recommendations, the OIG urged the lab to abandon the staffing structure in the Explosives Unit and elsewhere in the organization to make sure that examiners had adequate scientific qualifications. Also, the OIG convinced the FBI lab to abandon the distinction between "principal" and "auxiliary" examiners, a practice which had contributed to organizational dysfunction and problems in case reviews. Further, the OIG pointed out that technical reviews should be conducted by the most-qualified examiner, not necessarily the unit chief, and that the work of every examiner should be signed by that examiner. These reforms and related recommendations had a profound effect on the culture of the FBI Laboratory, which is now led by scientists, not former FBI field agents. The recommendations mirror many precepts associated with high-reliability organizations, such as deference to expertise over authority and a sensitivity to operations (i.e., the primacy of frontline staff and situational awareness).

ORGANIZATIONAL STRUCTURE

The reforms were partially responsive to concerns that forensic science organizations are too closely aligned with law enforcement. Prior to 1997, the FBI Laboratory was organized as a law enforcement entity and had a law enforcement culture reinforced by the presence and oversight of supervisory special agents. After 1997, the lab shifted its ethos and organizational structure to a more independent, scientific culture, but the lab remains an entity of the FBI. The 1987 Marvin Thomas wrongful conviction illustrates the drawbacks of a law enforcement culture in a crime lab. Thomas was accused of kidnapping and murdering Janet Miller in West Virginia. The victim's prints were found in the car of an alternate suspect but not Thomas' car. An initial FBI examination found nothing of significance in Thomas' car at all. Later, the seats were removed from the car and sent to the FBI lab, which found a bloodstain on the seat cover and a hair on the floor mat. The serology of the blood spot matched the victim and tied Thomas to the crime. The hair was also found to be consistent with the victim. The FBI examiner, Randall Murch, had not taken photographs of the evidence or documented his search and analysis. He said, "We believe that if the defense counsel and his experts wish to challenge us or reproduce our work, then they can make the test … [they can] re-test using their own methods in their own laboratories" (State v. Thomas, 1992). As the West Virginia Supreme Court noted in its decision overturning the conviction, a defense re-test is not possible when the samples are consumed by the government laboratory. Proper documentation is all that the defense or the court can rely on in such a case. Murch's actions prevented an effective cross-examination and undermined the scientific value of the FBI conclusions. The failure to preserve the evidence or document the work prevented a fair trial for Thomas and led directly to the decision to vacate the conviction. Afterward, Thomas was acquitted on retrial. Murch's statement was not unusual for the FBI in the pre-1997 period. Many examiner-agents took the side of law enforcement and the prosecution. This issue was at the heart of many of Whitehurst's allegations. The OIG took many steps to alleviate this issue and cause a cultural shift in the lab. It is uncertain whether those changes went far enough to ensure the full independence of the FBI Laboratory.

The OIG also recommended that the FBI Laboratory pursue ASCLD-LAB accreditation for the Explosives Unit and the other units of the laboratory. FBI Director Louis Freeh had directed that the lab would pursue accreditation in 1994, and the FBI Laboratory itself acknowledged that it should have pursued accreditation at least a decade earlier. In fact, the FBI lab had no formal quality assurance plan prior to 1992. Some individual units implemented quality assurance plans on their own, but the overall laboratory management relied on the use of sworn agents, unit chief oversight, and proficiency tests as quality assurance mechanisms. Accreditation was resisted due to the resource demands required and doubts from management about the value of accreditation. In addition, the courts did not (and still generally do not) require that examiners come from an accredited laboratory to testify. The FBI lab established a Quality Assurance Unit in 1995. The OIG report clearly did not expect accreditation and quality assurance to prevent any chance at future problems. They did, however, expect these measures to "enhance quality performance." In particular, accreditation requires specific policy, practice, training, review, and related measures that mitigate the probability of forensic errors. Today, the vast majority of forensic science organizations—including the FBI Laboratory—have achieved accreditation. There are also international forensic accreditation standards that apply in the United States and elsewhere, including ISO/IEC 17025, General Requirements for the Accreditation of Testing and Calibration Laboratories (ISO, 2017).

HOUSTON

Today, the city of Houston and surrounding Harris County are served by respected forensic laboratories, including the Harris County Institute of Forensic Sciences (Figure 12.2) and the fully independent Houston Forensic Science Center. Prior to 2010, the area's forensic science organizations were underfunded and poorly managed, resulting in many wrongful convictions.

FIGURE 12.2 Harris County lab. The Harris County Institute of Forensic Sciences (pictured) and Houston Forensic Science Center each occupy purpose-built facilities that reflect their independence and organizational requirements. For many years, the predecessor Houston Police Department Crime Laboratory suffered from poor management and funding, and their facility was so poor that water would often leak into the laboratories. Credit: Michelle Lynn Arnold, CC-BY-SA-4.0.

In 1985, African American Kevin Byrd was arrested for sexual assault in Houston, Texas. A sexual assault kit was collected and sent to the Houston Police Department Crime Laboratory (HPDCL), where analysts Robert Warkentin and James Bolding did hair and serology testing, respectively. Warkentin found only hairs from the victim and no foreign hairs that would inculpate or exculpate Byrd. Bolding used acid phosphatase and microscopic confirmation of semen to establish that the rape kit sample included a male fraction. He found no blood-type substances in the kit. Without separately testing a reference sample from the victim, he concluded that she was a nonsecretor and that the assailant was a nonsecretor. He did perform a reference test on Byrd, who was confirmed to be a nonsecretor. He testified, "It is possible that the defendant in this case is a semen donor." On cross-examination, Bolding admitted that he did not take an elimination sample from the husband. He did not do a P30 confirmation, but he did do a microscopic confirmation of sperm. In this case, as in many others, the HPDCL analyst failed to perform reference and elimination tests that were necessary to do a valid interpretation of the serology. Although Bolding did perform appropriate testing to confirm the male fraction in this case, the HPDCL failed to do so in many cases over decades of serology work. In 1994, about a decade after his trial, the county purged the warehouse of evidence in old cases but missed the evidence in the Byrd case. In 1997, DNA tests exonerated Byrd and he was released and given a pardon.

In 2007, after he had entered the private sector, Bromwich conducted a review of the HPDCL that demonstrated much deeper dysfunction than he observed at the FBI Laboratory (Bromwich, 2007). He found 139 cases in which no comparisons were made to known reference samples as in the Byrd case. He found 274 cases in which the lab didn't even attempt ABO (blood group) testing that could have been probative in the case. Between 1980 and 1992, 21% of the serology cases were unreliable in cases that led to a prison sentence for the defendant. Bromwich found major issues in about one-third of DNA cases that he reviewed, including four death penalty cases.

Bromwich's investigation began in 2005 after years of neglect forced a crisis in the Houston lab. Like many departments, the HPD did not view the crime laboratory as a priority. They failed to invest in staff improvements or training to ensure that the lab was producing high-quality results. The problems became public after a 2001 media report found that the lab analyzed only 25% of the sexual assault kits that they received. The City Council then allocated an additional $600,000 to deal with the backlog, but the police chief blocked the hiring of new personnel. He believed it was a "one time" pool of money and that the problem could be addressed with overtime compensation and outsourcing of rape kit analysis. In 2002, a criminalist, Jennifer LaCoss, resigned from the DNA/Serology section. She cited "horrendous" working conditions, poor salaries, and an "appalling" lack of support and staffing. LaCoss understood that a properly funded lab could solve many crimes with DNA cold hits, but her concerns were dismissed by police leadership. They felt that the new city funds and an expected federal grant would address her concerns. By December, the DNA/Serology unit would close. A local television station reviewed seven DNA and serology cases and discovered severe errors. William Thompson and Elizabeth Johnson, noted experts in DNA interpretation and statistics, assisted the media investigation. Internally, Bolding held that the lab conformed to national FBI guidelines, and the lab director trusted him. An external audit in December was led by Irma Rios, who was then the head of the DNA laboratory for the Texas Department of Public Safety. Rios and her team found that Bolding's assessment was wrong in almost every aspect. The audit cited a lack of quality assurance, no internal auditing system, no qualified technical leader, inadequate training, inadequate standard operating procedures, and poor documentation. The shocking findings surprised the lab and police leadership, but they still attempted to downplay the problems. Nonetheless, the Rios audit and subsequent political firestorm forced them to shut the section down.

JOSIAH SUTTON

Media accounts focused on Josiah Sutton, an African American man who was convicted of sexual assault in 1998 "based largely on flawed and misleading DNA work" (Bromwich, 2007). The evidence included samples from the victim's jeans, a rape kit, and a semen stain from the victim's vehicle. The HPDCL analyst, Christy Kim, used dqAlpha, Polymarker, and D1S80 analyses. These marker systems were little better than traditional serology, but few laboratories at the time could perform more powerful STR analysis. The stains were a mixture of the victim and the rapist, but it appears that Kim did not successfully perform a differential extraction so that a "clean" male fraction could be analyzed. In fact, the victim's DNA profile was observed in all of the evidence profiles, including sperm fractions from the vaginal swab and pubic hair combings. Kim found another male donor in the DNA profiles but didn't account for or report those results. Her controls failed in the dqAlpha testing, meaning that she didn't have enough template DNA. When she ran the victim's reference sample using dqAlpha, the test failed due to poor temperature control, thus demonstrating that she could not run the test reliably even with a clean reference sample. She used the faulty dqAlpha test to include Sutton as a contributor to the sample from the victim's jeans. She only conducted D1S80 testing on samples in which she had a positive association from the dqAlpha testing. When she did that testing, Sutton was excluded. Kim concluded that Sutton's profile was reflected in the DNA results and further said his profile was expected to occur in 1 out of 694,000 people among the black population. That statistic was in error on several fronts. Most importantly, it failed to recognize the difference between the uniqueness of Sutton's DNA and the likelihood that he was a donor to the evidence sample. These are two, very different propositions. Bromwich concluded that the accurate frequency estimate would have been that Sutton would be among the 1 in 14 members of the African American population who could be included in the evidence sample. There was no technical review of Kim's work. There was no written policy in the laboratory regarding technical reviews. Thompson, who had helped uncover the problems in the DNA lab, published a separate review of the DNA analysis in the Sutton case (Thompson, 2003). Thompson concluded that Sutton could be excluded based on the dqAlpha types found in the various evidence samples, but he was apparently unaware (at that time) of the severity of the issues in the HPDCL. The dqAlpha results were not reliable and could not be used to include or exclude anyone. Thompson has produced an excellent review of the Houston situation and similar scandals that were precipitated by organizational failures but often are blamed on "bad apples." At the Sutton trial, the defense did not present any independent analysis or testing. The defense lawyer took money to do so but never followed through. Kim testified simply that she found "Josiah Sutton's pattern" on the jeans and rape kit evidence. The cross-examination was inadequate in all respects. DNA testing eventually exonerated Sutton, who received a gubernatorial pardon. In 2006, Donald Young was identified as the perpetrator based on a CODIS cold hit.

BROADER PROBLEMS IN HOUSTON

Bromwich found some issues in the HPDCL's Controlled Substances Section and other units, such as their analysis of liquids and tablets from drug seizures. Two drug analysts were found to be dry-labbing in some cases, but the lab had difficulty removing or disciplining incompetent personnel. Bromwich was not aware that the HPD would be involved in a major drug case scandal a few years later. That issue did not involve errors in the crime laboratory. Rather, it related to the use of field test kits that are susceptible to false positives. Over 100 defendants were convicted—all from plea deals—without confirmatory testing in the lab. In many cases, confirmatory tests that didn't support the conviction were ignored or lost in poor communication between the crime lab and prosecutor's office. Bromwich reviewed firearms, trace evidence, and toxicology reports and questioned documents units and found only minor or isolated issues These HPDCL units lacked adequate documentation and quality assurance mechanisms.

The ballistics unit—particularly the work of examiner Robert Baldwin—was also found to reflect poor policies and procedures. For example, there was a misidentification in the Nanon Williams capital murder case. Baldwin had testified that both bullets recovered from the crime scene were .25 caliber bullets, thus absolving an alternate suspect who was found with a .22 Derringer pistol. Baldwin never test-fired the Derringer. Postconviction, an independent examiner found that the bullet recovered from the victim's head at autopsy was actually a .22 round that matched the Derringer. This was obviously material to the finding of guilt or innocence for Williams. Bromwich noted that the ballistics unit failed to account for the distortion of bullets due to impacts, failed to test-fire the Derringer, and relied on policies that did not require technical reviewers to actually review the evidence in question. Although

Williams' death sentence has been commuted to life, he remains in prison. Three times, a court has vacated his conviction, but the decisions were overturned on further appeal.

In general, the issues in other disciplines were minor in comparison with the gross errors in the HPDCL serology and DNA work. The DNA analysis was characterized by "the absence of a quality assurance program, inadequately trained analysts, poor analytical technique, incorrect interpretations of data, the characterizing of results as 'inconclusive' when that was not the case, and the lack of meaningful and competent technical reviews." The lab routinely reported inaccurate and misleading statistics in a manner similar to that observed in the Sutton case.

ROOT CAUSES

Bromwich outlined four key root causes of the problems in HPDCL. First, the police department and city of Houston had failed to provide adequate resources to the lab. The lab director, Donald Krueger, failed to communicate the severity of issues in the lab to police and city leadership, who showed little interest in any case. As in the FBI, the civilian employees of the lab were devalued relative to the sworn officers of the HPD itself. There were chronic staff shortages and the siloed nature of the various units meant there was little opportunity for advancement. Bromwich did not find individual misconduct, but he did observe severe training deficiencies. The infrastructure was also poor, with roof leaks that allowed water to leak into the crime lab over a six-year period from 1997 to 2003. Lab director Krueger avoided accreditation because he was aware the deficiencies would make the presence of outside inspectors problematic at best. For his part, Krueger was isolated from his staff. He relied on Bolding to manage the DNA/serology section with minimal oversight, despite the fact that Bolding lacked education, training, or experience in DNA analysis.

The lab units lacked an adequate quality control program. The standard operating procedures were developed in a haphazard way over many years without periodic reevaluation or review. Technical reviews were also haphazard, so incorrect testing and interpretation were not corrected. When quality reviews were conducted, they emphasized administrative issues and did not examine the results and interpretation of actual analyses.

The DNA/Serology section stood out as a "shambles" from its inception in the early 1990s. Although the lab had agreed to conform to national FBI standards linked to CODIS access, they did not follow through on these commitments. They did not arrange for external reviews on a biannual basis as required. Internal reviews conducted by Bolding failed to find deficiencies because Bolding was not competent or an independent auditor. For example, analysts continued to report false statistical interpretations in DNA analyses. The Rios audit in 2002 amply demonstrated the ramifications of technical incompetence and a lack of external oversight.

By the time the Bromwich report was issued, Rios had been named the new director of the Houston laboratory and had begun to implement fundamental reforms. Bromwich recognized the value of her improvements and made additional recommendations. Most importantly, his team had reviewed 850 serology and 180 DNA cases, and there was a need for follow-up to determine the extent of wrongful convictions that may have been associated with the crime lab scandal. They were already aware of Sutton and other cases. For example, George Rodriguez had been wrongfully convicted for a 1987 kidnapping and sexual assault. Faulty serological analysis had excluded a key suspect, who was identified by DNA analysis after Rodriguez had served 17 years in prison. By 2007, the lab's budget had doubled, but resource issues remained in firearms and evidence receiving sections. The lab established a formal quality assurance program, but that unit also required additional staffing to function efficiently. Bromwich noted that there remained training issues in the new Biology Section in the recognition of probative evidence, semen identification, DNA interpretation, and reporting language.

In 2012, the primary forensic services for the HPD moved to a new, nonprofit corporation, the Houston Forensic Science Center. The HSFC enjoys greater independence from law enforcement than most crime laboratories and has established a wide range of innovations. For example, HSFC has the most extensive in-house performance testing regime in forensic science (Hundl et al., 2020). Under a blind quality control program, they introduce samples into the HSFC workflow as a check on analyst performance. The approach reflects high-reliability organization principles, especially the "obsession with error." In other words, this program identifies performance gaps before they become problems with severe ramifications. In the pre-2002 Houston lab, problems were not proactively identified. In fact, they were allowed to fester and develop over many years. In the current structure, HSFC is able to mitigate—not eliminate—the possibility of severe errors before they occur.

The Texas Forensic Science Commission (TXFSC) was established in 2005 in the wake of the Houston scandal and a large number of wrongful convictions in Texas related to forensic science errors (Texas Forensic Science Commission, 2022). The TXFSC mandate has been expanded to include investigation of complaints involving forensic disciplines and the licensing of forensic practitioners within the state. The commission has now issued dozens of reports covering many laboratories and a broad array of disciplines. Many reports relate to self-disclosures from laboratories regarding deficiencies. Research has not been conducted to determine the full impact of TXFSC's work. Most observers agree that the Texas structure provides the most thorough and effective governance of forensic science in the United States. Certainly, no scandals of the order of the HPDCL have arisen in the intervening years.

DETROIT

Kym Worthy became the first black woman to head the Wayne County Prosecutor's Office in 2004. She inherited a situation with declining city finances, a troubled police department, and a dysfunctional crime laboratory (see Figure 12.3). Five years later, she handled two problems related to forensic evidence that were among the most extreme issues

FIGURE 12.3 Detroit Police HQ 1300 Beaubein. In 2013, the Detroit Police Department (DPD) moved out of their historic former headquarters at 1300 Beaubien Boulevard. When it was built in 1923, the building represented the forward-thinking innovation of the DPD. As the city's population and finances declined, the department's resources and leadership were deeply affected. The building became part of Detroit's bankruptcy settlement, and crime lab responsibilities were assumed by the state of Michigan. Credit: Mike Russell; Creative Commons Attribution-Share Alike 3.0 Unported license.

ever encountered in any jurisdiction. In March, an audit found that 10% of the firearms cases handled by the city crime lab contained identification errors. Then, in August, her office found a massive backlog of over 11,000 untested sexual assault kits in the police department warehouse.

The Michigan State Police (MSP) inspected the Detroit lab in June (2008) in accordance with criteria from the ASCLD/LAB accreditation program (Forensic Science Division, 2008). Ron Smith & Associates (RSA) assisted with the reexamination of 200 past cases handled by the Detroit firearms unit. At Worthy's request, they included 33 previously adjudicated cases identified by the Wayne County Prosecutor's Office. The results showed chronic shortfalls with respect to ASCLD/LAB standards (see https://anab.ansi.org/). ASCLD/LAB standards define three levels of standards which are part of an accreditation review:

Essential: Direct and fundamental impact on the work product and integrity of evidence
Important: Key quality indicator that may not directly impact the work product or integrity of evidence
Desired: Standards which enhance the professionalism of the laboratory

At the case level, ASCLD/LAB defines three levels of inconsistencies:

Class I: Immediate concern regarding the laboratory's work, such as an erroneous identification, false identification, or false positive
Class II: Issue relates to quality of work but not necessarily overall quality of laboratory work, such as a missed identification or false negative
Class III: Minimal significance, not likely to be systemic, such as administrative or transcription mistake

As noted in the MSP report, Class II or Class III inconsistencies may become a pattern that rises to the level of a Class I inconsistency. In any high-reliability organization, any Class III inconsistency is a red flag for managers and staff to initiate substantive reviews to prevent higher-level errors. In Detroit, they tolerated Class II inconsistencies in *most firearms examinations* and Class I inconsistencies in 10% of examinations.

In about two-thirds of cases, the Detroit lab was noncompliant with accreditation standards for ballistics units. In fact, the firearms unit scored only 42% compliance with the "Essential" criteria laid down by ASCLD/LAB. The MSP audit found a wide range of documentation and procedural errors. Evidence was "laid about in the unit unsecured and unprotected from possible loss and contamination." No standardized procedures were documented or followed. Technical reviews were "almost nonexistent." No audits or independent reviews had ever taken place. In many cases, the audit team could not get answers to simple questions concerning calibration and materials quality because the laboratory had not documented anything about these important issues. Examiners were reporting matches without notes, photographs, or other documentation of features and comparisons. An external vendor, Collaborative Testing Services, had administered a proficiency testing program. The CTS proficiency tests were not useful because the examiners took the test "as a group with the consensus answers submitted to the test provider[.]" The performance of individual examiners was not tested at all.

The MSP report did not develop a root-cause analysis of the Detroit lab issues. They did note the lack of training and employee development, lack of support from police and city leaders, the mismatch between resources and the volume of the work, and "the deplorable conditions of the facility." As in Houston, the lab had water leaks that compromised active cases and evidence storage. They detailed 66 deficiencies or "inconsistencies," as they are called in accreditation parlance. The Detroit lab did not value quality assurance. Their Quality Manual was basically the MSP quality manual with the Detroit lab's name on the front cover. The lab director served as the Quality Manager and the Safety Officer. In other words, the lab didn't have a Quality Manager or Safety Officer. The budget was inadequate. Case records did not have property receipts, which means that chain of custody was compromised on 90% of the cases. Interestingly, the MSP audit indicated that the firearms unit supervisor was generally supportive of the unit and the employees, who laid blame for the deficiencies on the lab director. The supervisor must share in the responsibility for the lack of accountability in the unit, although resource and organizational issues were clearly much broader problems. For example, the training budget for the firearms unit in 2007 was $0. No scientific organization can be successful under such conditions.

As in Houston, evidence tracking was woefully deficient in Detroit. There was no consistent documentation. There was insufficient space for storage of evidence. As a result, firearms evidence was "laid about the unit unsecured and unprotected from possible loss and contamination." Evidence overflowed into the offices, and access to the workspace was not restricted during normal business hours. Test fires were not secured and were found in case files in unsealed envelopes. The lab space was "grossly insufficient," and the ability to adequately perform casework was "almost nonexistent." The shooting tank was in the basement and was "dark, moldy, and cockroach infested." The facility was not a place to do effective forensic science, but it was also not a healthy and safe work environment. There was minimal personal protective equipment, and the sole fume hood was being used for overflow storage.

MSP did document the Class I inconsistencies found by RSA in their case reviews. They noted that the majority of firearms cases in the lab resulted in a match to evidence, which they dubbed "a highly uncommon result." Most ballistics cases do not produce a match to evidence. The MSP report did not say so, but it is clear that there was a basis to believe that some significant fraction of the matches were fraudulent. Some of the Class I errors were identifications or source conclusions that should have been "inconclusive." Others were more blatant errors. In one case, the Detroit examiners had said that a .40 S&W caliber cartridge case had been fired from a specific firearm, but the cartridge case hadn't been fired from any firearm. In some cases, the Detroit lab examiner had failed to make an association that should have been found. They found a Class I inconsistency in four of the 33 cases submitted for review by prosecutor Worthy.

Given the severe problems, it is remarkable that the Detroit police department and its forensic laboratory were operating at all. The police chief, Ella Bully Cummings, was a tough, reform-minded leader. She resigned in 2008 after becoming embroiled in a controversy in which the mayor's chief of staff was pulled over for a traffic stop. The forensic lab was closed and all functions were transferred to the MSP.

NEW YORK STATE POLICE

In 1991, David Harding interviewed for a job at the Central Intelligence Agency (CIA) and told his prospective employer about his willingness to commit perjury in the Shirley Kinge case. The wrongful conviction is detailed in the chapter on fingerprints (Roth, 1997). Harding and four other members of the New York State Police (NYSP) Troop C Identification Unit and two members of the Troop F unit had committed perjury and tampered with physical evidence over a decade of official misconduct (See Figure 12.4). The troopers were fired and prosecuted and served up to 18 years in prison. In 1997, New York's Deputy Attorney General, Nelson Roth, issued a 400-page report detailing the misconduct. Although there are other examples of misconduct among police and forensic examiners, the Roth report is among the most comprehensive and insightful examinations of the root causes. The investigation reviewed every positive match made the NYSP over a ten-year period and a random sampling of no-match cases.

Harding had fabricated evidence in seven cases. His conspirator in the Kinge case, Robert Lishansky, fabricated evidence in 22 cases. Prints were lifted from suspects or evidence and planted to frame them

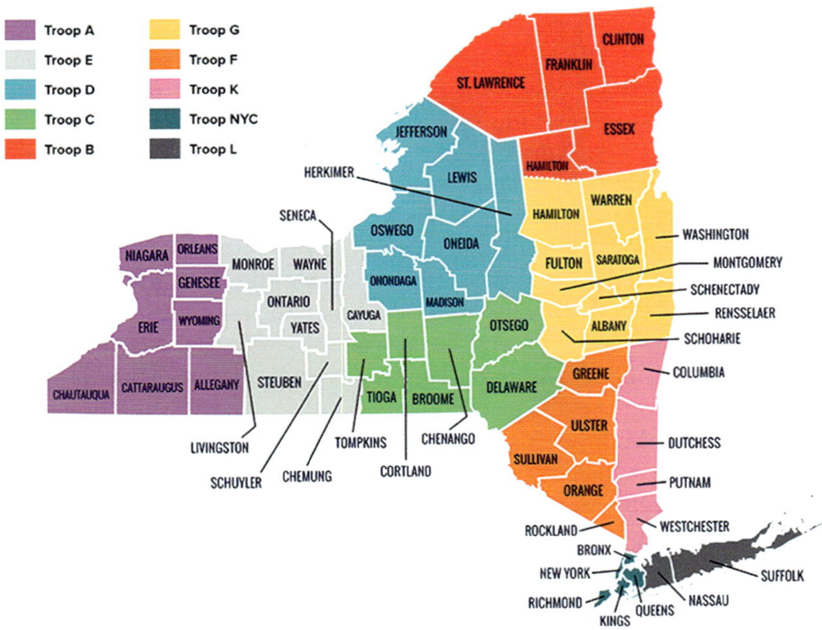

FIGURE 12.4 NYSP troop map. The fingerprint scandal involved multiple trooper units within the NYSP. Troops C and F were located in the lower part of upstate New York. Linus Rautenstrauch, a certified fingerprint examiner from Troop E to the west, refused to testify in the Kinge case and told the prosecutor his concerns about Harding and Troop C. The Roth review did not find fraudulent work in other units. Source: New York State Police.

for crimes. Examiners lied about the location where prints were found or manipulated photographs to depict a background different from the original print. Unit leaders were aware of the practices. It is clear that the NYSP chain of command was aware of or should have been aware of the issues in the latent print units. The perpetrators held that there was no organized plan of corruption, though one trooper, Craig Harvey, committed the first known fraudulent examination and rose to lead the Troop C unit as an NYSP Lieutenant. Roth said, "Vigilantism does not appear to be a major factor. Ego, laziness, craving for publicity and advancement, and gamesmanship appear to be likely explanations." This supposition aligns with other instances of forensic misconduct, such as the Boston drug lab scandal (Chapter 13, Drugs and Toxicology) and the Joyce Gilchrist misconduct (Chapter 3, under Serology).

More fundamentally, the NYSP did not detect the deviations from established protocols and regulations during periodic reviews. Leadership must have had some awareness of the issues because examiners from other NYSP units clearly alleged misconduct well before Harding's admissions to the CIA. Certified examiner Linus Rautensrauch refused to testify in the Shirley Kinge case and was dismissed by lead investigator David McElligott. This behavior is in stark contrast to the response of federal prosecutor Charles Burch in the Psinakis trial. Although Burch expressed his annoyance at Whitehurst's behavior in the trial, he also alerted FBI leadership of the poor forensic work in the case. Unfortunately, the unit leaders inside the FBI reacted poorly, just as McElligott did in the NYSP scandal. In many cases of laboratory dysfunction, supervisors knew that lower-level issues were present—what might be referred to as Class III inconsistencies. They dismissed the importance of lower-impact deficiencies that could be a sign of more serious problems in the units. As Roth observed, McElligott showed a lack of sensitivity about fingerprint evidence in the Kinge case that proved to be fabricated. The district attorney also used perjured testimony by Harding in a criminal retrial in the Mark Prentice wrongful conviction that had arisen from Harding's earlier misconduct.

Roth acknowledged that large organizations like the NYSP could not eradicate the possibility of corrupt officers or forensic examiners. Any policy that anticipated that they would always recruit the perfect cop was bound to fail. Instead, he held that NYSP leadership should emphasize the establishment and enforcement of written regulations and protocols. He said, "The deviations from Division regulations also violated basic (and common sense) protocols which would likely be apparent even to the most inexperienced officer. Had existing regulations been enforced, much of the misconduct in Troop C may have been prevented." To some extent, NYSP leadership did not show the awareness needed to enforce regulations. Rautenstrauch attended the Kinge crime scene for at least five days, observed the gasoline can after it was processed, and saw that it had no usable prints. He then notified the chain of command when he became suspicious of the prints that Harding supposedly found. The lead investigator, McElligott, knew that Harding had changed his finding of prints on the gasoline can between his first report and the preliminary hearing in the case. He knew that Rautenstrauch objected to Harding's documentation failures, which were clearly not aligned with NYSP regulations.

The NYSP hierarchy had plenty of red flags too. The Troop C unit had one of the lowest caseloads of any fingerprint unit but had an unusually high rate of positive latent print matches. Too often, lab scandals arise when managers are too pleased with performance metrics that lead to cleared cases and ignore the possibility that errors have been made. A high positive rate may be an indication of many things. In the NYSP, it was an indication of fraudulent work. In other places, it may reflect subjective decision thresholds that are prosecution-friendly or other biases (Busey et al., 2021).

Roth's recommendations centered on documentation and process. For example, every latent print should be photographed, the time and exact location of the print should be recorded, and an evidence tag should be attached to the prints. Roth described extensive improvements in documentation and chain of custody. He also laid out detailed responsibilities for senior investigators in fingerprint units, such as technical reviews, verifications, inventory, and so on. None of the recommendations were extreme. They were all oriented around doing business as a professional forensic science organization and expecting accountability for each person in each case.

Roth also described the negative role of police unions in the NYSP corruption scandal, saying they "played an intentionally hostile and destructive role." The Police Benevolent Association sent a representative to interviews with Troop C examiners, but that person was directly linked to some of the investigations himself. Another union representative continued to denounce the investigation publicly even after the examiner he was defending had confessed and been convicted. The representative used his NYSP position to refuse access to physical evidence in a case in which prints may have been fabricated. Ultimately, the authenticity of the print was confirmed without the union representative's cooperation. Roth believed that the union opposed any investigation of its members without regard to the substantive basis for that investigation. The union "viewed [investigators] as the enemy rather than as an integral part of a respected and honest department." The documentation of this attitude and the way that it can prevent accountability in cases of police misconduct is unusual. More broadly, many leaders in public crime laboratories face similar hurdles in discipline processes relating to misconduct.

US ARMY CRIMINAL INVESTIGATION LABORATORY

The US Army Criminal Investigation Laboratory (USACIL), now reorganized under the Defense Forensic Science Center, is the primary forensic laboratory handling cases within the military courts (Figure 12.5). Forensic analyst Phillip Mills started at USACIL in 1979 doing serology analyses while in the active-duty Army (Office of the Inspector General, 2013). Later, he moved to DNA work and also became a civilian employee of the lab. In 2002, he failed a hair-proficiency test. In December 2003, he cross-contaminated or switched samples within and between five cases. After retraining, he returned to casework but was permanently suspended when he was found falsifying test data. An administrative inquiry found that he had prepared a fictitious DNA

FIGURE 12.5 USACIL Mickey Mouse logo. It is unclear why a forensic science organization would choose to incorporate Mickey Mouse into its official logo. USACIL has maintained this logo despite the inevitable association of the lab with epithets that labeled it a "Mickey Mouse organization" after multiple organizational problems became public knowledge. USACIL is now organized under the Defense Forensic Science Center and US Army Criminal Investigation Division, both of which feature more traditional designs in keeping with their mission. Source: United States Army.

"quantitative testing record." Presumably, this means he uploaded a false profile into the CODIS system. A three-year, $1.4 million investigation ensued. Lab officials found errors in 55% of Mills' DNA results among those that could be reanalyzed. Unfortunately, policy had called for the routine destruction of evidence in older cases, so 83% of Mills' work could not be retested. At least one other USACIL DNA analyst had shown a "lack of attention to detail" that impacted casework.

The wrongful conviction of Roger House resulted from Mills' DNA testing errors (House v. United States, 2011). House was accused of rape arising from an incident on a military base in Tennessee in 2001. A rape kit was collected by the City of Memphis but did not show the presence of semen. Three used condoms were found in and around the house of one of the alleged rapists. Mills did the DNA testing of the condoms at USACIL. He found DNA that matched the alleged female victim on the outside of one condom. The profile of the biological material on the inside of that condom was consistent with House, but the match was incomplete and inconclusive. The profiles from another condom were even more compromised but also consistent with the alleged victim and

House. House was court-martialed. Although he was acquitted of rape, he was convicted of conduct unbecoming an officer and of making false statements under oath. He resigned his commission.

After Mills' misconduct was discovered, the evidence was retested. The alleged female victim's DNA profile was confirmed, but the DNA inside the condoms was attributed to an unknown male. House and his two co-defendants were all excluded as contributors. They were excluded from all of the evidence in the case, even as minor donors. The results were not shared with the defendants for another three years.

Other issues have arisen at USACIL, including a forensic document examiner, Allen Southmayd, who embezzled funds from the American Board of Forensic Document Examiners, and a firearms analyst, Michael Brooks, who was caught dry-labbing gunshot residue and destroying evidence (Turvey, 2013). The Army has conducted multiple internal investigations of alleged misconduct by laboratory managers, including six complaints over four years regarding racism, sexual harassment, assault, and fraud (Do you trust me now? 2011). Official reports concerning the resolution of these matters have been scarce, leading to speculation about the culture and conditions within the laboratory. Some observers claim that the lab has a culture "that is permissive of fraud and incompetence" related to the larger culture of military justice and law enforcement (Turvey, 2013). These claims lack an objective basis in actual reviews of USACIL.

The one cultural issue that has been substantiated is the systematic opposition to transparency. An independent, 2013 report from Defense Department OIG examined the failure to notify individuals about possibly compromised DNA evidence from the Phillip Mills investigation. While the Navy and Air Force notified or attempted to notify affected individuals, the Army only provided broad memoranda to military defense attorneys. Further, the OIG found that USACIL did not comply with evidence and control requirements. For example, some of the evidence in Mills' cases was found in an unsecured refrigerator years after he had resigned. Samples were also found in his old locker and a closet. The samples were retested and uploaded to CODIS, but questions about the chain of custody led to the deletion of the profiles from CODIS and NDIS. Other profiles had been uploaded by Mills and were also removed. The OIG found that the Army met the letter of its notification regulations but not the spirit. After the OIG investigation, specific notices were sent to the affected defendants and Army regulations were changed.

A separate media investigation by McClatchy Newspapers found that military officials had tried to avoid a "public scandal and protect criminal cases from outside legal attack, in part by keeping their inquiry of Mills in-house" (Taylor & Doyle, 2011). In response to the media investigation, the Army pointed out that $1.4 million had been devoted to the investigative response and said, "[W]e feel very strongly that we took immediate corrective action and have done everything possible to prevent this from happening in the future." That said, even the federal prosecutor, David Leta, who was responsible for determining whether Mills should face charges, said he was only made aware of the Army report on the matter when McClatchy informed him years after the fact. Also, USACIL bent over backwards to retain and retrain an employee who was clearly not well-suited to forensic analysis. Mills should never have been returned to the bench after his failures in DNA work and hair analysis. Also, USACIL did not implement or enforce necessary evidence storage and chain of custody protocols. Although USACIL had been accredited since 1985, it is unclear how it had passed accreditation reviews given these deficiencies. Finally, USACIL and Army leaders were clearly concerned with the political and judicial impacts of disclosures. Their subsequent damage-control actions failed to demonstrate transparency and a commitment to fundamental improvements in the lab. They treated the Mills issues as an isolated instance that could not possibly reflect more broadly on the management of USACIL. Although Mills must take responsibility for his actions, USACIL needed to take responsibility for the deficiencies that permitted Mills to produce forensic errors that impacted on casework.

There is nothing unique about USACIL's position in the military or law enforcement in this regard. Most organizations "circle the wagons" when they feel under attack. The conditions for transparency and accountability must be set prior to a crisis so an organization can mount a substantive response to an acute crisis. The primary failures at USACIL were management failures that occurred well before the House case or the OIG review. Managers failed to put into place a culture that accepted the inevitability of errors and systems to mitigate the possibility of errors. They did not treat lower-impact errors as signs of the possibility of deeper problems. When an acute crisis did arise, it is unsurprising that they threw money at the issue like water at a fire. The firefighter knows that prevention and response are both vital to the task. You do have to deal with the fire when it happens, but you also need to do everything ahead of time to prevent the fire and prepare yourself with the response tools. USACIL did not take this approach.

WASHINGTON, DC

This chapter does not cover every scandal ever alleged in a crime laboratory. It is limited to instances in which Class I errors—false positives—arose from forensic misconduct and were later investigated by independent, government entities. Many observers fail to make a distinction among classes of errors or types of deficiencies. Labs may experience deficiencies in accreditation reviews or other circumstances that can and must be addressed, but these matters do not rise to the same level as the Houston or Detroit scandals. Also, when thorough reviews have not been done, biased speculation tends to substitute for objective analysis. The observer assumes that the problems reflect the need for their preferred choice of reform. In some cases, these perceptions can be abused to block or even undo needed reforms.

In 2011, Washington, DC established an independent Department of Forensic Science (DFS) with a Forensic Sciences Advisory Board (FSAB) (Rudin & Inman, 2015). The structure was designed to address calls from the NAS and others to separate forensic services from law enforcement influence (Committee on Identifying the Needs of the Forensic Sciences Community, National Research Council, 2009). Former FBI analyst Max Houck was hired to run the lab, assisted by Christine Funk, a nationally recognized defense attorney (Rudin & Inman, 2015). The lab began operation in 2012 and immediately sought accreditation from the ANSI National Accreditation Board (ANAB). The ANAB audit of the DNA unit noted the need for corrective actions, but no finding was significant enough to prevent accreditation by October of 2013. Houck said, "The agency's creation has sent ripples of constructive discussion through the forensic and scientific community about our scientific independence, our melding of forensic and public health services, and the progressive view on having DFS as a 'science first' organization."

In the summer of 2013, two crimes in Northeast DC changed the course of the lab. Two suspects, Tavon Barber and De Aundre Williams, were alleged to have sexually assaulted a woman and committed two burglaries. A vehicle was stolen in connection with the first burglary. Fingerprints and a DNA sample from a cigarette butt were recovered. The DC lab concluded that the DNA sample was consistent with a mixture of Barber's and Williams' DNA profiles. Williams' DNA was also detected on door handles of the car. Barber's palmprint was found at the second robbery scene along with DNA from the victim and Williams. Barber also used the victim's credit card.

Before the trial in May of 2014, renowned DNA expert Bruce Budowle was brought in to review DFS's DNA work. Budowle and Houck had worked together at the FBI and collaborated on a landmark paper on the use of mitochondrial DNA on hair samples (Houck & Budowle, 2002). Budowle disagreed with the DFS interpretations of the DNA profiles from the stolen vehicle. He agreed with the allele calls but disagreed with the statistical calculations. For a sample from the car's gear shift which was associated with Barber, DFS said there was a 1 in 3290 chance that a randomly selected person had the same genetic traits. Budowle put the chance at 1 in 9. Budowle excluded some alleles that he thought couldn't be used reliably in the statistical calculation. As is often the case, the main issue revolved around mixture interpretation of secondary contributors. The FSAB reviewed the issue and made 12 recommendations for improvement in the DFS guidelines for mixture interpretation. They emphasized that the DFS approach was reliable but could be improved.

The US Attorney's Office (USAO) did not agree. Because Washington, DC is under federal jurisdiction, the USAO serves as the chief prosecutor. The USAO convened its own review panel that included Budowle. They also relied on a DNA analyst from Bode Laboratories in Virginia who, it was later discovered, was in a personal relationship with an assistant US attorney within the USAO. It is reasonable to believe that the appearance of conflict of interest should have prevented the involvement of both individuals in the review. The USAO panel questioned the DNA interpretation in the Barber/Williams case and four other cases and made five recommendations of their own. DFS did not learn of the recommendations until early 2014 after the USAO moved all of the Washington, DC DNA work to a California crime lab directed by another member of the USAO panel. Again, there is no public evidence that the potential conflict of interest was addressed. Shortly thereafter, Houck was reappointed by incoming mayor Muriel Bowser as head of the DFS. DFS issued a formal response to the USAO, saying, "The arguments and criticisms raised in the USAO report were not found to be persuasive. ... Unit personnel ... adhered to the Unit's DNA mixture interpretation guidelines..."

At this point, the dispute was public and reflected deep dysfunction in the relationships among the USAO, DFS, and the DC government. The Washington Post reported the USAO's decision on the DNA interpretation but misreported the essence of the issue. They said Barber was not the source of the DNA on the gear shift. In fact, Barber was always recognized as a possible contributor to the sample. The differences related to the statistical calculation only. The mayor requested a new USAO audit, which found nonconformities and directed that DNA testing be suspended until they were resolved. The FSAB urged the mayor to withhold judgment pending their own review of the matter. They clearly believed that the USAO had acted improperly, and the issues were related to political, not scientific, issues. Nonetheless, Bowser removed Houck in April of 2015. The following month, widely respected forensic educator, Jay Siegel, resigned from the FSAB in protest. In an open letter to Bowser, he said,

> The District of Columbia has an extensive and well-deserved reputation for political interference in a wide variety of its activities and

> processes. I hoped that this would not be the case with the DFS when I joined the Board. My hopes were misplaced. The actions ... the USAO have taken in this matter were clearly not based on scientific considerations since the Scientific Advisory Board had no chance to provide advice BEFORE you took such drastic actions. I cannot continue to serve as a member of the Science Advisory Board and I hereby resign, effective immediately.
>
> (J. A. Siegel to Mayor M. Bowser, "RE: Science Advisory Board, DC Division of Forensic Science", 27b May 2015)

In September, DFS hired the Bode employee from the USAO review as the new DNA unit manager. In 2016, the Washington Post reported that the DFS would no longer have the independence it was designed to enjoy. Prosecutors were given "direct access" to analysts to check the status of testing, overturning the Houck policy which had been designed to limit contextual bias concerns. In 2018, Barber's appeal for a new trial was rejected by the DC Court of Appeals. Overall, the evidence against Barber outweighed any uncertainty raised by the USAO criticisms.

The situation in Washington may be interpreted in a variety of ways. The USAO prosecutors may have felt the same way that Charles Burch felt in the Psinakis trial related to the Whitehurst allegations. They had a responsibility to act if poor forensic work impacted their cases. Unlike Burch, they took matters into their own hands and established a review committee that clearly lacked independence and objectivity. Their hamhandedness resulted in an outcome that has the hallmarks of bureaucratic squabbling, not leadership.

Further, media accounts failed to report the matter accurately. The disagreements were presented within a set of assumptions regarding laboratory scandals and other cases in which DNA mixture interpretation contributed to wrongful convictions. The accounts tended to reinforce the perception that the DC lab was mired in scandal, even though the lab position on mixture interpretation was defensible. The media accounts may have undermined a genuine attempt to establish positive reform in the Washington, DC crime laboratory.

It is impossible to know whether Budowle or Houck were right in their analysis of the statistics. The sample and reference profiles have not been made public, nor has there been any other independent review of the matter. The lab's Forensic Biology unit had no nonconformities by 2016. The DNA unit has led efforts to adopt the direct-to-DNA approach to sexual assault evidence and the exploration of next-generation sequencing. The FSAB still exists and meets regularly.

STUDY QUESTIONS

1. There are many approaches to describe organizational dysfunction. One useful approach identifies five root causes (Pearson Education, 2014):

    1. Misunderstood mission
    2. Lack of consensus on the nature of problems facing the team
    3. Misunderstood strategy
    4. Lack of team cohesion
    5. Lack of resources

    There are also five characteristics of high-reliability organizations (Weick & Sutcliffe, 2001):

    1. Preoccupation with failure
    2. Reluctance to simplify
    3. Every voice matters
    4. Resiliency
    5. Deference to expertise

    Finally, there are three types of accreditation inconsistencies (https://anab.ansi.org/):

    - Class I: Immediate concern regarding the laboratory's work, such as an erroneous identification, false identification, or false positive
    - Class II: Issue relates to quality or work but not necessarily overall quality of laboratory work, such as a missed identification or false negative
    - Class III: Minimal significance not likely to systemic, such as administrative or transcription mistake

    Consider the examples of organizational dysfunction described in this chapter.

    1. Describe an example of one of the kinds of organizational dysfunction
    2. Describe an example of a failure to reflect the principles of a high-reliability organization
    3. Describe an example of Class I, Class II, or Class III deficiencies

    How do these concepts relate to wrongful convictions? Can quality assurance mechanisms be used to mitigate the risk of forensic science errors and wrongful convictions? How does the culture of a laboratory mitigate or contribute to the risk of forensic science errors and wrongful convictions?

2. There are many other examples of organizational dysfunction in forensic science organizations and other criminal justice organizations. Many examples are described elsewhere in this text. Consider the recluse characteristics of organizational dysfunction, high-reliability organizations, and accreditation inconsistencies and how they relate to another case context.
3. Consider another type of dysfunctional organization outside of the criminal justice system. Do you see similar behaviors and problems? How would you address the issue if you were a part of a dysfunctional organization?

FURTHER READING

The chapter references provide a rich source of reading material on the subject of organizational dysfunction in forensic science organizations. The Bromwich reports are a good starting point. Bromwich's Houston report is especially useful for its case reviews and examination of the underlying issues. The OIG report on USACIL, MSP report on Detroit, and Roth report on NYSP all make excellent reading. The Rudin/Inman account of the Washington, DC lab situation should be required reading for anyone contemplating a career in forensic science.

REFERENCES

ABS Group. (2018). *Root Cause Analysis of Microscopic Hair Comparison Analysis*. Arlington, VA: Federal Bureau of Investigation.

Bromwich, M. (1997). *The FBI Laboratory: An Investigation into Laboratory Practices and Alleged Misconduct in Explosives-Related and Other Cases*. Washington, DC: US Department of Justice Office of the Inspector General.

Bromwich, M. (2007). *Final Report of the Independent Investigator for the Houston Police Department Crime Laboratory and Property Room*. Washington, DC: Fried, Frank, Harris, Shriver & Jacobson LLP.

Busey, T. A., Heise, N., Hicklin, R. A., Ulery, B. T., & Buscaglia, J. (2021). Characterizing Missed Identifications and Errors in Latent Fingerprint Comparisons Using Eye-tracking Data. *PloS One*, *16*(5), e0251674.

Committee on Identifying the Needs of the Forensic Sciences Community, National Research Council. (2009). *Strengthening Forensic Science in the United States: A Path Forward*. Washington, DC: National Academies Press.

Do You Trust Me Now? (2011, June 27). Retrieved from Law Office of Philip D. Cave: https://www.court-martial-ucmj.com/do-you-trust-me-now/

Forensic Science Division. (2008). *Audit of the Detroit Police Department Forensic Services Laboratory Firearms Unit*. Michigan State Police.

Houck, M. M., & Budowle, B. (2002). Correlation of Microscopic and Mitochondrial DNA Hair Comparisons. *Journal of Forensic Sciences*, *47*(5), 964–967.

House v. United States, 08–758C (United States Court of Federal Claims July 8, 2011).

Hundl, C., Neuman, M., Rairden, M., Rearden, P., & Stout, P. (2020). Implementation of a Blind Quality Control Program in a Forensic Laboratory. *Journal of Forensic Sciences*, *65*(3), 815–822.

ISO. (2017). *General Requirements for the Competence of Testing and Calibration Laboratories*, 3rd ed. ISO/IEC.

Michigan State Police. (2008). *Detroit Police Department Firearms Unit Preliminary Audit Findings*.

Office of the Inspector General. (2013). *Review of the DoD Response to Noncompliant Crime Laboratory Analyses*. Alexandria: US Department of Defense.

Pearson Education. (2014, July 3). *Five Common Causes of Organizational Dysfunction*. Retrieved from InformIT: https://www.informit.com/articles/article.aspx?p=2168986

Roth, N. (1997). *The New York State Police Evidence Tampering Investigation Report to the Honorable George Pataki*. Ithaca.

Rudin, N., & Inman, K. (2015). Could Your Lab Be Next? *The CAC News*.

State v. Thomas, 20676 (Supreme Court of Appeals of West Virginia July 15, 1992).

Taylor, M., & Doyle, M. (2011, March 20). Army Slow to Act as Crime-lab Worker Falsified, Botched Tests. *McClatchy Newspapers*.

Texas Forensic Science Commission. (2022). *FSC About Us*. Retrieved from Texas Judicial Branch: https://www.txcourts.gov/fsc/about-us/

Thompson, W. (2003). *Review of DNA Evidence in State of Texas v. Josiah Sutton (District Court of Harris County, Cause No. 800450)*. Irvine: KHOU.

Thompson, William C. (2008) Beyond bad apples: Analyzing the role of forensic science in wrongful convictions. *Sw. UL Rev.* 37, 1027–1050.

Turvey, B. (2013). *Forensic Fraud: Evaluating Law Enforcement and Forensci Science Cultures in the Context of Examiner Misconduct.* Cambridge: Academic Press.
Weick, K. E., & Sutcliffe, K. M. (2001). *Managing the Unexpected.* San Francisco: Jossey-Bass.

CHAPTER 13

Drugs and Toxicology

Forensic laboratories analyze materials seized during investigations to determine if they contain controlled substances. Forensic toxicologists analyze biological fluids to determine the presence of drugs or metabolites. Forensic examiners employ well-established methods for chemical analysis that may also be used in biomedical laboratories. The primary issues in wrongful convictions relate to the use of field-test methods, misconduct, and the interpretation of unusual case circumstances.

MISCONDUCT

The most serious misconduct case involved Annie Dookhan, a drug chemist with the Massachusetts Department of Public Health from 2003 until 2012. Dookhan routinely analyzed three to ten times the number of samples than the average chemist (Verner, 2012; Riccuiti, et al., 2014). In many cases, other analysts did not confirm her results when retesting samples. Lab management did paperwork audits only. They conducted only technical reviews, so systematic retesting of Dookhan's work was not performed. In 2011, lab leadership gave her a special project "in an attempt to slow her down." Another employee claimed Dookhan forged her initials on lab log records. In June of that year, an allegation that Dookhan had falsified records for 90 drug samples finally led to management follow-up. They did not notify any external parties, including the district attorney, until the following year. Even then, they claimed there was no evidence that Dookhan's results were wrong. The Massachusetts State Police took over the lab in July 2012 and discovered the numerous allegations against Dookhan. They interviewed her, and she confessed to serious misconduct. She had not conducted tests but reported results anyway, so-called "dry-labbing." She spiked unknowns with known drugs to get the result she expected in the sample. She falsified logs and reports and quality control documents. In November 2013, she pled guilty to 27 counts of obstruction of justice, evidence tampering, and perjury and was sentenced to three to five years in prison. She

DOI: 10.4324/9781003202578-13

had been responsible for 60,000 sample tests in 34,000 criminal cases involving 1,140 incarcerated defendants.

The full extent of wrongful convictions related to the Dookhan misconduct has not been established. District attorneys—under pressure from the courts and civil liberties advocates—mailed over 20,000 letters to defendants who may have been affected by the Dookhan misconduct. The vast majority of cases have never been readjudicated. One man, Leonardo Johnson, was arrested in 2009 for selling crack cocaine to an undercover police officer. Dookhan's analysis confirmed that the substance was cocaine, but it was actually a cashew nut (Otterburg, 2021). He served 15 months in prison and was eventually exonerated. He received compensation of $250,000 from the state of Massachusetts. He won a lawsuit against Dookhan for $2 million in 2017.

Another analyst, Sonja Farak, was implicated in a similar scandal in 2013. Farak worked at a forensic laboratory on the campus of the University of Massachusetts at Amherst. The lab was not accredited. Farak had been taking evidence from the lab for her personal use. A crack pipe was found under her desk and oxycodone and cocaine in her belongings. Eventually, Farak would plead guilty to heroin possession. Assistant attorney general Thomas Caldwell investigated and found serious deficiencies in lab operations, poor security, and poor management (Healey & Caldwell, 2016). The Massachusetts Supreme Court ruled that over 16,000 defendants were potentially affected by Farak's misconduct. Over 24,000 charges were dismissed.

When she was hired, Farak was not addicted to drugs. She may have become addicted due to exposure in the laboratory. She took drugs from reference and calibration samples initially. Later, she escalated by taking drugs from evidence bags, though she was careful to take amounts that were within the expected amounts for possible measurement errors, sample testing, and other losses. Some police departments did not seal their evidence bags, making it much easier for her to take the seized drugs for her personal use. Farak was able to continue her work while abusing drugs for many years, and many prosecutors reported that she seemed to perform her job well. Her performance was severely affected when she expanded to new drugs like methamphetamine. In part, Farak is a cautionary tale about the personal toll of forensic science on its practitioners. Also, it demonstrates that initial employment screening tests may be insufficient to discover misconduct arising from drug abuse.

Seized drug analysis requires the development and enforcement of thorough evidence control to prevent issues like the Farak scandal. Other analysts have used seized drugs for their personal use. David Peterson oversaw the St. Paul Laboratory in the Minnesota Bureau of Criminal Apprehension's Forensic Science Service and served as president of American Society of Crime Laboratory Directors (ASCLD) during

2004–2005. He had been stealing cocaine from the evidence locker to support his addiction for several years. The theft was discovered in early 2005. He was fired, removed as ASCLD president, and sentenced to six months in prison (Turvey, 2013). Lower-level laboratory officials in several other jurisdictions and commercial drug testing laboratories have been implicated in similar misconduct.

FIELD TESTING

Law enforcement officials use field test kits to make presumptive findings concerning the presence of seized drugs during the course of an arrest (Texas Forensic Science Commission, 2018). Drugs react with chemicals in the test kits and produce a color change. The kits are presumptive only, meaning that they should only be used to establish probable cause for a search or arrest. False positives can arise from reactions with sugar, cat litter, and other substances. False positives can also be caused by drug mixtures, additives, novel psychoactive substances, and the inherent subjectivity of judgments about a color change. Confirmatory testing is needed to determine the actual content of any seized material. In practice, lab confirmations may be delayed by backlogs or inefficient management. Defendants are often habitual offenders who accept plea deals to resolve a case with a reduced sentence. Prosecutors and courts do not practice great care on individual cases. Case throughput is emphasized.

Field test kits have contributed to wrongful convictions in many jurisdictions. In Houston, Texas, over 100 individuals have been identified who were wrongfully convicted on the basis of field test kit errors. In each case, the forensic laboratory did not confirm the presence of the drug that was thought to be present on the basis of the test kit result. The problems continued for years because defendants lacked the knowledge or resources to challenge the broken system. They generally relied on public defenders who had limited knowledge of the limitations of the test kits. The contradictory lab reports were ignored by prosecutors or lost in the noise of law enforcement communications. The situation was exacerbated by Texas law that permitted conviction and jail time for possession of tiny amounts of controlled substances.

Amy Albritton was an unusual defendant. She was white and had no criminal history. During a routine traffic stop, a syringe and "crumb" were seized from her vehicle. The crumb tested positive for cocaine using a cobalt thiocyanate field test (see Figure 13.1). She said that her defense attorney advised her to take a plea deal that would result in a 30-day jail sentence. A trial could have resulted in a two-year sentence even though the crumb was only 20 milligrams. She took the advice. Six months later, the Houston Police Department crime laboratory tested the evidence

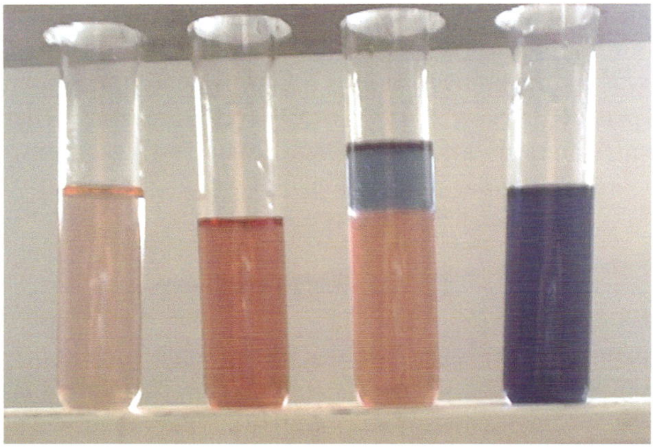

FIGURE 13.1 Cobalt thiocyanate. A solution of cobalt thiocyanate will turn blue in the presence of cocaine. The test is among the most common colorimetric tests, but there is a wide variety. For example, the Marquis reagent colorimetric test can be used to detect amphetamines or morphine. All colorimetric tests may produce false positive and false negative results, even under controlled laboratory conditions. Source: FK1954 Wikimedia.

using a gas chromatograph mass spectrometer (GCMS) and found no controlled substances. She was not notified and was not officially exonerated until six years after her initial arrest.

A more typical case involved 38-year-old Kendrick Mable, an African American man with prior convictions. He was arrested in 2014 based on a field test that was positive for PCP. He pled guilty to possession of a controlled substance and was sentenced to two years in prison (Ex parte Mable, 2014). The Houston Forensic Science Center found that the seized material did not contain any controlled substance. The Texas Court of Criminal Appeals granted his habeas appeal and vacated the conviction, but they did not do so on the basis of actual innocence. They held that "it is possible that he intended to possess a controlled substance (which is not alone an offense) or that he attempted to possess a controlled substance (which is a[mong] lesser included offenses of possession)." In other words, the court believed that he may have meant to buy drugs but got scammed instead. The court vacated the conviction on the basis that his plea was not "a voluntary and intelligent choice" because he did not know about the subsequent crime lab testing. He was allowed to withdraw his plea, and the prosecutor dismissed the charge. This legal maneuver was replicated in almost every seized-drug case in Houston after the Mable exoneration.

The Houston situation was unique only to the extent that so many convictions were vacated. Other jurisdictions have faced similar problems with the misuse of field drug tests. In 2019, start quarterback Shai Werts was arrested for cocaine possession based on a cobalt thiocyanate color test, but crime lab testing showed the substance was not cocaine or any controlled substance. Afterward, Savannah police did a review of 42 cases involving cocaine or ecstasy field tests, of which nine were false positives and three had false negatives. The extent of wrongful convictions involving faulty drug tests has not been fully determined. A very large number of kits are used each year, and few states have laws to prevent plea-deal convictions on the sole basis of a presumptive test. National forensic science standards require more testing, but standards do not have the force of law. Crime labs are aware of the problem, but prosecutors and courts are free to do as they wish and often show minimal awareness of scientific standards. Defendants often rely on public defenders who are either unaware of the test kit problem or unable to challenge it effectively. Like Kendrick Mable, many defendants lack the resources or background to assert their rights.

QUALITY ASSURANCE

As with other forensic disciplines, seized drug analysis may be unreliable in a poorly managed laboratory without necessary quality assurance controls. The Delaware drug lab scandal is a case in point. Jermaine Dollard was arrested for drug trafficking on June 13, 2012 (Jermaine Dollard and Keisha Dollard v. Callery et al., 2018). A canine inspection indicated the presence of narcotics. Two kilograms of a white powder were found in a concealed compartment. At the time, the state's Forensic Services Laboratory was housed with the Office of the Chief Medical Examiner for the State of Delaware (OCMED), which in turn was under the Department of Health and Social Services. Theoretically, this gave the lab independence from law enforcement and a place within a "scientific" organization. In practice, it meant that it was isolated and devalued. The chief medical examiner was busy with other priorities and did not engage in strategic planning, budget formulation, or employee reviews (Andrews International, 2014). The evidence in the Dollard case was given to Irshad Bajwa, who prepared a lab report and testified that the seized powder was cocaine. Dollard was convicted on multiple drug counts and sentenced to 20 years in prison.

While Dollard's appeal was pending, poor evidence handling in the OCMED came to light in another case. During the criminal trial of Tyrone Walker, a witness opened an exhibit that was supposed to contain 67 blue oxycodone pills and instead contained 16 pink pills. There was evidence that Bajwa had altered the evidentiary worksheet in the Walker case. Other issues were soon discovered. Evidence handling and administrative specialists never received training. Evidence was stored in offices. Documentation and chain of custody were not maintained. Eventually, the Delaware Superior Court ordered a retest of the evidence in the Dollard case. It turned out the material was just confectioner's sugar. The charges were then dismissed. His lawsuit was dismissed post-conviction because the lab was found to have made an honest mistake, not a deliberate or fraudulent one.

REVIEW OF DELAWARE OCMED

The state conducted an official review of the Forensic Sciences Laboratory and OCMED (Andrews International, 2014). In addition to the inadequate supervision and management practices, the OCMED leadership team was found to be dysfunctional. They did not communicate and exhibited open animosity with each other. The review report stated, "The OCMED functions as multiple 'silos' with little communication among the various disciplines. This has contributed to low morale, an almost complete lack of unity of purpose, and a culture of indifference." The OCMED leadership valued the pathology and toxicology units and did not view their oversight of other laboratory units as a priority or even a part of their work responsibilities. Morale was low, and salaries were not aligned with other states. A senior DNA analyst was making only $59,000, which was found to be about $30,000 less than a similar position would receive in neighboring Maryland or a small state like Oklahoma. Quality assurance standards require continuing education for scientific personnel, but the funding was not commensurate with the need. Analysts were provided only $300 to travel to scientific meetings, which would not cover the cost of workshops or basic expenses. In general, quality assurance was not valued. For example, the Quality Assurance Manager was not included in OCMED leadership meetings and was not counted as an integral part of the management team.

Interestingly, the review found that the large majority of staff within the Controlled Substances (CS) unit were well-qualified, even though pay was inadequate. There were significant reforms needed in the security of the facility and evidence and chain-of-custody policies and procedures. The key issue was that the CS unit lacked effective leadership, which weakened the quality assurance program. For example, proficiency testing was done as a group instead of individually. Employees collaborated during the test to ensure they all obtained the same correct result. This practice mirrored the experience of the dysfunctional Detroit ballistics unit, which also did "group" proficiency testing. That practice is less than useful. It can be used to support a false contention that proficiency testing has been done. In fact, no individual in the Delaware controlled substance or Detroit ballistic units had been subject to actual proficiency testing.

After the review and action by the state legislature, a new Chief Operating Officer was hired to oversee and manage the nonmedical and non-forensic science functions of the OCMED. A Forensic Science Commission was established to provide oversight. A wide range of quality assurance and management improvements were enacted. The FBI Laboratory's evidence management and operations policies were used as a model to improve the basic operations of the facility (FBI Laboratory, 2009). The recommendations covered every discipline, including pathology and toxicology.

TOXICOLOGY

Toxicology covers a wide range of analyses in biological matrices. Although it is most often associated with postmortem evaluations, the most common toxicological analysis is performed to analyze blood alcohol levels in drunk driving cases. Many of these analyses are done using breathalyzers by police officers. The crime lab may oversee the training of the officers and the maintenance and calibration of the instruments. Inevitably, problems will arise from the countless thousands of such tests that are performed each year.

A typical case arose in Idaho in 2014. Carlos Cruz-Romero nearly hit two vehicles after swerving across two lanes of traffic (State of Idaho v. Carlos Adrian Cruz-Romero, 2016). He admitted to drinking six beers and the breathalyzer returned results of 0.097 and 0.096. He was charged with felony Driving Under the Influence and related charges. The officer had used an Intoxilyzer 5000EN breathalyzer. The machine had failed calibration tests on several dates but the forensic lab found nothing wrong with the machine or the calibration test solution. It passed calibration before and after the Cruz-Romero test and was considered to be working properly at that time. The appeals court overturned Cruz-Romero's DUI conviction on the basis that the machine's prior and subsequent malfunctioning was relevant and should have been considered by the court. It also held that

Cruz-Romero didn't require an expert witness to question the functioning of the Intoxilyzer. The court summarized,

> Evidence that this machine had a history of inexplicably testing out of tolerance has probative value as to whether the machine was working properly at the time of Cruz-Romero's test. The evidence should have been presented to the trier of fact, who would have been in the position to assess all of the evidence on the issue of whether the breathalyzer result established Cruz-Romero's guilt beyond a reasonable doubt.
>
> (State of Idaho v. Carlos Adrian Cruz-Romero, 2016)

Cruz-Romero's charges were dismissed. He was deported in 2016 based on his immigration status.

LOW-LEVEL DEFICIENCIES

These issues—even when they are limited to Class III deficiencies—may undermine the confidence in the functioning of a forensic laboratory. The Washington State Patrol (WSP) Forensic Laboratory Services Bureau (FLSB) was led by Barry Logan from 1999 to 2008. Logan is among the most respected forensic toxicologists in the world. He appointed Ann Marie Gordon as lab manager in 2003. The lab had a practice of having junior toxicologists prepare and test the simulator solutions used to do calibration checks of breathalyzer instruments (Washington v. Amach, 2008). That was not a problem. The lab manager would also certify to having prepared and tested the solutions, which was not acceptable practice. The technicians who did the work should have been the ones to take formal responsibility for their own work, even if the lab manager signed off as a reviewer. Gordon told Logan she opposed the practice but continued to follow it. In 2007, Logan discovered the problem when anonymous tips were directed to the chief of the WSP. There was no evidence that the solutions were wrong or produced misleading results in any conviction. Nonetheless, Gordon had certified that she had performed the work that was actually done by her subordinates. The courts varied in their response to the problem. The District Court of King County issued a scathing decision that claimed that the FLSB handling of breathalyzer problems created a "culture of compromise" and said Gordon had committed fraud that undermined hundreds of DUI cases. Gordon resigned in 2007 immediately after the problem was found. Logan resigned a year later. The situation has been the subject of extended (and questionable) criticism alleging a "culture of fraud, incompetence, and compromise [that] was created and sustained during the overlapping tenures of Barry Logan and Ann Marie Gordon." (Turvey, 2013). Both Logan and Gordon were subsequently employed as forensic scientists in other jurisdictions. Logan serves as the Chief Scientist of NMS Labs, the largest commercial forensic laboratory in the drug testing arena. Through his work as Executive Director of the Frederic Rieders Family Foundation, he delivers Borkenstein training, named after the inventor of the Breathalyzer. Logan was nearly dismissed from the forensic profession over the handling of calibration solutions in breathalyzers. Fortunately, his expertise and hard-won experience are still available to the professionals who perform breathalyzer testing.

Quality assurance and lab deficiencies may lead to more serious consequences. The case of Eric Smith demonstrates these issues. Smith was a 40-year-old major in the Army, serving as a doctor at the Madigan Army Medical Center (MAMC) at Joint Base Lewis-McChord in Washington State in 2011 (United States v. Eric Smith, 2015). He failed a urine drug test, which was positive for a cocaine metabolite. The MAMC samples were sent to the Forensic Toxicology Drug Testing Laboratory at Tripler Army Medical Center in Hawaii (Figure 13.2). After the Tripler test came back positive, he requested a drug test of his hair. Because hair incorporates drugs during growth, it can be used as a qualitative test for past drug use. The hair test came back negative.

FIGURE 13.2 Tripler AMC Front. The Tripler Army Medical Center contains the Forensic Toxicology Drug Testing Laboratory, an unaccredited laboratory that performs a large number of drug tests for the military. The Tripler medical pathology department maintains relevant accreditations, including accreditation by the College of American Pathologists (CAP). Tripler does not maintain a CAP accreditation as a forensic drug testing laboratory. Source: US Army.

The military considers a failed drug test as evidence of drug use and grounds for criminal sanction. Smith's defense counsel noted that there was significant risk of cross-contamination in the toxicological analysis. The court discounted the hair test on the basis that it is only useful for the determination of chronic use by a drug abuser. It is the case that the primary cocaine metabolite, Benzoylecgonine, is not efficiently incorporated into hair during growth. Cocaine itself is incorporated into hair and easily detected using modern laboratory methods. The defense counsel pointed out that Smith was not required to take the drug test and had actually volunteered for it. Also, Smith suffered from anxiety and panic disorders that would have been exacerbated by cocaine use, so he was unlikely to abuse the drug. Smith had had his appendix removed the prior summer and had to return for three subsequent surgeries due to poor medical treatment at MAMC. He had been taking 30 prescribed medications each day, but none that contained cocaine or a similar chemical. He was sentenced to two years in military prison and forfeiture of all pay and allowances.

In 2013, the military court granted Smith the opportunity to retest the sample. The sample was sent to NMS Laboratories, which was under the direction of Barry Logan at the time. NMS was an accredited laboratory, while the military Tripler lab was not (Save Our Heroes, 2016). The sample retest showed that the level of Benzoylecgonine had actually increased from 620 ng/L to 710 ng/L, an unusual result because the chemical would typically degrade over time. Additional testing found that the sample contained DNA from two individuals. In other words, the DNA testing confirmed that the sample had been contaminated during collection, processing, or storage. Smith had been rude to the junior noncommissioned officer who supervised the collection of his urine sample. The collection site at Joint Based Lewis-McChord had also had problems with chain-of-custody. Despite its claim of a zero false positive rate, Tripler had typical quality assurance problems that are associated with an unaccredited laboratory. They had no satisfactory answer to explain the two major DNA contributors found in the Smith sample (Maria Delacruz vs. Tripler Army Medical, 2007).

A military appeals court later set aside the verdict based on inadequate defense related to the failure to use the hair test evidence to its fullest effect. Smith was forced to continue to fight with Army administrative authorities that failed to account for the clearance of his wrongful conviction and the evidence that his urinalysis test was invalid on the basis of contamination. His former supervisor, Colonel Steven Smith (no relation), had served as a Medical Review Officer (a trained and certified physician who reviews drug testing results). Colonel Smith wrote on Major Smith's behalf that MROs were aware of

> significant issues and concerns for the integrity of our testing program... It was clear to me that on more than one occasion, test specimens' chain of custody was compromised at local levels. When an adverse event occurs, there are clearly cover-ups instituted that usually only involve one or two people.
>
> (Save Our Heroes, 2016)

Major Smith was largely cleared by a board of inquiry in 2016, but his medical privileges were never restored by the military and no follow-up investigation of the issues raised in the Smith case is known to have occurred (Ashton & Bernton, 2016).

CYNTHIA SOMMER

Toxicology laboratories require the maintenance of strict controls to limit contamination and ensure the integrity of forensic results. In the 2002 case of the death of 23-year-old Todd Sommer in San Diego, California, there was uncertainty regarding whether he had been poisoned with arsenic (Sommer v. United States, 2013). His wife, Cynthia Sommer, was implicated as a possible murder suspect after she collected a life insurance settlement and appeared to behave irresponsibly after the death. Marine forensic pathologist Dr. Stephen Robinson issued the cause of death as probable cardiac arrhythmia. He saved tissue specimens, which were securely stored. Dr. Allen Burke at the Armed Forces Institute for Pathology (AFIP) determined that Sommer's heart was "morphologically normal."

The samples were tested for heavy metals by Dr. Jose Centeno in the AFIP's Environmental Division. Although other parts of the AFIP had experience in forensic work, the Environmental Division was not set up to manage chain of custody or other requirements associated with forensic analysis. Centeno was an experienced and highly published researcher in arsenic toxicology. He found highly elevated levels of arsenic in Sommer's liver and kidney specimens. The levels were over ten times those ever observed in a human being. Oddly, Sommer had not exhibited any symptoms of arsenic poisoning before his death, except for severe gastrointestinal distress. There were no signs of arsenic poisoning in any other tests or autopsy findings, such as blood vessel or organ damage. The samples were later sent to NMS Labs, which confirmed the presence of arsenic. Al Poklis, an independent expert, told the Navy Criminal Investigative Service (NCIS) that the results were probably invalid because arsenic attacks all bodily tissues and the levels found by the AFIP would have quickly killed any human or any animal, no matter how healthy. Medical examiner Dr. Glenn Wagner disagreed and felt that a healthy and strong young person like Sommer could continue to "walk around with a high level of arsenic in his body." The case proceeded to trial and conviction. Cynthia Sommer's conviction was vacated before sentencing based on inadequate defense.

Backup samples had been preserved by Robinson from the original autopsy and were sent to the Quebec Toxicology Center, which reported finding no arsenic at all. It was later established that at least 16 breaks in chain of custody occurred after AFIP received the samples. The AFIP lab lacked protocols to limit contamination that could produce false positives for arsenic. Centeno was unable to determine if the samples had been contaminated at AFIP and, if so, how. A postconviction lawsuit by Cynthia Sommer alleged that AFIP covered up the problems in its work to avoid "public embarrassment" and protect Centeno's "professional image." That lawsuit was dismissed because there was some basis to conclude that arsenic poisoning may have occurred even with the discordant autopsy findings and issues with the AFIP lab. The court decision said that everyone "did their best."

PATRICIA STALLINGS

Some wrongful convictions have helped the field to identify improvements in quality assurance and proficiency testing. The 1989 Patricia Stallings case is a clear example. She was convicted of murdering her 5-month-old son, Ryan, when a lab test showed ethylene glycol—antifreeze—in his blood. When he was three months old, Ryan presented with lethargy and blood acidosis with a blood pH of 7.02. The lab test showed ethylene glycol and acetone concentrations of 180 mg/L and 215 mg/L, respectively (Panel Discussion: Toxicology Mimics in the Critically Ill Patient, 2016). Doctors assumed the child was poisoned, and he was moved to foster care. In the days after Stallings was allowed to visit him, Ryan experienced a second episode of acidosis, and his ethylene glycol level was measured to be 911 mg/L. The child died at that time. A level of 911 mg/L is thought to be clinically impossible to achieve, let alone survive. There was also an extended time between Stallings' visit and her son's test. Because ethylene glycol is quickly metabolized, it is unclear how she could have been responsible for the child's exposure. Ryan's autopsy also showed calcium oxalate in his brain and other organs, an indication of ethylene glycol poisoning.

Stallings was arrested and eventually gave birth to a second child. That child was diagnosed with methylmalonic acidemia (MMA), a genetic disorder which is found in about 1 in 50,000 births. Among other things, MMA produces lethargy and severe ketoacidosis. The key indicator is elevated levels of propionic acid. Two analytical laboratories, SmithKline and St. Louis University, had analyzed Ryan's blood samples with gas chromatography with flame ionization detection (GC-FID), which is a sensitive and reliable technique. Unfortunately, the GC elution times for propionic acid and ethylene glycol are almost identical. The labs could have differentiated the two chemicals by a number of techniques, such as sampling of headspace vapor (which would have detected only ethylene glycol), co-elution with standards, use of a different GC column, or detection with mass spectrometry. The standard technique now uses GCMS, which easily differentiates the fragmentation pattern of the two chemicals.

After her second son's diagnosis, St. Louis University researcher, William Sly, used a co-elution procedure with Ryan's sample to generate a "double-headed" GC peak that clearly showed the detection of propionic acid, not ethylene glycol. Stallings' conviction was vacated. She settled a lawsuit against the analytical labs for an unknown amount. Her second son died of MMA 20 years later. Today, MMA is diagnosed using testing at birth. Treatment includes restriction of dietary protein and other interventions that may avoid long-term complications. Physicians are guided to consider the possibility of metabolic acidosis as part of the differential diagnosis in poisoning cases. The College of American Pathologists administers a proficiency testing program to toxicology laboratories that tests their ability to distinguish propionic acid from ethylene glycol. Labs are expected to confirm their results using a second analytical method, especially if the findings will be relevant as a forensic conclusion.

MOTHERISK

The Stallings case also suggests that research and clinical toxicological laboratories may have difficulty when performing analyses for forensic purposes. Forensic toxicology presents different challenges to the analyst than would be encountered in research or clinical work. In many instances, the quality assurance requirements are more stringent. While the analytical laboratories in the Stallings case were well-regarded, they may not have anticipated the challenges that can arise in criminal cases. Such laboratories may be accredited to perform clinical toxicology. That does not automatically imply that they are qualified to perform forensic toxicology testing.

The Motherisk Drug Testing Laboratory at Toronto's Hospital for Sick Children (SickKids) provides a clear example of this issue (Beaman, 2015; Lang, 2015). Under the leadership of Dr. Gideon Koren, SickKids developed the Motherisk laboratory in the mid-1980s to perform clinical testing to provide objective, clinical information to support pediatric medicine. They were well-positioned to do this work. Koren and his colleagues were well-respected physicians and researchers who regularly published research and clinical case reports (Pimlott, 2020). Their most groundbreaking work involved the assessment of the safety of prescription and over-the-counter drugs during pregnancy and breastfeeding.

SickKids inevitably encountered situations in which children may have been exposed to drugs of abuse. (Beaman, n.d.). Starting in the mid-1990s, they conducted extensive hair testing for SickKids and child aid societies for use in child protection cases. Between 2005 and 2015, they tested over 24,000 samples from over 16,000 individuals for child protection purposes. Most cases didn't extend to criminal charges, so the lab didn't view itself as a forensic laboratory. Motherisk was never accredited as a forensic toxicology laboratory and never fully conformed to the guidelines of forensic hair testing as promulgated by the Society of Hair Testing (Cooper, Kronstrand, & Kintz, 2011). Nonetheless, many parents lost custody of their children due to the findings of the Motherisk lab. The lab results were used in a range of child protection legal proceedings, meaning that their work constituted an application of forensic science.

The case of Tamara Broomfield fundamentally changed the direction of SickKids and Motherisk. Broomfield took her two-year-old son to the emergency room at her local hospital on August 1, 2005. A hair test on the child showed that he had ingested large amounts of cocaine over the preceding 14 months. On April 1, 2009, Broomfield was convicted of aggravated assault, failure to provide the necessaries of life, and two counts related to giving cocaine to her son. The Motherisk lab's hair testing was key evidence in the latter two convictions. On appeal, Dr. Craig Chatterton, the Deputy Chief Toxicologist for the Office of the Chief Medical Examiner in Edmonton, Alberta, challenged the Motherisk findings. Chatterton held that their techniques and analyses were flawed and results invalid. The Court of Appeal reversed the two convictions related to the hair testing in 2014. She did not appeal her other convictions.

The Ontario government then conducted an independent investigation of Motherisk led by Susan Lang (Lang, 2015). In 2016, a Motherisk Commission was formed after Lang's report of severe deficiencies at Motherisk. In 2018, Judith Beaman issued the final report of the Motherisk Commission, *Harmful Impacts: The Reliance on Hair Testing in Child Protection Report of the Motherisk Commission*, a 300-page deconstruction of the events and problems that led to the Broomfield wrongful convictions and other miscarriages of justice over two decades (Beaman, n.d.).

It was not the first time that a public inquiry had criticized oversight at Motherisk. In 2008, an inquiry found that Motherisk pediatric pathologist Dr. Charles Smith had produced unreliable findings in 20 out of 45 criminal cases (Goudge, 2008). As described by the Goudge report commissioned by the Ontario Attorney General, Smith was appointed to be the director of a newly established Ontario Pediatric Forensic Pathology Unit at SickKids in 1992. Just the prior year, a 12-year-old girl was acquitted on a charge of manslaughter in a case in which the trial judge strongly criticized Smith's methodology and conclusions (Goudge, 2008). The Goudge report found that Smith had not been formally trained as a forensic pathologist or been board-certified in that field. That wasn't uncommon at that time because many autopsies in Ontario were being performed by fee-for-service pathologists without the necessary training or certification. At SickKids, the assumption was that pediatric pathologists were best suited to perform autopsies on children, not certified forensic pathologists. Smith himself said that he did not view forensic pathology as a separate discipline that could inform his work, and he had little or no exposure to the larger community of forensic pathologists.

The Goudge report also found that SickKids and the criminal justice system exercised poor oversight over Smith and the Motherisk lab. Smith routinely failed to prepare adequately for court or share his documentation as required in criminal proceedings. He routinely opined on matters outside his expertise, such as a 1997 case in which a child was attacked and killed by a pit bull. Smith mistakenly concluded that the child was murdered by stab wounds inflicted by her mother. The case became controversial among forensic pathologists, and her body was exhumed for a second autopsy. That autopsy concluded that the dog had caused many—and probably all—of the child's wounds. The charges against her mother were then dropped.

The Lang and Beaman reports made findings about the oversight of the Motherisk toxicology laboratory that were similar to the conclusions of the Goudge report the previous decade (Lang, 2015). The lab relied on hair testing, which has inherent limitations that require careful sample preparation, testing, and interpretation. For example, there may be contamination on the surface of the hair. Forensic hair testing labs wash the hairs using protocols that preserve the drugs and drug metabolites while removing surface contamination. Motherisk never washed hair samples. Motherisk also never established written test procedures that governed hair analysis.

Most critically, Motherisk relied in most cases on enzyme-linked immunoassay (ELISA) tests. ELISA tests use antibodies that link preferentially to the analyte of interest. In hair testing, the antibodies in the ELISA test are designed to find drugs and drug metabolites. The antibodies are linked to enzymes that change color when the analyte is attached to the antibody. The color change is an indication that the analyte is present in the sample. ELISA tests are cheap and sensitive but are subject to problems from cross-reactivity. In other words, if another chemical is similar to the analyte, then it may also bind to the antibody and give a false positive indication in the test. The ELISA test is also nonlinear, especially at low and high concentrations. In other words, a doubling of concentration may not double the ELISA response.

For these reasons, forensic toxicologists rely on ELISA to do presumptive tests only. A presumptive test is a screening test that can be used on a large number of samples very quickly. If a sample gives a positive indication on a presumptive test, then it is subject to confirmation testing—usually involving chromatographic separation and mass spectrometry identification. The Motherisk lab misinterpreted the word, "presumptive," to mean that the test provided a preliminary positive indication. That is not the case. In a forensic science context, "presumptive" just means the sample passed the screening test; it does not mean the lab can report that the test is a positive or that legal proceedings can rely on that tentative result as if it were a valid and reliable conclusion. The Motherisk staff and leadership did not appear to appreciate this distinction. They reported ELISA results as if they were reliable enough to make conclusions about the presence of drugs in a hair sample. In many cases, this misrepresentation led to children being taken from their parents. In the Broomfield case, it led to a criminal conviction.

The reliance on ELISA testing at Motherisk has been interpreted by some observers to be a contextual bias effect in which the context of a child protection case influenced the decision to rely on the presumptive ELISA test (Dror, 2020). There is very little basis for that claim. Motherisk staff relied on presumptive ELISA tests as a matter of flawed policy and failure to conform to minimal toxicology standards. There is little evidence that this decision was based on the context of specific child protection cases. On the other hand, there is evidence that Motherisk relied on its respected position within the medical and research communities. Even when they made simple and tragic mistakes, they believed that they were doing scientifically sound work. They were blind to their mistakes because they regarded themselves to be experts in forensic toxicology on the basis of their expertise in clinical toxicology.

Motherisk also treated the level of ELISA response as a semi-quantitative indicator of the amount of drug that had been ingested by the child. So, if the ELISA response were high, Motherisk would report their interpretation that the high ELISA response reflected the level and frequency of an individual's drug use. Hair testing cannot be reliably used in that way. There are significant variations in how drugs and drug metabolites are incorporated into hairs among individuals. Some people may incorporate more of a certain drug into their hair. Their hair may have more or less contamination or may have morphological differences that change the amount of drug that is extracted (Tsanaclis & Wicks, 2018). Therefore, even with the best analytical instrumentation, hair testing is qualitative. It can be used to determine if and when a person ingested a drug but can't be used to say how much they took. Again, the Motherisk staff and leadership did not appear to appreciate this problem. They would send the "bare test results" to customers without providing any interpretation of the data. Naturally, many child protection and medical staff took the results to mean that the ELISA responses were an indication of how much of a drug had been ingested. This misleading impression led to many miscarriages of justice in child protection cases.

It should be noted that Motherisk did send some samples to independent testing labs for confirmation testing, although there was no consistent policy. Even in that case, Motherisk staff failed to distinguish between presumptive and confirmation testing. If the confirmation testing agreed with the presumptive test, then that was noted on the test report but the original presumptive test result was still relied on as if it were the most reliable result. Typically, they would report the ELISA result and attach a footnote in the results report stating that the result was "confirmed." Sometimes, they did report the actual confirmation results, but the reporting practices were wildly inconsistent. Finally, Motherisk would often misinterpret the results of confirmation testing. For example, they adopted the use of fatty acid ethyl esters in 2007 to determine past alcohol use. That practice was acceptable, although it is now recommended to include ethyl glucuronide testing also to provide a more reliable result. On the other hand, Motherisk misapplied the cutoffs to assess the external confirmation tests and ignored gross differences between ELISA results and the confirmation tests. For example, some GCMS confirmation results differed by as much as 300% from the ELISA results, which should have been a red flag for the organization about the reliability of its analyses.

Critically, it is not clear if the results of Motherisk drug testing were evaluated by a medical review officer. MROs review positive drug test results in other contexts, such as workplace drug testing. It is unlikely that the scientific interpretation issues at Motherisk would have continued if their results were subject to review by trained and certified MROs. (For more information about medical review officers, see the Further Reading section.)

The essential issues at Motherisk involved a lack of oversight and a lack of leaders and staff trained in forensic analysis. They had minimal written policies and procedures or quality assurance practices to ensure the consistency of sampling, analysis, and interpretation. SickKids was a hospital with a reputation for excellence, and everyone just assumed that such a respected institution had the relevant expertise. Unfortunately, even SickKids management made this incorrect assumption. Significant changes arose from the hair toxicology review. Motherisk was shut down, and the state of Ontario required all forensic laboratories to be accredited, among other requirements of the subsequent Forensic Laboratories Act (2018).

VIRGINIA LEFEVER

The interpretation of toxicological results may be difficult in criminal cases. Circumstances may present diagnostic issues that would not be present in a noncriminal medical evaluation. The forensic toxicologist must determine if poison is present but must also consider the broader circumstances that may have contributed to the cause of death. In 1988, 41-year-old William LeFever died of a drug overdose in Newark, Ohio. His wife, Virginia LeFever, claimed that he had committed suicide by overdosing on antidepressants (State v. LeFever, 1991). William LeFever had a long history of drug and alcohol abuse, including prescription drug abuse of phenobarbital, Percoset, and Endep (a form of amitriptyline). According to Virginia LeFever, her husband had overdosed on amitriptyline and had been self-harming. He was taken to the hospital and died shortly thereafter. His body was covered in bruises.

Toxicologist James Ferguson and forensic pathologist Dr. Patrick Fardal determined that William LeFever had been injected with amitriptyline in his left buttock. The injection site and lower colon had large amounts of amitriptyline and an injection site was visible. Two types of strychnine rat poison were also found in the colon. The Newark Police Department seized evidence from the home, including two garbage bags which contained "Smoke-em" pesticides. Additional toxicological testing found that William LeFever had been poisoned with amitriptyline and nortriptyline by intramuscular injection and further poisoned with sulfur oxide, arsenic, and strychnine by pulmonary and rectal routes. He had apparently been exposed to chronic, oral arsenic poisoning. Presumably, there was an attempt to poison him in small doses over an extended period of time. When that did not work, poisons were administered by injection, enema, and gas exposure to "Smoke-em" pesticide. He was undoubtedly incoherent for an extended period prior to hospitalization, but the injection must have occurred shortly before his death. The appeals court wrote,

> Appellant's theory of innocence (i.e., a suicide) would require the trial court to accept the argument that despite his incoherent state, Mr. LeFever was somehow able to rectally administer himself a dose of arsenic. The most generous thing that can be said about that possibility is that it is inconceivable.
>
> (LeFever v. Ferguson, 2013)

Interestingly, none of the poisons were in the decedent's stomach at the time of death. He didn't get an oral overdose of the drugs; they entered his body by other means.

Virginia LeFever was convicted at a bench trial in 1990 of aggravated murder and sentenced to life in prison. Twenty years later, her conviction was vacated when it was discovered that Ferguson had lied about his credentials in hundreds of cases over 26 years as the county's head toxicologist. He never received a purported doctorate from Ohio State University and only received a bachelor's degree after 25 years of study. He failed chemistry seven times. Ferguson was convicted and jailed for his perjury. His toxicological testimony was ruled invalid, and those findings were the basis for the LeFever conviction. Ferguson had also written a book in the period leading up to the trial, *Angel of Mercy or Angel of Death?* about the case and speculated that Virginia LeFever may have been responsible for the death of two of her children, her father-in-law, and her sister-in-law, all of whom allegedly died under her care (LeFever v. Ferguson, 2016). In granting a new trial for Virginia LeFever, the court expressly doubted her innocence but held that Ferguson's dishonesty had resulted in an unfair trial. The prosecution dismissed the charges due to the passage of time and the need to rely on Ferguson's original work in the case. Virginia LeFever and her son sued Ferguson in federal court. The lawsuit failed because the court held that Ferguson's testimony was scientifically valid even if he had misrepresented his credentials. Ferguson had shown bias and lied about his degree, but the substance of his toxicological findings was nonetheless valid.

STUDY QUESTIONS

1. Consider the Anthony Coppolino case (covered in Chapter 11, Forensic Pathology) and the Virginia LeFever case (LeFever v. Ferguson, 2016). The two cases each involved difficult toxicological interpretations based on the theory that lethal drugs had been administered but not orally. Compare and contrast the issues in the cases, including those related to cognitive bias,

professional standards, and uncertainties about the guilt of the defendants.

2. What types of quality assurance mechanisms may have prevented the Dookhan or Farak drug scandals in Massachusetts? Consider the views of the National Commission of Forensic Science concerning performance testing and human performance (National Commission of Forensic Science, 2016).
3. The Dollard, Sommers, Broomfield, and Stallings cases had an unusual common element—the forensic test laboratories were all independent of law enforcement. Do you believe the labs were biased toward the prosecution despite their independence? What were the strengths and weaknesses exhibited by the independent labs? What do these cases suggest about proposed reforms to make crime laboratories independent of law enforcement?

FURTHER READING

The Delaware Attorney General's review of the issues in Delaware provides a clear justification to link wrongful convictions to lapses in management and quality assurance (Andrews International, 2014). Jermaine Dollard's civil appeal raised important issues related to the liability of forensic scientists and their organizations when misconduct is implicated in wrongful convictions (Jermaine Dollard and Keisha Dollard v. Callery et al., 2018).

The Boston drug lab scandal was well-covered by the Boston Bar Association in their 2014 report (Riccuiti, et al., 2014). The Massachusetts Office of the Attorney General also issued a report that was mostly a documentation of the issues (Verner, 2012).

The issues with drug test kits have received extensive attention. The 2018 Texas Forensic Science Commission report is the most thorough examination (Texas Forensic Science Commission, 2018).

Toxicological interpretation may present difficulties during a death investigation. Gill and Stajic provided a useful starting point for consideration of "classical mistakes" made by forensic pathologists in forensic toxicology (Gill & Stajic, 2012). ANSI/ASB has now established guidelines for forensic toxicology testimony that are well-received in the field (ANSI/ASB, 2019). For more insight into the interpretation of drug testing, the reader should consider the extensive resources associated with the community of medical review officers. The two certification bodies are the Medical Review Officer Certification Council (https://www.mrocc.org) and the American Association of Medical Review Officers (https://www.aamro.com).

REFERENCES

Andrews International. (2014). *Review of the Office of the Chief Medical Examiner: Report for the Department of Health and Social Services*. State of Delaware.

ANSI/ASB. (2019). *Guidelines for Opinions and Testimony in Forensic Toxicology*. ANSI/ASB.

Ashton, A., & Bernton, H. (2016, March 7). Panel Backs JBLM Doctor Who Was Jailed Over Contaminated Drug Test. *The News Tribune*.

Beaman, J. (2015). *Harmful Impacts: The Reliance on Hair Testing in Child Protection Report of the Motherisk Commission*. Toronto: Ministry of the Attorney General.

Chung, W., Tormoehlen, L., and Morgan, B. (2016) *Panel Discussion: Toxicology Mimics in the Critically Ill Patient*. Huntington Beach: American College of Medical Toxicology.

Cooper, G., Kronstrand, R., & Kintz, P. (2011). Society of Hair Testing guidelines for testing in hair. *Forensic Science International*, 218(1–3), 20–24.

Dror, I. E. (2020). Cognitive and Human Factors in Expert Decision Making: Six Fallacies and the Eight Sources of Bias. *Analytical Chemistry*, *92*(12), 7998–8004.

Ex parte Mable, 443 S. W. 3d 129 (Court of Criminal Appeals of Texas September 17, 2014).

Ex parte Overton, WR-75,804-02 (Court of Criminal Appeals of Texas September 17, 2014).

FBI Laboratory. (2009). *FBI Evidence Management and Operations Policy Implementation Guide*. Quantico: FBI Laboratory.

Forensic Laboratories Act. (2018). *2018, S.O. 2018, c. 3, Sched. 8*. Ontario. Retrieved from ontario.ca/laws/statute/18f03

Gill, J., & Stajic, M. (2012). Classical Mistakes in Forensic Toxicology Made by Forensic Pathologists. *Acad Forensic Pathol*, 2(3), 228–234.

Goudge, S. (2008). *Inquiry into Pediatric Forensic Pathology in Ontario*. Toronto: Attorney General of Ontario.

Healey, M., & Caldwell, T. (2016). *Investigative Report Pursuant to Commonwealth v. Cotto, 471 Mass. 97 (2015)*. Boston: Office of the Attorney General, Commonwealth of Massachusetts.

Jermaine Dollard and Keisha Dollard v. Callery et al, N16C-01-102 AML (Superior Court of Delaware April 16, 2018).

Lang, S. (2015). *Report of the Motherisk Hair Analysis Independent Review*. Toronto, ON: Toronto Ministry of the Attorney General.

LeFever v. Ferguson, 2:11-cv-935 (US District Court for the Southern District of Ohio, Eastern Division July 15, 2013).

LeFever v. Ferguson, 14-3905/3906 (United States Court of Appeals for the Sixth Circuit April 15, 2016).

Maria Delacruz vs. Tripler Army Medical, 05–00571 (US District Court for the District of Hawaii 07 24, 2007).
National Commission of Forensic Science. (2016). *Views of the Commission Optimizing Human Performance in Crime Laboratories through Testing and Feedback*. Washington, DC: US Department of Justice and US Department of Commerce.
Otterburg, K. (2021, 07, 1). *Massachusetts 2017*. Retrieved from National Registry of Exonerations: https://exonerations.newkirk-center.uci.edu/groups/group-exonerations/massachusetts-2017
Pimlott, N. (2020). The Legacy of Motherisk. *Can Fam Physician*, *66*(11), 787.
Riccuiti, M., Joyce, K., Lopez, S., Lunt, L., Miller, C., Murphy, M., & Smith, M. (2014). *Report of the Boston Bar Association Drug Lab Crisis Task Force*. Boston, MA: Boston Bar Association.
Savage, J., WTOC Investigates: Field drug tests producing false results, WTOC, 12 Dec 2019, https://www.wtoc.com/2019/12/12/wtoc-investigates-field-drug-tests-producing-false-results/.
Save Our Heroes. (2016, September 2). Army Major Eric Smith forced to Fight for his Job – De Facto Prosecution Continues After O. *Save Our Heroes*.
Sommer v. United States, 09cv2093-CAB (United States District Court for the Southern District of California December 5, 2013).
State of Idaho v. Carlos Adrian Cruz-Romero, 42994 (Court of Appeals of the State of Idaho March 31, 2016).
State v. LeFever, CA-3535 (Court of Appeals of Ohio, Fifth Appellate District, Licking County November 18, 1991).
Texas Forensic Science Commission. (2018). *Report in Compliance with HB-34 (85th Legislature)*. Austin: Texas Forensic Science Commission.
Tsanaclis, L., & Wicks, J. (2018). Hair Analysis When External Contamination Is in Question: A Review of Practical Approach for the Interpretation of Results. *Forensic Science International*, *285*, 105–110.
Turvey, B. (2013). *Forensic Fraud: Evaluating Law Enforcement and Forensci Science Cultures in the Context of Examiner Misconduct*. Cambridge: Academic Press.
United States v. Eric Smith, Amry 20120918 (US Army Court of Criminal Appeals July 17, 2015).
Verner, J. (2012). *Re: William A. Hinton State Laboratory*. Boston: Commonwealth of Massachusetts Office of the Attorney General.
Washington v. Amach, 21 (District Court of King County January 30, 2008).

CHAPTER 14

Digital Evidence

Criminal investigations increasingly rely on the exploitation of digital evidence. The general public routinely uses cell phones and other information systems in their daily lives. Criminal offenders are no different in this regard. The use of digital evidence has been complicated by the wide variety of digital evidence types. Surveillance video, cell phones, computers, and audio recordings have all played roles in wrongful conviction cases. Digital evidence examiners may be trained and certified under a diverse range of standards, organizations, and technical specialties. Some important efforts have established useful guideposts, such as the Scientific Working Group on Digital Evidence (SWGDE, www.swgde.org) and the OSAC Digital/Multimedia Scientific Area Committee (https://www.nist.gov/osac/digitalmultimedia-scientific-area-committee).

Courts have been highly variable in their acceptance of various forms of digital evidence. Judges realize that they lack the technical background to assess the validity of the offered evidence (Kessler, 2010). They have been particularly skeptical concerning the use of software that may alter evidence, such as video encryption and compression algorithms. Fundamentally, each of these tools may be considered a novel method. They incorporate algorithms that are not necessarily validated. The user may not be trained—and is often not certified—to use the tools in a valid and reliable way. This issue applies to digital evidence manipulation and interpretation, but it also applies to the use of software to process other evidence. For example, DNA mixture interpretation uses algorithms to enable the analyst to deconvolve major and minor contributors. Judges and juries may or may not recognize the novelty or limitations of the algorithms that form the basis for evidence presented in court.

Wrongful convictions provide some insight into the practical problems for criminal justice practice that ensue from the rapid adoption of digital systems in society as a whole. In some wrongful conviction cases, the digital evidence was exculpatory. In other cases, the evidence was inculpatory but other factors led to the exoneration of the defendant.

DOI: 10.4324/9781003202578-14

In many cases, the courts failed to assess the technical reliability and probative value of digital evidence testimony. Two examples will be provided here.

LISA ROBERTS

In 2002, the body of 25-year-old Jerri Williams was found in Kelley Point Park in Portland, Oregon (Roberts v. Howton, 2014). Deputy Medical Examiner Cliff Nelson determined that she had been strangled to death and noted contusions on her right arm and leg. A pillowcase was found near the body. Deputy Medical Examiner Duane Bigoni estimated the time of death to be 11:40 am. Her body had been found at 2:55 pm.

Lisa Roberts was the girlfriend of the victim, and police alleged that Roberts had killed Williams due to jealousy over a relationship with Terry Collins, a former girlfriend of the victim. Roberts and Collins each had a history of domestic violence. Roberts had previously been involved in other criminal activity, including a failed kidnapping scheme. Police believed that Roberts killed Williams at home, took the body to the park, and dumped it there. The story was supported by circumstantial evidence and cell phone tower evidence that was used to reconstruct her movements on the day of the murder. Roberts' DNA was found on the pillowcase next to Williams' body in the park and under the victim's fingernails. There was also exculpatory DNA evidence in the form of vaginal swabs that showed the presence of spermatozoa from an unknown male. Before the case went to trial, Roberts pled guilty to manslaughter in the first degree and admitted that she had strangled Williams to death. She was sentenced to 15 years in prison.

Despite her plea, Roberts had said that she had not been anywhere near Kelley Point Park on the day of the murder. Witness accounts and the cell phone tower data contradicted that claim. Roberts filed a postconviction habeas petition challenging the cell phone tower data and police investigation. On the morning of the murder, Roberts had exchanged calls with Jennifer Locke, the daughter of Terry Collins. One call, made by Roberts at 10:28 in the morning, connected to a cell phone tower at 2001 Kotobuki Way, approximately three miles from Kelley Point Park. Roberts had said the closest she had come to the park was the intersection of I-205 and Marine Drive, which was over 12 miles away from both the park and the cell phone tower. At 10:36 am, a friend, Julia Patterson, called Collins when she observed Roberts driving Collins' red pickup truck on Marine Drive roughly halfway between the park and the intersection with I-205. A Verizon Wireless technician said that the call had to have been placed near Kelley Point Park.

Postconviction, Special Agent Michael Bethers from the Oregon Department of Justice did a more thorough analysis. He was certified by the National Technical Investigators Association and a member of the FBI's Law Enforcement Technology Forum. He noted a previous call at 10:27 am that hit a cell tower at 415 E. 13th Street, which was closer to downtown Vancouver but still much closer to the park than the intersection of Marine Drive with I-205. He said,

> For Petitioner's statement that she was not west of I-205 on the day of Ms. Williams' murder to be accurate, the call to Locke would have had to bypass or "defeat" numerous other cell towers between petitioner's purported location at the time of the call and the Kotobuki Way and East 13th Street towers. From my knowledge of cell phone systems, tower data, the number of cell tower sites available in the relevant geographic area, and what is well accepted in the field of [call detail records], it is not possible for a telephone call to bypass or "defeat" that many other towers.

As Bethers accurately described, cell towers cover only the immediate area around the cell site and the general direction of a cell phone can be inferred because each cell site is divided into sectors that are roughly 120 degrees wide. Roberts had also claimed the 10:28 am call may have come from near Withycombe, her place of employment. There is a cell tower less than a mile from Camp Withycombe and all of Roberts' previous calls from her job used that tower. The camp was actually in Clackamas, more than 20 miles away. There are dozens of Verizon towers between Clackamas and Portland, so the chance that she made a call from Clackamas that used a tower in Portland was exceedingly remote. In fact, it is unlikely that a tower will pick up a call more than a few miles away. There is no statistical likelihood estimate or other quantitative basis for a geolocation based on cell tower data, but Bethers' report was based on valid and reliable technical analysis.

Postconviction experts for the defense were Jeff Fischbach and Manfred Schenk. They pointed out that the Kotobuki Way tower was 55 feet tall, one of the tallest towers in the area, and could have a range of 10 miles depending on call load at the time. They also said that a cell tower could not be used to pinpoint a person's location, but that was never at issue. The tower data was used to impeach Roberts' alibi and show that she was in the vicinity of the park, not pinpointing her location in the park. They claimed that a network analysis would be required in the case and that the Kotobuki Way tower hit was "not reliable proof that a call originated from that discrete area." Roberts' defense team also claimed that the Kotobuki Way and East 13th Street towers were over nine miles apart, so she could not have driven between them in two-and-a-half minutes. That claim was invalid because the towers were only 3.42 miles apart even though they were 9.3 miles apart in driving distance. Roberts could easily have traveled a sufficient distance between the tower coverage areas on the morning of the murder.

The prosecution and defense experts agreed that there were many variables that could impact a cell tower's range, including tower geometry, local topography, software issues, and call volume. They disagreed concerning the constraints on Roberts' location from the tower data and the probabilities associated with those constraints. Even a sophisticated network analysis—as suggested by the defense experts—would include significant uncertainties and produce a qualitative, not quantitative, answer. No research has been done to support validated, statistical estimates regarding cell tower location hypotheses. Bethers' testimony was a reliable analysis based on the best technical information available. The defense raised misleading objections to the Bethers testimony.

The appeals court had other, new forensic evidence in the Roberts case. It was discovered that the vaginal swab contained contributions from Ed Mills and Brian Tuckenberry. Mills' and Tuckenberry's DNA profiles were also identified in the victim's fingernail clippings. The new evidence came in the form of Y-STR analyses conducted in 2013 under the orders of a federal District Court judge. Mills was known to solicit Williams for sex. Tuckenberry had been convicted in 2010 of raping his former girlfriend and had a history of domestic violence, including strangulation. The District Court held that Roberts had received ineffective counsel during the events that led to her guilty plea, in part because the defense counsel had not investigated the uncertainties related to the cell tower evidence. The lawyer had not hired an expert to review the data, and the court held that Roberts may have insisted on going to trial if she knew that the tower evidence could be challenged. The court did not "take sides" on the issue of the dueling experts on the tower evidence during the postconviction proceeding except to acknowledge the credibility of the competing prosecution and defense theories. The court did not find that Roberts had established her innocence—even with the DNA evidence in hand—only that her original plea was based on inadequate defense counsel (Roberts v. Howton, 2014). Prosecutors dismissed the charges but stated that they felt she was guilty.

The postconviction digital evidence debate in the Roberts case is instructive. Digital evidence can play a key role, just as other types of forensic evidence, in the investigation and adjudication of a crime. The courts are poorly equipped to understand and use digital evidence. The complexity of digital evidence may exacerbate the imbalance between the prosecution and defense: the digital divide contributes to the adversarial deficit.

Also, the field has struggled to deal with the inherent uncertainties of digital evidence examination. Like fire debris and forensic pathology, digital evidence examination often considers contextual information that may bias interpretation. Despite the digital nature of the evidence, the interpretations are usually subjective and qualitative. This paradox is appreciated by some in the digital evidence community but is not well understood by the courts.

GEORGE CORTEZ

The digital evidence field continues to experience "growing pains." Many digital evidence units are not accredited. Many examiners work outside a forensic context and act more as rapid response investigators, not forensic examiners. Police and prosecutors may not use or be aware of digital evidence units that can provide reliable forensic analyses.

The George Cortez case provides a clear example of the dysfunction that may result from the shortcomings in governance, training, and standards (Philadelphia Event Review Team, 2019). Cortez was arrested for murder in Philadelphia, Pennsylvania in 2011, convicted on a range of related charges, and sentenced to life without parole. The case involved eyewitness testimony that likely confused Cortez with his brother, who would later confess to the murder. Cortez's wife said that he was with her the entire night of the murder and even had a video that Cortez had taken with her phone (Melamed, 2019). During Cortez's trial, the judge ordered that the defense hand the phone over to the prosecution so that the video could be extracted and shown on the court's television system. The District Attorney then ordered a full forensic analysis of the phone. That analysis led the prosecution to claim that the time-stamp information on the phone had been falsified. In the interest of courtroom efficiency, the defense did not object to that claim. Cortez was convicted. Four years later, he was exonerated based on his brother's confession and a review of the evidence in the case. Two months after his release, he was shot on the street and killed. His brother is serving an 18-to-36-year prison sentence for the original murder (Commonwealth v. Cortez, 2017).

SENTINEL EVENT ANALYSIS

The case provides a unique opportunity to understand the root causes of wrongful convictions because the Quattrone Center for the Fair Administration of Justice conducted a sentinel event review of the case in 2019 (Philadelphia Event Review Team, 2019). Their review assumed that a "just culture" is one "that recognizes that competent professionals make mistakes and acknowledges that even competent professionals will develop unhealthy norms (e.g., shortcuts, 'routine rule violations'), but has zero tolerance for reckless behavior." Their goal was

> not to punish or find blame with any individual or agency, but solely to understand how our system could ultimately convict George Cortez and then conclude that the conviction was in error based on the specifics of this case and its subsequent appeal.
>
> (Philadelphia Event Review Team, 2019)

The review panel found that the investigational phase of the case included several contributing factors, including inaccurate witness identification, inadequate recordkeeping, and tunnel vision about alternate suspects. The trial phase was compromised by the handling of the cell phone evidence.

The review panel found several contributing factors to the cell phone error. Cortez's wife's cell phone was a flip phone with a very small (2" by 2") screen, so it was impossible for the defense counsel to show it to the jury. The judge then ordered the phone to be given to the prosecution for extraction of the file so it could be shown on a television in the courtroom. The discussions concerning the cell phone transfer from the defense to the prosecution were held off the record without the benefit of the court reporter. This meant that any confusion or erroneous follow-up could not be judged against the original record.

The District Attorney's Office (DAO) then exceeded the judge's instructions to conduct a broader search than was ordered. The DAO had an internal Technical Services Unit (TSU) that performed the actual analysis. There was confusion about the prosecutor's instructions, but the TSU expert did not confine his work to the video file. He extracted all of the photos and videos on the phone. After analyzing the files, the TSU expert opined that the data on the phone had been manually altered. The key video was in an unexpected position in the video list. It was not numbered in order relative the file next to it and had a nonstandard title. In a previous case, defendants had manipulated the phone's date/time-stamp feature to support their alibi. The expert assumed Cortez had done the same. The phone extraction software arranged the video files by their numeric file names, not necessarily in chronological order. The second file in the list had an earlier date than the first one, so the analyst concluded that it had been altered.

The TSU issued its report the evening before the final day of trial. Because the defense did not request a continuation, there was no opportunity to get an appropriate review of the forensic data and opinion. The interests of "judicial efficiency" overrode the interests of the defendant.

The judge knew that another trial was on the docket soon after the Cortez case and worried that an extended trial would inconvenience the jury. The judge said the DAO's actions were a "by-product" of the video extraction process and were therefore admissible. The defense objection was overruled. The video was shown to the jury. The defense rested without any request for an extension to review the TSU report.

As in the Roberts case, the trial attorneys and the judge lacked the technical knowledge required to evaluate the TSU expert's opinions. The defense counsel did attempt a cross-examination that established that the TSU expert could not actually establish the date and time of video. In fact, he acknowledged that a user could have changed the dates on the files to anything they wished. The Quattrone review team noted that the court could (and should) have found a neutral expert to review the cell phone findings, which would have clarified the probative value of the cell phone data.

Finally, the original cell phone and file extracted by the DAO TSU were not retained as evidence. Postconviction, even without the phone, the defense team was able to establish that the flip phone software did not work as described in the TSU report. The numeric names were not changed when the phone date was manipulated. The postconviction defense team also established that the phone automatically adjusted the screen clock for daylight savings time but not the embedded time codes associated with video files. Thus, the videos were timecoded one hour earlier than they were created. These two glitches were sufficient to explain the results observed by the TSU expert.

The Quattrone review did not further extend its consideration of the root causes of the forensic errors in the Cortez case. The TSU was placed in the DAO, which is not equipped to oversee forensic science professionals. It is unknown if the lab was accredited. The training and certification status of the analysts is unknown. The quality assurance mechanisms used by the unit are unknown. It is clear that they had little or no formal process for the acceptance of evidence, the standards for evidence analysis, or evidence storage and retention. Although there were issues with regard to the court process during the Cortez case, the more important root causes related to the failure of the DAO to use the ample resources for digital forensic analysis in Philadelphia, including the Digital Media Evidence Unit within the police department's Office of Forensic Science and the Philadelphia Regional Computer Forensics Laboratory funded by the FBI. Instead, they used their own Technical Services Unit, which specialized in electronic surveillance, not forensic science. This approach is not unusual. Law enforcement agencies have not prioritized the difficult task of building state-of-the-art digital evidence units to deliver validated and reliable findings to inform investigation and adjudication of crime. The full impact of the gaps in practice are not fully known, at least with respect to the impact on wrongful convictions.

STUDY QUESTIONS

1. Take a look at the pictures on your cell phone. How could they be used to track your movements or activities? If they are synced on a separate device, examine the time codes and metadata. Do they agree with your recollection of the time, place, or other aspects of the picture or video? How might a digital evidence examiner be misled by the content or metadata associated with your cell phone information?
2. Sentinel event analysis may be applied in many situations. Read the sentinel event review (SER) papers in the references to learn more about the approach taken by the University of Pennsylvania in criminal justice contexts. Then select one of the situations in Chapter 12, Organizational Dysfunction, and develop an SER based on the documentation you have available. What kinds of information are most helpful to understanding a sentinel event? How might this be useful in other contexts?

FURTHER READING

In addition to their report on the Cortez case, John Hollway and colleagues have developed SERs to examine other cases and issues in policing. Their 2019 paper, Applying Sentinel Event Reviews to Policing, provides an introduction to this important topic (Hollway et al., 2019). It is evident that wrongful convictions implicate a broad set of issues in forensic science and more broadly in policing. Hollway and others advocate for a culture of continuous learning in policing (Hollway, 2021). This is consistent with calls for a "research culture" in forensic science organizations (Koehler, et al., 2011).

SWGDE and the OSAC Digital Evidence Subcommittee have developed extensive standards for digital evidence (see https://www.nist.gov/osac/digital-evidence-subcommittee). NIJ has a long-standing research program in the area (Novak, 2021). The FBI Regional Computer Forensic Laboratory program was created in 2000 and has expanded to include 17 full-service laboratories and training centers in addition to the long-standing one in Philadelphia (see https://www.rcfl.gov/).

There is a dearth of research and attention in the understanding of digital forensic evidence from a systems perspective. A 2017 master's thesis by Nina Sunde, Non-technical Sources of Errors When

Handling Errors When Handling Criminal Investigation, examined the "non-technical" errors that may contribute to errors in digital evidence (Sunde, 2017). Sunde and Dror have examined human factors—such as cognitive bias—that may affect digital evidence interpretation (Sunde & Dror, 2019). Much work remains to be done.

REFERENCES

Commonwealth v. Cortez, 650 EDA 2016 (Superior Court of Pennsylvania November 28, 2017).

Hollway, J. F. (2019). Applying Sentinel Event Reviews to Policing. *Criminology & Public Policy*, *18*(3), 705–730.

Hollway, J. F. (2021). *Instilling a Culture of Continuous Learning from Criminal Justice Systems Errors: A Multi-Stakeholder Sentinel Event Review Process in Philadelphia*. Philadelphia, PA: National Institute of Justice.

Kessler, G. (2010). *Judges' Awareness, Understanding, and Application of Digital Evidence*. Ft. Lauderdale, FL: Nova Southeastern University.

Koehler, J., Mnookin, J., Cole, S., Fisher, B., Dror, I., Houck, M., ... & Siegel, J. (2011). The Need for a Research Culture in the Forensic Sciences. *UCLA Law Review*, *58*, 725–780.

Melamed, S. (2019, April 9). Philly Agencies Grapple with a Wrongful Conviction. Can They Learn from Their Mistakes? *The Philadelphia Inquirer*.

Novak, M. (2021, December 16). *Improving the Collection of Digital Evidence*. Retrieved from National Institute of Justice: https://nij.ojp.gov/topics/articles/improving-collection-digital-evidence#citation--0

Philadelphia Event Review Team. (2019). *Report of the Philadelphia Event Review Team on Commonwealth v. George Cortez*. Philadelphia, PA: Quattrone Center for the Fair Administration of Justice.

Roberts v. Howton, 3:08-cv-01433-MA (United States District Court for the District of Oregon April 9, 2014).

Sunde, N. (2017). *Non-technical Sources of Errors When Handling Errors When Handling Criminal Investigation*. Trondheim, Norway: Norwegian University of Science and Technology.

Sunde, N., & Dror, I. (2019). Cognitive and Human Factors in Digital Forensics: Problems, Challenges, and the Way Forward. *Digital Investigation*, *29*, 101–108.

CHAPTER 15

Themes and Root Causes of Forensic Science Errors in Wrongful Convictions

Wrongful convictions can be assessed based on the prevalence of causes and conditions that are observed in historical cases. Until recently, researchers lacked sufficient case data on which to base substantive conclusions. Known wrongful convictions were too rare to make generalized observations. As a result, wrongful convictions have been a kind of Rorschach test. Observers tended to make conclusions that fit their prior assumptions and biases about issues in policy and practice. Some might say that wrongful convictions were tragic but isolated instances of criminal justice errors. Others might say that wrongful convictions demonstrated the incompetence or corruption of the system. The case evidence was seldom the driving factor behind such judgments.

There are now over 3,000 wrongful convictions, including more than 700 that have been associated with false or misleading forensic evidence by the National Registry of Exonerations (University of California Irvine Newkirk Center for Science & Society, University of Michigan Law School, and Michigan State University College of Law, 2020). There is ample evidence to support objective analysis of forensic science errors in wrongful convictions. Prior sections of this text have examined specific disciplines and types of cases. Here, generalized themes and root causes are discussed. In this context, a "theme" is an idea that is commonly observed but is not necessarily a causative factor. For example, errors are inevitable, and that idea has deep implications for the management of forensic laboratories and the handling of forensic science by the criminal justice system. However, the idea does not describe the cause of any specific error.

DOI: 10.4324/9781003202578-15

THEME: HINDSIGHT IS 20-20

There remains a speculative aspect to any causative factor. Wrongful convictions provide observational, not empirical data, with all of the limitations that are implied. Reasonable disagreements should be expected concerning the interpretation of the observational data in wrongful convictions. Wrongful conviction analysis will necessarily be retrospective and selective. The old maxim, "Hindsight is 20/20" should be taken as a precaution, not a statement of fact. By definition, the wrongful conviction is only detected after the injustice has been done. Other uncertainties also apply. There are many innocent people who have been convicted and never exonerated. And there are guilty people who are freed because a court found that their trial was fundamentally unfair. Just as forensic science is subject to inevitable errors, the criminal justice system may be even more subject to error. Those who assess wrongful convictions and forensic science errors are subject to error too and may be limited by their priors and biases. Therefore, one should take great care in generalizing about the causes and correlates of a specific wrongful conviction or about sets of wrongful convictions.

THEME: ERRORS ARE INEVITABLE

There is no human endeavor that is free from error. Forensic methodologies may be subject to continual improvement to mitigate the possibility of errors, but there is no way to completely eliminate the possibility. Many forensic science organizations now recognize that a zero-error rate is unachievable. Further, a zero-error rate objective detracts from a healthy culture of accountability and encourages misconduct and cover-ups.

THEME: FORENSIC SCIENCE ORGANIZATIONS ARE HIGH-RELIABILITY ORGANIZATIONS

Forensic science organizations are high-reliability organizations (HROs) (Weick & Sutcliffe, 2001). An HRO must plan for and adapt to challenging, disruptive events that entail high-consequence risks. Unlike a research laboratory, the forensic laboratory does not handle clean, well-controlled samples. They get what can be recovered from a suspected crime scene. The latent evidence may be contaminated or mixed with multiple sources. Each criminal case may present unexpected circumstances because criminal activity involves inherent uncertainties. The probative value of the evidence is uncertain. A particular piece of latent evidence may be the most important element in a case or wholly irrelevant. The consequences of error may be as severe as a wrongful conviction or the failure to apprehend a violent offender.

Cause: Lower-Level Deficiencies May Lead to Serious Errors if Left Unresolved

Wrongful convictions demonstrate that HRO principles are directly relevant to the management of a forensic science organization. HROs are preoccupied with small failures. Wrongful convictions demonstrate that lower-level deficiencies are often present in laboratories that produce erroneous forensic results. The effect is most easily observed in analyses related to seized drugs and toxicology. These disciplines have thorough quality assurance and accreditation systems to identify deficiencies. The experience of dysfunctional forensic organizations is also instructive. The Detroit and Houston lab scandals were associated with a large array of "small" deficiencies that were discounted or ignored. The situation produced detected wrongful convictions after chronic policy and practice shortfalls were allowed to continue over many years. Some forensic science organizations—including the Houston Forensic Science Center—have taken steps to *induce* errors in a controlled manner through performance testing (Hundl et al., 2020). This reflects an HRO mindset and is likely to limit severe deficiencies in those organizations.

Example: See the discussion of quality assurance issues in toxicology laboratories in Chapter 13.

Cause: Forensic Science Organizations May Not Conduct Root-Cause Analysis of Serious Deficiencies

HRO principles provide a structure for the analysis of forensic science errors in wrongful convictions. HROs avoid simplification. Forensic scientists work in complex environments, so the root causes of errors are likely to be complex. The best root cause analysis is conducted by organizations or independent investigators with unfettered access to an organization's people and records. In such a circumstance, it is possible to collect enough information to conduct a thorough analysis of the complex factors that may be at work in a particular situation. Unfortunately, most wrongful convictions have not been subject to publicly disclosed root cause analyses.

Example: The histories of the Detroit and Houston laboratories are discussed in Chapter 12.

Cause: Front-Line Forensic Examiners May Be Devalued Relative to Managers or Sworn Personnel

HROs put a priority on operations and defer to front-line expertise. In other words, nobody understands a complex professional environment better than the front-line people who work in that environment. The best root-cause analysis should consider the views of forensic science experts and the views of those with intimate knowledge of the day-to-day situation. One of the clearest examples comes from the New York State Police fingerprint scandal in the 1990's (Roth, 1997) Front-line examiners noticed the poor performance, lack of training, and other deficiencies in the unit that was producing fraudulent latent print comparisons. They knew what was going on. They told police leaders about it. They told the prosecutor about it. Those "leaders" did not defer to the experts on the front line, and wrongful convictions necessarily followed. A similar circumstance could be described in a wide range of wrongful conviction cases.

> *Example: See the case history of the Whitehurst allegations and the gap between "sworn" and "civilian" scientists inside the FBI in Chapter 12.*

Cause: The Organization May Lack Adequate Quality Assurance Mechanisms to Prevent Forensic Science Errors

The implications in current forensic science practice are profound. Over the last 20 to 30 years, labs have increasingly implemented accreditation and quality assurance (QA) mechanisms to improve the reliability of forensic analysis. These efforts should be considered a direct and important response to the challenge of wrongful convictions. When properly implemented, QA provides constant feedback to the organization concerning deficiencies and needed corrective actions. To be successful, QA must be an everyday priority for the laboratory and be seen as a response to the inevitability of errors. It should not be a reason to punish people who are associated with nonconformance, but it can be used in combination with performance metrics to identify system issues and needed changes.

> *Example: See the discussion of the quality assurance and chain of custody issues in the DNA analysis work in O.J. Simpson case in Chapter 4.*

Cause: Governance Mechanisms Must Promote Transparency and Accountability in Forensic Science Organizations

To the greatest extent possible, these processes should be transparent to stakeholders. Forensic science organizations—like other HROs—must be resilient. They must be able to acknowledge problems, manage crises, and implement reforms. The history of wrongful convictions suggests that some forensic science organizations have avoided transparency and public accountability. It has been argued that transparency will be used by defense lawyers to raise questions about valid and reliable forensic results. Also, it is noted that the media and politicians may indulge in venal and uninformed criticisms of crime labs. Finally, many labs report to entities—such as law enforcement agencies—that lack the expertise or desire to provide effective oversight. These concerns are often real, but they are not sufficient reason to avoid transparency and accountability. The Texas Forensic Science Commission (TXFSC) requires labs to disclose any professional negligence or misconduct. The commission publishes these reviews on its website. This level of transparency may cause stress in Texas forensic science organizations, but that is the point. Stress improves the resiliency of the organizations and the reliability of forensic results. Unfortunately, such transparency is not implemented in many forensic laboratory systems.

Example: See the Stephan Cowans latent print misidentification case in Chapter 7.

THEME: CURRENT GOVERNANCE MECHANISMS DO NOT PROVIDE ADEQUATE OVERSIGHT OF FORENSIC SCIENCE PRACTITIONERS AND ORGANIZATIONS

Texas learned this lesson the hard way. The state has produced more wrongful convictions related to forensic science errors than any other US jurisdiction. In many cases, problems were covered over or ignored. TXFSC is now one of the strongest governance entities in forensic science in the world. The United Kingdom Forensic Regulator provides similar oversight, as do national-level entities elsewhere. About a dozen states have some kind of forensic science commission, though none have the level of authority enjoyed by the TXFSC. The National Forensic Science Commission was disbanded in 2017 and had little or no power to enforce its recommendations in any case.

Cause: Some Forensic Experts Exist Outside the Governance Mechanisms of the Forensic Science Community

Many forensic practitioners work outside the governance of a public forensic science organization. They may be consultants, medical experts, or examiners within law enforcement units. For example, many fingerprint and digital evidence examiners are organized within police agencies. Many wrongful convictions associated with these disciplines relate to poor management and oversight, not the inherent difficulties of the fields. Also, many medical professionals have produced expert testimony in criminal trials related to pediatric abuse and other issues. Their findings and testimony are not subject to significant review outside the medical community, which does not prioritize oversight of medical input into judicial proceedings. Almost all bite mark testimony in wrongful convictions came from consultants who practiced as dental professionals. Their reports and testimony were seldom subject to any review by a forensic science organization. They experienced little or no accountability from any governing authority. Even the American Board of Forensic Odontology (ABFO) had very little influence, as evidenced by the contribution of uncertified bite mark examiners to wrongful conviction cases.

Example: See the history of Michael West and the governance of bite mark comparison in Chapter 6.

Cause: Some Forensic Disciplines Exist Outside the Governance Mechanisms of the Forensic Science Community

In the United States and other countries that use the CODIS system, DNA analysis is subject to strict quality controls. The National DNA Index System (NDIS) promulgates regulations that every laboratory must follow for the testing and analysis of any DNA profile that is uploaded to CODIS. The system is not completely comprehensive; some local agencies maintain local databases that fall outside CODIS. Rapid DNA and certain genealogical matches may not conform to NDIS guidelines. Nonetheless, DNA profiles introduced into any trial proceedings almost always conform to NDIS guidelines, making DNA analysis the only forensic discipline with that type of national governance. Other systems—such as the national fingerprint and ballistics databases—do not have similar requirements. Forensic toxicologists conform to American Board of Forensic Toxicology requirements, which are dispositive in almost all instances. Other disciplines have certification boards, but many courts will accept testimony from examiners regardless of certification status. The American Academy of Forensic Sciences Standards Board promulgates a growing list of standards for forensic practice, but the enforcement of these standards depends on adoption by individual laboratories, laboratory systems, or jurisdictions. Governance gaps are readily observed in wrongful convictions, especially in dysfunctional organizations. Such gaps also enable individual examiners to produce negligent or fraudulent work without accountability. In extreme cases—such as canine detection—entire fields of practice have been undermined by governance failures that permit unscrupulous examiners to practice over many years.

Example: Chapter 5 includes a discussion of the misuse of canine detection in wrongful convictions.

THEME: ALL ERRORS BY INDIVIDUALS RELATE TO SYSTEM DEFICIENCIES

Many people assume that wrongful convictions are primarily caused by corruption and incompetence. Misconduct certainly plays a role in many cases, but it would be a mistake to assume that everyone involved in a wrongful conviction was corrupt or incompetent. When assessing root causes, one must consider how misconduct was able to occur. What deficiencies existed in training, accountability, organizations, or systems? A fuller understanding of deficiencies provides a clearer path to the definition of reforms or corrective actions.

THEME: MOST INDIVIDUALS WHO CONTRIBUTED TO A WRONGFUL CONVICTION MADE HONEST MISTAKES

More fundamentally, no rational person becomes involved in criminal justice so that they can put innocent people in prison. The vast majority of professionals believe that they are contributing to just outcomes. Each observer is subject to the same biases and problems that impacted the individuals who contributed to a wrongful conviction. Further, if there is one human flaw evident in wrongful convictions, it is arrogance based on the wrong assumption that justice was being served. Just as arrogance led to many wrongful convictions, arrogance may lead to errors in the assessment of the root causes of wrongful convictions. One way to avoid this problem is to acknowledge the inevitability of errors and the problem of universal human fallibility. When asserting that errors are inevitable, the necessary corollary is that any of us put into the same situation could have made the same mistakes. We should assume that we could have made the same mistakes as the people who were involved in wrongful convictions.

Cause: "Bad apple" Examiners Cause Wrongful Convictions

Nonetheless, some wrongful convictions are closely tied to incompetent or fraudulent examiners, so-called "bad apples." Among others, Fred Zain, Michael West, Joyce Gilchrist, and Amy Dookhan produced false results in wrongful convictions over many years. They continued to operate because they were affiliated with organizations that were broken and dysfunctional. There may have been a lack of resources, accountability, governance, or effective management. In most cases, effective quality assurance mechanisms and technical reviews would have detected the problems and prevented these individuals from contributing to multiple wrongful convictions. At some level, there was a lack of institutional will to make changes. That may be at the level of the crime laboratory, but ineffective executive and judicial oversight are at least as common.

Examples: Fred Zain and Joyce Gilchrist are discussed in the history of serological analysis in Chapter 3.

Cause: The Forensic Examiner May Have Lacked Training in the Application of the Forensic Discipline

Untrained individuals may produce errors in a variety of ways. They may be more subject to cognitive bias, misinterpretation, or overconfidence. They may fail to apply standards in a rigorous and reproducible manner. In essence, they are not applying validated science because they are unable to reliably follow standards (or standard operating procedures). Forensic analysis must be reliable across the entire chain of custody of the evidence. Forensic professionals must perform their work at a very high level of skill and reliability in order to produce trustworthy results for criminal proceedings. In wrongful convictions, many forensic examiners were not trained to perform the work they were assigned. Training deficiencies produce unacceptable gaps between the forensic discipline's reliability *in the ideal* and the reliability *as applied*. The application of an idealized set of scientific principles will always lead to some loss of reliability due to real-world variability and human error. When a forensic professional lacks training, their reliability as applied may be so poor that they produce serious errors that impact wrongful convictions.

Example: Many latent print errors have been associated with untrained examiners who failed to apply the standards of the discipline. See Chapter 7.

Cause: The Examiner May Have Lacked Rigorous Certification

Education and training are not sufficient to ensure that a forensic examiner is able to produce reliable forensic results. In some cases, the education and training may be deficient. In other cases, the examiner may not be well-suited to the knowledge, skills, abilities, and other attributes (KSAO) associated with the discipline. KSAO gaps often manifest in poor adherence to accepted standards and the use of unvalidated methods, inevitably leading to forensic errors. Ideally, every examiner would be subject to certification to ensure that they are able to perform their work up to a research-based standard. Certification regimes are in place in many disciplines, but the requirements for certification are not uniform across the forensic community. Further, many certifications do not entail rigorous testing. For example, what does it mean for a fingerprint examiner to be able to complete "difficult" comparisons? Latent print certification tests do not provide much insight into the relative ability of an examiner to perform at a high level. Other disciplines also lack that level of clarity. In some laboratories, certification has been even less useful because examiners took the test as a group, thus covering any individual deficiencies.

Example: Uncertified forensic pathologists demonstrated this issue in the Larry Souter case in Chapter 11's discussion of variability and bias in forensic pathology.

Cause: The Forensic Examiner May Have Been Subject to Cognitive Bias

Cognitive bias may arise in many forms that impact the reliability of forensic examination. The examiner may be biased by contextual information about the case or pressure to solve a high-profile case. This may extend to knowledge of other forensic results, which also may provide a biasing context to influence forensic interpretation. The examiner may be subject to target bias in which the features of a known source are "teased" to fit the features of an unknown source of crime scene evidence. Laboratory verification and review processes may be biased by the conclusions of the original examiner, whose error is thereby overlooked. In addition, there may be biases introduced in the communication and coordination processes associated with the criminal investigation. These biases may extend to the discounting of exculpatory forensic results, even by defense attorneys. This is not an exhaustive list, which would include a wide range of individual, organizational, and system factors.

Regardless of the source, human bias is an inevitable part of the criminal justice system and forensic science in practice. That does not imply that heroic efforts are needed to eliminate human judgment from forensic science. Algorithms have biases that are different from human biases and may be more pernicious and subject to more serious errors. Automated systems also must interface with humans at some level, meaning that no system can be deployed that completely eliminates human bias effects in criminal justice practice. Instead, forensic science organizations need to adopt appropriate reforms that mitigate the risks associated with cognitive bias in balance with other considerations.

> *Examples: See the Willingham and Kluppelberg cases and other issues in cognitive bias in fire debris investigation in Chapter 9.*

Cause: Subjective Interpretation Frameworks May Exacerbate Cognitive Bias Effects and Lead to Forensic Errors

Some disciplines have subjective interpretation frameworks at the conclusion level, including forensic pathology, forensic medicine, fire debris investigation, and document examination. These disciplines consider contextual information as part of their interpretative analysis. Conclusions are often subject to uncertainties due to lack of complete information or gaps in scientific knowledge. In some cases, an examiner may be able to make multiple, valid conclusions—some of which might be compatible with the prosecution theory of a case and some of which may be compatible with the defense theory of a case. These inherent characteristics necessarily imply that these disciplines are more vulnerable to cognitive bias. Subjective interpretation disciplines—especially forensic pathology and forensic medicine—have continued to contribute to wrongful convictions up to the present day. This may be due to the variability, bias, and complexity of their interpretation frameworks and the difficulty of establishing standards that mitigate the associated difficulties.

> *Example: Forensic medicine in pediatric abuse investigation is based on subjective interpretation frameworks that may be heavily influenced by moral panic about the victimization of children. See Chapter 10.*

Cause: Forensic Examiners May Produce Fraudulent Results

Official misconduct has been associated with many wrongful convictions and every type of criminal justice practitioner, including forensic scientists. Forensic examiners may produce fraudulent results to "prove" a case against a defendant who was presumed to be guilty. They may cover for their own incompetence or those of their colleagues. They may engage in criminal activity themselves. More commonly, the individuals will be seeking professional advancement or the glory that comes from solving a difficult case. Venality is more common than sociopathy. Wrongful convictions arise from individuals who believe that their misconduct is justified to get ahead, and the means justifies the ends. As outlined above, forensic science organizations require quality control mechanisms that identify fraudulent work. Further, labs must maintain a culture of openness and accountability. Incentive structures should encourage valid and reliable analysis, not glory and case clearance. Professionals should feel that their substantive concerns are addressed by management. In most cases of official misconduct, other forensic scientists observed the warning signs of fraud but their concerns were brushed aside. This resulted in wrongful convictions, but it also led to deep scars in the fabric of the associated organizations.

Example: See the case examples provided in Chapter 12, such as the New York State Police fingerprint scandal, or the discussion of the Massachusetts drug scandals in Chapter 13.

Cause: Other Criminal Justice Practitioners May Engage in Official Misconduct and Misuse Forensic Evidence

Corrupt police investigators, prosecutors, and judges do exist. Their misconduct may extend to their use of forensic evidence. They may manufacture evidence. They may suppress exculpatory forensic evidence. They may lie to a suspect about the nature of forensic evidence to elicit a false confession. More simply, a prosecutor may mischaracterize evidence in court to produce a clearly false understanding of the evidence. Misconduct may include the use of laboratories or consultants who are outside the systems of accountability followed by traditional forensic science organizations. These experts may be biased or manipulated to produce invalid results favorable to the prosecution. It is important to distinguish between official misconduct and honest mistakes. Honest mistakes are much more common and may be associated with inadequate understanding of evidence, poor investigative practices, and a lack of professionalism. Many gaps remain in investigation practices in police departments. Courts have demonstrated that they are poorly equipped to use forensic evidence reliably and effectively.

Example: See the discussion of sexual assault investigations in the pre-DNA era in Chapter 3.

THEME: SYSTEM ERRORS ARE THE PRIMARY CAUSE OF FORENSIC SCIENCE ERRORS

The processing and use of forensic evidence begins at the crime scene and continues through the adjudication of a case. An error may arise at any point along the way. The error may not even relate to the work of a forensic examiner. An error may arise from:

- Collection, storage, and chain of custody of evidence
- Misuse or misunderstanding of forensic evidence among law enforcement officers or officers of the court
- Communication to the laboratory or analyst about the case or evidence processing
- Communication from the laboratory or analyst about the forensic evidence

These origin points relate to the systems that are used to support forensic analysis, not forensic analysis itself. They are system problems, and system problems are much more prevalent in wrongful convictions than issues within the analytical framework of the disciplines. There are notable exceptions, with bite mark analysis being the most obvious and prominent.

Within the analysis framework itself, an error may arise from the method employed, the way the method is performed in the laboratory, or the interpretation of the evidence. Often, observers—including the courts—assume that errors arise from inherent uncertainties in forensic methods. Although these errors do occur, they are not the primary cause of forensic errors in wrongful convictions.

For example, there has been an emphasis on the error rate of latent print analysis. There are reasonable grounds for this concern. Latent print analysis includes elements of subjective interpretation. No statistical framework has been developed to characterize latent print conclusions. Historically, the fingerprint community has claimed a "zero error rate." Arguably, the high-profile Mayfield case error arose from the inherent uncertainties of latent print identification when faced with close nonmatches. Nonetheless, most wrongful convictions associated with latent print analysis are not associated with identification errors. And almost all identification errors have been related to misconduct or the work of untrained, uncertified examiners. Many wrongful convictions are associated with the failure to consider exculpatory latent prints. It is laudable to seek to improve the underlying scientific foundation of latent print analysis, but system improvements are much more likely to prevent wrongful convictions.

THEME: FORENSIC SCIENCE ERRORS MAY ARISE AT ANY POINT IN THE CRIMINAL JUSTICE SYSTEM AND ARE NOT NECESSARILY ERRORS BY FORENSIC SCIENTISTS

The NRE has adopted careful language—False or Misleading Forensic Evidence—when referring to forensic science issues that may have contributed to a wrongful conviction. This phrasing suggests that many types of system errors may have been present in a case. A forensic examiner may have presented an incorrect result or communicated the result in a misleading way. Alternatively, other practitioners may have played the primary role in the error.

In wrongful convictions, system issues may be pervasive from crime scene to courtroom. Even if an analyst does their job perfectly, a police investigator or officer of the court may misunderstand or misuse the evidence. Of course, "all of the above" is also possible. False or misleading forensic evidence may include errors by forensic scientists *and* other criminal justice system practitioners. In some cases, the situation may be very complex and not subject to easy analysis, especially when relying on a limited public record.

Cause: A Forensic Science Error May Be Related to Crime Scene Investigation, Police Investigation, or an Officer of the Court

To illustrate, it is useful to examine some causes related to forensic science errors outside the purview of the forensic scientist in a crime laboratory. The figure describes causes, not root causes. For example, the chain of custody may not be maintained, but root cause analysis would entail the investigation of the underlying factors (such as lack of standards, lack of enforcement of standards, training, resource limitations, etc.). The list is not exhaustive but does include the primary issues (Table 15.1).

THEME: THE CRIMINAL JUSTICE SYSTEM IS POORLY EQUIPPED TO HANDLE FORENSIC EVIDENCE RELIABLY

As the graphic illustrates, officers of the court face many pitfalls in the reliable use of forensic evidence. Many wrongful convictions have been overturned due to these errors. In some cases, guilty defendants were released because of flawed forensic testimony or mistakes in the handling of forensic science by the court. Justice requires that everyone receive a fair trial, including guilty defendants. Also, the public rightly expects

TABLE 15.1 Causes related to forensic science errors outside the purview of the forensic scientist in a crime laboratory.

Crime Scene	Police investigation	Prosecution	Defense	Judge
• Evidence not collected • Evidence not stored or preserved correctly • Poor crime scene Analysis • Evidence not sent to laboratory • Evidence lost, destroyed, or contaminated • Chain of custody compromised	• Failure to request forensic analysis • Failure to collect reference or elimination samples • Forensic evidence ignored • Forensic evidence suppressed • Forensic evidence misrepresented to suspect or others	• Forensic evidence is suppressed or ignored. • Scientific or statistical validity Of forensic • Evidence is mischaracterized. • Source attribution is mischaracterized • Prosecution interferes with forensic analysis.	• Inadequate pre-trial discovery or preparation • Incompetent advice concerning plea • Failure to recognize/ present exculpatory evidence • Failure to obtain independent expert review or analysis • Inadequate cross-examination or trial • Inadequate direct appeal	• Novel or faulty method accepted into evidence • Faulty testimony accepted over objection • Faulty jury instructions • Failure to provide adequate resources for a forensic expert to the defense

competent policing and forensic analysis in every case. That said, these criminal justice practitioners are unlikely to have education or training in science or the application of science to forensic analysis. They are not in a good position to use forensic evidence reliably.

Cause: Police Investigators May Exhibit Tunnel Vision and Continuation Bias in Which They Ignore or Discount Forensic Evidence That Detracts from Their Original Hypothesis

The consequences are easily observed in wrongful convictions. There are thousands of law enforcement agencies with widely varying governance, so it is possible for just about anything to be adopted into practice somewhere. For example, police dogs have been misused in fire debris investigation, drug detection, and scent lineups, all of which have contributed to wrongful convictions. Many police agencies use manipulative interrogation techniques. Police have misrepresented forensic evidence to elicit false confessions. In a stunningly large number of cases, police investigators have ignored or discounted forensic evidence. In some cases, this was due to deliberate misconduct. More commonly, they were just exhibiting tunnel vision and a failure to appreciate the implications of exculpatory forensic evidence. In these cases, forensic evidence may be the best opportunity innocent suspects have to clear their name. Forensic analysis is much more objective than other types of evidence. In some respects, hair and serology evidence "failed" because their probative value was so weak that they were too easily discounted. It is much more difficult to dismiss exculpatory DNA in most circumstances. It should be noted that there is a pecking order in law enforcement, and forensic science is not at the top of it. Sworn police officers may be dismissive of exculpatory results from civilian forensic scientists. The forensic scientist may not feel that they can challenge the direction of an investigation.

Example: See the discussion of the Madrid bombing investigation in Chapter 7.

Cause: Forensic Laboratories May Not Communicate the Probative Value of Forensic Evidence to Police Investigators and Fact Finders

More recently, the walls between crime labs and police have been strengthened due to concerns about the effect of contextual bias on the objectivity of forensic examiners. These concerns have validity, of course, but such barriers may exacerbate the tunnel vision and biases of detectives and other criminal justice practitioners. This is not idle speculation; many wrongful convictions are associated with exculpatory evidence that was present and known prior to conviction. Paradoxically, the root cause of some forensic errors may be the failure to build walls between investigation and forensic analysis, and the root cause of other forensic errors may be the failure to tear down walls between forensic analysis and investigation. Many laboratories have implemented evidence management systems—not just information technology solutions but rather organizational systems—designed to improve workflow efficiency. These professionals may also serve a different purpose to manage the flow of contextual information to analysts and enable reliable communication to investigators. This may help police make better use of forensic evidence.

Examples: See the Orlando Bosquette and Barry Laughman serology cases in Chapter 3.

Cause: Courts Have Accepted Forensic Methods with Inadequate Scientific Foundations

Unproven methods have been introduced in many trials, such as lip print identification. There has been extraordinary variability in the acceptance of some methods, such as voiceprint analysis. Courts have failed to act as gatekeepers for analyses that have produced dozens of wrongful convictions, such as bite mark comparison. Some invalid methods have been addressed but not by the court system. Firearms identification was transformed by law enforcement and scientific researchers. Fire debris investigation was reformed by dogged empirical work and experts who were willing to challenge the status quo as NFPA 921 developed. The courts have consistently lagged developments in DNA analysis. Judges have conflated issues related to statistics, mixture interpretation, new marker systems, and other developments. The field did not improve because the courts demanded it. Key researchers and forensic scientists led the way, and the courts have kept up in fits and starts.

Example: There are several examples in Chapter 5 on unsubstantiated methods, such as the misuse of Child Sexual Abuse Accommodation Syndrome.

Cause: Courts Have Failed to Limit the Scope of Expert Testimony to the Technical Area That Was Subject to Voir Dire

The courts have also failed to understand the scope of an individual examiner's expertise. The list of examples from wrongful convictions is quite vast. A latent print examiner has no special knowledge about the age of a print. A forensic pathologist cannot tell you whether the shooter was left- or right-handed. Dogs are not better than mass spectrometers at detection of volatile organic compounds, and so on. Many, unqualified "experts" have testified despite a lack of any proven expertise. A fingerprint examiner with training in collection of ten-prints was permitted to testify as a latent print examiner. Serologists were often permitted to testify in DNA cases without necessary training. Researchers have introduced novel, unproven methods without establishing the appropriate basis of the technique as a forensic method relevant outside the research laboratory. These have all happened in wrongful conviction cases.

Example: See the Steven Chaney discussion in Chapter 7, which involved invalid testimony about the age of a latent print. The Houston lab issues are discussed in detail in Chapter 12.

Cause: Courts Do Not Consider Input from Scientific Bodies Concerning the Admissibility and Scope of Expert Testimony

It is possible that Daubert, Frye, and Federal Rules of Evidence have not been applied consistently and reliably in criminal courts (though it appears they have been more successful in civil courts). The Federal Rules of Evidence have been updated with the intent to improve the judge's gatekeeper function but with little effect. One study found that federal district judges didn't even apply the correct preponderance standard in 65% of cases (Bernard, 2022). This statistic is all the more alarming given that federal judges are usually more rigorous in their evidence review than state and local judges. A new amendment shifting the burden for admissibility and compelling judicial review of the basis of admissibility seeks to solve this issue. It does not address the fundamental problem: scientists are in the best position to determine the validity of a scientific method, but the courts do not recognize the authority of any particular scientific body for this purpose. In some sense, the root cause of many wrongful convictions is the inadequacy of judicial review mechanisms as applied to admissibility of expert testimony.

Example: See the discussion of voiceprint comparison and the David Shawn Pope case in Chapter 1. Also, the experience with Composition Bullet Lead Analysis in Chapter 5 raises similar issues.

THEME: THERE IS AN ADVERSARIAL DEFICIT IN WHICH DEFENDANTS DO NOT HAVE ACCESS TO ADEQUATE EXPERTISE IN THE UNDERSTANDING AND REVIEW OF FORENSIC EVIDENCE

The adversarial deficit between prosecution and defense is a root cause of many wrongful convictions. The adversarial deficit is a systemic issue in which prosecutors have more resources and capabilities than defense lawyers. The adversarial deficit may mean that a defendant does not have access to adequate counsel and forensic expertise to mount a successful defense. This issue arises in successful direct appeals or habeas corpus appeals. In many instances, the basis for these appeals is inadequate defense related to forensic evidence. The appeals court will recognize an adversarial deficit that prevented a fair trial. It is likely that this problem is far more widespread than is observed in detected wrongful convictions.

Cause: Defense Attorneys May Not Have the Expertise to Use Forensic Evidence Effectively

Defense attorneys usually do not have any background in science, and they may fail to appreciate the implications of forensic science analyses. This tendency has undoubtedly been exacerbated by the increasing complexity of science and technology in society. Forensic science has become more complex hand-in-hand with the broader societal trend. Digital evidence poses new challenges every day. DNA has evolved to include advanced algorithms for mixture interpretation and may soon use next-generation sequencing. The issue is worse in the disciplines that rely on contextual information to make subjective interpretations, such as forensic medicine, forensic pathology, and fire debris investigation. Thousands of research papers are published relevant to these disciplines each year. Experts may struggle to keep up with changes. Many defense lawyers don't stand a chance. Many defense attorneys in wrongful convictions have stated flatly that they did not understand the forensic evidence and were not prepared to challenge it or use it successfully. The complexity of science has also given rise to increasing specialization among experts. That makes it harder to find the right expert, more expensive to retain the expert, and much more difficult to challenge the expert's qualifications and testimony effectively. Public defenders are at an extreme disadvantage because they must rely on court discretion to provide resources to retain an appropriate expert. As seen in many wrongful convictions, judges (or state laws) do not provide sufficient funds for this purpose.

Example: The digital evidence cases in Chapter 14 demonstrate that inadequate defense remains an issue in cases involving advanced technology.

Cause: Defense Attorneys May Not Have the Resources to Review or Challenge Forensic Evidence

In many cases, the forensic evidence will privilege the prosecution. This is due to the inherent dynamics of modern criminal investigation. First, crime labs are often located within police agencies or at least have close working relationships with police and prosecutors. Independent consultants and commercial labs may depend on the contractual relationship they have with police or prosecutors. That may also lead to a prosecution bias in their analysis. Fundamentally, many prosecutions require favorable forensic results if they are to proceed to trial. For example, a murder charge is not likely to be successful if a forensic pathologist has concluded that a death was the result of accident, suicide, or natural causes (although such manner determinations are public health, not legal, conclusions). As a result, a murder prosecution will almost always include some support from autopsy findings and a forensic pathologist. A successful defense may attempt to advance a theory of an alternative suspect. An easier route might be to challenge a homicide finding by the forensic pathologist, but that might require substantial effort to review the death certificate and other circumstances by expensive, independent experts. The experts may end up agreeing with their colleague. In other cases, the medical or scientific uncertainties may lead different experts to make different interpretations from the same set of facts. Many wrongful convictions arise when defense attorneys are unwilling or unable to navigate these difficulties and develop a reasonable challenge to a subjective forensic interpretation. Innocence organizations have become more adept at discovering and challenging these interpretations, but of course those resources are only applied in specific cases in the postconviction phase.

Example: Most forensic pathology and forensic medicine cases discussed in Chapters 10 and 11 implicate the resource challenges for defense attorneys when challenging forensic expert testimony.

THEME: THERE ARE IMPORTANT DIFFERENCES AMONG THE FORENSIC DISCIPLINES WITH RESPECT TO THEIR VULNERABILITY TO ERRORS

All forensic disciplines—even DNA—could benefit from improvements in their underlying scientific foundation and practice standards. Science demands that the process is never truly complete because our understanding can always improve based on new empirical data and insights.

Cause: Feature Distortions May Be Comparable to Source Feature Variability in Some Pattern Evidence Disciplines and Require Further Scientific Study

Some disciplines have weaker scientific foundations overall, including bite mark comparison, handwriting comparison, and blood spatter analysis. These disciplines also face challenges related to the distortions inherent to the latent evidence in their disciplines. In short, real-world evidence exhibits variations that are difficult to distinguish from source features. Friction ridge identification and firearms examination share similar challenges related to scientific understanding and feature distortions. The experience of wrongful convictions suggests that these issues can be mitigated by careful adherence to rigorous practice standards. The history of hair comparison suggests that pattern evidence disciplines must prioritize the development and enforcement of research-based testimony standards.

Example: Bite mark comparison and its fundamental limitations are described in Chapter 6.

Cause: Examiners May Not Account for Analysis and Interpretation Uncertainties in Highly Reliable Forensic Disciplines

In general, DNA, toxicology, and seized drug analysis have an excellent scientific foundation. The application of these disciplines is aided by the ability of examiners to distinguish source features very reliably, although mixtures and quality assurance issues may still lead to forensic science errors. The history of serological typing suggests that these disciplines should prioritize the development of reliable interpretation frameworks and thorough training to ensure that these frameworks are applied in practice.

Example: See the discussion of testimony errors in hair comparison and serological typing in Chapter 3.

Cause: Subjective Disciplines May Lack Standards and Governance to Account for Bias, Variability, and Scientific Validity

Finally, as outlined above, the reliability of forensic pathology, forensic medicine, forensic psychology, and other disciplines may be compromised by subjective interpretation frameworks that are susceptible to cognitive bias, examiner variability, and the use of invalid interpretation frameworks. In some areas of practice, these disciplines lack sufficient, research-based standards for interpretation and testimony, a problem which has contributed to many wrongful convictions. The disciplines also lack sufficient governance to develop and enforce such standards. As one example, there is no standard to reconcile the variability of post-mortem interval determinations across environmental variables and measurement modalities, even though substantial scientific research has been conducted to elucidate the relevant issues.

Examples: See the Monroe and Robbins case histories in Chapter 11 on forensic pathology.

Cause: Unvalidated Forensic Methods Contribute to Forensic Errors and Wrongful Convictions

Law enforcement agencies and forensic science organizations may adopt unproven approaches to improve their effectiveness. This may lead to important innovations, but it may also contribute to wrongful convictions when the method proves to be unreliable. Some researchers have called these methods "junk science," but that is not a valid term in the assessment of scientific theories. Everything in our modern world was at one time a technology with an inadequate scientific foundation. We should consider the validity of an idea based on the current empirical foundation and maintain an open mind if new information changes our understanding. That said, forensic science must have higher standards than the general scientific community. Lives are at stake, and errors have immediate implications for the real people whose lives depend on the reliability of the criminal justice system. Fundamentally, forensic science is the application of validated scientific methods to produce information relevant to legal proceedings. By "validated," we may mean several things. First, the method is based on empirical and observation data that has been subject to sustained and reproducible research. Second, the method answers questions that may be formulated as falsifiable hypotheses. Third, the method has been reduced to practice and subjected to standards that are applied by forensic examiners in a valid and reliable manner. Finally, the method has been studied in idealized and applied frameworks with reasonable ecological validity. Some wrongful convictions have relied on forensic methods that did not meet any of these criteria, such as dog scent line-ups and wink response.

Examples: The chapter on unsubstantiated science discusses the histories of canine detection and the wink response.

THEME: RELIABLE FORENSIC SCIENCE REQUIRES THE DEVELOPMENT AND ENFORCEMENT OF SCIENTIFIC STANDARDS

Standards are rules for the application of validated science in real-world applications. In some sense, the forensic scientist is more like an engineer than a scientist because the job is not to do experiments but rather to apply science to practical problems. Thus, standards help the forensic "engineer" apply scientific knowledge in a reproducible manner. In practice, forensic science relies on consensus bodies to establish standards. Standards may specify laboratory methods, interpretation frameworks, and communication. Forensic scientists must be willing and able to apply standards in all three of these phases of work. Forensic science organizations must have mechanisms to ensure that the standards are implemented and enforced. These mechanisms commonly fall under the broad category of quality assurance.

Cause: Forensic Science Errors May Result from Failure to Develop and Enforce Scientific Standards Related to Forensic *Methods*

A method standard includes the instructions for the conduct of a forensic test. The standard may include criteria for the quality or suitability of forensic evidence or tools used in the conduct of the test. It also may refer to other standards that govern elements of the overall method. Properly designed, the standard reflects the idealized, laboratory-based methods that were subject to scientific research. It is not sufficient for such standards to be developed by consensus bodies. Implementation mechanisms must also be in place to ensure that the standards are followed in practice. This may include discipline-level mechanisms (such as conformity assessment) and organizational mechanisms (such as accreditation and certification). Forensic errors and wrongful convictions may arise from the absence of method standards or nonconformance due to inadequate implementation and enforcement.

> *Example: See the discussions of simultaneous prints in Chapter 7 and the Patricia Stallings toxicology case in Chapter 13.*

Cause: Forensic Science Errors May Result from Failure to Develop and Enforce Scientific Standards Related to Forensic *Interpretation*

Standards establish the limits of validity for the interpretation of the results obtained from forensic methods. Misinterpretation can lead to individualization or classification errors even when a method is otherwise applied reliably. Thus, the method will produce valid results, but the examiner will fail to incorporate all of the relevant considerations into the final analysis. For example, the examiner may have failed to consider elimination samples or other variables. Also, the examiner may produce an invalid or misleading probability related to the physical, chemical, or biological populations involved in the interpretation. Most importantly, the interpretation must be based on hypotheses that are formulated at the correct level of crime, activity, source, and sub-source populations. Finally, the method may entail systemic and random uncertainties or other limitations that scope the probative value of the evidence. Interpretation standards may be difficult to develop and enforce. Many examiners may make honest interpretation mistakes that lead to serious forensic errors and wrongful convictions.

Example: The history of "shaken baby syndrome" is closely related to the lack of adequate interpretation standards. See Chapter 10.

Cause: Forensic Science Errors May Result from Failure to Develop and Enforce Scientific Standards Related to Forensic Reports and Testimony

Testimony and report errors are common in wrongful convictions. A forensic scientist may exaggerate the probative value or provide misleading statistics, misrepresent the scientific basis for forensic methods and interpretations, or exclude relevant information about forensic results, methods, or interpretations. Courts have struggled to deal with this issue. Legal standards are broad and do not reflect the distinction between invalid methods and invalid communication. Further, prosecutors, defense attorneys, and judges are not qualified to assess the merit of scientific propositions as represented in forensic reports and testimony. The forensic science community has not adopted comprehensive testimony standards across the forensic disciplines. In the past, many forensic science organizations enforced broad testimony requirements that were primarily based on comportment, not the substance of testimony. More recently—largely in response to concerns raised by wrongful convictions—the field has developed and enforced testimony standards. Many examiners remain concerned when such standards become too narrow and constrictive. Many critics maintain that the standards may produce further misunderstandings. For example, jurors may place great weight on forensic testimony due to its perceived scientific force, so examiners should avoid language that unduly reinforces those perceptions. Ideally, testimony standards will balance the probative value of forensic results with a clear understanding of the limitations of the analysis. Forensic examiners who demonstrate that level of "calibration" are trusted by jurors. Forensic examiners who failed to do so have contributed to many wrongful convictions.

Example: Many wrongful convictions related to hair comparison were the result of failures to develop and enforce testimony standards in the field (see Chapter 3).

THEME: NEW SCIENCE AND TECHNOLOGY CAN IMPROVE THE PROBATIVE VALUE OF FORENSIC EVIDENCE AND PREVENT WRONGFUL CONVICTIONS

New science and technology have had a profound impact on forensic science. Examples include the use of the comparison microscope in firearms comparison, adoption of mass spectrometry for chemical analysis, and development of DNA for biological analysis. In each case, these technologies supplanted old methods that produced less probative results and contributed to wrongful convictions. For example, hair comparison and serology were associated with many wrongful convictions prior to the adoption of DNA in the 1990s. Automated databases have extended these gains to produce reliable cold hits to DNA, latent print, and ballistic evidence. These advances have improved the reliability of forensic evidence, but they have also had a profound and positive impact on criminal investigation. Arguably, new forensic technology has improved criminal investigation more than any other innovation. Scientific research has also improved standards in key disciplines. Fire debris investigation has been revolutionized by the adoption of research-based standards to guide interpretation. Pediatric abuse investigation has also improved as scientific research has impacted the substance and scope of interpretation standards. Much work remains to be done, but science and technology innovations have prevented wrongful convictions and will continue to be an important part of future system improvements.

Cause: Validated Methods May Adopt Innovations That Are Not Validated or Recognized by the Courts

The promise of new technology must be balanced against the possibility of forensic errors. It is important that new methods be validated prior to use. This includes incremental improvements. In an era of increasingly specialized science, forensic methods may incorporate novel ideas that have not yet been validated. Great care should be taken before the implementation of any new method, interpretation framework, communication standard, or other reform. Even well-meaning reforms—such as the adoption of statistical methods or contextual bias controls—may introduce unforeseen problems into complex systems and should be fully researched and validated prior to adoption. Innovation is not just about good ideas. If wrongful convictions teach us anything, it is that effective justice requires great care and diligence by every professional working in the field.

Example: See the history of the adoption of new methods in DNA analysis since the early 1990s in Chapter 4.

REFERENCES

Bernard, E. (2022). *Analysis: Say Goodbye to 'Daubert Motion', Hello to New Rule 702(1).* Bureau of National Affairs.

Hundl, C., Neuman, M., Rairden, M., Rearden, P., & Stout, P. (2020). Implementation of a blind quality control program in a forensic laboratory. *Journal of Forensic Sciences*, *65*(3), 815–822.

Roth, N. E. (1997). *New York State Police Evidence Tampering Investigation.* Ithaca: State of New York.

University of California Irvine Newkirk Center for Science & Society, University of Michigan Law School, & Michigan State University College of Law. (2020, January 28). Retrieved from The National Registry of Exonerations: https://www.law.umich.edu/special/exoneration/Pages/about.aspx

Weick, K. E., & Sutcliffe, K. M. (2001). *Managing the Unexpected.* San Francisco: Jossey-Bass.

Index

For Product Safety Concerns and Information please contact our EU representative GPSR@taylorandfrancis.com Taylor & Francis Verlag GmbH, Kaufingerstraße 24, 80331 München, Germany